Collins

Quiz Night

Published by Collins
An imprint of HarperCollins Publishers
Westerhill Road
Bishopbriggs
Glasgow G64 2QT

www.harpercollins.co.uk

First Edition 2018

10 9 8 7 6

ISBN 978-0-00-829028-3

www.harpercollins.co.uk

Typeset by Puzzler Media

Printed and bound by CPI Group (UK) Ltd, Croydon, CR0 4YY

A catalogue record for this book is available from the British Library.

If you would like to comment on any aspect of this book, please contact us at the above address or online.
E-mail: puzzles@harpercollins.co.uk

Introduction

What makes a good quiz? A witty and amusing host and a choice of interesting categories are good places to start.

You could combine the hosting talents of Alexander Armstrong and Jeremy Paxman but you need a great set of questions too.

That's where *Collins Quiz Night* comes in. We've taken the hassle out of creating the perfect quiz by providing 10,000 questions on all manner of subjects in an easy-to-use format.

There's something on offer for everyone, too, from easy questions for those taking their first tentative steps from quizzing base camp right up to super-tricky testers for those experienced trivia travellers heading for the highest peaks of general knowledge.

Let's get going.

The quizzes

The book is divided into two parts, each with 250 quizzes. Half of the quizzes are based on themes ranging from biology to buildings, geography to golf, nature to numbers and a whole host of subjects in between. The rest of the quizzes are pot luck and contain a little bit of everything.

The quizzes in each part of the book are grouped together depending on how tricky we think they are. The easy ones come first, followed by medium and finally hard.

Easy

With a wide range of themes on offer in our easy section, you're bound to find some questions and quizzes easy and others a bit harder. It's not all straightforward in this section though: watch out for a few themes that aren't quite as obvious as the title suggests. Quiz 251 marks the start of the second easy section.

Medium

You'll get a good general knowledge workout when you tackle our medium quizzes. Classic themes that appeared in the easy section are repeated here, but you'll most likely need some extra thinking time to complete the quizzes at this level. The second medium section starts at Quiz 401.

Hard

You'll really need to work those little grey cells when you venture into our hard quiz section, so set aside plenty of time. An enthusiast's knowledge would be a definite advantage on some of the themed quizzes. When you've toiled your way through the first section, the second hard section begins at Quiz 476.

The answers

Each quiz header tells you where the answers are printed. They're mostly just a couple of pages away, for example the answers to Quiz 1 appear at the bottom of Quiz 3. The exceptions are the last two quizzes in each part of the book, which appear at the bottom of the first two quizzes in that part.

Running a quiz

When you're running a quiz night, there's a great sense of satisfaction to be had in doing a job well, and a little bit of effort beforehand will go a long way to making sure that your quiz goes without a hitch.

❖ Plan: consider how many questions you want to ask in the time available, making sure you leave enough thinking time between questions. Once you've done that, pick a good range of subjects so that there's something for everyone.

❖ Rehearse: Go through all the questions you're going to be asking beforehand, checking any potentially tricky pronunciations and making sure your timings work. Note down all the questions (notes look better in a quiz environment than reading from a book) and answers. Every effort has been made to ensure that all the answers in *Collins Quiz Night* are correct. Despite our best endeavours, mistakes may still appear. If you see an answer you're not sure is right, or if you think there's more than one possible answer, then do check.

❖ Paper and writing implements: make sure you prepare enough sheets of paper for everyone to write on, including scrap paper, and have plenty of pens to hand for those who need them.

❖ Prizes: everyone likes a prize. No matter how small, it's best to have one on offer.

Good luck! We hope you enjoy *Collins Quiz Night*.

Contents

Easy Quizzes

Medium Quizzes

Hard Quizzes

Easy Quizzes

Medium Quizzes

Hard Quizzes

QUIZ 1 – Pot Luck

ANSWERS ON PAGE 3

1 What is the French word for "water"?

2 Who had hits with *Rock DJ* and *Radio*?

3 Which musical term means "quickly"?

4 A nonagon has how many sides?

5 Which actor played nine members of the same family in the 1949 black comedy *Kind Hearts and Coronets*?

6 What name is given to a baby kangaroo?

7 What is the Earth's only natural satellite?

8 In which street did the Great Fire of London start?

9 Which group had a hit in 1978 with *Night Fever*?

10 Midsummer Day falls in which month?

11 Which cartoon bear lives in the village of Nutwood?

12 How many cents are there in a Canadian dollar?

13 Which is the world's largest desert?

14 Which Jewish greeting means "peace"?

15 Who played Gary Strang in the TV series *Men Behaving Badly*?

16 What term is given to a small bar of gold bullion?

17 Which actor was known as "Duke"?

18 Sir Arthur Conan Doyle created which detective?

19 What was the given name of America's President Lincoln?

20 Who was the "doubting" apostle?

Answers to QUIZ 249 – Pot Luck

1 Togo
2 1896
3 Maurice Ravel
4 Aar (or Aare)
5 Van Morrison
6 Hardwick Hall
7 Absorbed radiation dose
8 Arthur Balfour
9 The Weeknd
10 Dis Pater (or Pluto)
11 Tobias Smollett
12 Cretaceous
13 The Sheaf
14 Aragon
15 Saturn
16 Amos
17 Guarani
18 Jean-Jacques Rousseau
19 Bayview
20 Emilia

QUIZ 2 – Food and Drink

ANSWERS ON PAGE 4

Easy

1 Cheddar cheese is named after a village in which county?

2 What term is used to describe food that is served set alight?

3 Which herb is traditionally served with lamb?

4 What do Americans call jam?

5 Which Indian side dish is made from cucumber, mint and yoghurt?

6 Which insect lends its name to a cocktail made from crème de cacao and crème de menthe?

7 What is the British name for the eggplant?

8 Comice is a variety of which fruit?

9 What style of Indian food is cooked in a clay oven?

10 Which popular pasta sauce is made with bacon, egg and cream?

Medium

11 What type of food can be served sunny side up?

12 Which patty of fried minced meat is named after its German city of origin?

13 Bara brith is a traditional tea bread from which country?

14 What does a barista serve?

15 Which French term describes a dry wine?

16 Which salad plant is usually grown with mustard?

17 From which flower is saffron obtained?

18 What is a Chinese cooking pan called?

19 What is the name of the Russian metal urn used for making tea?

20 Which Middle Eastern dip is made from chickpeas and sesame seeds?

Hard

Answers to QUIZ 250 – Europe

1 Mainz
2 Liège
3 Avernus
4 Portugal
5 Andorra
6 Have a nice day!
7 Vienna
8 Ennis
9 Bulgaria
10 Unter den Linden
11 Avignon
12 North Utsire
13 Iceland
14 La Fenice (The Phoenix)
15 Suir
16 Livy
17 Warsaw
18 Strait of Messina
19 1956
20 Robert Louis Stevenson

QUIZ 3 – Pot Luck

ANSWERS ON PAGE 5

1 What colour is the flag that traditionally denotes surrender?
2 Who wrote the 1967 novel *Where Eagles Dare?*
3 Flamenco dancing is associated with which country?
4 What type of food is lollo rosso?
5 At which historical landmark would you find Traitor's Gate?
6 What is a school's shared occupancy bedroom called?
7 What is the county town of Cornwall?
8 Which actress played Clara Oswald in *Doctor Who*?
9 What decoration is known in the USA as "frosting"?
10 Which group's hits include *Holding Back the Years* (1985) and *Stars* (1991)?
11 What type of creature is a house martin?
12 What name is given to the spike of a fork?
13 Which metal has the symbol Fe?
14 Which town in south-east Ireland is famed for its crystal?
15 What is the currency unit of Mexico?
16 What word describes a musical note played slightly lower than it should be?
17 Who presented the TV series *Time Team*?
18 How is 2018 written in Roman numerals?
19 What is the penultimate radio alphabet code letter?
20 Who was the leader of the Soviet Union during WWII?

Answers to QUIZ 1 – Pot Luck

1 *Eau*
2 Robbie Williams
3 Presto
4 Nine
5 Sir Alec Guinness
6 Joey
7 The Moon
8 Pudding Lane
9 The Bee Gees
10 June
11 Rupert
12 100
13 Sahara
14 Shalom
15 Martin Clunes
16 Ingot
17 John Wayne
18 Sherlock Holmes
19 Abraham
20 Thomas

Easy

Medium

Hard

QUIZ 4 – Geography

ANSWERS ON PAGE 6

Easy

1 Which mountainous principality lies between France and Spain?
2 In which city is the Taj Mahal?
3 What is the name of modern-day Persia?
4 Which city is the capital of Romania?
5 The shamrock is the emblem of which country?
6 What are the native inhabitants of New Zealand known as?
7 Which language is spoken in the south-western part of Cyprus?
8 What is the longest river wholly in France?
9 "The Windy City" is the nickname of which US city?
10 Which sea lies between Italy and Croatia?

Medium

11 Which international airport is located in Bedfordshire?
12 Giza is a city in which country?
13 In which Australian state is Brisbane?
14 In which North American mountain range are Banff and Jasper located?
15 What is the capital of Vietnam?
16 Which Portuguese island is famous for its dessert wine?
17 What is the currency unit of Switzerland?
18 The World Heritage site of Ephesus is in which modern country?
19 In which English county is Ross-on-Wye?
20 Which South American country has Lima as its capital?

Hard

Answers to QUIZ 2 – Food and Drink

1 Somerset
2 Flambé
3 Mint
4 Jelly
5 Raita
6 Grasshopper
7 Aubergine
8 Pear
9 Tandoori
10 Carbonara
11 Fried egg
12 Hamburger
13 Wales
14 Coffee
15 Sec
16 Cress
17 Crocus
18 Wok
19 Samovar
20 Hummus

QUIZ 5 – Pot Luck

ANSWERS ON PAGE 7

1 Who was the lead singer with The Police?
2 Who starred in the TV series *Murder, She Wrote*?
3 Which Biblical character was betrayed by Delilah?
4 What is the name for toasted Italian-style sandwiches?
5 What name is given to a gnawing mammal such as a rat or mouse?
6 Who is the patron saint of England?
7 What is the common name of sodium chloride?
8 Who was the first president of the USA?
9 What does the "A" of "VAT" stand for?
10 Which chess pieces move in L-shapes?
11 The cartoon character Popeye is associated with which vegetable?
12 Which Canadian police go on horseback?
13 Which classic film and book series includes *The Two Towers*?
14 Charles I and James I belonged to which royal House?
15 Which type of ship flies the Jolly Roger flag?
16 Which Welsh singer's debut hit was *Lost in France* in 1976?
17 A Manx cat is missing which feature that most cats have?
18 What is the national airline of Australia?
19 What term is given to a plant that lives for one year?
20 Which ocean is the world's largest?

Answers to QUIZ 3 – Pot Luck

1 White
2 Alistair MacLean
3 Spain
4 Lettuce
5 Tower of London
6 A dormitory
7 Truro
8 Jenna Coleman
9 Icing
10 Simply Red
11 A bird
12 Tine
13 Iron
14 Waterford
15 Peso
16 Flat
17 Sir Tony Robinson
18 MMXVIII
19 Yankee
20 Joseph Stalin

QUIZ 6 – Films

ANSWERS ON PAGE 8

1 Who voiced the title character in the 2009 film *Fantastic Mr Fox*?
2 What does the second M in the film company MGM stand for?
3 Which actor starred in the 1959 film *Ben-Hur*?
4 Which film was mistakenly announced as the winner of the Best Picture Oscar at the 2017 ceremony?
5 Which 1960 Sir Alfred Hitchcock film is famed for its shower scene?
6 Who found fame as Bella Swan in the *Twilight Saga*?
7 Which creature featured in the 1975 film *Jaws*?
8 Who starred as a prison guard in the 1999 film *The Green Mile*?
9 What was the name of the Volkswagen in the 1968 Disney film *The Love Bug*?
10 What is the subtitle of the second *Terminator* film, released in 1991?
11 The 1955 film *Rebel Without a Cause* starred which actor?
12 Which film is based on the life of the Trapp Family Singers?
13 Who starred in the 2010 film *Black Swan*?
14 Which *Toy Story* character has the catchphrase "To Infinity, and Beyond!"?
15 Who co-starred with Robert Redford in *Butch Cassidy and the Sundance Kid*?
16 Which actress played Bobbie in the 1970 film *The Railway Children?*
17 What is the nickname of India's film industry?
18 How does James Bond like his martini?
19 Ryan Gosling starred in a 2017 sequel to which 1982 sci-fi film?
20 Who played Gandalf in *The Lord of the Rings* trilogy?

Answers to QUIZ 4 – Geography

1 Andorra
2 Agra
3 Iran
4 Bucharest
5 Republic of Ireland
6 Maori
7 Greek
8 Loire
9 Chicago
10 The Adriatic
11 Luton
12 Egypt
13 Queensland
14 The Rockies
15 Hanoi
16 Madeira
17 Franc
18 Turkey
19 Herefordshire
20 Peru

QUIZ 7 – Pot Luck

ANSWERS ON PAGE 9

1 Which museum houses the *Mona Lisa*?

2 In which town is the Royal and Ancient Golf Club?

3 What term is given to the heating process which destroys disease-producing bacteria in milk?

4 What is the name given to the Central Criminal Court in London?

5 A kumquat is what colour?

6 What is the capital of the US state of Hawaii?

7 What title was traditionally given to the most senior nurse in a hospital?

8 Harry Potter was played on screen by which actor?

9 Who wrote the play *Blithe Spirit* (1941)?

10 What was the language of ancient Rome?

11 What, according to the proverb, gathers no moss?

12 Cheddar Gorge is part of which range of hills?

13 Who topped the UK singles chart in 1999 with *Baby One More Time*?

14 Which sign of the zodiac is represented by the Ram?

15 Which group's first chart-topper was 1995's *Some Might Say*?

16 The New Zealand rugby team perform what ritual before a match?

17 What, proverbially, is the mother of invention?

18 Which 1942 Disney film featured Thumper the rabbit?

19 Who is the patron saint of travellers?

20 What unit is used in measuring the height of a horse?

Answers to QUIZ 5 – Pot Luck

1 Sting
2 Dame Angela Lansbury
3 Samson
4 Panini
5 Rodent
6 St George
7 Salt
8 George Washington
9 Added
10 Knights
11 Spinach
12 Mounties
13 *The Lord of the Rings*
14 Stuart
15 Pirate
16 Bonnie Tyler
17 A tail
18 Qantas
19 Annual
20 Pacific

QUIZ 8 – History

ANSWERS ON PAGE 10

1 The euro was first adopted as an official currency on New Year's Day in which year?
2 Which spa town was founded by the Romans as Aquae Sulis?
3 Which Elizabethan seaman was captain of the *Golden Hind*?
4 Where were the Hanging Gardens, one of the Seven Ancient Wonders of the World?
5 Which was originally the tenth month in the Roman calendar?
6 During which battle was Horatio Nelson (Viscount Nelson) killed?
7 What nickname was given to a Parliamentary soldier in the English Civil War?
8 What acronym denoted the forces' showbiz organisation in WWII?
9 What was the profession of "Capability" Brown?
10 Which civilisation inhabited Peru before the Spanish conquest?
11 Who was the first person to fly the Atlantic solo?
12 Which organisation was founded by William Booth?
13 In which year did the *Titanic* sink?
14 Which 19th-century movement is associated with William Morris?
15 Which Italian volcano destroyed Pompeii in AD 79?
16 What type of transport was a penny-farthing?
17 Which king succeeded Elizabeth I?
18 Which medal was awarded to Malta in 1942?
19 Who was the last president of the Soviet Union?
20 What was the name of the census commissioned by William the Conqueror in 1085?

Answers to QUIZ 6 – Films

1 George Clooney
2 Mayer
3 Charlton Heston
4 *La La Land*
5 *Psycho*
6 Kristen Stewart
7 Great white shark
8 Tom Hanks
9 Herbie
10 *Judgment Day*
11 James Dean
12 *The Sound of Music*
13 Natalie Portman
14 Buzz Lightyear
15 Paul Newman
16 Jenny Agutter
17 Bollywood
18 Shaken, not stirred
19 *Blade Runner*
20 Sir Ian McKellen

QUIZ 9 – Pot Luck

ANSWERS ON PAGE 11

1 What name is given to the central aisle of a church?
2 Where were the 2016 Summer Olympics held?
3 In which county is St Albans?
4 With which band did Ronan Keating find fame?
5 Who is the god of mischief in Norse mythology?
6 What is the fourth book of the New Testament?
7 To which side of a boat does the term starboard refer?
8 Who released the album and single *Let's Get It On* in 1973?
9 What is Paddington Bear's sandwich of choice?
10 Someone born on August 1 has which birth sign of the zodiac?
11 Which river flows through Dublin?
12 Who is Bart Simpson's father in *The Simpsons*?
13 What name is given to the central tower of a castle?
14 What do milliners produce?
15 Who wrote *Charlie and the Chocolate Factory* (1964)?
16 Rickets is caused by the lack of which vitamin?
17 What is the currency unit of South Africa?
18 Which large vein is found in the neck?
19 What is the name of Jack's hill-climbing companion in the nursery-rhyme?
20 Which wading bird was worshipped by the ancient Egyptians?

Answers to QUIZ 7 – Pot Luck

1 The Louvre
2 St Andrews
3 Pasteurisation
4 Old Bailey
5 Orange
6 Honolulu
7 Matron
8 Daniel Radcliffe
9 Sir Noël Coward
10 Latin
11 A rolling stone
12 Mendips
13 Britney Spears
14 Aries
15 Oasis
16 Haka
17 Necessity
18 *Bambi*
19 St Christopher
20 Hand

QUIZ 10 – Music

ANSWERS ON PAGE 12

Easy

1 Ziggy Stardust was the alter ego of which singer?
2 Which character on a musical stave determines pitch?
3 Which duo wrote the opera *Trial by Jury*?
4 What is the name of Elvis Presley's Memphis estate?
5 Which singer's backing band were called The Wailers?
6 What was the title of Lady Gaga's first UK chart-topper?
7 Which singer/songwriter had an early hit with *Crocodile Rock*?
8 Which song title was a hit in 1993 for Mariah Carey and in 2002 for Enrique Iglesias?
9 The video to which 2012 song by Psy became the first YouTube video to reach a billion views?
10 Which Bizet opera, first performed in 1875, is set in Spain?

Medium

11 Who had a hit in 1982 with *Come on Eileen*?
12 Jason Orange was a member of which group until 2014?
13 Which musical term means "smoothly flowing"?
14 Who had 1984 hits with *Penny Lover* and *Stuck on You*?
15 Roger Daltrey founded and fronted which band?
16 What type of instrument is a bongo?
17 What name is given to the final passage in a musical work?
18 Which Britpop band had a 1994 hit with *Parklife*?
19 Which group topped the charts in 1966 with *Paperback Writer?*
20 What cry for help has been a hit for both Abba and Rihanna?

Hard

Answers to QUIZ 8 – History

1 1999
2 Bath
3 Sir Francis Drake
4 Babylon
5 December
6 Trafalgar
7 Roundhead
8 ENSA
9 Landscape designer
10 Inca
11 Charles Lindbergh
12 The Salvation Army
13 1912
14 Arts and Crafts
15 Vesuvius
16 A bicycle
17 James I
18 The George Cross
19 Mikhail Gorbachev
20 The Domesday Book

QUIZ 11 – Pot Luck

ANSWERS ON PAGE 13

1 With which town is Brighton joined to make an official city name?
2 What was Archimedes' famous cry of discovery?
3 Which band had a hit in 1982 with *Save a Prayer*?
4 Of which country is Damascus the capital?
5 Which engineer built the Great Western Railway?
6 What is a young lion called?
7 Who played Gordon Gekko in the *Wall Street* films?
8 Of which English county is Chelmsford the county town?
9 Which figure of Greek myth flew too close to the Sun?
10 Which misnamed war lasted from 1337 until 1453?
11 Which disorder is marked by difficulty in recognising written words?
12 What is the principal ingredient of chow mein?
13 Lex Luthor is the enemy of which comic-book hero?
14 What is the capital of the US state of Georgia?
15 Who composed the *1812 Overture*?
16 What term is given to two under par for a hole in golf?
17 Dennis Quaid and Jake Gyllenhaal starred in which 2004 disaster film?
18 What is the name of the slender tower on a mosque?
19 Which is the largest continent?
20 What is the name of the dog in *Peter Pan?*

Easy

Medium

Hard

Answers to QUIZ 9 – Pot Luck

1 The nave
2 Rio de Janeiro
3 Hertfordshire
4 Boyzone
5 Loki
6 John
7 Right
8 Marvin Gaye
9 Marmalade
10 Leo
11 The Liffey
12 Homer
13 The keep
14 Hats
15 Roald Dahl
16 Vitamin D
17 Rand
18 Jugular
19 Jill
20 Ibis

QUIZ 12 – Nature

ANSWERS ON PAGE 14

1 Which soft-bodied crustacean lives in the empty shells of other molluscs such as whelks?

2 Which Australian marsupial feeds on eucalyptus leaves?

3 Which type of elephant has the largest ears?

4 How many limbs do squid have?

5 What term is used to describe the vast treeless plains of the Arctic?

6 Which fish is associated with the Sargasso Sea?

7 What type of creature lives in a holt?

8 Which flower yields digitalis?

9 Which chemical element is found in kelp?

10 Which is the world's largest antelope, native to South Africa?

11 Zephyr, sirocco and chinook are all types of what?

12 Which oil, derived from flax, is used in putty?

13 Which type of lizard has the ability to change its colour?

14 What is an insect called in the early stage of development?

15 What is "Old Faithful" in Yellowstone National Park?

16 Which African carnivore has a call that sounds like laughter?

17 Which type of amphibian has varieties including crested, fire belly and spotted?

18 In which direction does the sun rise?

19 Which wild cat has tufts on its ear tips?

20 Which river runs through America's Grand Canyon?

Answers to QUIZ 10 – Music

1 David Bowie
2 Clef
3 Gilbert and Sullivan
4 Graceland
5 Bob Marley
6 *Just Dance*
7 Sir Elton John
8 *Hero*
9 *Gangnam Style*
10 *Carmen*
11 Dexys Midnight Runners
12 Take That
13 Legato
14 Lionel Richie
15 The Who
16 Drum
17 Coda
18 Blur
19 The Beatles
20 SOS

QUIZ 13 – Pot Luck

ANSWERS ON PAGE 15

1 What is a level or grade in judo called?
2 Which fish has varieties including brown and rainbow?
3 Who directed the 2008 film *Slumdog Millionaire*?
4 What was the title of ABBA's first UK chart-topper?
5 What is the French word for "thank you"?
6 What title is given to the supreme commander of the British navy?
7 *Dinnerladies* was created by and starred which comedienne?
8 What does the Richter scale measure?
9 Which vitamin is most abundant in carrots?
10 What is a baby swan called?
11 Which Womble was named after a Siberian city?
12 Proverbially, which reptile cries insincere tears?
13 In which county is Bexhill?
14 What is the American term for a holiday?
15 What familiar short name is used for London's police force?
16 Which retired athlete's autobiography is entitled *Faster than Lightning*?
17 What is the *Flying Scotsman*?
18 Which animated pair had *A Grand Day Out* in 1989?
19 Which river flows through Stoke?
20 Who wrote the play *The Winter's Tale*?

Answers to QUIZ 11 – Pot Luck

1 Hove
2 Eureka!
3 Duran Duran
4 Syria
5 Isambard Kingdom Brunel
6 A cub
7 Michael Douglas
8 Essex
9 Icarus
10 The Hundred Years War
11 Dyslexia
12 Noodles
13 Superman
14 Atlanta
15 Tchaikovsky
16 Eagle
17 *The Day After Tomorrow*
18 Minaret
19 Asia
20 Nana

Easy

1 Who played Pam in *Gavin & Stacey*?

2 In which London borough was *Only Fools and Horses* set?

3 What was the name of Ricky Gervais' character in *The Office*?

4 Which part-improvised series featured siblings Ben, Karen and Jake?

5 Which actress played Grace in *Will & Grace*?

6 In which sitcom did Simon Bird play the character Will McKenzie?

7 Which sitcom was set on Craggy Island?

8 Who played Manuel in *Fawlty Towers*?

9 Who co-starred with Zoë Wanamaker in *My Family?*

10 In which city was *Bread* set?

Medium

11 Which profession features in *Damned*?

12 Which US medical sitcom starred Zach Braff and Sarah Chalke?

13 Which series starred Dame Judi Dench and Geoffrey Palmer as Jean and Lionel?

14 David Hyde Pierce played which character in *Frasier*?

15 Which country is the setting for the TV sitcom *Two Doors Down*?

Hard

16 What was the name of Paul Eddington's character in *The Good Life*?

17 What was the nickname of the company clerk in *M*A*S*H?*

18 Officer Crabtree, famed for his French mispronunciation, appeared in which sitcom?

19 Which actor provided the narration for *Twenty Twelve* and *W1A*?

20 Who played Miranda's mother in the sitcom *Miranda*?

Answers to QUIZ 12 – Nature

1 Hermit crab
2 Koala
3 African
4 Ten (eight arms, two tentacles)
5 Tundra
6 Eel
7 Otter
8 Foxglove
9 Iodine
10 Eland
11 Wind
12 Linseed
13 Chameleon
14 Larva
15 A geyser
16 Hyena
17 Newt
18 East
19 Lynx
20 Colorado

QUIZ 15 – Pot Luck

ANSWERS ON PAGE 17

1 What colour is turmeric?
2 Which creature is said to be caught by the early bird?
3 Who wrote *The Three Musketeers*?
4 What was the name of the Soviet space station launched in 1986?
5 The Shambles is a street in which English city?
6 Who was the chief Greek god on Mount Olympus?
7 What substance makes up the outer layer of a tooth?
8 Yaffle is a dialect name for which bird?
9 "Simian" refers to which type of animal?
10 Which section of an orchestra includes flutes?
11 "The Gunners" is the nickname of which football team?
12 What term is given to a bishop's high hat?
13 In which county is Sherwood Forest?
14 Which actress starred in the TV series *Hannah Montana*?
15 Which singer was originally named Anna Mae Bullock?
16 In the PG Wodehouse novels, who is Bertie Wooster's manservant?
17 Who had a 1978 hit with *Song for Guy*?
18 What is a Scottish water sprite in the form of a horse called?
19 Who were the Rockers' 1960s rivals?
20 The Woolpack pub is featured in which long-running TV series?

Answers to QUIZ 13 – Pot Luck

1 Dan
2 Trout
3 Danny Boyle
4 *Waterloo*
5 *Merci*
6 Admiral of the Fleet
7 Victoria Wood
8 Magnitude of earthquakes
9 Vitamin A
10 Cygnet
11 Tomsk
12 Crocodile
13 East Sussex
14 Vacation
15 Met
16 Usain Bolt
17 Steam locomotive
18 Wallace and Gromit
19 Trent
20 William Shakespeare

Easy

Medium

Hard

QUIZ 16 – UK Politics

ANSWERS ON PAGE 18

Easy

1 What is the title of the official printed record of Parliamentary proceedings?
2 Who was the first female Speaker of the House of Commons?
3 Who was Prime Minister at the outbreak of WWII?
4 On which day of the week are British elections usually held?
5 Who became the UK's first Green Party MP in 2010?
6 Who was Gordon Brown's Chancellor of the Exchequer?
7 In which Lincolnshire town was Baroness Margaret Thatcher born?
8 Which former Prime Minister is associated with the country house of Chartwell?
9 What exclamation is heard in the House of Commons to signal Members' agreement?
10 Which former MP was elected Mayor of Greater Manchester in May 2017?

Medium

11 What is the maximum period between general elections in the UK?
12 Which London street is home to the Ministry of Defence?
13 What term is given to a seat in the House of Lords for an independent or minor party member?
14 Who was Prime Minister from 1990 to 1997?
15 In the House of Commons, what colour are the seats?
16 What was the nickname of the 1940s Labour politician Aneurin Bevan?
17 What are the initials of the government's industrial mediation body?
18 What is the name of the Speaker's seat in the House of Lords?
19 On which occasion does the Chancellor traditionally brandish a red case?
20 In 2017 who became leader of the Liberal Democrats for the second time?

Hard

Answers to QUIZ 14 – Sitcoms

1 Alison Steadman
2 Peckham
3 David Brent
4 *Outnumbered*
5 Debra Messing
6 *The Inbetweeners*
7 *Father Ted*
8 Andrew Sachs
9 Robert Lindsay
10 Liverpool
11 Social work
12 *Scrubs*
13 *As Time Goes By*
14 Niles (Crane)
15 Scotland
16 Jerry Leadbetter
17 Radar
18 *'Allo, 'Allo!*
19 David Tennant
20 Patricia Hodge

QUIZ 17 – Pot Luck

ANSWERS ON PAGE 19

1 What is the capital of Portugal?
2 Who were Gladys Knight's backing group?
3 What term is given to a blacksmith's iron block?
4 What is a grinding tooth called?
5 Which soft, bland foodstuff is made from soya beans?
6 In a limerick, which lines should rhyme with the second line?
7 What is the longest river in South America?
8 Which Cumbrian town is famous for its mint cake?
9 In which month is Armistice Day?
10 What is the name of the Marquess of Bath's stately home in Wiltshire?
11 Which ballet features the *Dance of the Sugar Plum Fairy*?
12 How many fiddlers does Old King Cole have in the nursery rhyme?
13 Who wrote *Far from the Madding Crowd* (1874)?
14 Which fictional village is the setting for *The Archers*?
15 What is the largest planet in our solar system?
16 Toxteth is an area of which English city?
17 What is the musical term for a range of eight notes?
18 Which actor starred in the 1984 film *Footloose*?
19 What is the Irish name for Ireland?
20 What are young goats called?

Answers to QUIZ 15 – Pot Luck

1 Yellow
2 The worm
3 Alexandre Dumas (père)
4 Mir
5 York
6 Zeus
7 Enamel
8 Green woodpecker
9 Monkey
10 Woodwind
11 Arsenal
12 Mitre
13 Nottinghamshire
14 Miley Cyrus
15 Tina Turner
16 Jeeves
17 Sir Elton John
18 Kelpie
19 The Mods
20 *Emmerdale*

QUIZ 18 – Human Biology

ANSWERS ON PAGE 20

Easy

1 What is the name of the red pigment in blood?

2 Which hormone, secreted by the pineal gland, induces sleepiness?

3 Which of the five senses might be impaired as a result of laryngitis?

4 In which organs of the body would you find aqueous and vitreous humour?

5 Which muscle is found at the front of the upper arm?

6 Which molecule, in the form of a double helix, transfers genetic characteristics?

7 Which parts of the body are technically called the nares?

8 Which condition occurs as a result of alopecia?

9 Which vital organ neutralises harmful substances in the blood?

10 Which disease, also called infantile paralysis, is prevented by swallowing a vaccine-treated sugar cube?

Medium

11 The umbilicus is the clinical name for what part of the body?

12 Which nerve transmits visual information from the retina to the brain?

13 What is the "soft spot" on a baby's head called?

14 Which is the outermost layer of the skin?

15 What is the common name for the scapula?

16 What is the science of the structure of the body?

17 Encephalology is the study of disorders of which part of the body?

18 What is the medical term given to low blood sugar?

19 Which word meaning "dog-like" applies to a human tooth?

20 What do the letters BMI stand for in the context of personal health?

Hard

Answers to QUIZ 16 – UK Politics

1 Hansard

2 Baroness Betty Boothroyd

3 Neville Chamberlain

4 Thursday

5 Caroline Lucas

6 Alistair Darling

7 Grantham

8 Sir Winston Churchill

9 Hear, hear

10 Andy Burnham

11 Five years

12 Whitehall

13 Crossbench

14 Sir John Major

15 Green

16 Nye

17 ACAS

18 The Woolsack

19 Budget Day

20 Sir Vince Cable

QUIZ 19 – Pot Luck

ANSWERS ON PAGE 21

1 Which medical instrument is used to listen to the heart?

2 *Firework* was a 2010 hit for which singer?

3 Who co-starred with Jodie Foster in the 1991 film *The Silence of the Lambs*?

4 Which northern Italian town is famous for its cured pork and cheese?

5 Which pre-decimal British coin was worth twelve old pence?

6 What is the capital city of Turkey?

7 Which Sunday precedes Easter by a week?

8 Which is Amsterdam's airport?

9 What is the study of disease called?

10 Which is the world's largest bird?

11 Which legendary musician led children from Hamelin?

12 In the TV series *Dallas*, who played Bobby Ewing?

13 Which elite regiment's motto is "Who Dares Wins"?

14 What do Americans call a full stop?

15 Who was Eric Morecambe's comedy partner?

16 Which Latin word is the "A" of "AD"?

17 In which Scottish city would you find the Royal Mile?

18 What is a period of six balls in cricket?

19 Which imaginary line around the Earth is at Latitude 0°?

20 Which car company has a rampant lion as its logo?

Answers to QUIZ 17 – Pot Luck

1 Lisbon
2 The Pips
3 Anvil
4 Molar
5 Tofu
6 First and fifth
7 Amazon
8 Kendal
9 November
10 Longleat
11 *The Nutcracker*
12 Three
13 Thomas Hardy
14 Ambridge
15 Jupiter
16 Liverpool
17 Octave
18 Kevin Bacon
19 Eire
20 Kids

QUIZ 20 – Sport

ANSWERS ON PAGE 22

Easy

1 What name is given to the New Zealand international rugby team?

2 Who was the first man to run the mile in under four minutes?

3 Which of the grand slam tennis tournaments is played on clay?

4 Which country failed to qualify for the FIFA World Cup in 2018, its first absence since 1958?

5 The Henley Regatta takes place on which river?

6 Which name is applied to the Wolverhampton and Bolton football teams?

7 Which indoor game is played with a shuttlecock?

8 Which famous cricket venue is in St John's Wood, London?

9 Which part of a dartboard is worth 50 points?

10 What is the thrower called in a game of baseball?

Medium

11 How many players are there in a rugby union team?

12 Where were the 2014 Winter Olympics held?

13 What is the home ground of Liverpool FC?

14 What are the final odds offered before a horse race?

15 Strikes and spares feature in which indoor sport?

16 Which athletics contest comprises ten events?

17 Which winter sport is associated with the Cresta Run?

18 Who won the Masters Snooker title for a record seventh time in 2017?

19 Which cricketing trophy is played for every two years by England and Australia?

20 What is the name of the rubber disc used in ice hockey?

Hard

Answers to QUIZ 18 – Human Biology

1 Haemoglobin
2 Melatonin
3 Speech
4 The eyes
5 Biceps
6 DNA
7 The nostrils
8 Baldness
9 The liver
10 Polio
11 The belly button
12 Optic nerve
13 Fontanelle
14 Epidermis
15 Shoulder blade
16 Anatomy
17 The brain
18 Hypoglycaemia
19 Canine
20 Body Mass Index

QUIZ 21 – Pot Luck

ANSWERS ON PAGE 23

1 In which London borough is Heathrow Airport situated?
2 Who had a hit in 1977 with *When I Need You*?
3 Which ornamental fabric has a Chantilly variety?
4 Which large body of water surrounds the North Pole?
5 In the TV series *Happy Days*, who played the Fonz?
6 What yarn is derived from the Angora goat?
7 Who invented the miner's safety lamp?
8 What is the English name of the Catholic prayer to Our Lady?
9 Which infectious viral disease causes inflammation of the face's salivary glands?
10 Which sauce is traditionally eaten with roast beef?
11 A plant of the genus *Urtica* has what common name?
12 Which species of eel shares a name with a Scottish firth?
13 Where in the human body is the patella?
14 Who was Arthur of Camelot's wife?
15 Chestnut and oyster are varieties of which food item?
16 What is the capital of Finland?
17 With which musical instrument is Vanessa Mae associated?
18 What, according to the proverb, is better than no bread?
19 Which actress played Lucy in the 1985 film *A Room With A View*?
20 What is a trumpet-quietening device known as?

Answers to QUIZ 19 – Pot Luck

1 Stethoscope
2 Katy Perry
3 Sir Anthony Hopkins
4 Parma
5 Shilling
6 Ankara
7 Palm Sunday
8 Schiphol
9 Pathology
10 Ostrich
11 Pied Piper
12 Patrick Duffy
13 SAS
14 Period
15 Ernie Wise
16 *Anno*
17 Edinburgh
18 Over
19 Equator
20 Peugeot

QUIZ 22 – Communications

Easy

1 What does the "C" stand for in the initials BBC?
2 Who invented the World Wide Web?
3 Which word represents the letter "T" in the standard radio phonetic alphabet?
4 Which was the first programme to be broadcast on Channel 4?
5 What was the name of the world's first adhesive postage stamp?
6 What does DAB stand for in relation to radios?
7 Which is the most frequently used letter in the English language?
8 What was the world's first teletext information service, started by the BBC in 1974?
9 In which year did the UK complete the switch to digital television?
10 By what system is a letter sent if labelled "par avion"?
11 What does SMS stand for in relation to texting?
12 Who invented the telephone?
13 What does "fax" stand for?
14 Which country developed emojis?
15 Which letter is represented in Morse Code by a single dash?
16 How much did a standard first class stamp cost in the UK at the beginning of 2018?
17 Who was the first person to produce a printed book in English?
18 On a standard keyboard, what is the topmost left letter?
19 Which London thoroughfare was traditionally associated with newspapers?
20 In 1973, which company became the first to mass-produce the handheld mobile phone?

Medium

Hard

Answers to QUIZ 20 – Sport

1 The All Blacks
2 Sir Roger Bannister
3 The French Open
4 Italy
5 The Thames
6 Wanderers
7 Badminton
8 Lord's
9 The bull
10 Pitcher
11 15
12 Sochi (Russia)
13 Anfield
14 Starting price
15 Tenpin bowling
16 Decathlon
17 Bobsleigh
18 Ronnie O'Sullivan
19 The Ashes
20 Puck

QUIZ 23 – Pot Luck

ANSWERS ON PAGE 25

1 Which city is the capital of India?
2 Who was the Greek goddess of retribution?
3 What term is given to the central part of a wheel?
4 In which Welsh county is Bangor?
5 Who had a hit in 2009 with *Bad Romance*?
6 What title is given to a person who owns a large estate in Scotland?
7 Which English naval hero was commander of *HMS Victory*?
8 The football ground of Elland Road is in which city?
9 What is the term for an official who leads prayers in a mosque?
10 What is the American term for a narrow rocky valley?
11 Who was the composer of *The Planets* suite?
12 What is the state capital of Tennessee?
13 In the 2012 film *Les Misérables*, who played Jean Valjean?
14 Where does an arboreal creature live?
15 In which county is Loughborough?
16 What is the medical term for short-sightedness?
17 Which Ealing comedy was remade in 2004 with Tom Hanks in the starring role?
18 What is the word of Indian origin for an equestrian show?
19 Which peach variety has a smooth yellow and red skin?
20 What is the capital of Japan?

Answers to QUIZ 21 – Pot Luck

1 Hillingdon
2 Leo Sayer
3 Lace
4 Arctic Ocean
5 Henry Winkler
6 Mohair
7 Sir Humphry Davy
8 Hail Mary
9 Mumps
10 Horseradish
11 Nettle
12 Moray
13 The knee
14 Guinevere
15 Mushroom
16 Helsinki
17 Violin
18 Half a loaf
19 Helena Bonham Carter
20 Mute

QUIZ 24 – Film Music

ANSWERS ON PAGE 26

1 Who sang *Gangsta's Paradise*, featured in the 1995 film *Dangerous Minds*?

2 Who won an Oscar for the score to the film *ET: the Extra-Terrestrial*?

3 Who sang the theme song to the 1984 film *Ghostbusters*?

4 The song *Bright Eyes* was the theme tune to which 1978 animated film?

5 The 1945 film *Brief Encounter* featured which composer's *Concerto No 2 in C Minor*?

6 Which film theme song was a hit for Phil Collins in 1984 and Steve Brookstein in 2005?

7 Who had a second hit with *Unchained Melody* in 1990 as a result of the film *Ghost*?

8 Who composed *The Pink Panther* theme?

9 Which group topped the charts for 15 weeks in 1994 with *Love is All Around*, from *Four Weddings and a Funeral*?

10 Who wrote *I Will Always Love You*, Whitney Houston's hit from *The Bodyguard*?

11 Which song used in *Despicable Me* 2 was a 2014 hit for Pharrell Williams?

12 Who sang *My Heart Will Go On*, the theme song to *Titanic*...?

13 ...and who composed the score?

14 Berlin's *Take My Breath Away* featured in which 1986 film?

15 Which 2002 James Bond film had a theme tune performed by Madonna?

16 *Let It Go* is a song from which 2013 animated film?

17 Who composed the score for the 1966 film *The Good, The Bad and The Ugly*?

18 *Everything is Awesome* by Tegan and Sara was from which 2014 film?

19 Which song used in *Robin Hood: Prince of Thieves* topped the UK charts for 16 weeks?

20 Vangelis won an Oscar for which 1981 British film's soundtrack?

Easy

Medium

Hard

Answers to QUIZ 22 – Communications

1 Corporation
2 Sir Tim Berners-Lee
3 Tango
4 *Countdown*
5 Penny Black
6 Digital Audio Broadcasting
7 E
8 Ceefax
9 2012
10 Airmail
11 Short Message Service
12 Alexander Graham Bell
13 Facsimile
14 Japan
15 T
16 65p
17 William Caxton
18 Q
19 Fleet Street
20 Motorola

QUIZ 25 – Pot Luck

ANSWERS ON PAGE 27

1 Which ship famously sank off the Portsmouth coast in 1545?
2 In which country was Russell Crowe born?
3 What was the name of the first "talkie" film, released in 1927?
4 What modern measurement of length is equivalent to just over a yard?
5 The city of Hull lies on which estuary?
6 What term describes lines lying in the same plane and not intersecting?
7 What is the French term for the South of France?
8 The Gurkhas hail from which mountainous Asian country?
9 What is the collective noun for a group of owls?
10 Of which European country is The Hague the seat of government?
11 Which group had a hit in 1992 with *November Rain*?
12 Which author created the character of Tom Sawyer?
13 What name is given to a female horse?
14 In which city is Central Park?
15 Who was the god of war in Roman mythology?
16 What is the common name for the tiny piece of silicon used in circuits?
17 Who was the lead singer with The Jam?
18 Of which country is Budapest the capital?
19 Which salad is made from tuna, French beans, olives and eggs?
20 Which screen legend starred in the film *The Seven Year Itch*?

Answers to QUIZ 23 – Pot Luck

1 New Delhi
2 Nemesis
3 The hub
4 Gwynedd
5 Lady Gaga
6 A laird
7 Horatio Nelson (Viscount Nelson)
8 Leeds
9 Imam
10 Gulch
11 Gustav Holst
12 Nashville
13 Hugh Jackman
14 In a tree
15 Leicestershire
16 Myopia
17 *The Ladykillers*
18 Gymkhana
19 Nectarine
20 Tokyo

Easy
Medium
Hard

QUIZ 26 – Maths

ANSWERS ON PAGE 28

Easy

1 How many sides does an octagon have?

2 What unit of time is 1440th of a day?

3 What term is given to the distance from the centre of a circle to its outside edge?

4 What is 0.025 expressed as a fraction?

5 What unit of land is ten thousand square metres?

6 Which mathematical diagram of intersecting circles was invented by British logician, John?

7 What term is given to the mathematics of shapes?

8 What name is given to a triangle that has two equal sides?

9 Which imperial length measurement is equal to 2.54 centimetres?

10 How many degrees are there in a right angle?

Medium

11 What term is given to an angle of between 90 and 180 degrees?

12 What is the square root of 169?

13 Which metric unit of weight is equivalent to 1000 kilograms?

14 How many sides are there on a rhombus?

15 Which branch of mathematics is concerned with theoretical rather than practical aspects?

16 Which shape has long straight sides and two equal-sized circular ends?

17 What term is given to a graph shown as a circle divided into sections?

18 What is the decimal equivalent of the binary number 110?

19 Which unit of quantity is equal to twelve dozen?

20 What term is given to the top line of a fraction?

Hard

Answers to QUIZ 24 – Film Music

1 Coolio
2 John Williams
3 Ray Parker Jr
4 *Watership Down*
5 Rachmaninov
6 *Against All Odds*
7 Righteous Brothers
8 Henry Mancini
9 Wet Wet Wet
10 Dolly Parton
11 *Happy*
12 Celine Dion
13 James Horner
14 *Top Gun*
15 *Die Another Day*
16 *Frozen*
17 Ennio Morricone
18 *The Lego Movie*
19 *(Everything I Do) I Do It for You*
20 *Chariots of Fire*

QUIZ 27 – Pot Luck

ANSWERS ON PAGE 29

1 Who was the original host of the TV series *QI*?

2 Proverbially, what is it that blows nobody any good?

3 Bangkok is the capital of which south-east Asian country?

4 Which syrupy liqueur is an ingredient of the cocktail Kir Royale?

5 What is the modern name for Ceylon?

6 What is the term for money paid to the courts as security?

7 The Blockheads were the backing band for which singer?

8 Which town in Warwickshire is associated with Shakespeare?

9 Who was the Greek god of pastures and nature?

10 In rounders, which player stands behind the batter?

11 Which is the largest cathedral in the world?

12 Which English conflict lasted from 1642 to 1646?

13 Who was the director of *2001: A Space Odyssey*?

14 *Mrs Brown's Boys* was created by which comedian?

15 The Serpentine is in which area of London?

16 What was Jack's surname in the TV series *24*?

17 What is the highest award at the Cannes Film Festival?

18 Who won the men's singles title at Wimbledon in 1974 and again in 1982?

19 Which motor-racing circuit is situated near Swanley in Kent?

20 What is a solution of water strongly impregnated with salt called?

Easy Medium Hard

Answers to QUIZ 25 – Pot Luck

1 The *Mary Rose*
2 New Zealand
3 *The Jazz Singer*
4 Metre
5 The Humber estuary
6 Parallel
7 Midi
8 Nepal
9 Parliament
10 Netherlands
11 Guns N' Roses
12 Mark Twain
13 A mare
14 New York
15 Mars
16 Microchip
17 Paul Weller
18 Hungary
19 Niçoise
20 Marilyn Monroe

QUIZ 28 – Art

ANSWERS ON PAGE 30

1 Which art museum is located in London's Bankside area?
2 Who decorated the ceiling of the Sistine Chapel in the 16th century?
3 Who created the art installation *My Bed* in 1998?
4 Which pop artist said that everyone would be famous for 15 minutes?
5 Which 18th-century artist painted the satirical sketches *A Rake's Progress*?
6 Which colour is obtained by mixing red and blue paint?
7 *The Angel of the North* sculpture is near which town?
8 What brownish-orange hair colour is named after a Renaissance painter?
9 What was Picasso's first name?
10 *The Monarch of the Glen* (1851) is a painting by which British artist?
11 Which French painter was famed for his pictures of water lilies?
12 Which artist painted *The Night Watch* (1642)?
13 What is the support for an artist's canvas called?
14 Which artist painted *The Fighting Temeraire* (1838)?
15 In which city can Leonardo da Vinci's *The Last Supper* be seen?
16 Which Cornish seaside town has a branch of the Tate gallery?
17 George Stubbs is famous for his paintings of which type of animal?
18 Who sculpted *The Kiss* (1882)?
19 In which city is the Uffizi gallery?
20 Which French artist (b.1848) is famous for his paintings of Tahiti?

Answers to QUIZ 26 – Maths

1 Eight
2 Minute
3 Radius
4 Fortieth
5 Hectare
6 Venn
7 Geometry
8 Isosceles
9 An inch
10 90
11 Obtuse
12 13
13 Tonne
14 Four
15 Pure maths
16 Cylinder
17 Pie chart
18 Six
19 Gross
20 Numerator

QUIZ 29 – Pot Luck

ANSWERS ON PAGE 31

1 Which female rank is equivalent to a knight?
2 What is the national bird of the USA?
3 What is the fourth letter of the Greek alphabet?
4 Which Italian dish consists of slices of raw meat or fish?
5 For what type of comedy plays was dramatist Georges Feydeau famous?
6 Which is the second largest of the Great Lakes by surface area?
7 Which southern county gave its name to a geological period?
8 Which wild flower has a seed head known as a clock?
9 What is the Spanish word for “donkey”?
10 Epiphany is celebrated in which month?
11 What is the capital city of Belgium?
12 What was the surname of the butler in *Downton Abbey*?
13 On which river does Chester stand?
14 Linen is obtained from which plant?
15 What is the lowest male singing voice?
16 Vulpine refers to which animal?
17 What is the nickname of Norwich City FC?
18 Of which family did John Galsworthy write a series of novels between 1906 and 1921?
19 *Tapestry* was a 1971 album by which singer/songwriter?
20 What, according to the proverb, is the sincerest form of flattery?

Answers to QUIZ 27 – Pot Luck

1 Stephen Fry
2 An ill wind
3 Thailand
4 Cassis
5 Sri Lanka
6 Bail
7 Ian Dury
8 Stratford-upon-Avon
9 Pan
10 Backstop
11 St Peter's, Vatican City
12 The First English Civil War
13 Stanley Kubrick
14 Brendan O'Carroll
15 Hyde Park
16 Bauer
17 Palme d'Or
18 Jimmy Connors
19 Brands Hatch
20 Brine

QUIZ 30 – Celebrity

ANSWERS ON PAGE 32

Easy

1 Which TV scientist played in the 1990s band D Ream?

2 Who is the youngest of the Kardashian sisters?

3 Which girl group was formed as a result of the programme *Popstars: The Rivals*?

4 In which US state was Nicole Kidman born?

5 Which reality TV star won the 2017 series of the winter sports competition *The Jump*?

6 Angelina Jolie is the daughter of which actor?

7 Which intrepid TV presenter first found fame on *Castaway 2000*?

8 Which guitarist graduated with a physics PhD in 2008, having originally begun his studies in the 1970s?

9 The TV series *Cradle to Grave* is a biopic of which TV and radio presenter's early life?

10 What is the name of David and Victoria Beckham's second son?

Medium

11 What is the surname of Oscar-winning film-making brothers Joel and Ethan?

12 Which comedian featured on the 2005 version of Tony Christie's *Is This the Way to Amarillo*?

13 In which country was Cate Blanchett born?

14 Which Oscar-winning actor is a founder member of the band Thirty Seconds to Mars?

15 On which talent show did Simon Cowell first appear as a judge?

16 Which group was Beyoncé part of before going solo?

17 Dakota Johnson is the daughter of which actress?

18 Which Hollywood actress was Miss USA runner-up in 1986?

19 By what name is Stefani Germanotta better known?

20 Arnold Schwarzenegger was Governor of which US state from 2003 to 2011?

Hard

Answers to QUIZ 28 – Art

1 The Tate Modern
2 Michelangelo
3 Tracey Emin
4 Andy Warhol
5 William Hogarth
6 Purple
7 Gateshead
8 Titian
9 Pablo
10 Sir Edwin Landseer
11 Claude Monet
12 Rembrandt
13 An easel
14 JMW Turner
15 Milan
16 St Ives
17 Horses
18 Auguste Rodin
19 Florence
20 Paul Gauguin

QUIZ 31 – Pot Luck

ANSWERS ON PAGE 33

1 Who wrote the 1936 novel *Jamaica Inn*?
2 What term is used to describe sloping type?
3 What alias does Superman use?
4 The Isle of Dogs is part of which area of London?
5 Which US state has Denver as its capital?
6 In Roman numerals, what number is represented by LXXV?
7 Which bird is traditionally seen as an emblem of peace?
8 What is the common name for the crane fly?
9 What was the title of Phil Collins and Philip Bailey's 1985 no.1 hit?
10 What is a gavotte?
11 Wales has which patron saint?
12 What general disorder does the suffix "itis" indicate?
13 What, according to the proverb, should you not look in the mouth?
14 Which was the only one of Disney's Seven Dwarfs without a beard?
15 Which TV series is set in the fictional Cornish village of Portwenn?
16 In which year did Concorde make its first flight?
17 Who starred in the 2003 film *School of Rock*?
18 What was the name of Victor's wife in the TV series *One Foot in the Grave*?
19 Which member of a rowing team is responsible for steering?
20 The cities of Glasgow and Edinburgh are linked by which motorway?

Answers to QUIZ 29 – Pot Luck

1 Dame
2 Bald eagle
3 Delta
4 Carpaccio
5 Farces
6 Huron
7 Devon
8 Dandelion
9 Burro
10 January
11 Brussels
12 Carson
13 Dee
14 Flax
15 Bass
16 Fox
17 Canaries
18 Forsyte
19 Carole King
20 Imitation

QUIZ 32 – At the Double

ANSWERS ON PAGE 34

Easy

Medium

Hard

1 What name is given to the short stiff skirt worn by a ballerina?

2 Who is Yogi Bear's best friend?

3 What term is given to a ditch used as an invisible garden boundary?

4 In which decade did the ra-ra skirt first become popular?

5 Couscous is made from which type of grain?

6 How many wheels are there on a tuk-tuk?

7 Who wrote the 2012 novel *Me Before You*?

8 Which bird has the Latin name *Troglodytes troglodytes*?

9 What was the name of the frog in the 1960s children's series *Hector's House*?

10 The can-can dance originated in which country?

11 Who had a 1974 hit with *Rebel Rebel*?

12 Tête-à-Tête is a dwarf variety of which flower?

13 Which radio alphabet code word follows "papa"?

14 Which group had a 1983 hit with *Mama?*

15 Which long-extinct bird was native to Mauritius?

16 What type of transport might be described as "ro-ro"?

17 What type of creature is the cartoon character Pepé Le Pew?

18 In the TV series *Teletubbies*, what colour is Laa-Laa?

19 Which group had a 1965 hit with *California Dreamin'*?

20 "Toto, I've a feeling we're not in Kansas anymore" is a quote from which film?

Answers to QUIZ 30 – Celebrity

1 Brian Cox
2 Khloé
3 Girls Aloud
4 Hawaii
5 Spencer Matthews
6 Jon Voight
7 Ben Fogle
8 Brian May
9 Danny Baker
10 Romeo
11 Coen
12 Peter Kay
13 Australia
14 Jared Leto
15 *Pop Idol*
16 Destiny's Child
17 Melanie Griffith
18 Halle Berry
19 Lady Gaga
20 California

QUIZ 33 – Pot Luck

ANSWERS ON PAGE 35

1 In which US state is Disney World?
2 What word represents the letter "F" in the radio phonetic alphabet?
3 Which sport is played at Headingley and The Oval?
4 Which versatile pungent bulb is said to ward off vampires?
5 What term is given to a female deer?
6 What is the German word for "Mrs"?
7 *Joey* was a spin-off from which TV series?
8 St Austell can be found in which English county?
9 Which imperial liquid measure is equivalent to eight pints?
10 In which country was porcelain first made?
11 Which group topped the UK charts in 1978 with *Dreadlock Holiday*?
12 What word is used in the US for a lift that travels between floors?
13 Which long-running drama series is set in Weatherfield?
14 In the Bible, which archangel foretells the birth of Jesus to Mary?
15 Which period covers the years 1901-10 in Britain?
16 Which British fashion designer launched the miniskirt?
17 In the nursery rhyme, how many men did the Grand Old Duke of York have?
18 Which alcoholic drink is produced from fermented honey?
19 In the TV series *CSI*, what does the "I" stand for?
20 Which author created the character Tracy Beaker?

Answers to QUIZ 31 – Pot Luck

1 Dame Daphne du Maurier
2 Italic
3 Clark Kent
4 Docklands
5 Colorado
6 75
7 Dove
8 Daddy-long-legs
9 *Easy Lover*
10 An 18th-century dance
11 St David
12 Inflammation
13 A gift horse
14 Dopey
15 *Doc Martin*
16 1969
17 Jack Black
18 Margaret
19 Cox
20 M8

QUIZ 34 – Science Fiction

ANSWERS ON PAGE 36

Easy

1 Which 2004 Will Smith film is based on short stories by Isaac Asimov?
2 What is the name of the villainous computer network in the *Terminator* films?
3 Who played the lead role in the 2015 film *The Martian*?
4 What was the title of the 2016 film released as part of the *Star Wars* franchise?
5 The 1990 film *Total Recall* features a mining colony on which planet?
6 Who played the hero Galen in the TV series *Planet of the Apes*?
7 What giant creatures featured in the 1954 film *Them!*?
8 The 1968 film *Barbarella* featured which famous actress?
9 Who played Jean-Luc Picard in the TV series *Star Trek: the Next Generation*?
10 Which actor starred in the 2002 film *Minority Report*?

Medium

11 The Cylons featured in which TV series of the 1970s and 2000s?
12 Which famous author wrote *The Time Machine* and *The War of the Worlds*?
13 Who wrote *The Hitch-Hiker's Guide to the Galaxy*?
14 Which famous sci-fi character was played by Sylvester Stallone and later by Karl Urban?
15 How did the extra-terrestrials communicate in *Close Encounters of the Third Kind*?
16 What colour were the tall humanoids in *Avatar*?
17 Which actress starred in the 2016 sci-fi film *Arrival*?
18 Which TV series has featured the alien Sontarans, Ice Warriors and Silurians?
19 Which rock group provided the soundtrack to the 1980 film *Flash Gordon*?
20 What does Babylon 5 refer to in the title of the TV series?

Hard

Answers to QUIZ 32 – At the Double

1 Tutu
2 Boo-Boo
3 Ha-ha
4 1980s
5 Semolina
6 Three
7 Jojo Moyes
8 Wren
9 Kiki
10 France
11 David Bowie
12 Daffodil
13 Quebec
14 Genesis
15 The dodo
16 A ferry (roll-on, roll-off)
17 A skunk
18 Yellow
19 The Mamas & the Papas
20 *The Wizard of Oz*

QUIZ 35 – Pot Luck

ANSWERS ON PAGE 37

1 Sicily and Cyprus lie in which sea?
2 On which course is the classic horse race the Oaks run?
3 What was the name of the cow in *The Magic Roundabout*?
4 Which point is the southernmost tip of Britain?
5 What type of fruit is an ogen?
6 Which Caribbean island has Havana as its capital?
7 What name is given to a pale, dry sherry?
8 Which girl's name is the French word for "she"?
9 According to the song, who sold "cockles and mussels, alive, alive-o"?
10 Which of Handel's oratorios contains the "Hallelujah" chorus?
11 What title is given to the head of a monastery?
12 Who is Charlie Brown's blanket-carrying friend?
13 Which sign of the zodiac is represented by the Archer?
14 Which German city hosted the 1972 Olympic Games?
15 Who recorded the 1990 hit *Unbelievable*?
16 Ancient poets gave which name to the drink of the gods?
17 Which of the Cinque Ports shares its name with a cereal crop?
18 What is the line behind which darts players stand?
19 What is the given name of Ms Harker, the heroine of *Dracula*?
20 Where is the headquarters of London's Metropolitan Police?

Answers to QUIZ 33 – Pot Luck

1 Florida
2 Foxtrot
3 Cricket
4 Garlic
5 Doe
6 Frau
7 *Friends*
8 Cornwall
9 Gallon
10 China
11 10cc
12 Elevator
13 *Coronation Street*
14 Gabriel
15 Edwardian
16 Dame Mary Quant
17 10,000
18 Mead
19 Investigation
20 Dame Jacqueline Wilson

QUIZ 36 – France

ANSWERS ON PAGE 38

1 On which river does Paris stand?
2 What is the term for a French police officer?
3 Which French stew of fish and vegetables originated in Marseille?
4 Which French port is linked to Newhaven by ferry?
5 *Jaune* is French for which colour?
6 Which former French royal house is also the name of a variety of American whiskey?
7 What name is given to the Parisian underground?
8 Of which former duchy and province of France was William the Conqueror a duke?
9 On which Parisian thoroughfare does the Tour de France finish?
10 Which novelist wrote *Les Misérables* (1862)?
11 What is the French phrase for the dish of the day in a restaurant?
12 Which town in the north of the country is associated with racing and lace?
13 What is the French word for "snail"?
14 In which year of the late 20th century did France host the FIFA World Cup?
15 Which singer (b.1915) was nicknamed the "Little Sparrow"?
16 Which Parisian landmark was begun by Napoleon to celebrate his victories?
17 Which French wine classification is the highest level for Burgundy?
18 The "little black dress" was popularised by which French fashion designer?
19 Which French term means "baked in a pastry coating"?
20 At which venue is the French Grand Slam tennis tournament played?

Answers to QUIZ 34 – Science Fiction

1 *I, Robot*
2 Skynet
3 Matt Damon
4 *Rogue One*
5 Mars
6 Roddy McDowall
7 Ants
8 Jane Fonda
9 Sir Patrick Stewart
10 Tom Cruise
11 *Battlestar Galactica*
12 HG Wells
13 Douglas Adams
14 Judge Dredd
15 Music (tones)
16 Blue
17 Amy Adams
18 *Doctor Who*
19 Queen
20 Space station

QUIZ 37 – Pot Luck

ANSWERS ON PAGE 39

1 Which element combines with oxygen to make water?
2 Which fairy-tale character met the three bears?
3 In which county is the seaside town of Cromer?
4 What is the eastern Mediterranean flaky pastry used to make strudel?
5 Who is Popeye's girlfriend?
6 Which group released *The Lexicon of Love II* album in 2016?
7 According to the rhyme, on what day was Solomon Grundy born?
8 Pumpernickel bread is from which country?
9 What is the colour of the ball worth three points in snooker?
10 Which unit of weight is used for gems and gold?
11 What is the name of Sherlock Holmes' housekeeper?
12 What term is given to a fish's breathing organs?
13 Who played the Prime Minister in the 2003 film *Love Actually*?
14 What is the dead skin at the base of a nail called?
15 According to the saying, what die hard?
16 In which TV series did Lea Michele play Rachel Berry?
17 Portland is the name of the largest city in Maine and which other US state?
18 Who was the main presenter of the long-running consumer series *That's Life*?
19 Which constellation is known as the Hunter?
20 Des Moines is the capital of which US state?

Answers to QUIZ 35 – Pot Luck

1 Mediterranean
2 Epsom
3 Ermintrude
4 Lizard Point
5 A melon
6 Cuba
7 Fino
8 Elle
9 Molly Malone
10 *Messiah*
11 Abbot
12 Linus
13 Sagittarius
14 Munich
15 EMF
16 Nectar
17 Rye
18 Oche
19 Mina
20 New Scotland Yard

QUIZ 38 – George

ANSWERS ON PAGE 40

1 Winston Smith and Emmanuel Goldstein are characters in which George Orwell novel?
2 George Cole played Flash Harry in which series of films?
3 George the pink hippo appeared in which children's TV series?
4 In which month is the feast day of St George?
5 Who duetted with George Michael in 1991 on *Don't Let the Sun Go Down on Me*?
6 Which British monarch's reign saw the American War of Independence?
7 Which actor's only outing as James Bond was in *On Her Majesty's Secret Service*?
8 What was George and Mildred's surname in the 1970s sitcom?
9 Which English engineer was known as "the Father of Railways"?
10 Which English spymaster features in John le Carré's *Tinker, Tailor, Soldier, Spy*?
11 Who was French president from 1969 to 1974?
12 What was the surname of George Takei's *Star Trek* character?
13 In which 1946 film did James Stewart star as George Bailey?
14 Georges Simenon created which fictional detective?
15 Which actor played TV's Inspector George Gently?
16 Who played the title role in the 1994 film *The Madness of King George*?
17 What was the name of George Wendt's character in the TV series *Cheers*?
18 Which 1980s TV series starred George Peppard as Hannibal Smith?
19 Which type of instrument did George Formby play?
20 What is the capital of the country Georgia?

Answers to QUIZ 36 – France

1 The Seine
2 Gendarme
3 Bouillabaisse
4 Dieppe
5 Yellow
6 Bourbon
7 Métro
8 Normandy
9 Champs-Élysées
10 Victor Hugo
11 *Plat du jour*
12 Chantilly
13 *Escargot*
14 1998
15 Édith Piaf
16 Arc de Triomphe
17 Grand cru
18 Coco Chanel
19 En croute
20 Roland Garros (Paris)

QUIZ 39 – Pot Luck

ANSWERS ON PAGE 41

1 In which county is Henley-on-Thames?
2 What was the nickname of rock 'n' roll pianist Antoine Domino?
3 What is toxicology the study of?
4 Who hosted *Ready Steady Cook* before Ainsley Harriott?
5 What is a cutting tooth called?
6 What term is given to a tennis serve that cannot be returned?
7 Which Cornish town is the home of Gilbert and Sullivan's pirates?
8 The 1986 film *Crocodile Dundee* starred which actor in the title role?
9 What is the official language of Chile?
10 What is the US equivalent of "Ltd"?
11 What term is given to the scientific study of birds?
12 Which New Testament book precedes Romans?
13 The 1974 novel *Jaws* was written by which author?
14 Which cup was sought by King Arthur's knights?
15 What is a dried plum called?
16 Which trophy is contested by male US and European golfers every two years?
17 *Nutbush City Limits* was a hit for which separating duo in 1973?
18 What is the chess term for a deadlock?
19 Which is the largest living primate?
20 What metal is an alloy of iron and carbon?

Answers to QUIZ 37 – Pot Luck

1 Hydrogen
2 Goldilocks
3 Norfolk
4 Filo
5 Olive Oyl
6 ABC
7 Monday
8 Germany
9 Green
10 Carat
11 Mrs Hudson
12 Gills
13 Hugh Grant
14 Cuticle
15 Old habits
16 *Glee*
17 Oregon
18 Dame Esther Rantzen
19 Orion
20 Iowa

QUIZ 40 – Trees

ANSWERS ON PAGE 42

1 What is the popular name given to the fruit of the horse chestnut tree?

2 The oil from which tree native to Australia has medicinal uses including clearing congestion?

3 What name is given to a botanical tree garden such as Westonbirt?

4 The berries of which tree are used to flavour gin?

5 Which tree shares its name with a US ski resort?

6 Which tree traditionally provides the leaves used for making honorary wreaths?

7 What is the term given to a tree's liquid?

8 Which country has a cedar tree on its national flag?

9 The wood of which tree is traditionally used to make cricket bats?

10 What term is given to a tree that is leafy all year round?

11 Which Californian tree has a seven-letter name that contains all five vowels?

12 The branch of which tree signifies an offer of reconciliation?

13 Which tree is also known as the rowan?

14 What term is given to a fruit tree trained on stakes?

15 For what use is the Norway Spruce tree most well-known?

16 Acorns are the fruit of which tree?

17 Which tree "bears the crown" in the lyrics of a well-known seasonal song?

18 What name is given to the cylindrical flower cluster that forms on trees such as birch or hazel in spring?

19 What is the maple tree genus?

20 What term is given to the concentric marks on a tree trunk?

Answers to QUIZ 38 – George

1 *Nineteen Eighty-Four*
2 St Trinian's
3 *Rainbow*
4 April
5 Sir Elton John
6 George III
7 George Lazenby
8 Roper
9 George Stephenson
10 George Smiley
11 Georges Pompidou
12 Sulu
13 *It's a Wonderful Life*
14 Maigret
15 Martin Shaw
16 Sir Nigel Hawthorne
17 Norm
18 *The A-Team*
19 Ukulele (or banjolele)
20 Tbilisi

QUIZ 41 – Pot Luck

ANSWERS ON PAGE 43

1 Which period of fasting precedes Easter?
2 Which mushroom-like organisms are studied by mycologists?
3 In which year did Madonna have her first UK top ten hit with *Holiday*?
4 What is the canine symbol of Great Britain?
5 Which bloodsucking worm was once used in medicine?
6 In the name of the charity ROSPA, what does the "A" stand for?
7 Which musical centres around the character of Sally Bowles?
8 What title is given to an army chaplain?
9 Which number is written as XC in Roman numerals?
10 Where were the summer Olympic Games of 1980 held?
11 What jelly is made from seaweed and used in glue-making?
12 What was the middle name of the poet Shelley (b.1792)?
13 Which French wine-growing region is also a deep red colour?
14 Jacob Marley is a character in which Dickens novel?
15 Which US city suffered a massive earthquake in 1906?
16 What type of creature is a painted lady?
17 What term is given to the highest part of a tropical rainforest?
18 Who was elected Mayor of London in 2016?
19 Which band had a hit in the mid-1980s with *Take On Me*?
20 What is the name of the Royal Military Academy near Camberley in Surrey?

Answers to QUIZ 39 – Pot Luck

1 Oxfordshire
2 Fats
3 Poisons
4 Fern Britton
5 An incisor
6 Ace
7 Penzance
8 Paul Hogan
9 Spanish
10 Inc
11 Ornithology
12 Acts
13 Peter Benchley
14 The Holy Grail
15 Prune
16 Ryder Cup
17 Ike and Tina Turner
18 Stalemate
19 Gorilla
20 Steel

QUIZ 42 – Literature

ANSWERS ON PAGE 44

Easy

1 How many lines are there in a sonnet?

2 For what type of book is Samuel Pepys best known?

3 Which author created the Secret Seven?

4 Who wrote the 1899 novel *Heart of Darkness*?

5 Whom did Gepetto the woodcarver create?

6 In which Dickens novel does Miss Havisham, who was jilted on her wedding day, appear?

7 Who is Scotland's national poet?

8 Which creature raced against the hare in Aesop's fable?

9 Who wrote *Salem's Lot*, *Cujo* and *It*?

10 Which bear admitted to "having very little brain"?

Medium

11 What is Sherlock Holmes' address?

12 What is the name of the girl who flies to Neverland with Peter Pan?

13 Who wrote the 1961 novel *The Prime of Miss Jean Brodie*?

14 Which Tennyson poem begins "Come into the garden"?

15 Elizabeth Bennet is the main character in which 1813 novel?

16 What is the family's surname in the 1868 novel *Little Women*?

17 Which classic novel features the character of Catherine Earnshaw?

18 Which novel by Richard Adams was made into an animated film in 1978?

19 CS Lewis penned stories set in which imaginary land beyond the wardrobe?

20 Which author created Inspector Wexford?

Hard

Answers to QUIZ 40 – Trees

1 Conker
2 Eucalyptus
3 Arboretum
4 Juniper
5 Aspen
6 Laurel
7 Sap
8 Lebanon
9 Willow
10 Evergreen
11 Sequoia
12 Olive
13 Mountain ash
14 Espalier
15 Christmas tree
16 Oak
17 Holly
18 Catkin
19 *Acer*
20 Growth rings

QUIZ 43 – Pot Luck

ANSWERS ON PAGE 45

1 *Smooth Operator* was a 1980s hit for which singer?
2 What name is given to a male goose?
3 What was the first name of French philosopher Sartre (b.1905)?
4 Which kind of building can be found at Westminster, Woburn and Whitby?
5 Which offence in the US might be "grand" or "petty"?
6 Who starred in the 2003 film *Hulk*?
7 In which county is Preston?
8 In which month is Twelfth Night?
9 Which salad is made from romaine lettuce, croutons and Parmesan?
10 What name is given to a Freemasons' meeting place?
11 Who played Carrie in *Sex and the City*?
12 Which word can be an island, a coffee bean or a computer language?
13 *The Catcher in the Rye* (1951) was written by which novelist?
14 Which city, near the Pyramids, is the capital of Egypt?
15 Which fatty substance is found in wool?
16 What nickname is given to a private in the Royal Engineers?
17 Which ex-*Neighbours* actor had a hit in 1991 with *Any Dream Will Do*?
18 What is the German equivalent of the title "Miss"?
19 Which Spanish Surrealist painted *The Persistence of Memory* (1931)?
20 How many pounds are there in a stone?

Answers to QUIZ 41 – Pot Luck

1 Lent
2 Fungi
3 1984
4 Bulldog
5 Leech
6 Accidents
7 *Cabaret*
8 Padre
9 90
10 Moscow
11 Agar
12 Bysshe
13 Burgundy
14 *A Christmas Carol*
15 San Francisco
16 A butterfly
17 Canopy
18 Sadiq Khan
19 A-Ha
20 Sandhurst

QUIZ 44 – Crime

ANSWERS ON PAGE 46

1 The 1995 film *Rogue Trader* was based on whose autobiography?

2 Which Scottish legal officer performs the functions of public prosecutor and coroner?

3 For what crime was Al Capone jailed in 1931…?

4 …and what was the nickname of the team of agents, led by Eliot Ness, who investigated his crimes?

5 What name is given in the UK to an establishment where criminal cases are tried by a judge and jury?

6 What were Bonnie and Clyde's surnames?

7 In which city was John F Kennedy assassinated?

8 Which former UK politician unsuccessfully attempted to fake his own death in 1974?

9 In which year did the Great Train Robbery take place in the UK?

10 Which criminal organisation is known in the USA as Cosa Nostra?

11 What term is given to the likeliest perpetrator of a crime?

12 Who has responsibility for maintaining the law in a US county or independent city?

13 Which murderer was the subject of the 1985 film *Dance with a Stranger?*

14 What did Colonel Thomas Blood famously steal in 1671?

15 Which phrase describes a court case held behind closed doors?

16 What term is given to the head of a prison in the UK?

17 Who played OJ Simpson in the 2016 *American Crime Story* dramatisation *The People v. O.J. Simpson*?

18 Which term describes evidence which may not be brought before a court of law?

19 Which Roman statesman was murdered on the Ides of March?

20 The term "Triad" is used to describe criminal gangs in which country?

Answers to QUIZ 42 – Literature

1 14
2 A diary
3 Enid Blyton
4 Joseph Conrad
5 Pinocchio
6 *Great Expectations*
7 Robert Burns
8 Tortoise
9 Stephen King
10 Winnie-the-Pooh
11 221b Baker Street
12 Wendy
13 Dame Muriel Spark
14 *Maud*
15 *Pride and Prejudice*
16 March
17 *Wuthering Heights*
18 *Watership Down*
19 Narnia
20 Baroness Ruth Rendell

QUIZ 45 – Pot Luck

ANSWERS ON PAGE 47

1 Who presented the long-running children's series *Animal Magic*?
2 Which is the second-largest city in Pakistan?
3 The Goat represents which star sign?
4 What term is given to a grotesquely carved water-spout found on churches?
5 What is the common name for the delphinium?
6 Where are the headquarters of Surrey County Cricket Club?
7 What is the measurable unit of work or energy in the CGS system?
8 Which London hotel was built by theatrical impresario Richard D'Oyly Carte?
9 In which US state is San Francisco?
10 Which red gem is January's birthstone?
11 Which beetle was sacred to the ancient Egyptians?
12 Who directed the 1946 film *It's a Wonderful Life*?
13 What reaping tool is associated with Old Father Time?
14 What was Mel B's Spice Girls' nickname?
15 What kind of animal is a dromedary?
16 Which waters separate Anglesey from the Welsh mainland?
17 Merino is a breed of which animal?
18 What is the family name of Juliet in Shakespeare's *Romeo and Juliet*?
19 What is the currency unit of Israel?
20 "Bob" was a slang term for which pre-decimal coin?

Answers to QUIZ 43 – Pot Luck

1 Sade
2 Gander
3 Jean-Paul
4 Abbey
5 Larceny
6 Eric Bana
7 Lancashire
8 January
9 Caesar
10 Lodge
11 Sarah Jessica Parker
12 Java
13 JD Salinger
14 Cairo
15 Lanolin
16 Sapper
17 Jason Donovan
18 Fräulein
19 Salvador Dali
20 14

QUIZ 46 – Football

ANSWERS ON PAGE 48

Easy

1 Who was the manager of Manchester United from 1945 until 1969?

2 Which club, nicknamed “The Seagulls”, made their Premier League debut in 2017?

3 What term is given to the scoring system where the first goal scored in extra time wins the match?

4 Which European team plays its home games at Camp Nou?

5 How many points are awarded for a win in an FA league game?

6 What name is given to a match between two local teams?

7 Who captained England to victory in the 1966 FIFA World Cup?

8 What colour shirts and shorts do Chelsea players usually wear?

9 In football, what is another name for an upright?

10 In which year did the infamous “Hand of God” incident occur?

Medium

11 Where was the home ground of Arsenal FC until 2006?

12 For which football club did Gary Lineker play professionally from 1978 to 1985?

13 Which stadium is the home of Rangers FC?

14 In which Italian city is the football club Juventus based?

15 Who was the first non-Englishman to manage the England national team?

16 Which football team is known as “the Toffees”?

17 Which hymn is traditionally sung at the FA Cup final?

18 Who captained Portugal to their UEFA European Championship win in 2016?

19 Which Premier League team played home games at Wembley during the 2017-18 season?

20 Which colour card does a football referee show as a warning?

Hard

Answers to QUIZ 44 – Crime

1 Nick Leeson
2 Procurator fiscal
3 Tax evasion
4 The Untouchables
5 Crown court
6 Parker and Barrow
7 Dallas
8 John Stonehouse
9 1963
10 The Mafia
11 Prime suspect
12 Sheriff
13 Ruth Ellis
14 Crown Jewels
15 *In camera*
16 Governor
17 Cuba Gooding Jr
18 Inadmissible
19 Julius Caesar
20 China

QUIZ 47 – Pot Luck

ANSWERS ON PAGE 49

1 Which cocktail is mainly made from gin and cherry brandy?

2 Who won the men's singles title at Wimbledon in 1981, 1983 and 1984?

3 Sudoku puzzles originate from which country?

4 Matt LeBlanc starred as himself in which sitcom with Stephen Mangan and Tamsin Greig?

5 In the Bible, which city's walls were blown down by trumpets?

6 In which body of water is the island of Mustique?

7 What is the term given to a speculative opening move in chess?

8 What is the name of Postman Pat's black and white cat?

9 What initials denote the index of the top 100 UK companies?

10 Which yobbish plasterer was an early Harry Enfield TV creation?

11 Which Turkish dish has doner and shish varieties?

12 To which family of fish does the barbel belong?

13 Who first played Ripley in the 1979 film *Alien?*

14 What surname is shared by former *EastEnders* actors Martin and Ross?

15 Which lasagne-loving ginger cartoon cat is friends with a dog named Odie?

16 What was Thailand's name until 1939?

17 In which county is the seaside town of Whitstable?

18 Which author's novels include *Polo* and *Riders*?

19 What is a potter's oven called?

20 Which Cambridge college is famed for its choir's Christmas carol-singing?

Answers to QUIZ 45 – Pot Luck

1 Johnny Morris
2 Lahore
3 Capricorn
4 Gargoyle
5 Larkspur
6 The Oval
7 Erg
8 Savoy
9 California
10 Garnet
11 Scarab
12 Frank Capra
13 Scythe (or sickle)
14 Scary
15 Camel
16 Menai Strait
17 Sheep
18 Capulet
19 Shekel
20 Shilling

QUIZ 48 – Television

ANSWERS ON PAGE 50

1 In which fictional town is the soap *Home and Away* set?
2 Who was the original host of the quiz show *Blockbusters*?
3 Who starred as Jonathan Pine in the 2016 TV series *The Night Manager*?
4 Which animated canine graduated from Dogwarts University?
5 Who played Lady Mary in *Downton Abbey*?
6 Which celebrity won the first series of *Strictly Come Dancing*?
7 Fozzie Bear featured in which series?
8 Who replaced Margaret Mountford on the TV series *The Apprentice*?
9 Which charity benefits from Red Nose Day?
10 Who returned as the main *Gardeners' World* presenter for the second time in 2011?

11 Peter Dinklage is best known for playing Tyrion Lannister in which TV show?
12 Who was Andy Pandy and Looby Loo's companion in the children's series?
13 What was the first name of Ricky Tomlinson's character in *The Royle Family*?
14 Who played Nicholas Brody in the TV series *Homeland*?
15 Which series starred James Gandolfini as the boss of a crime family?
16 Who played Mr Big in *Sex and the City*?
17 *Holby City* is a spin-off from which other TV drama?
18 Which 1970s TV detective was played by Telly Savalas?
19 Who starred in the TV series *House*?
20 Whom did Rachel Riley replace as the maths expert on *Countdown*?

Answers to QUIZ 46 – Football

1 Sir Matt Busby
2 Brighton and Hove Albion
3 Golden goal
4 Barcelona
5 Three
6 Derby
7 Bobby Moore
8 Blue
9 Goalpost
10 1986
11 Highbury
12 Leicester City
13 Ibrox
14 Turin
15 Sven-Göran Eriksson
16 Everton
17 *Abide with Me*
18 Cristiano Ronaldo
19 Tottenham Hotspur
20 Yellow

QUIZ 49 – Pot Luck

ANSWERS ON PAGE 51

1 Which duo had a 1986 hit with *Edge of Heaven*?
2 Which animal is known as a moose in the USA?
3 Who wrote the 1847 novel *Wuthering Heights*?
4 Which London Underground line is coloured red on maps?
5 What is the fifth sign of the zodiac?
6 What is the official language of the Canadian province of Quebec?
7 In the nursery rhyme *Mary, Mary, Quite Contrary*, what colour are the bells in her garden?
8 What name is given to an official population count?
9 What is the nickname of Sheffield Wednesday FC?
10 What is proverbially said to be as good as a feast?
11 Which port is the largest coastal city in Belgium?
12 Which Staffordshire university is situated near Stoke-on-Trent?
13 What is the only English town to appear in the title of a Shakespeare play?
14 In the children's series *Roobarb and Custard,* what kind of animal was Roobarb?
15 Which drink is associated with California's Napa Valley?
16 Which flaky white cheese is produced in North Yorkshire?
17 Which actress starred in the *Nanny McPhee* films?
18 In the nursery rhyme, which stoat-like animal goes "pop"?
19 What kind of boat has twin parallel hulls?
20 What is the name of London's famous botanical gardens?

Answers to QUIZ 47 – Pot Luck

1 Singapore Sling
2 John McEnroe
3 Japan
4 *Episodes*
5 Jericho
6 Caribbean Sea
7 Gambit
8 Jess
9 FTSE
10 Loadsamoney
11 Kebab
12 Carp
13 Sigourney Weaver
14 Kemp
15 Garfield
16 Siam
17 Kent
18 Jilly Cooper
19 Kiln
20 King's

QUIZ 50 – Mythology

ANSWERS ON PAGE 52

Easy

1 Who, in Greek mythology, were the older gods who preceded the Olympians?
2 Which chemical element is named after the Roman god of communication?
3 What was the name of the Roman goddess of the hunt?
4 Which Norse god was Thor's father?
5 Who was the Greek goddess of love...?
6 ...and who was her Roman counterpart?
7 What did Prometheus steal from the gods?
8 What flower is named after a mythical, self-absorbed youth?
9 Who was the Roman sun god?
10 Which lost continent of legend is said to have sunk below the sea?
11 What is the alternative name for Jupiter, the supreme god of the Romans?

Medium

12 What, in Greek mythology, was a female spirit that tormented evil-doers?
13 Which Gorgon's name is also used for a jellyfish?
14 Which three-pronged spear is traditionally carried by Neptune?
15 Where in the Mediterranean was home to the Minotaur?
16 Which god of property boundaries gave his name to a station at the end of the line?
17 Who was the Roman god of love?
18 What is the name of the resting place for the souls of slain heroes in Norse mythology?
19 What was the name of Jason's ship, in Greek mythology?
20 After which Anglo-Saxon god was Wednesday named?

Hard

Answers to QUIZ 48 – Television

1 Summer Bay
2 Bob Holness
3 Tom Hiddleston
4 Gromit
5 Michelle Dockery
6 Natasha Kaplinksy
7 *The Muppet Show*
8 Baroness Karren Brady
9 Comic Relief
10 Monty Don
11 *Game of Thrones*
12 Teddy
13 Jim
14 Damian Lewis
15 *The Sopranos*
16 Chris Noth
17 *Casualty*
18 Kojak
19 Hugh Laurie
20 Carol Vorderman

QUIZ 51 – Pot Luck

ANSWERS ON PAGE 53

1 What is the world's fastest land animal?

2 What is the name of the commemorative pillar near Pudding Lane in London?

3 What is the science of moral principles?

4 Which puppet fox has the catchphrase "Boom! Boom!"?

5 Where in the body is the hippocampus?

6 What name is given to a sporting event consisting of a series of boat or yacht races?

7 Who was the goddess of the dawn in Roman mythology?

8 In which city is Beverly Hills?

9 Maraschino liqueur is made from which fruit?

10 Which group sang *Lonely This Christmas* in 1974?

11 What is the capital city of Estonia?

12 What volcanic rock forms the Giant's Causeway in Northern Ireland?

13 What is Cockney rhyming slang for "hair"?

14 Which old tax-collecting government department changed its name in 2005?

15 Who was the mid-5th-century king of the Huns?

16 What is the name of Homer Simpson's mother in *The Simpsons*?

17 What is the "season of mists and mellow fruitfulness", according to Keats?

18 Who composed the music for *Star Wars*?

19 In which county is Crewe?

20 Leghorn is a breed of what animal?

Answers to QUIZ 49 – Pot Luck

1 Wham!
2 Elk
3 Emily Brontë
4 Central
5 Leo
6 French
7 Silver
8 Census
9 The Owls
10 Enough
11 Ostend
12 Keele
13 Windsor
14 Dog
15 Wine
16 Wensleydale
17 Dame Emma Thompson
18 Weasel
19 Catamaran
20 Kew

QUIZ 52 – Royalty

ANSWERS ON PAGE 54

Easy

1 Which Royal House opposed the House of York in the Wars of the Roses?
2 What was the name of 18 French kings?
3 Elizabeth Woodville married which king?
4 Who was king of England during WWII?
5 Which 11th-century English king was nicknamed "the Unready"?
6 What is the name of the royal residence in Norfolk?
7 Who was Queen Victoria's consort?
8 Which king of England was defeated at the Battle of Hastings?
9 What was George I's native language?
10 Which castle built for Edward I is situated on the south-eastern shore of Anglesey?
11 What was the name of the ruling dynasty of Scotland from 1371 to 1714?
12 Which king signed the *Magna Carta*?
13 Who was Queen of England from 1558 to 1603?
14 In which royal residence can you view Queen Mary's dolls' house?
15 Which English king, according to legend, burned the cakes?
16 In which city were the remains of Richard III found in 2012?
17 Mary of Teck was the wife of which British monarch?
18 What was the family nickname of both Edward VII and George VI?
19 In which year did Edward VIII abdicate?
20 What was the name of Henry VIII's first wife?

Medium

Hard

Answers to QUIZ 50 – Mythology

1 Titans
2 Mercury
3 Diana
4 Odin
5 Aphrodite
6 Venus
7 Fire
8 Narcissus
9 Sol
10 Atlantis
11 Jove
12 Fury
13 Medusa
14 Trident
15 Crete
16 Terminus
17 Cupid
18 Valhalla
19 *Argo*
20 Woden

QUIZ 53 – Pot Luck

ANSWERS ON PAGE 55

1 Cathay is an old name for which country?
2 What kind of rays cause skin to go brown in the sun?
3 What is the Latin name of the prayer Hail Mary, set to music by many composers?
4 Which 2002 romcom starred Nia Vardalos and John Corbett?
5 Which city hosted the 2018 Winter Olympics?
6 How is actor Nicolas Coppola better known?
7 What cake is traditionally eaten during the Easter period in the UK?
8 Which city is the capital of the Tyrol?
9 Which bird is the emblem of the RSPB?
10 Who composed the piece known as the *Minute Waltz* (1847)?
11 What school is associated with a collar, a crop and the wall game?
12 Who is the Greek goddess of victory?
13 What are the announcements in church of a forthcoming wedding called?
14 Which group had a hit in 1985 with *Road to Nowhere*?
15 What is the name of Tokyo's financial index?
16 Which classic weepie starred Ali MacGraw and Ryan O'Neal?
17 What was the nickname of revolutionary Ernesto Guevara?
18 What term is given to a spindle that joins two wheels?
19 Which iconic fashion doll was launched in 1959?
20 In which county is Robin Hood's Bay?

Answers to QUIZ 51 – Pot Luck

1 Cheetah
2 Monument
3 Ethics
4 Basil Brush
5 In the brain
6 Regatta
7 Aurora
8 Los Angeles
9 Cherry
10 Mud
11 Tallinn
12 Basalt
13 Barnet Fair
14 Inland Revenue (to HM Revenue and Customs)
15 Attila
16 Mona
17 Autumn
18 John Williams
19 Cheshire
20 Chicken

QUIZ 54 – Yellow

ANSWERS ON PAGE 56

Easy

1 Yellowfin is a species of which fish?
2 What is the real name of TV's Keith Lemon?
3 Which Dutch town is famous for its cheese which usually has a yellow coating?
4 Princess Jasmine is a character in which 1992 Disney film?
5 In Formula 1, what does a single yellow flag warn a driver to do?
6 Which insect transmits the disease yellow fever?
7 Which is the largest of the Canary Islands?
8 Which buttercup-like flower has greater and lesser varieties?
9 Which US state is also known as the "Yellowhammer State"?
10 Meadowlark Lemon (1932-2015) was a professional player in which sport?

Medium

11 The yellow jersey is worn by the leader of which sporting event?
12 Which group sang *Tie a Yellow Ribbon Round the Ole Oak Tree* in 1973?
13 Which fictional sleuth has a secretary called Miss Lemon?
14 In which US state is Yellowstone National Park mainly situated?
15 How many points are awarded for potting the yellow ball in the game of snooker?
16 Who played Saffron in the TV series *Absolutely Fabulous*?
17 The Beatles released *Yellow Submarine* as a double A-sided single with which other song?
18 Which fish of the plaice family has a lemon variety?
19 Which actor starred in the 2004 film *Lemony Snicket's A Series of Unfortunate Events*?
20 In which area of London is Canary Wharf?

Hard

Answers to QUIZ 52 – Royalty

1 Lancaster
2 Louis
3 Edward IV
4 George VI
5 Ethelred
6 Sandringham
7 Albert
8 Harold II (Godwinson)
9 German
10 Beaumaris
11 Stewart
12 King John
13 Elizabeth I
14 Windsor Castle
15 Alfred the Great
16 Leicester
17 George V
18 Bertie
19 1936
20 Catherine of Aragon

QUIZ 55 – Pot Luck

ANSWERS ON PAGE 57

1 Which word meaning "poet" is commonly applied to Shakespeare?
2 Dom Perignon is a brand of which drink?
3 Which branch of science deals with the elements and their compounds?
4 Which spectacular North American cascade divides Canada and the USA?
5 Which French fashion designer introduced the New Look in 1947?
6 Which two academic qualifications were replaced by the GCSE exam?
7 In which county is Hexham?
8 Which military force was founded by Trotsky?
9 Which nursery rhyme character had no food for her dog?
10 What style of bay window is also the name of an Oxford college?
11 Which adventure hero visited the *Kingdom of the Crystal Skull* in 2008?
12 What is the capital city of Morocco?
13 What is "eight" in Spanish?
14 An Orcadian is a resident of which group of islands?
15 Who was the original presenter of the UK version of *MasterChef*?
16 What name is given to scissors that leave a zigzag instead of a straight edge?
17 Which male singing voice falls between tenor and bass?
18 What imperial measure is just over half a litre?
19 Which small horse is slang for £25?
20 Which food item is associated with the town of Melton Mowbray?

Answers to QUIZ 53 – Pot Luck

1 China
2 Ultraviolet
3 *Ave Maria*
4 *My Big Fat Greek Wedding*
5 Pyeongchang
6 Nicolas Cage
7 Simnel cake
8 Innsbruck
9 Avocet
10 Chopin
11 Eton
12 Nike
13 Banns
14 Talking Heads
15 Nikkei
16 *Love Story*
17 Che
18 Axle
19 Barbie®
20 North Yorkshire

1 What is the capital city of Scotland?
2 Which canal, completed in 1822, links Inverness and Fort William?
3 What is the name of the old Roman barrier along the Scottish/English border?
4 Who is the patron saint of Scotland?
5 Carnoustie is a famous venue for which sport?
6 Which Shakespeare play is traditionally thought to bring bad luck to its actors?
7 Which city is also known as "the Granite City"?
8 What is the longest river in Scotland?
9 On which island is there a monastery founded by St Columba?
10 Which Celtic language is spoken in many parts of the Western Isles of Scotland?
11 Which Scottish village was the traditional destination for runaway couples?

12 Which 1983 film set in a Scottish village featured music by Mark Knopfler?
13 What name is given to a turnip in Scotland?
14 A sequel to which 1996 film set in Scotland was released in January 2017?
15 Which fabric pattern is particularly associated with Scotland?
16 What is the name of the largest island in the Firth of Clyde?
17 Up till 2008, which coin had a Scottish thistle with a crown on top on the reverse?
18 In which council region is St Andrews?
19 What is the name of the Scottish rugby team's home ground?
20 Which palace is situated just north of Perth?

Answers to QUIZ 54 – Yellow

1 Tuna
2 Leigh Francis
3 Gouda
4 *Aladdin*
5 Slow down
6 Mosquito
7 Tenerife
8 Celandine
9 Alabama
10 Basketball
11 Tour de France
12 Dawn
13 Hercule Poirot
14 Wyoming
15 Two
16 Julia Sawalha
17 *Eleanor Rigby*
18 Sole
19 Jim Carrey
20 Docklands

QUIZ 57 – Pot Luck

ANSWERS ON PAGE 59

1 What is the collective noun for a group of lions?
2 Who won the fourteenth series of *Strictly Come Dancing* in 2016?
3 Which German sports car manufacturer created the Carrera model?
4 What term is given to a case for holding arrows?
5 What is the sixth colour of the rainbow?
6 Which Formula 1 team signed Lewis Hamilton as a young driver in 2007?
7 What is the capital of Spain?
8 Which title was assumed by Oliver Cromwell in 1653?
9 What is the last letter of the Greek alphabet?
10 Who were "on the run" according to the title of the 1990 Robbie Coltrane film?
11 What are the two official languages of Sri Lanka?
12 Which liqueur was originally made by Carthusian monks?
13 Which group had a 1980 hit with *Baggy Trousers*?
14 Which National Theatre auditorium was named after the first actor to be made a life peer?
15 What name is given to a bird of prey's hooked claw?
16 Where is the Sea of Tranquility?
17 The word for which system of weights and measures can also refer to an empire?
18 Which vegetable has pearl and Spanish varieties?
19 Which 1990s interior design show was presented by Carol Smillie from 1996 to 2003?
20 Which musical instruction means "very quickly"?

Answers to QUIZ 55 – Pot Luck

1 Bard
2 Champagne
3 Chemistry
4 Niagara Falls
5 Christian Dior
6 CSE and GCE
7 Northumberland
8 Red Army
9 Old Mother Hubbard
10 Oriel
11 Indiana Jones
12 Rabat
13 Ocho
14 Orkney
15 Loyd Grossman
16 Pinking shears
17 Baritone
18 Pint
19 Pony
20 Pork pie

Easy

1 What is the tallest living mammal?
2 Which animal is known as "the ship of the desert"?
3 What name is given to a badger's burrow?
4 Is a carp a freshwater or sea fish?
5 What term is given to animals that eat food of both plant and animal origin?
6 Which bird shares its name with a chess piece?
7 What is a young hare called?
8 Which seabird is traditionally thought to bring bad luck to sailors?
9 The capybara is native to which continent?
10 Threshers and hammerheads are types of what?
11 What type of creature is a devil's coach-horse?
12 Which is the largest living land mammal?
13 Which bird has long-eared, snowy and barn species?
14 A copperhead is what type of creature?
15 What is the alternative name for the viper?
16 Which spotted cat, related to the leopard, is the largest big cat in the Americas?
17 Are polar bears found in the Arctic or Antarctic?
18 Which sea mammal has bottlenose, short-beaked and spinner species?
19 A drey is home to which animal?
20 Which insect lives in an organised colony known as a formicary?

Medium

Hard

Answers to QUIZ 56 – Scotland

1 Edinburgh
2 Caledonian
3 Hadrian's Wall
4 St Andrew
5 Golf
6 *Macbeth*
7 Aberdeen
8 Tay
9 Iona
10 Gaelic
11 Gretna Green
12 *Local Hero*
13 Neep
14 *Trainspotting*
15 Tartan
16 Arran
17 5p
18 Fife
19 Murrayfield
20 Scone

1 In which room in a church are the ceremonial robes housed?

2 Who succeeded James I (James VI of Scotland) as king of England, Ireland and Scotland?

3 What term is given to the introduction of a poem or play?

4 Who captained the 2012 European Ryder Cup team?

5 What did the Fairy Godmother use to create Cinderella's coach?

6 Which name represents "C" in the radio phonetic alphabet?

7 Who played Wonder Woman in the 1970s TV series?

8 What is the study of the mind called?

9 What is another name for ascorbic acid?

10 Which 15th-century Florentine politician and writer's name is synonymous with devious ambitiousness?

11 Which peninsula lies between the Mersey and Dee estuaries?

12 King Edward is a variety of which vegetable?

13 What branch of medicine is concerned with resistance to disease?

14 Who wrote the 1970 song *Big Yellow Taxi*?

15 Which group had a hit in 1995 with *Wonderwall*?

16 In which country is the ancient city of Petra?

17 What is the location of Kubla Khan's pleasure dome in Coleridge's famous poem?

18 Who starred in the 1990 film *Home Alone*?

19 What name was given to a rioting machine-wrecker of the early 19th century?

20 What is the term for the pointed front part of a ship's bow?

Answers to QUIZ 57 – Pot Luck

1 Pride
2 Ore Oduba
3 Porsche
4 Quiver
5 Indigo
6 McLaren
7 Madrid
8 Lord Protector
9 Omega
10 Nuns
11 Tamil and Sinhalese
12 Chartreuse
13 Madness
14 Olivier
15 Talon
16 On the Moon
17 Imperial
18 Onion
19 *Changing Rooms*
20 Prestissimo

QUIZ 60 – Transport

ANSWERS ON PAGE 62

Easy

1 What type of bicycle is designed for two riders?
2 Which car manufacturer has a rampant horse for its logo?
3 In the tyre pressure measure PSI, what does the "I" stand for?
4 Which group had a hit with *Car Wash* in 1976?
5 What term is given to the cheapest accommodation on a ship?
6 Which liquid is put into car batteries?
7 Gondolas are associated with which city?
8 Which classic car caper film was remade in 2003?
9 Who wrote the novel *Trainspotting*?
10 What is the French term applied to a two-door car with a sloping rear?

Medium

11 Who directed the 1951 thriller *Strangers on a Train*?
12 How many horses pull a troika?
13 Which US city has the only cable car system to still be operated manually?
14 Who was the Scottish inventor of the pneumatic bicycle tyre?
15 What three-masted ship was used by Spanish and Portuguese traders in the 15th and 16th centuries?
16 Which company launched a rocket with a car attached to it in February 2018?
17 Who wrote the novel *Three Men in a Boat*?
18 On which famous train did Dame Agatha Christie set one of her novels?
19 Which small car was designed by Sir Alec Issigonis?
20 Queen released *Bicycle Race* as a double A-side single with which other song?

Hard

Answers to QUIZ 58 – Animal World

1 Giraffe
2 Camel
3 Sett
4 Sea fish
5 Omnivores
6 Rook
7 Leveret
8 Albatross
9 South America
10 Sharks
11 Beetle
12 Elephant
13 Owl
14 A snake
15 Adder
16 Jaguar
17 The Arctic
18 Dolphin
19 Squirrel
20 Ant

QUIZ 61 – Pot Luck

ANSWERS ON PAGE 63

1 What is the common name for the obverse of a coin?

2 Traditionally drunk at Christmas, what is the drink of yolk, beer and spirit?

3 What is the usual background colour of motorway signs?

4 What is held in a creel?

5 A blast furnace is mainly used to produce which metal?

6 Who won the Wimbledon men's singles title in 1975?

7 What is the principal religion of Iran?

8 Who wrote the 2001 novel *Life of Pi*?

9 Which town is the capital of the Isle of Man?

10 What nationality was psychologist Carl Jung?

11 The postcode prefix LS denotes which English city?

12 Which actor topped the charts in 1997 with *Men in Black*?

13 What machine is used for turning and shaping wood?

14 In which county is the beauty spot of Box Hill?

15 Which animal is said to be unable to change its spots?

16 Nichelle Nichols played which *Star Trek* lieutenant?

17 What, in law, is written defamation of character?

18 Which part of the body was Achilles' weakness?

19 On which London road would you find the Royal Courts of Justice?

20 Which group won *The X Factor* in 2011?

Answers to QUIZ 59 – Pot Luck

1 Vestry
2 Charles I
3 Prologue
4 José Maria Olazabal
5 Pumpkin
6 Charlie
7 Lynda Carter
8 Psychology
9 Vitamin C
10 Machiavelli
11 Wirral
12 Potato
13 Immunology
14 Joni Mitchell
15 Oasis
16 Jordan
17 Xanadu
18 Macaulay Culkin
19 Luddite
20 Prow

QUIZ 62 – Nursery Rhymes

ANSWERS ON PAGE 64

1 What did Jack plaster his head with after falling down the hill?
2 Where was the cow in the rhyme *Little Boy Blue*?
3 How many full bags of wool did the black sheep have?
4 Where was Doctor Foster when he stepped in a puddle?
5 What colour was Mary's lamb's fleece?
6 Was it Jack Sprat or his wife who could eat no lean?
7 Where was the queen eating bread and honey in *Sing a Song of Sixpence*?
8 What did Little Tommy Tucker have to sing for?
9 Where had the pussy cat been to see the Queen?
10 What did Little Jack Horner find in his Christmas pie?
11 In the rhyme *Hey Diddle Diddle*, what did the dish run away with?
12 Who was the third man in the tub with the butcher and the candlestick maker?
13 Who pulled the pussy out of the well after Little Johnny Green had put her in there?
14 Where did Bobby Shaftoe wear his silver buckles?
15 Who sat on a wall and had a great fall?
16 Which creature was climbing up the spout?
17 How much did Johnny earn a day in *Seesaw Margery Daw*?
18 Who took the kettle off after Polly put it on?
19 Which two creatures were fighting for the crown all around the town?
20 Who found Lucy Locket's pocket?

Answers to QUIZ 60 – Transport

1 Tandem
2 Ferrari
3 Inch
4 Rose Royce
5 Steerage
6 Distilled water
7 Venice
8 *The Italian Job*
9 Irvine Welsh
10 Coupé
11 Sir Alfred Hitchcock
12 Three
13 San Francisco
14 John Dunlop
15 Galleon
16 SpaceX
17 Jerome K Jerome
18 The *Orient Express*
19 Mini
20 *Fat Bottomed Girls*

QUIZ 63 – Pot Luck

ANSWERS ON PAGE 65

1 The character of Mrs Robinson appears in which 1967 film?

2 How many lines are there on a stave of music?

3 What is the common name for a turf accountant?

4 Who had a hit in 1973 with *Paper Roses*?

5 What was the fabled city of gold sought by Spanish conquistadors?

6 A champagne bottle which has the capacity of two ordinary bottles is given what name?

7 What type of business is London's Lombard Street most associated with?

8 Which brand of yeast and vegetable extract takes its name from a French metal cooking pot?

9 *The Music of the Night* is a song from which musical?

10 Which adjective describes energy created by atomic fission?

11 What term was applied to lively, fashionable young women of the 1920s?

12 In what county is Stonehenge located?

13 What is the name of the Washington headquarters of the US armed forces?

14 What term is given to a flower that blooms year after year?

15 In which 1960s TV series did Patrick McGoohan play "Number Six"?

16 Which imperial length measurement is equivalent to three feet?

17 What was the Irish currency unit before the euro?

18 In which Scandinavian country is the city of Uppsala located?

19 The Tower of London is an example of which style of architecture?

20 What letter is furthest to the right on the bottom row on a standard keyboard?

Answers to QUIZ 61 – Pot Luck

1 Heads
2 Eggnog
3 Blue
4 Fish
5 Iron
6 Arthur Ashe
7 Islam (Shia)
8 Yann Martel
9 Douglas
10 Swiss
11 Leeds
12 Will Smith
13 Lathe
14 Surrey
15 Leopard
16 Uhura
17 Libel
18 His heel
19 The Strand
20 Little Mix

QUIZ 64 – Third Place

ANSWERS ON PAGE 66

Easy

1 Which is the third planet from the Sun?
2 Who was Henry VIII's third wife?
3 Which is China's principal river and the third longest river in the world?
4 In a medley race, which is the third of the four swimming styles?
5 Which is Spain's third largest city?
6 The book and screenplay *The Third Man* was written by which English author?
7 Who won a third term as US President in 1940?
8 Which is the third largest of the Channel Islands?
9 Who wrote the third of the New Testament gospels?
10 Who starred in the 1977 film *Close Encounters of the Third Kind*?

Medium

11 What is the third-highest rank in the peerage?
12 Third place in an Olympic event is awarded which colour medal?
13 What is the third letter of the Greek alphabet?
14 What does the acronym U3A stand for?
15 What is Italy's third largest lake?
16 Which is the third novel in the *Lord of the Rings* series?
17 What is the third sign of the zodiac?
18 Which is the third largest of the Balearic Islands?
19 In the nativity story, which third Wise Man accompanied Caspar and Melchior?
20 Which is the third largest US state, by land area?

Hard

Answers to QUIZ 62 – Nursery Rhymes

1 Vinegar and brown paper
2 In the corn
3 Three
4 Gloucester
5 White as snow
6 His wife
7 Parlour
8 His supper
9 London
10 A plum
11 The spoon
12 The baker
13 Little Johnny Stout
14 At his knee
15 Humpty Dumpty
16 Itsy Bitsy Spider
17 A penny
18 Sukey
19 The lion and the unicorn
20 Kitty Fisher

QUIZ 65 – Pot Luck

ANSWERS ON PAGE 67

1. Which prison reformer was depicted on the Bank of England £5 note from 2002 to 2017?
2. The island of Key West is in which US state?
3. What is the name of the marshy area of East Anglia?
4. Which living ingredient makes bread rise?
5. Michelangelo's statue of David is in which Italian city?
6. Which acid is found in milk?
7. Which animal has species called Bewick's, whooper and mute?
8. What is the name of the double-dot mark used to modify a vowel in German?
9. Who played President Bartlet in the TV series *The West Wing*?
10. The 2008 Olympic Games were held in which country?
11. A golden anniversary celebrates how many years of marriage?
12. Which actress starred in the 1990 film *Misery*?
13. What term is given to substances in the periodic table?
14. Who won the first series of *Pop Idol*?
15. What name was given to a woman doing farm work to support the war effort during WWII?
16. What is a whist competition or tournament called?
17. In which county is Folkestone?
18. What was the name of Henry VIII's elder daughter?
19. Which children's TV series featured a lion called Parsley and an owl called Sage?
20. Which prefix means "to a factor of one million"?

Easy

Medium

Hard

Answers to QUIZ 63 – Pot Luck

1. *The Graduate*
2. Five
3. A bookmaker
4. Marie Osmond
5. El Dorado
6. Magnum
7. Finance
8. Marmite®
9. *The Phantom of the Opera*
10. Nuclear
11. Flappers
12. Wiltshire
13. Pentagon
14. Perennial
15. *The Prisoner*
16. Yard
17. The punt
18. Sweden
19. Norman
20. M

QUIZ 66 – Astronomy

ANSWERS ON PAGE 68

Easy

1 Which planet is closest to the Sun?

2 "The Swan" is the common name for which constellation?

3 What term is given to an interstellar cloud of dust and gas?

4 Which heavenly body was "demoted" from planet status in 2006?

5 What phenomenon occurs when the Moon passes between the Sun and the Earth?

6 In which county is the Jodrell Bank Observatory?

7 What term is given to the second-brightest star in a constellation?

8 A shooting star can also be referred to as what one-word term?

9 What is the name of Earth's galaxy?

10 Which word for the universe is also the name of a garden flower?

Medium

11 What word means "bear" in major and minor constellations?

12 What is the point in the heavens opposite the zenith?

13 Which type of star emits regular bursts of radio waves?

14 What name is given to a field of extremely strong gravitational pull in space?

15 What is another name for the North Star or Pole Star?

16 Hale-Bopp is an example of which heavenly phenomenon?

17 The space telescope launched in 1990 was named after which astronomer?

18 Which constellation forms a W-shape in the sky?

19 What term is given to the small celestial bodies between the orbits of Mars and Jupiter?

20 Which constellation's name is Latin for "crab"?

Hard

Answers to QUIZ 64 – Third Place

1 Earth
2 Jane Seymour
3 Yangtze
4 Breaststroke
5 Valencia
6 Graham Greene
7 Franklin D Roosevelt
8 Alderney
9 Luke
10 Richard Dreyfuss
11 Earl
12 Bronze
13 Gamma
14 University of the Third Age
15 Como
16 *The Return of the King*
17 Gemini
18 Ibiza
19 Balthazar
20 California

1 How many days did it take to tour the world in the title of the Jules Verne novel?

2 What was the surname of the father and daughter who appeared in the film *On Golden Pond*?

3 What is the next highest prime number above 13?

4 What is the surname of the police chief in *The Simpsons*?

5 What is the name of the chapel at Windsor Castle?

6 What name is given to a group of eight musicians?

7 What is a young horse called?

8 In the Beatles song, what is the name of the meter maid?

9 What is the capital of Saudi Arabia?

10 Which nut is obtained from the hickory tree?

11 Who won Olympic gold medals in the decathlon in 1980 and 1984?

12 What is the trunk of the human body called?

13 "I've been alone with you inside my mind" is the opening lyric from which song?

14 In the context of education, where is the UEA located?

15 What condition does pluvius insurance cover?

16 Which city of South Wales is known locally as Abertawe?

17 Which condiment contains cauliflower, onion and gherkin, seasoned with mustard and turmeric?

18 Which fairy-tale character, locked in a tower by a witch, lets down her long golden hair?

19 What is used to make the soles of espadrilles?

20 Who co-starred with Tom Hanks in *Sleepless in Seattle*?

Easy

Medium

Hard

Answers to QUIZ 65 – Pot Luck

1 Elizabeth Fry
2 Florida
3 Fens
4 Yeast
5 Florence
6 Lactic
7 Swan
8 Umlaut
9 Martin Sheen
10 China
11 50
12 Kathy Bates
13 Elements
14 Will Young
15 Land girl
16 (Whist) Drive
17 Kent
18 Mary
19 *The Herbs*
20 Mega

QUIZ 68 – Television Costume Drama

ANSWERS ON PAGE 70

1 Which 2013-16 series, starring Jeremy Piven, followed the life of a famous retailer?
2 Who played the title role in the series *Foyle's War*?
3 Which Tolstoy novel was adapted for TV in 2016 and starred James Norton?
4 Which US series set in South Dakota starred Ian McShane as Al Swearengen?
5 Which 1970s costume drama, set in Eaton Square, was revived in 2010?
6 What is the name of the convent in *Call the Midwife*?
7 Which series was named after the home belonging to the Crawley family?
8 Jonathan Rhys Meyers starred as which monarch in the 2007-10 series *The Tudors*?
9 Who played Charles Ryder in the 1981 adaptation of *Brideshead Revisited?*
10 What was The Halcyon in the 2017 ITV drama series?
11 Which series was set in the fictional village of Aidensfield?
12 Which 1970s drama series about the Roman Empire starred Derek Jacobi in the title role?
13 Who originally played Robin of Loxley in the 1980s series *Robin of Sherwood*?
14 Damian Lewis played Major Richard Winters in which WWII drama series?
15 The BBC series *The Hollow Crown* are adaptations of which playwright?
16 Sir Mark Rylance played which historical figure in the series *Wolf Hall*?
17 Which drama series, revived in 2015, is based on the novels by Winston Graham?
18 What is the title of the Netflix drama series about Elizabeth II?
19 Who played Athos in the 2014 TV series *The Musketeers*?
20 Which *The X-Files* actress appeared in the BBC 2005 adaptation of *Bleak House*?

Easy

Medium

Hard

Answers to QUIZ 66 – Astronomy

1 Mercury
2 Cygnus
3 Nebula
4 Pluto
5 Eclipse
6 Cheshire
7 Beta
8 Meteor
9 Milky Way
10 Cosmos
11 Ursa
12 Nadir
13 Pulsar
14 Black hole
15 Polaris
16 Comet
17 Edwin Hubble
18 Cassiopeia
19 Asteroids
20 Cancer

QUIZ 69 – Pot Luck

ANSWERS ON PAGE 71

1 Which Pacific state dropped "Western" from its name in 1997?
2 Which jubilee did Queen Elizabeth II celebrate in February 2017?
3 What is the capital of Iraq?
4 What was the surname of Shakespeare's wife?
5 What term is given to prayer cushions for kneeling on?
6 What is four score and ten?
7 What name is given to copies of a book published at one time?
8 On the original version of the quiz show *Fifteen to One*, who asked the questions?
9 Which bread roll of Jewish origin is in the shape of a ring?
10 Which style of architecture is epitomised by Bath's Royal Crescent?
11 What is the main alcoholic ingredient of a Pink Lady cocktail?
12 Which Native American chief was the subject of a Longfellow poem?
13 Which spicy peanut sauce is a feature of Asian cuisine?
14 In which European country is the Black Forest?
15 Which light wood is much used in model-making?
16 Which theatre term indicates movement away from the audience?
17 What is the opposite of "yin" in Chinese philosophy?
18 The town of Dunstable is in which county?
19 What kind of bet puts money on a horse finishing in the first three places?
20 Which Somerset town, legendary burial place of King Arthur, is famous for its music festival?

Answers to QUIZ 67 – Pot Luck

1 80
2 Fonda (Henry and Jane)
3 17
4 Wiggum
5 St George's
6 Octet
7 Foal
8 Rita
9 Riyadh
10 Pecan
11 Daley Thompson
12 Torso
13 *Hello* (Lionel Richie)
14 Norwich (University of East Anglia)
15 Rain
16 Swansea
17 Piccalilli
18 Rapunzel
19 Rope
20 Meg Ryan

ANSWERS ON PAGE 72

QUIZ 70 – Also Known As

Easy

1 Which chemical element is also known as quicksilver?
2 Boz was a pen-name of which famous author?
3 What is the stage name of singer Alecia Moore?
4 Which African mammal is also known as the antbear?
5 How is the building at London's 30 St Mary Axe commonly known?
6 Pontoon, twenty-one and vingt-et-un are alternative names for which card game?
7 What is the official name for an Oscar?
8 Who is the comic-strip alter ego of Peter Parker?
9 Acton, Currer and Ellis Bell were the pen names of which sisters?
10 What plant is also known as the Michaelmas daisy?
11 What name was used by the unspeaking Marx brother whose birth name was Adolph?

Medium

12 The Granta is another name for which East Anglian river?
13 What is the Indian term for a vegetable also known as "ladies' fingers" and "okra"?
14 Which breed of dog is also known as the German shepherd?
15 How were Graeme Garden, Bill Oddie and Tim Brooke-Taylor collectively known?
16 In which city is Storkyrkan, officially named Sankt Nicolai kyrka?
17 Which musician's real name is Vincent Furnier?
18 What was the real name of writer George Orwell?
19 Which American wild cat is also known as a cougar or mountain lion?
20 Which British city has the nickname "Auld Reekie"?

Hard

Answers to QUIZ 68 – Television Costume Drama

1 *Mr Selfridge*
2 Michael Kitchen
3 *War and Peace*
4 *Deadwood*
5 *Upstairs, Downstairs*
6 Nonnatus House
7 *Downton Abbey*
8 Henry VIII
9 Jeremy Irons
10 A hotel
11 *Heartbeat*
12 *I, Claudius*
13 Michael Praed
14 *Band of Brothers*
15 William Shakespeare
16 Thomas Cromwell
17 *Poldark*
18 *The Crown*
19 Tom Burke
20 Gillian Anderson

QUIZ 71 – Pot Luck

ANSWERS ON PAGE 73

1 Liverpool and Birkenhead are linked by which tunnel?
2 Which word means both a fencing sword and a thin metal sheet?
3 What was Elvis Presley's middle name?
4 Who played the title role in the 1970s children's TV series *Catweazle*?
5 Chilli was originally native to which country?
6 What name is given to an official with the power to evict people from their houses?
7 Who wrote the nonsense poem *The Hunting of the Snark*?
8 The *Back to the Future* films starred which actor as Marty McFly?
9 How many sheets of paper are there in a ream?
10 Ni is the chemical symbol for which element?
11 Which French president succeeded Jacques Chirac?
12 Which actor starred in the 1955 thriller *To Catch A Thief*?
13 What is the name of the game that Americans call tic-tac-toe?
14 In which year did Kate Bush have a no.1 hit with *Wuthering Heights*?
15 What does the letter "O" stand for in the phrase "SWOT analysis"?
16 Sauchiehall Street is in which city?
17 Which spoof soap included the character of Mrs Overall?
18 The remote and uninhabited interior of Australia is given what name?
19 What term is given for the standard score for each golf hole and for the entire course?
20 What type of animal is a Tamworth?

Answers to QUIZ 69 – Pot Luck

1 Samoa
2 Sapphire (65 years)
3 Baghdad
4 Hathaway
5 Hassocks
6 90
7 Edition
8 William G Stewart
9 Bagel
10 Georgian
11 Gin
12 Hiawatha
13 Satay
14 Germany
15 Balsa
16 Upstage
17 Yang
18 Bedfordshire
19 Each-way
20 Glastonbury

QUIZ 72 – Notable Occasions

ANSWERS ON PAGE 74

Easy

1 Which American national holiday is celebrated in late November?
2 The Up Helly Aa festival is held in which group of islands?
3 What name is given to the Hindu Festival of Lights?
4 The Eisteddfod festival takes place in which country?
5 What is the Jewish candelabrum traditionally used during Hanukkah?
6 Which Christian feast is celebrated on January 6?
7 ANZAC Day is marked by which two countries?
8 The Day of the Dead festival is celebrated in which country?
9 What religious festival is celebrated ten days before Yom Kippur?
10 St Patrick's Day is celebrated in which month?
11 Which Chinese Year started in February 2018?

Medium

12 In the Christian church, what is the period before Christmas called?
13 Which Scottish celebration takes place on January 25?
14 What is the Shrove Tuesday festival in New Orleans called...?
15 ...and what does its name mean in English?
16 What term is given to the seven days before Easter in the Christian church?
17 What name is All Hallows Eve more commonly known as?
18 At what age does a bar mitzvah usually take place?
19 Which Muslim festival marks the end of Ramadan?
20 Which saint's feast day is celebrated on December 26?

Hard

Answers to QUIZ 70 – Also Known As

1 Mercury
2 Charles Dickens
3 Pink
4 Aardvark
5 The Gherkin
6 Blackjack
7 Academy Award
8 Spider-Man
9 The Brontë sisters
10 Aster
11 Harpo
12 The Cam
13 Bhindi
14 Alsatian
15 The Goodies
16 Stockholm
17 Alice Cooper
18 Eric Blair
19 Puma
20 Edinburgh

 ANSWERS ON PAGE 75

1 What was the first name of English composer Vaughan Williams?

2 Palaeontology is the study of which objects?

3 Which measurement of distance is the equivalent of 1.61 kilometres?

4 Who was Stan Laurel's comedy-film partner?

5 Which decade saw the imposition of the three-day week in the UK to conserve fuel supplies?

6 Daventry is in which county?

7 What is the official language of Brazil?

8 Which Indonesian holiday island lies off the eastern tip of Java?

9 According to the proverb, what comes before a fall?

10 Which critically panned 2003 film starred Ben Affleck and Jennifer Lopez?

11 What do the initials "REM" stand for in relation to sleep?

12 The musical *Chess* was written by Sir Tim Rice along with two members of which group?

13 What is the chief city of Majorca?

14 The character of Mrs Merton was created by which actress?

15 "The backbone of England" describes which range of hills?

16 Who wrote the book *The Snowman* (1987)?

17 What is the first name of TV's Grampa Simpson?

18 Which old entertainment company had a large gong as its company logo?

19 How many years of marriage are celebrated at a ruby wedding anniversary?

20 Merlot grapes produce what colour wine?

Answers to QUIZ 71 – Pot Luck

1 The Mersey Tunnel
2 Foil
3 Aaron
4 Geoffrey Bayldon
5 Mexico
6 Bailiff
7 Lewis Carroll
8 Michael J Fox
9 500
10 Nickel
11 Nicolas Sarkozy
12 Cary Grant
13 Noughts and crosses
14 1978
15 Opportunities
16 Glasgow
17 *Acorn Antiques*
18 Outback
19 Par
20 A pig

QUIZ 74 – Harry Potter

ANSWERS ON PAGE 76

Easy

1 Which Hogwarts Minister did Robert Hardy play in the films?
2 Who is Harry's corpulent cousin...?
3 ...and what are the names of that cousin's parents?
4 What is the name of Harry's owl?
5 Harry's wand is made from which wood?
6 What is Hermione's surname?
7 What did Harry get for Christmas in his first term at Hogwarts?
8 How many players are on each team in a game of Quidditch?
9 Professor McGonagall was played by which actress in the films?
10 What was "*Philosopher's*" changed to in the title of the US version of the first book?

Medium

11 What is the first name of Hogwarts headmaster Mr Dumbledore?
12 What is a person from a non-magical family called?
13 Where do students eat their dinner at Hogwarts?
14 What is the first name of Harry's creator?
15 What model was Harry's first broomstick?
16 The fourth book in the series has what subtitle?
17 Which English castle was used as Hogwarts in the films?
18 Which play, set 19 years later than the books, premiered in London in 2016?
19 The Leaky Cauldron is what type of building?
20 Who played Sirius Black in the films?

Hard

Answers to QUIZ 72 – Notable Occasions

1 Thanksgiving
2 The Shetland Islands
3 Diwali
4 Wales
5 Menorah
6 Epiphany
7 Australia and New Zealand
8 Mexico
9 Jewish New Year
10 March (17th)
11 Dog
12 Advent
13 Burns Night
14 Mardi Gras
15 Fat Tuesday
16 Holy Week
17 Hallowe'en
18 13
19 Eid
20 Stephen

QUIZ 75 – Pot Luck

ANSWERS ON PAGE 77

1 What is the name of Goneril and Cordelia's sister in Shakespeare's *King Lear*?
2 What is a series of games that makes up part of a tennis match called?
3 Which US watercourse is nicknamed "Ol' Man River"?
4 What term is given to a military unit headed by a colonel?
5 *Casa di Giulietta* and its balcony are a feature of which Italian city?
6 For which 1985 James Bond film did Duran Duran provide the theme tune?
7 What term applies to someone who doesn't eat or use animal products?
8 In music, how should a piece marked "largo" be played?
9 Who is Betty's husband in *The Flintstones*?
10 Chocolate, ginger and pineapple are varieties of which culinary herb?
11 What is the Spanish title for a married woman?
12 By what name is the larva of a butterfly or moth known?
13 Who starred as Joy Adamson in the 1966 film *Born Free*?
14 In the Bible, who was the second son of Adam and Eve?
15 What is an ancient Celtic priest known as?
16 What sort of creature is a merganser?
17 Which group was fronted by Frankie Valli?
18 Warwickshire County Cricket Club has which ground as its home?
19 What is the name of the royal residence on the River Dee in Scotland?
20 What kind of musical instrument is a tom-tom?

Answers to QUIZ 73 – Pot Luck

1 Ralph
2 Fossils
3 A mile
4 Oliver Hardy
5 1970s
6 Northamptonshire
7 Portuguese
8 Bali
9 Pride
10 *Gigli*
11 Rapid Eye Movement
12 ABBA
13 Palma
14 Caroline Aherne
15 Pennines
16 Raymond Briggs
17 Abe
18 Rank Organisation
19 40
20 Red

QUIZ 76 – Formula 1

ANSWERS ON PAGE 78

1 What does DRS stand for?
2 What driver safety measure was introduced in 2018?
3 Former team owner Eddie Jordan became a presenter on which motoring series in 2016?
4 Which country hosted the first race of the 2018 season?
5 What is the governing body of Formula 1?
6 Which former driver turned commentator is famous for his pre-race grid walk?
7 Who became team principal of Mercedes in 2013?
8 Nico Rosberg represented Germany, but which country did his father Keke drive for?
9 What is the name of Red Bull's junior team?
10 Which European principality first hosted its street circuit Grand Prix in 1929?
11 Who won the World Championship every year from 2010 to 2013?
12 A green flag being shown indicates what to the drivers?
13 What relation was Ayrton Senna to former F1 driver Bruno Senna?
14 At which track has the British Grand Prix been held since 1987?
15 In the 2016 season who became the youngest ever winner of an F1 race...?
16 ...and what is his nationality?
17 Which car number is associated with Lewis Hamilton?
18 What nationality is former World Champion Fernando Alonso?
19 Which company has been the sole supplier of tyres to F1 since 2011?
20 The 2009 World Championship was won by which British driver?

Answers to QUIZ 74 – Harry Potter

1 Cornelius Fudge
2 Dudley Dursley
3 Vernon and Petunia
4 Hedwig
5 Holly
6 Granger
7 An invisibility cloak
8 Seven
9 Dame Maggie Smith
10 *Sorcerer's*
11 Albus
12 Muggle
13 The Great Hall
14 Joanne
15 Nimbus 2000
16 *The Goblet of Fire*
17 Alnwick
18 *Harry Potter and the Cursed Child*
19 A pub
20 Gary Oldman

QUIZ 77 – Pot Luck

ANSWERS ON PAGE 79

1 The rear inner surface of the eye has what name?

2 What is the Spanish equivalent of champagne?

3 What is the name of the Californian river which flows into a desert of the same name?

4 Which of Disney's dwarfs is known for his shyness?

5 From which city does Neapolitan ice cream originate?

6 What was the title of the 1982 chart-topping single by Renée and Renato?

7 What name is given to one of the original inhabitants of Australia?

8 The 1988 Summer Olympics were staged in which Asian city?

9 In which National Park would you find Buckler's Hard and Lymington?

10 What is the US term for a curriculum vitae?

11 Which assembled group recorded the 1984 charity song *Do They Know It's Christmas?*?

12 The name of which sheltering device is the Italian for "little shade"?

13 For what is the Victoria Cross awarded, as inscribed on the medal itself?

14 How many players are there in a rugby league team?

15 Which private was played by John Laurie in the original TV series of *Dad's Army*?

16 What number is represented by the Roman numerals IX?

17 Which salad is made from apple, celery, walnuts and mayonnaise?

18 What is the ancient citadel of Athens called?

19 In which country was the actor Richard Burton born?

20 Which Disney elephant learned to fly using his huge ears?

Answers to QUIZ 75 – Pot Luck

1 Regan
2 A set
3 Mississippi
4 Regiment
5 Verona
6 *A View to a Kill*
7 Vegan
8 Very slowly
9 Barney (Rubble)
10 Mint
11 Señora
12 Caterpillar
13 Virginia McKenna
14 Abel
15 Druid
16 A duck
17 The Four Seasons
18 Edgbaston
19 Balmoral
20 Drum

Easy

1 Where was the Open University founded?

2 What are the initials of the UK professional doctors' organisation?

3 J Edgar Hoover once headed which crime-fighting agency?

4 Who was the General Secretary of the TUC from 1973 to 1984?

5 Wisley gardens in Surrey are owned by which organisation?

6 Who was appointed Managing Director of the International Monetary Fund in 2011?

7 Which conservation organisation has oak leaves as its symbol?

8 In which year was the United Nations formed?

9 What do the initials RAC stand for in a motoring context?

10 Which agency is responsible for World Heritage Sites?

Medium

11 Which branch of the Red Cross operates in Muslim countries?

12 The film *Calendar Girls* featured which organisation?

13 What name is given to a member of the Society of Friends?

14 What is the name of the British actors' union?

15 Which voluntary organisation features in the TV series *Saving Lives at Sea*?

16 "Nation shall speak peace unto nation" is the motto of which organisation?

17 What does the "T" of NATO stand for?

18 What is the symbol of the World Wide Fund for Nature?

19 The Lodge, Sandy, Bedfordshire is the headquarters of which conservation charity?

20 The General Synod is the governing body of which organisation?

Hard

Answers to QUIZ 76 – Formula 1

1 Drag Reduction System
2 Halo
3 *Top Gear*
4 Australia
5 FIA
6 Martin Brundle
7 Toto Wolff
8 Finland
9 Toro Rosso
10 Monaco
11 Sebastian Vettel
12 Track clear
13 Uncle
14 Silverstone
15 Max Verstappen
16 Dutch
17 44
18 Spanish
19 Pirelli
20 Jenson Button

QUIZ 79 – Pot Luck

ANSWERS ON PAGE 81

1 What was the name of Stacey's best friend in the TV series *Gavin & Stacey*?
2 What is a seven-part ensemble called?
3 Grave, acute and circumflex are examples of what?
4 What is the main ingredient of tahini?
5 Which river flows through Worcester?
6 Who had a hit in 1978 with *Copacabana*?
7 Scottish warlord Robert MacGregor had what nickname?
8 Which meringue-based dessert was named after a Russian ballerina?
9 What category of road signs are triangular with a red border?
10 In song, what do you pack up in your old kit bag?
11 What term is used for an American pharmacy dispenser?
12 In which county is Leamington Spa?
13 Which Scottish city gives its name to a variety of fruit cake?
14 Wookey Hole in Somerset is famous for what natural features?
15 Which 2003 Christmas comedy starred Will Ferrell?
16 What term is given to the use of needles to relieve pain?
17 What is the young of the eel called?
18 The single postcode letter B is used for which English city?
19 Who wrote *A Room with a View* (1908)?
20 For what is London's Billingsgate Market famous?

Answers to QUIZ 77 – Pot Luck

1 Retina
2 Cava
3 Mojave
4 Bashful
5 Naples
6 *Save Your Love*
7 Aborigine
8 Seoul
9 The New Forest
10 Résumé
11 Band Aid
12 Umbrella
13 Valour
14 13
15 Private Frazer
16 Nine
17 Waldorf
18 Acropolis
19 Wales
20 Dumbo

QUIZ 80 – Video Games

ANSWERS ON PAGE 82

Easy

1 Which Nintendo® hedgehog is capable of running at tremendous speeds?

2 Which popular free-to-play location-based augmented reality game was released on July 6, 2016?

3 Who is the Nintendo® gorilla who was originally conceived as an enemy of Mario?

4 What is the name of the star of the *Tomb Raider* games...?

5 ...and who portrayed her on screen in 2001 and 2003?

6 In which 2011 game does play focus on the breaking and placing of blocks?

7 What is the title of the 2D table tennis sports game first released in 1972 as an arcade game?

8 Who is Mario's younger brother, often dressed in a green shirt?

9 Microsoft®'s gaming brand has what name?

10 What is the title of the falling-block matching puzzle game first released in 1984?

Medium

11 In which year did Nintendo® release the Wii™?

12 In which 1978 game does the player defend the world from aliens?

13 In which game does the player navigate a maze while avoiding ghosts and eating dots?

14 In which year was the Nintendo® Game Boy™ released in Europe?

15 Who starred in the 2010 film adaptation of *Prince of Persia: The Sands of Time*?

16 In which 1985 game does the player attempt to make deliveries from a bicycle along a suburban street?

17 Which popular warfare game was first released for Microsoft® Windows in 2003?

18 Released in 1981, which arcade video game involves directing amphibians to their homes?

Hard

19 Which 2012 animated film featured a game character who wanted to become a hero?

20 What is the name of the video gaming brand created and owned by Sony?

Answers to QUIZ 78 – Organisations

1 Milton Keynes
2 BMA
3 FBI
4 Len Murray
5 The Royal Horticultural Society
6 Christine Lagarde
7 The National Trust
8 1945
9 Royal Automobile Club
10 UNESCO
11 Red Crescent
12 The Women's Institute
13 Quaker
14 Equity
15 RNLI
16 BBC
17 Treaty
18 Giant panda
19 RSPB
20 The Church of England

QUIZ 81 – Pot Luck

ANSWERS ON PAGE 83

1 Which French term means "in a group, all together"?
2 Which Welsh resort lies between Prestatyn and Colwyn Bay?
3 Collectively, what term is applied to geese on land?
4 *Rolling in the Deep* was a 2010 hit for which singer?
5 What is the name of the volcano which is the highest point of Japan?
6 What ingredients give a quiche Lorraine its flavour?
7 Which animated character lives on Mossy Bottom Farm?
8 In 1909, Louis Blériot became the first person to fly over which body of water?
9 What is the capital city of Lebanon?
10 What is the focal point of an earthquake?
11 Which is India's most sacred river?
12 Campanology is more commonly known by what name?
13 Which actor starred, alongside Paul McGann, in the 1987 film *Withnail & I*?
14 What is fermented to make the Japanese drink sake?
15 *Every Breath You Take* was a chart-topper for The Police in which year?
16 Which wide-angled lens used in photography has a curved front?
17 In linguistics, what is the name given to a describing word?
18 Which fortified wine takes its name from the Spanish town of Jerez?
19 Vince Clarke and Andy Bell formed which pop duo?
20 Which golfer won The Masters in 2017?

Answers to QUIZ 79 – Pot Luck

1 Nessa
2 Septet
3 Accents
4 Sesame seeds
5 Severn
6 Barry Manilow
7 Rob Roy
8 Pavlova
9 Warning signs
10 Your troubles
11 Druggist
12 Warwickshire
13 Dundee
14 Caves
15 *Elf*
16 Acupuncture
17 Elver
18 Birmingham
19 EM Forster
20 Fish

QUIZ 82 – Mountains

ANSWERS ON PAGE 84

Easy

1 What is the highest mountain in Great Britain?
2 Which mountain was carved with the faces of four US presidents?
3 Table Mountain overlooks which city?
4 Which mountains form the backbone of South America?
5 France and Spain are divided by which range?
6 What is the name of the active volcano that stands above the Bay of Naples?
7 What is the second highest mountain in the world?
8 Who was with Sir Edmund Hillary when he reached the summit of Everest in 1953?
9 On which mountain is it said that Noah's Ark came to rest?
10 In which European country is Mount Olympus?
11 On which continent are the Atlas Mountains?

Medium

12 What term is given to a Scottish mountain that is over 3,000 feet high?
13 Which mountain range is known as "the backbone of Italy"?
14 The Columbia Icefield is in which range of mountains?
15 Where is Olympus Mons, the highest mountain in our Solar System?
16 Which continent is separated from Europe by the Ural mountains?
17 What is the highest mountain in England?
18 The longest mountain range in the world is beneath which ocean?
19 Where is Mauna Kea?
20 In which range would you find the highest 14 mountains in the world?

Hard

Answers to QUIZ 80 – Video Games

1 Sonic
2 *Pokémon™ Go*
3 Donkey Kong
4 Lara Croft
5 Angelina Jolie
6 *Minecraft*
7 *Pong*
8 Luigi
9 Xbox
10 *Tetris®*
11 2006
12 *Space Invaders*
13 *Pac-Man™*
14 1990
15 Jake Gyllenhaal
16 *Paperboy*
17 *Call of Duty*
18 *Frogger*
19 *Wreck-it-Ralph*
20 PlayStation®

QUIZ 83 – Pot Luck

ANSWERS ON PAGE 85

1 What are Canterbury bells?
2 What is the everyday term for the tibia?
3 According to the song title, in which London square is a nightingale said to sing?
4 Who is Jack Worthing's alter ego in a famous Oscar Wilde comedy?
5 An Australian rugby union player is given the nickname of which marsupial?
6 On which continent would you find the country of Lesotho?
7 Which fairy-tale character pricked her finger on a spindle?
8 Which is the largest of Italy's lakes?
9 What is Latin for "and the rest"?
10 Which archaeological period followed the predominance of bronze?
11 Who starred in the film *Gandhi*?
12 What type of creature is a wrasse?
13 What is the title of dignity in Portugal and Brazil?
14 In ice hockey what shape is a puck?
15 Who founded the Boy Scouts?
16 Who had a 1984 hit with *I Feel For You*?
17 Of which Scottish island is Portree the largest town?
18 What is an irrational fear of open places called?
19 What nickname is given to the southern states of the USA?
20 From which biblical paradise were Adam and Eve expelled?

Easy Medium Hard

Answers to QUIZ 81 – Pot Luck

1 En masse
2 Rhyl
3 Gaggle
4 Adele
5 Fuji
6 Cheese and bacon
7 Shaun the Sheep
8 English Channel
9 Beirut
10 Epicentre
11 The Ganges
12 Bell-ringing
13 Richard E Grant
14 Rice
15 1983
16 Fisheye
17 Adjective
18 Sherry
19 Erasure
20 Sergio García

QUIZ 84 – The Romans

ANSWERS ON PAGE 86

Easy

1 Which British queen and leader of the Iceni led a revolt against the Romans?
2 What is the name of the large ancient amphitheatre in Rome?
3 In which county is the Roman fort of Housesteads?
4 Which number is represented by “L” in Roman numerals?
5 Vulcan was the god of which element?
6 What name was given to the 15th of certain months in the Roman calendar?
7 The character of Maximus was played by which actor in the 2000 film *Gladiator*?
8 A Roman mansion was known by what general name?
9 What general name was given to the oar-propelled boat used by the ancient Romans?
10 What was the Roman name for the Iberian peninsula?
11 What decorative feature was often seen on the floors of Roman houses?

Medium

12 The Roman remains at Chedworth are in which county?
13 Who played the title role in the 1960 film *Spartacus*?
14 What was the Roman name for Ireland?
15 Who was emperor when fire destroyed half of Rome in AD 64?
16 Which poet wrote *Metamorphoses*?
17 In a Roman bathhouse was the *caldarium* a hot or cold bath?
18 What name was given to a square where business and political matters were discussed?
19 Which English city was called Deva in Roman times?
20 What title was given to Roman emperors?

Hard

Answers to QUIZ 82 – Mountains

1 Ben Nevis
2 Mount Rushmore
3 Cape Town, South Africa
4 The Andes
5 The Pyrenees
6 Vesuvius
7 K2 (also called Mount Godwin-Austen)
8 Sherpa Tensing Norgay
9 Mount Ararat
10 Greece
11 Africa
12 A Munro
13 Apennines
14 Rockies
15 Mars
16 Asia
17 Scafell Pike
18 Atlantic Ocean
19 Hawaii
20 The Himalayas

QUIZ 85 – Pot Luck

ANSWERS ON PAGE 87

1 How many players are there in a netball team?
2 What is the capital of Northern Ireland?
3 Which French word is used for a large creamy layered cake?
4 The Space Needle is a landmark in which US city?
5 How many pockets does a snooker table have?
6 What is the leader of a Cub pack called?
7 In *The Avengers* series of films who plays Tony Stark?
8 Which type of sweet is a rose-flavoured jelly coated with icing sugar?
9 What word is used to describe an inactive volcano?
10 In a military context, what does the “A” of SAS stand for?
11 What is the name of the New York stock exchange?
12 Which islands off Cornwall include St Mary’s and St Martin’s?
13 *Private Life* and *Slave to the Rhythm* were hits for which actress and singer?
14 What is the second book of the Old Testament?
15 What is the North American term for a saloon car?
16 The Bantu language is spoken on which continent?
17 Who duetted with Meat Loaf on the single *Dead Ringer for Love*?
18 Which word meaning “to strike noisily” is also the location of Ireland West Airport?
19 Which word follows *Titus* in the title of a Shakespeare play set in Rome?
20 Inhabitants of Manchester are known by what name?

Answers to QUIZ 83 – Pot Luck

1 Flowers
2 Shin bone
3 Berkeley
4 Ernest
5 Wallaby
6 Africa
7 Sleeping Beauty
8 Garda
9 *Et cetera*
10 The Iron Age
11 Sir Ben Kingsley
12 A fish
13 Dom
14 Circular
15 Lord Robert Baden-Powell
16 Chaka Khan
17 Skye
18 Agoraphobia
19 Dixie
20 The Garden of Eden

QUIZ 86 – Classic Novels

ANSWERS ON PAGE 88

Easy

1 Which North Yorkshire fishing port is associated with Dracula?
2 Anna Sewell created which fictional horse?
3 Who wrote *The Mill on the Floss* (1860)?
4 Mr Bumble in *Oliver Twist* holds which parish position?
5 Who wrote the 1954 novel *Lucky Jim*?
6 Which character in *The Wind in the Willows* was obsessed with motor cars?
7 Alice's pet cat has what name in *Alice's Adventures in Wonderland* (1865)?
8 Who wrote *The Tenant of Wildfell Hall* (1848)?
9 What is the surname of Atticus, hero of *To Kill a Mockingbird* (1960)?
10 What is the title of the only novel written by Oscar Wilde?
11 Which American historical event provides the backdrop to *Gone with the Wind*?

Medium

12 Who is the main character in *The Pilgrim's Progress* (1678)?
13 What is the name of the youngest Bennet sister in Jane Austen's *Pride and Prejudice*?
14 How many steps are there in the title of the 1915 adventure book and film?
15 Who is the heroine of *Vanity Fair* (1847)?
16 In the Robert Louis Stevenson novel, what was the name of Henry Jekyll's alter ego?
17 Who wrote the novel *Ivanhoe* (1820)?
18 What is the first name of F Scott Fitzgerald's character Gatsby?
19 What was Jane Eyre's profession?
20 Who wrote the 1939 novel *The Grapes of Wrath*?

Hard

Answers to QUIZ 84 – The Romans

1 Boudicca
2 The Colosseum
3 Northumberland
4 50
5 Fire
6 Ides
7 Russell Crowe
8 Villa
9 Galley
10 Hispania
11 Mosaic
12 Gloucestershire
13 Kirk Douglas
14 Hibernia
15 Nero
16 Ovid
17 Hot
18 A forum
19 Chester
20 Caesar

QUIZ 87 – Pot Luck

ANSWERS ON PAGE 89

1 What is a baby deer called?

2 Who is the Irish pirate, Hook's sidekick, in *Peter Pan*?

3 The *Four Seasons* concertos were written by which composer?

4 Which fictional Gordon famously declared on film that "greed is good"?

5 How many players are in a cricket team?

6 What term describes a plant with a two-year life cycle?

7 Which river runs through Newcastle and Gateshead?

8 What type of creature is a taipan?

9 What does PAYE stand for?

10 Which US gangster was known as "Scarface"?

11 What is the art of knotting string to make decorative items?

12 In which pursuit was Gary Kasparov a World Champion?

13 What term is given to the art of clear diction and expressive speech?

14 *Wind Beneath My Wings* was a 1988 hit for which singer and actress?

15 What is the capital of Bulgaria?

16 What acronym is given to the catering organisation in the armed forces?

17 Which is the largest US state?

18 The outer bark of which tree is used for making bottle stoppers?

19 Who is the actor brother of Daniel, Stephen and William Baldwin?

20 Which type of constrictor snake is also the name of something worn around the neck?

Easy

Medium

Hard

Answers to QUIZ 85 – Pot Luck

1 Seven
2 Belfast
3 Gateau
4 Seattle
5 Six
6 Akela
7 Robert Downey Jr
8 Turkish delight
9 Dormant
10 Air
11 Dow Jones
12 Isles of Scilly
13 Grace Jones
14 Exodus
15 Sedan
16 Africa
17 Cher
18 Knock
19 *Andronicus*
20 Mancunians

QUIZ 88 – Superheroes

ANSWERS ON PAGE **90**

Easy

1. What fictional substance is Superman's main weakness?
2. What is Wonder Woman's real name...?
3. ...and who played her in the 2017 film *Wonder Woman*?
4. Which Marvel character has the catchphrase, "Don't make me angry. You wouldn't like me when I'm angry"...?
5. ...and what is the name of his alter ego?
6. What is the name of the newspaper that Clark Kent/Superman works for?
7. In the 2014 film, *Guardians of the Galaxy*, which tree-like alien was voiced by Vin Diesel?
8. What is the name of the DC superhero whose main power is superhuman speed...?
9. ...and who plays him in the TV series that started in 2014?
10. Who played the title role in the 2017 film *Spider Man: Homecoming*?

Medium

11. The TV series *Legends of Tomorrow* features which time-travelling spaceship?
12. Which Marvel team debuted in their first comic in 1961?
13. Who plays the title role in Marvel's 2015 film *Ant-Man*?
14. Captain America usually carries which offensive and defensive item?
15. Which actor has starred as the hero in the 2011 film *Green Lantern* and 2016 film *Deadpool*?
16. What is the name of Ray Palmer's superhero?
17. Superman's adopted parents have which first names?
18. Who played Lois Lane in the TV series *Lois & Clark: The New Adventures of Superman*?
19. The character of Thermoman from planet Ultron featured in which sitcom?

Hard

20. Who plays Storm in the *X-Men* film series?

Answers to QUIZ 86 – Classic Novels

1. Whitby
2. Black Beauty
3. George Eliot
4. Beadle
5. Sir Kingsley Amis
6. Toad
7. Dinah
8. Anne Brontë
9. Finch
10. *The Picture of Dorian Gray*
11. Civil War
12. Christian
13. Lydia
14. 39
15. Becky Sharp
16. Edward Hyde
17. Sir Walter Scott
18. Jay
19. Governess
20. John Steinbeck

QUIZ 89 – Pot Luck

ANSWERS ON PAGE 91

1 In which country was the 2010 Ryder Cup played?
2 Na is the symbol for which chemical element?
3 What is a more common name for the New World?
4 What is the white substance around an egg yolk?
5 Stubbornness is particularly associated with which animal?
6 Which Swiss city is the second-largest home of the United Nations?
7 Which creamy dessert is named after a famous English public school?
8 The films *Groundhog Day* and *Lost in Translation* both starred which actor?
9 Which Amsterdam football club shares its name with a hero of the Trojan War?
10 Tangier is a city in which country?
11 In which West Sussex city is there a Festival Theatre?
12 What do Americans call the numbers at the end of their address?
13 Which 1966 Sir Michael Caine film was remade with Jude Law in 2004?
14 Which part of speech adds information about an action?
15 What is Japanese horseradish also called?
16 In folklore, which astronomical phase is associated with the sighting of werewolves?
17 How many official languages are there in Switzerland?
18 Which German car maker has a four-ring trademark?
19 The Rose of Texas is what colour, according to the song?
20 Which Italian title is often applied to a distinguished conductor?

Answers to QUIZ 87 – Pot Luck

1 Fawn
2 Smee
3 Vivaldi
4 Gekko (in Wall Street)
5 Eleven
6 Biennial
7 Tyne
8 Snake
9 Pay As You Earn
10 Al Capone
11 Macramé
12 Chess
13 Elocution
14 Bette Midler
15 Sofia
16 NAAFI
17 Alaska
18 Cork
19 Alec
20 Boa

QUIZ 90 – Rock Music

ANSWERS ON PAGE 92

Easy

1 Peter Gabriel and Phil Collins were members of which band?

2 Which band, fronted by Rod Stewart, had a 1971 hit with *Stay with Me*?

3 The Pink Floyd classic *Money* is from which album?

4 Which *American Idol* finalist subsequently provided lead vocals for Queen?

5 Which group had a hit in 1972 with *Silver Machine*?

6 Which iconic frontman was born Farrokh Bulsara in 1946?

7 Dave Grohl of the Foo Fighters was previously the drummer for which influential 1990s band?

8 Ultravox and Thin Lizzy have both featured which musician?

9 The band Bon Jovi were formed in which US state, the title of their fourth album?

10 Who had hits in the 1970s with *School's Out* and *Elected*?

Medium

11 Which band had a 1967 hit with *Light My Fire*?

12 Which group won the Mercury Music Prize for their 2008 album *The Seldom Seen Kid*?

13 The Guns N' Roses cover of which Bond theme was a hit in 1991?

14 Which rock group sang *My Generation* in 1965?

15 *I Predict a Riot* and *Ruby* were hits for which group?

16 Which UK band had chart success with *Whole Lotta Love* in 1969?

17 Which group opened Live Aid in 1985?

18 *Gimme All Your Lovin'* was a 1983 hit for which US band?

19 Which 1975 Ken Russell film was based on an album by The Who?

20 In which city were the band Def Leppard formed?

Hard

Answers to QUIZ 88 – Superheroes

1 Kryptonite
2 Diana Prince
3 Gal Gadot
4 The Hulk
5 Dr Bruce Banner
6 *The Daily Planet*
7 Groot
8 The Flash
9 Grant Gustin
10 Tom Holland
11 *The Waverider*
12 The Fantastic Four
13 Paul Rudd
14 His shield
15 Ryan Reynolds
16 The Atom
17 Martha and Jonathan
18 Teri Hatcher
19 *My Hero*
20 Halle Berry

QUIZ 91 – Pot Luck

ANSWERS ON PAGE 93

1 Goal attack and goal defence are positions in which sport?

2 Who co-starred with Morgan Freeman in *The Bucket List*?

3 Carisbrooke Castle is on which island?

4 What was the round space in which gladiators fought?

5 *Signorina* is the form of address to an unmarried woman in which language?

6 Which word links a religious painting with a symbol on a computer screen?

7 Who had a hit with *Silver Lady* in 1977?

8 Which fibrous silicate mineral was used as a fire-resistant material until it was found to be harmful?

9 In aviation, what function does the black box serve?

10 Which material is associated with the Highland region of Harris?

11 Who won the men's singles title at Wimbledon in 1987?

12 Which children's comic featured Desperate Dan and Korky the Cat?

13 By which initials are Royal Dutch Airlines known?

14 What term is given to treatment of a disease by the use of water?

15 Who is the first actress to play the lead role in the TV series *Doctor Who*?

16 In which island group is Kos?

17 Someone described as a brunette has what colour hair?

18 Arborio is a type of which food?

19 What was the Roman name for Britain?

20 On which day of the week do Muslims gather to pray together?

Answers to QUIZ 89 – Pot Luck

1 Wales
2 Sodium
3 The Americas
4 Albumen
5 Mule
6 Geneva
7 Eton mess
8 Bill Murray
9 Ajax
10 Morocco
11 Chichester
12 Zip code
13 *Alfie*
14 Adverb
15 Wasabi
16 Full moon
17 Four
18 Audi
19 Yellow
20 Maestro

QUIZ 92 – Points of the Compass

ANSWERS ON PAGE 94

1 What colour is the Northern line on London Underground maps?
2 Which character was Adam West famous for playing on TV?
3 Which long-running BBC drama series features the location of Albert Square?
4 In which body of water is Dogger Bank?
5 Norfolk, Suffolk and Cambridgeshire make up which region of England?
6 Which country co-hosted the 2002 FIFA World Cup with Japan?
7 *Gold Digger* was a 2005 hit for which rapper?
8 Which actor starred in the 1959 thriller *North by Northwest*?
9 What is the name of the US military academy in New York State?
10 The West Indies is surrounded by which sea?
11 Which is the nearest city and port to the New Forest?
12 Which castle is the seat of the Dukes of Northumberland?
13 *Stay Another Day* was a hit for which group in 1994?
14 What is the administrative capital of South Africa?
15 Which US state is nicknamed "The Mountain State"?
16 Who wrote the 1855 novel *North and South*?
17 What term refers to the area around the North Pole?
18 The longest pleasure pier in the world is found in which English town?
19 What is the capital of New South Wales?
20 In which London borough is the Globe Theatre?

Answers to QUIZ 90 – Rock Music

1 Genesis
2 Faces
3 *Dark Side of the Moon*
4 Adam Lambert
5 Hawkwind
6 Freddie Mercury
7 Nirvana
8 Midge Ure
9 New Jersey
10 Alice Cooper
11 The Doors
12 Elbow
13 *Live and Let Die*
14 The Who
15 Kaiser Chiefs
16 Led Zeppelin
17 Status Quo
18 ZZ Top
19 *Tommy*
20 Sheffield

QUIZ 93 – Pot Luck

ANSWERS ON PAGE 95

1 The dingo is a wild dog from which country?

2 What was the name of the Titan in Greek mythology who held the world on his shoulders?

3 Which dance style was spelled out by an Ottawan hit of 1980?

4 What name is given to a Viking ship?

5 "Per ardua ad astra" is the motto of which of the services?

6 Which Devon town is famous for its carpets?

7 "The king of beasts" describes which animal, native to Africa?

8 Which Scottish football club shares its name with a playing card suit?

9 What is the name of the saxophone-playing member of TV's Simpson family?

10 What word precedes "Kush" to denote an Asian mountain range?

11 Ludlow Castle is an example of what type of architecture?

12 Which 1982 Roxy Music album shares a name with an island in Arthurian legend?

13 In which county is the town of Blandford Forum?

14 Who wrote the 1953 play *Waiting for Godot*?

15 A crocodile is the logo of which sports clothing company?

16 The invasion of which country began the First Gulf War in 1991?

17 What city in Colorado sounds like a large rock?

18 In the 1999 romcom *Notting Hill*, who played Hugh Grant's scruffy flatmate?

19 What is the capital city of Chile?

20 What was Brotherhood of Man's winning Eurovision entry in 1976?

Answers to QUIZ 91 – Pot Luck

1 Netball
2 Jack Nicholson
3 Isle of Wight
4 Arena
5 Italian
6 Icon
7 David Soul
8 Asbestos
9 Flight recorder
10 Tweed
11 Pat Cash
12 *Dandy*
13 KLM
14 Hydrotherapy
15 Jodie Whittaker
16 Dodecanese
17 Brown
18 Rice
19 Britannia
20 Friday

QUIZ 94 – Animated Films

ANSWERS ON PAGE 96

Easy

1 Which Disney film features the panther Bagheera?

2 What type of fish is Nemo in the 2003 film *Finding Nemo*?

3 Who voiced the character of Joy in the 2015 film *Inside Out*?

4 In which 1970 Disney film does the character Thomas O'Malley appear?

5 *Early Man* is a 2018 film produced by which studio?

6 In which 2009 film did a pensioner travel in a house lifted by balloons?

7 What is the name of the princess in the 1959 Disney film *Sleeping Beauty*?

8 The 2013 film *Frozen* is based on the story *The Snow Queen* by which author?

9 What was the title of the first feature-length film produced by Pixar?

10 What is the name of Disney's Little Mermaid?

Medium

11 Who voiced the title character in the 2018 film *Peter Rabbit*?

12 *Minions* (2015) is a spin-off from which series of films?

13 In which part-animated 2007 Disney film did Amy Adams play a princess who found herself in New York?

14 What was the title of the 2013 prequel to *Monsters Inc.*?

15 Who voiced the title character in the 2011 film *Puss in Boots*...?

16 ...and in which 2004 film did the character first appear?

Hard

17 Which 2002 film featured a woolly mammoth?

18 Who is Stitch's best friend in the 2002 Disney film?

19 What is the name of the hero of the *How to Train Your Dragon* series of films?

20 Which film features the song *Walking in the Air*?

Answers to QUIZ 92 – Points of the Compass

1 Black
2 Batman
3 *EastEnders*
4 North Sea
5 East Anglia
6 South Korea
7 Kanye West
8 Cary Grant
9 West Point
10 Caribbean
11 Southampton
12 Alnwick
13 East 17
14 Pretoria
15 West Virginia
16 Elizabeth Gaskell
17 Arctic Circle
18 Southend-on-Sea
19 Sydney
20 Southwark

1 What does QI stand for in the name of the TV panel game?

2 What term is given to a baby with five siblings of the same age?

3 Who was *Crying* at the top of the charts in 1980?

4 Which word meaning "having a jagged edge" comes from the Latin word for "saw"?

5 A yarmulke is a type of what item of clothing?

6 Which race is run over a distance of just over 13 miles?

7 Morocco has four Imperial cities: Fez, Meknes, Rabat and which other?

8 A Hawaiian garland of flowers is given what name?

9 What term is given to a brief film or TV role by a prominent actor?

10 Which 1989 Sir John Hurt film was about the Profumo affair?

11 Bet Gilroy is a former landlady of which fictional TV pub?

12 Which Irish castle has a famous stone that claims to confer the power of eloquent speech?

13 What are training shoes called in the US?

14 What was the name of Mark Hamill's character in the *Star Wars* films?

15 Jarvis Cocker fronted which 1990s group?

16 What is the nationality of opera singer Andrea Bocelli?

17 Which is the highest mountain in Wales?

18 The musical *We Will Rock You* features songs by which group?

19 Which river flows through Hereford?

20 Which kind of volcanic rock is used for exfoliating hard skin?

Answers to QUIZ 93 – Pot Luck

1 Australia
2 Atlas
3 Disco
4 Longboat
5 RAF
6 Axminster
7 Lion
8 Hearts
9 Lisa
10 Hindu
11 Norman
12 Avalon
13 Dorset
14 Samuel Beckett
15 Lacoste
16 Kuwait
17 Boulder
18 Rhys Ifans
19 Santiago
20 *Save Your Kisses For Me*

Easy

Medium

Hard

QUIZ 96 – Science

ANSWERS ON PAGE 98

1 How many chambers are there in a human heart?
2 Which element has the chemical symbol Au?
3 What is Earth's closest star?
4 The first cloned mammal was given what name?
5 Which adjective relates to the kidneys?
6 Which physicist is known for his theory of relativity?
7 Hydroelectric generators are powered by what substance?
8 What is the coloured part of the eye?
9 What term is given to an instrument for measuring heights?
10 Diabetes is treated with which substance?
11 What is the chemical opposite of an acid?
12 When the sound barrier is broken what noise occurs?
13 Who was the first man on the moon?
14 What term is given to a scientist who specialises in plants?
15 German measles has what medical name?
16 What term is given to a six-sided plane figure?
17 Tinnitus affects which part of the body?
18 Which chemical is used to disinfect swimming pools?
19 What is the medical name for the windpipe?
20 What does the "I" stand for in the astronomical abbreviation ISS?

Answers to QUIZ 94 – Animated Films

1 *The Jungle Book*
2 A clownfish
3 Amy Poehler
4 *The Aristocats*
5 Aardman Animations
6 *Up*
7 Aurora
8 Hans Christian Andersen
9 *Toy Story*
10 Ariel
11 James Corden
12 *Despicable Me*
13 *Enchanted*
14 *Monsters University*
15 Antonio Banderas
16 *Shrek 2*
17 *Ice Age*
18 Lilo
19 Hiccup
20 *The Snowman*

QUIZ 97 – Pot Luck

ANSWERS ON PAGE 99

1 About which fictional otter did Henry Williamson write?

2 Which Californian grape variety is used to make pinkish white wine?

3 Which imperial weight measure approximates to 28 grams?

4 Which Jamaican-American singer had hits in 2000 with *It Wasn't Me* and *Angel?*

5 What is the chemical symbol for phosphorus?

6 In which county is The Wrekin hill?

7 What term was given to early 1980s groups such as Duran Duran and Spandau Ballet?

8 Epping is on which London Underground line?

9 What was the first name of Jane Leeves' character in the TV series *Frasier*?

10 What is the term for the Asian dot of forehead colour?

11 LaGuardia airport serves which city?

12 Which style of music with a syncopated rhythm is associated with the composer Scott Joplin?

13 In which country is the Lada car made?

14 Which actor won an Oscar for his starring role in the 2008 film *Milk*?

15 Which TV choirmaster formed the Military Wives Choir?

16 A Chinese boat and unsolicited mail are linked by which word?

17 In which town in South Wales is the *Parc y Scarlets* rugby stadium?

18 Which popular girls' comic featured *The Four Marys*?

19 What was the stage name of Ian Kilmister of Motorhead?

20 Which UK Prime Minister said "A week is a long time in politics"?

Answers to QUIZ 95 – Pot Luck

1 Quite Interesting
2 Sextuplet
3 Don McLean
4 Serrated
5 Skullcap
6 Half-marathon
7 Marrakesh
8 A lei
9 Cameo
10 *Scandal*
11 Rovers Return
12 Blarney
13 Sneakers
14 Luke Skywalker
15 Pulp
16 Italian
17 Snowdon
18 Queen
19 Wye
20 Pumice

QUIZ 98 – Golf

ANSWERS ON PAGE 100

1 Arnold Palmer, Jack Nicklaus and which other golfer were known as "The Big Three"?

2 The long grass on a golf course is referred to by what name?

3 What colour jacket is awarded to the winner of The Masters tournament?

4 Virginia Water in Surrey is home to which famous golf course?

5 Which animal's limb is used to describe a hole that bends between the tee and the green?

6 "The Great White Shark" is a nickname of which Australian golfer?

7 Which peg is used to support a golf ball?

8 The 2016 Ryder Cup was won by which team?

9 Ailsa Craig is a hole on which Scottish course?

10 What term is given to an area of sand designed as a course obstacle?

11 In which country is the Celtic Manor course?

12 The clubhouse or pub on a golf course is referred to as which hole?

13 What is Tiger Woods' real first name?

14 What is a scratch golfer's handicap?

15 What is the lowest level of par given to a hole?

16 How is a shot described which a right-handed player pulls to the left, as opposed to a slice?

17 A seaside course is given what name?

18 In 2009 which US golfer came close to winning The Open at the age of 59?

19 What nationality is Ernie Els?

20 What is the name of the trophy presented to the winner of The Open tournament?

Easy

Medium

Hard

Answers to QUIZ 96 – Science

1 Four
2 Gold
3 The Sun
4 Dolly (a sheep)
5 Renal
6 Albert Einstein
7 Water
8 The Iris
9 Altimeter
10 Insulin
11 Alkali
12 Sonic boom
13 Neil Armstrong
14 Botanist
15 Rubella
16 Hexagon
17 The ears
18 Chlorine
19 The trachea
20 International

QUIZ 99 – Pot Luck

ANSWERS ON PAGE 101

1 Which New York department store features in the film *Miracle on 34th Street*?

2 What, in tennis, is a service obstructed by the net?

3 The lychee is a fruit from which country?

4 Which child star sang *On the Good Ship Lollipop* in the 1934 film *Bright Eyes?*

5 What were the initials of the former Soviet secret service?

6 What are the leather shorts worn with braces popular with both men and boys in Bavaria called?

7 Which mid-Kent town has an "International" station?

8 In UK road signs, what does a red circle with a white horizontal bar forbid?

9 Who played Ronni Mitchell in *EastEnders?*

10 Geronimo was a member of which Native American tribe?

11 In which body of water are the Maldives?

12 Which small musical instrument did Larry Adler play?

13 What type of rock is associated with Blaenau Ffestiniog in North Wales?

14 "Adam's Ale" is a term for which liquid?

15 Who was the original host of the series *Room 101*?

16 Which district of south London is famous for its Common and Junction?

17 In which county is Shepton Mallet?

18 Who was Dudley Moore's 1960s comedy partner?

19 Proverbially, what does a stitch in time save?

20 In which country is Penang?

Answers to QUIZ 97 – Pot Luck

1 Tarka
2 Zinfandel
3 An ounce
4 Shaggy
5 P
6 Shropshire
7 New Romantics
8 The Central Line
9 Daphne (Moon)
10 Bindi
11 New York
12 Ragtime
13 Russia
14 Sean Penn
15 Gareth Malone
16 Junk
17 Llanelli
18 *Bunty*
19 Lemmy
20 Harold Wilson (Baron Wilson of Rievaulx)

QUIZ 100 – Horses

ANSWERS ON PAGE **102**

Easy

1 What name is given to the occupation of a person who fits horseshoes?
2 What is the female parent of a horse called?
3 Bucephalus belonged to which leader?
4 Which joint on a horse is the equivalent of a human ankle?
5 What is the name for an old Russian or Ukrainian warrior, famed for his horsemanship?
6 The stirrup supports which part of the body when riding a horse?
7 What word describes a horse with a bay or chestnut coat dotted with grey and white?
8 What was the name of the Lone Ranger's horse?
9 The Clydesdale originates from which country?
10 Which creature of Greek mythology was half-human, half-horse?

Medium

11 Annual horse trials are held at which Lincolnshire stately home?
12 Young racehorses between 12 and 24 months old are given what name?
13 What was the name of the winning horse in the 2018 Grand National?
14 Which equestrian pace comes between walk and canter?
15 Doncaster has been the venue for which annual horse race since 1776?
16 Which word means "related to or connected with horses"?
17 What part of a bridle goes into the horse's mouth?
18 Black Bess belonged to which highwayman?
19 Which was the winged horse in Greek mythology that gave its name to a constellation?
20 Which Ford car is named after a wild horse?

Hard

Answers to QUIZ 98 – Golf

1 Gary Player
2 The rough
3 Green
4 Wentworth
5 Dog-leg
6 Greg Norman
7 Tee
8 United States
9 Turnberry
10 Bunker
11 Wales
12 19th
13 Eldrick
14 Zero
15 Three
16 Hook
17 Links
18 Tom Watson
19 South African
20 Claret jug

QUIZ 101 – Pot Luck

ANSWERS ON PAGE 103

1 Who was "educated" in a 1950s radio series?

2 What is the unit of currency in Turkey?

3 The name of which small domestic fowl is also used to describe a weight in boxing?

4 Which French term describes a pervasive feeling of boredom and languor?

5 Who played the title role in the 2006 film *Marie Antoinette*?

6 November 2 marks which Catholic festival?

7 What four-letter term can describe both a bathing beach and an outdoor swimming pool?

8 Who sang the 1972 song *Walk on the Wild Side*?

9 The TV series *Downton Abbey* was created by which screenwriter?

10 What gymnastic apparatus has two rails, at different heights?

11 What name is given to a person who scavenges at low tide?

12 In the novel *Moby-Dick*, who is the captain of the Pequod?

13 In which US state do the Amish mainly live?

14 What name is given to the checkerboard diamond pattern often used on socks?

15 In the TV series *Last of the Summer Wine*, what was Nora's surname?

16 Who is Roald Dahl's fictional champion of the world?

17 Which Irish town gives its name to a famous illuminated book of Latin Gospels?

18 Which fruit shares its name with the official form of the Chinese language?

19 What is the stiff bristle on an ear of barley called?

20 Emmental cheese originates from which country?

Answers to QUIZ 99 – Pot Luck

1 Macy's
2 Let
3 China
4 Shirley Temple
5 KGB
6 Lederhosen
7 Ashford
8 Entry
9 Samantha Womack
10 Apache
11 Indian Ocean
12 Harmonica
13 Slate
14 Water
15 Nick Hancock
16 Clapham
17 Somerset
18 Peter Cook
19 Nine
20 Malaysia

QUIZ 102 – Diamonds and Pearls

ANSWERS ON PAGE 104

Easy

1 On which Hawaiian island is Pearl Harbor situated?
2 Diamondback can refer to a terrapin and which other reptile?
3 The playing area in which sport is known as a diamond?
4 A pearl anniversary marks how many years of marriage?
5 Which actress starred in the 2003 film *Girl With a Pearl Earring...*?
6 ...and who wrote the 1999 novel on which it is based?
7 Diamonds are a form of which element?
8 Pearls are formed by which creature?
9 Are diamonds a major or minor suit in contract bridge?
10 Who wrote the opera *The Pearl Fishers*?

Medium

11 Who had hits with *Sweet Caroline* and *Love on the Rocks*?
12 Pearl is a birthstone for which month?
13 Who starred in the 2006 film *Blood Diamond*?
14 In which year did Queen Elizabeth II celebrate her diamond jubilee...?
15 ...and in which year did Queen Victoria celebrate the same jubilee?
16 Who had a 1977 hit with *Pearl's a Singer*?
17 In a Beatles song, who was "in the sky with diamonds"?
18 Who played James Bond in *Diamonds are Forever...*?
19 ...and who performed the theme song?
20 Who released a 1991 album entitled *Diamonds and Pearls*?

Hard

Answers to QUIZ 100 – Horses

1 Farrier
2 Dam
3 Alexander the Great
4 Fetlock
5 Cossack
6 Foot
7 Roan
8 Silver
9 Scotland
10 Centaur
11 Burghley
12 Yearlings
13 Tiger Roll
14 Trot
15 The St Leger
16 Equine
17 Bit
18 Dick Turpin
19 Pegasus
20 Mustang

QUIZ 103 – Pot Luck

ANSWERS ON PAGE 105

1 Which aromatic spice is obtained from the shell of nutmegs?

2 Where is a cummerbund worn?

3 A marlin is what type of creature?

4 Which compound is added to toothpaste?

5 Which religion is associated with Krishna?

6 Who sang the theme song to the TV series *Dad's Army*?

7 Which area of Liverpool is home to the Grand National?

8 Jule Styne and Stephen Sondheim wrote which musical based on the true story of a famous striptease artist?

9 What is the name of Porky Pig's cartoon duck companion?

10 In the Middle Ages, what name was given to a person who studied the art and craft of turning base metals into gold?

11 Who starred in the TV series *Doctor Foster*?

12 Which city of New York State shares its name with the American bison?

13 What name is given to radioactive material produced by nuclear explosions?

14 The flowers of the laburnum tree are which colour?

15 Which overhead train system runs on one track?

16 How many players are there in a volleyball team?

17 What word denotes a Mexican state and a small breed of dog?

18 What term is given to a piece of leather used for sharpening razors?

19 The 1963 film *The Great Escape* starred which actor as "The Cooler King"?

20 Which strongly flavoured blue-veined cheese is named after a Cambridgeshire village?

Answers to QUIZ 101 – Pot Luck

1 Archie
2 Lira
3 Bantam
4 Ennui
5 Kirsten Dunst
6 All Souls' Day
7 Lido
8 Lou Reed
9 Julian Fellowes (Baron Fellowes of West Stafford)
10 Asymmetric or uneven bars
11 Mudlark
12 Ahab
13 Pennsylvania
14 Argyle
15 Batty
16 Danny
17 Kells
18 Mandarin
19 Awn
20 Switzerland

Easy

1 Where does the Ceremony of the Keys take place every night?

2 How many bronze lions are there in Trafalgar Square?

3 What is the name of the ferris wheel on the banks of the Thames, built to celebrate the millennium?

4 What exactly is Big Ben?

5 What is the official residence of the Prime Minister in London...?

6 ...and who lives at the next-door house one number higher?

7 Who was the architect of St Paul's Cathedral?

8 Which river crossing is "falling down" in a popular nursery rhyme?

9 Rotten Row is in which area of London?

10 In which famous building are coronations held?

Medium

11 By what name is the statue in the middle of Piccadilly Circus known?

12 What gift from the Norwegian people is placed in Trafalgar Square every year?

13 Which silent film star is immortalised by a statue in Leicester Square?

14 What is the name of the ceremony that takes place on the forecourt of Buckingham Palace?

15 The London Underground has what nickname?

16 What Egyptian obelisk stands on the Thames Embankment?

17 Battersea is in which borough?

18 In which year did London buses stop accepting cash fares?

19 Which Beatles album is named after a London street?

Hard

20 Which famous financial institution can be found on London's Threadneedle Street?

Answers to QUIZ 102 – Diamonds and Pearls

1 Oahu
2 Rattlesnake
3 Baseball
4 30
5 Scarlett Johansson
6 Tracy Chevalier
7 Carbon
8 Oyster
9 Minor
10 Bizet
11 Neil Diamond
12 June
13 Leonardo DiCaprio
14 2012
15 1897
16 Elkie Brooks
17 Lucy
18 Sir Sean Connery
19 Dame Shirley Bassey
20 Prince

QUIZ 105 – Pot Luck

ANSWERS ON PAGE 107

1 Which English dynasty began with Henry VII and ended with Elizabeth I?

2 Lowestoft is in which county?

3 Which saint is celebrated on February 14?

4 *Coz I Luv You* was the first UK no.1 for which band?

5 What time of day does the adjective "crepuscular" refer to?

6 What was the river crossed by ferryman Charon in Greek mythology?

7 Cuthbert, Dibble and Grubb are firemen in which fictional town?

8 What name is given to the fleshy hanging part at the back of the soft palate?

9 What is conscription called in the USA?

10 What is the national language of Pakistan?

11 Who took over from John Nettles as Midsomer's Inspector Barnaby?

12 Which parasitic plant is associated with kissing at Christmas?

13 A macchiato is what type of drink?

14 What was the name of the central family in *The Godfather*?

15 What term is given to a touchdown in rugby?

16 What is a proviso or part of a sentence?

17 What was the Black Bottom, popular in the US in the 1920s?

18 Mount Ararat is in which country?

19 Which wedding anniversary is celebrated with china?

20 What is the main ingredient of guacamole?

Answers to QUIZ 103 – Pot Luck

1 Mace
2 Round the waist
3 Fish
4 Fluoride
5 Hinduism
6 Bud Flanagan
7 Aintree
8 Gypsy
9 Daffy
10 Alchemist
11 Suranne Jones
12 Buffalo
13 Fallout
14 Yellow
15 Monorail
16 Six
17 Chihuahua
18 Strop
19 Steve McQueen
20 Stilton

QUIZ 106 – Famous Buildings

ANSWERS ON PAGE 108

Easy

1 In which London borough is The Shard?
2 The CN tower is in which Canadian city?
3 Which Royal Palace is located in Edinburgh?
4 For which performing arts building is Sydney Harbour renowned?
5 Which palace on the River Thames is famous for its maze?
6 St Basil's Cathedral stands in which Russian square?
7 On which body of water is Urquhart Castle located?
8 What is Lancashire's highest landmark and tourist attraction?
9 The Notre-Dame cathedral in Paris is an example of which type of architecture?
10 Which Scottish castle is the main setting for Shakespeare's *Macbeth*?
11 In which Gulf state is the Burj Khalifa skyscraper?
12 The Hall of Mirrors is a famous gallery in which French palace?
13 In which year was Buckingham Palace first opened to the public?
14 The Lincoln Memorial is situated in which US city?
15 Which English cathedral was struck by lightning in July 1984?
16 What is the name of the 13th-century Moorish palace near Granada, Spain?
17 The Petronas Towers, one of the world's tallest buildings, are in which city?
18 Which famous building do Beefeaters guard?
19 The Duke of Wellington's tomb is in which London building?
20 In which Italian region is the Leaning Tower of Pisa?

Medium

Hard

Answers to QUIZ 104 – London

1 The Tower of London
2 Four
3 London Eye
4 A bell
5 10 Downing Street
6 The Chancellor of the Exchequer
7 Sir Christopher Wren
8 London Bridge
9 Hyde Park
10 Westminster Abbey
11 Eros
12 A Christmas tree
13 Sir Charlie Chaplin
14 Changing of the Guard
15 The Tube
16 Cleopatra's Needle
17 Wandsworth
18 2014
19 *Abbey Road*
20 Bank of England

QUIZ 107 – Pot Luck

ANSWERS ON PAGE **109**

1 Which day of the week is first alphabetically?

2 Which word means both a unit of measurement and the rhythm of a piece of poetry?

3 What were people encouraged to do for Victory in a WWII slogan?

4 Hugo Weaving played which wise elf in the *Lord of the Rings* series of films?

5 What is the radio operators' code word for the letter between tango and victor?

6 What is a broad ditch surrounding a castle called?

7 Crème de menthe liqueur has what flavour?

8 Which Atlantic colony gives its name to a type of shorts?

9 Who sang 99 *Red Balloons* in 1984?

10 What type of substance induces insensitivity to pain?

11 What does the "D" of "CD" stand for?

12 What was there "under the Sun" in the title of a 1982 Poirot film?

13 The Lombardy poplar tree is native to which country?

14 What was the name of Su Pollard's character in the TV series *Hi-de-Hi!*?

15 What is the square root of 100?

16 Jessica Tandy co-starred with which actor in the film *Driving Miss Daisy*?

17 What is the official examination of a company's books called?

18 What archaic word for "letter" is used in the New Testament for St Paul's to the Thessalonians, for instance?

19 How many years are celebrated at a bicentenary?

20 How many carats are there in pure gold?

Answers to QUIZ 105 – Pot Luck

1 Tudor
2 Suffolk
3 Valentine
4 Slade
5 Twilight
6 Styx
7 Trumpton
8 Uvula
9 Draft
10 Urdu
11 Neil Dudgeon
12 Mistletoe
13 Coffee
14 Corleone
15 Try
16 Clause
17 Dance
18 Turkey
19 20th
20 Avocado

QUIZ 108 – Dance

ANSWERS ON PAGE 110

Easy

1 What is the London home of the Royal Ballet?

2 Which Irish dance shares its name with a device designed to hold a component during machining?

3 Which dance in triple time derives its name from the German word for "roll"?

4 What was the first name of early Hollywood choreographer Mr Berkeley?

5 *Let's Dance* was a hit for which singer in 1983?

6 Which English choreographer famously created a version of *Swan Lake* with male swans?

7 For which occasion was *Riverdance* originally created in 1994?

8 Which former ballerina joined the judging panel of *Strictly Come Dancing* in 2012?

9 In which traditional English form of dance are bell pads worn on the shins?

10 The 1970s pogo was associated with which form of music?

Medium

11 In which city is the Bolshoi ballet based?

12 Who choreographed the original Broadway production of *Chicago*?

13 In which country was Carlos Acosta born?

14 Which 2000 film starred Jamie Bell as a boy who wanted to dance?

15 Who choreographed the 1970s dance troupe Hot Gossip...?

16 ...and which singer did they back on the 1978 song *I Lost My Heart to a Starship Trooper*?

17 The bossa nova dance originates from which South American country?

18 Who was the original presenter of *Strictly Come Dancing: It Takes Two*?

19 In ballet, what is a dance for two people called?

20 Which "dance" was a hit for Terry Wogan in 1978?

Hard

Answers to QUIZ 106 – Famous Buildings

1 Southwark
2 Toronto
3 Holyrood
4 Sydney Opera House
5 Hampton Court
6 Red Square
7 Loch Ness
8 Blackpool Tower
9 Gothic
10 Glamis
11 Dubai
12 Versailles
13 1993
14 Washington DC
15 York Minster
16 Alhambra
17 Kuala Lumpur
18 Tower of London
19 St Paul's Cathedral
20 Tuscany

QUIZ 109 – Pot Luck

ANSWERS ON PAGE 111

1 The mystery of *The Body in the Library* was solved by which fictional sleuth?

2 Who starred in the 2008 film *The Duchess*?

3 Who played Queen Elizabeth I in the TV series *Blackadder II*?

4 Which US senator was notorious for his 1950s "witch-hunts"?

5 "Pulmonary" relates to which organs of the body?

6 Which actress co-starred with Tom Hanks in the 2017 film *The Post*?

7 Which five-line humorous verse is named after a place in Ireland?

8 The Archbishop of Canterbury's residence is in which London palace?

9 What name was given to Schubert's eighth symphony?

10 Which 1960s group was fronted by Reg Presley?

11 The Bernabéu football stadium is located in which city?

12 What type of vehicle is a Chinook?

13 What is the first name of the Bond villain Blofeld?

14 What word can refer to both a coat peg and a boxing punch?

15 *Open Arms* was a hit for which singer in 1996?

16 In which county is the racecourse of Market Rasen?

17 Which biblical character had a wife who was turned into a pillar of salt?

18 In 1908 who, along with Mills, founded a publishing company famous for romantic novels?

19 Who played Chandler in the TV series *Friends*?

20 What is the monetary unit of Denmark and Norway?

Answers to QUIZ 107 – Pot Luck

1 Friday
2 Metre
3 Dig
4 Elrond
5 Uniform
6 Moat
7 Peppermint
8 Bermuda
9 Nena
10 Anaesthetic
11 Disc
12 Evil
13 Italy
14 Peggy
15 Ten
16 Morgan Freeman
17 Audit
18 Epistle
19 200
20 24

QUIZ 110 – James

ANSWERS ON PAGE 112

Easy

1 Who took over as host of *The Late Late Show* on CBS in 2015?

2 Who won *The X Factor* in 2012?

3 Who wrote the children's story *James and the Giant Peach*?

4 Which TV presenter featured in his *Man Lab* and told *Toy Stories*?

5 Which word describes the reign of James I?

6 What household item is Sir James Dyson famous for making?

7 What was the name of Polly James' character in the TV series *The Liver Birds*?

8 In which film did Pierce Brosnan first appear as James Bond?

9 *Chaos and the Calm* is a 2015 album by which singer/songwriter?

10 Which Greek hero shares his name with the title of a novel by James Joyce?

11 In which country is James Clavell's novel *Shogun* set?

Medium

12 Who was the fourth US president?

13 Who played Lady Rose in the TV series *Downton Abbey*?

14 Who had a 2005 hit with *Goodbye My Lover?*

15 On which London thoroughfare is St James's Palace?

16 Which crime writer created the character of Adam Dalgliesh?

17 In the New Testament, James was the brother of which other apostle?

18 Who was UK Prime Minister from 1976 to 1979?

19 Which musical instrument is associated with Sir James Galway?

20 Who played Idi Amin's personal physician in the 2006 film *The Last King of Scotland*?

Hard

Answers to QUIZ 108 – Dance

1 Royal Opera House
2 Jig
3 Waltz
4 Busby
5 David Bowie
6 Sir Matthew Bourne
7 The Eurovision Song Contest
8 Dame Darcey Bussell
9 Morris dancing
10 Punk
11 Moscow
12 Bob Fosse
13 Cuba
14 *Billy Elliot*
15 Arlene Phillips
16 Sarah Brightman
17 Brazil
18 Claudia Winkleman
19 *Pas de deux*
20 *The Floral Dance*

QUIZ 111 – Pot Luck

ANSWERS ON PAGE 113

1 The spicy soup mulligatawny originated in which country?
2 From whom do all Jews trace their ancestry?
3 Which clergyman created Thomas the Tank Engine?
4 Which date in spring is traditionally seen as a day on which to play pranks?
5 In which fairground game are wooden balls thrown at a dummy?
6 Who was comic-strip hero Dan Dare's arch-enemy?
7 What name is given to a narrow strip of land connecting two land areas?
8 Which UK Prime Minister was in office at the time of "Black Wednesday"?
9 Which Tolkien heroine did Liv Tyler play in the *Lord of the Rings* films?
10 What is one circuit of a track in a race called?
11 What term is given to a column made from a single stone?
12 Who wrote the 1969 autobiography *I Know Why the Caged Bird Sings*?
13 In the adage, what sort of hands does the devil find work for?
14 What is the first name of Woody Guthrie's folk-singer son?
15 English singer Alfie Boe (b.1973) is from which county?
16 What type of food is a bloomer?
17 Indicating an anonymous party in a US court case, what is the surname of "John"?
18 Which dessert has a French name meaning "froth"?
19 What word can mean a Turkish commander or a brand of cooker?
20 Which Christmas song features a "one-horse open sleigh"?

Answers to QUIZ 109 – Pot Luck

1 Miss Marple
2 Keira Knightley
3 Miranda Richardson
4 Joseph McCarthy
5 Lungs
6 Meryl Streep
7 Limerick
8 Lambeth
9 The *Unfinished*
10 The Troggs
11 Madrid
12 Helicopter
13 Ernst
14 Hook
15 Mariah Carey
16 Lincolnshire
17 Lot
18 Boon
19 Matthew Perry
20 Krone

QUIZ 112 – Technology

ANSWERS ON PAGE 114

Easy

1 What does AI stand for?

2 Which video hosting site was founded in 2005?

3 Google, Bing and Yahoo are what type of online resource?

4 Which social networking site doubled the length of posts which users could make in 2017?

5 Who was the co-founder of Apple, portrayed by Michael Fassbender in a 2015 film?

6 What do AR and VR stand for?

7 The three laws of robotics were invented by which sci-fi writer?

8 In what year was the iPad first released?

9 Mark Zuckerberg co-founded which social media site?

10 In what year was the World Wide Web invented?

Medium

11 The "Deep Blue" computer beat the reigning world champion in what game in 1996?

12 Which test was developed in 1950 to determine a machine's ability to exhibit behaviour indistinguishable from a human's?

13 What does GPS stand for?

14 Which cryptocurrency and worldwide payment system first came into existence in 2009?

15 Which machine located near Geneva was built to create and study the Higgs boson?

16 A pilotless aircraft operated by remote control is given what name?

17 For what does the acronym WYSIWYG stand in relation to electronic display?

18 Which computer programming language is named after the mathematician daughter of Lord Byron?

Hard

19 What name for a mechanical person comes from the Czech word for "forced labour"?

20 What does HTML stand for?

Answers to QUIZ 110 – James

1 James Corden
2 James Arthur
3 Roald Dahl
4 James May
5 Jacobean
6 Vacuum cleaner
7 Beryl
8 *GoldenEye*
9 James Bay
10 Ulysses
11 Japan
12 James Madison
13 Lily James
14 James Blunt
15 Pall Mall
16 PD James (Baroness James of Holland Park)
17 John
18 James Callaghan (Baron Callaghan of Cardiff)
19 Flute
20 James McAvoy

QUIZ 113 – Pot Luck

ANSWERS ON PAGE 115

1 What is the name of the Scottish National Park region north-east of Loch Lomond?
2 Who composed the 19th-century piece *Air on a G String*?
3 What was the surname of US newspaper tycoon William Randolph (b.1863)?
4 What term is given to a pocket-watch chain?
5 What is a dotterel?
6 What is the firing mechanism in a car's engine called?
7 *Porgy and Bess* is a 1935 opera by which composer?
8 Which is the National Book Town of Wales?
9 From which country does the fandango dance originate?
10 What is a native of England, Wales or Scotland called?
11 Which island-based TV series starred Matthew Fox as a plane-crash survivor?
12 What name links an Israeli port with an orange?
13 Julia Roberts co-starred with which actor in the 1990 film *Pretty Woman*?
14 Which Lewis Carroll character gave a tea-party?
15 What was the name of Michael Crawford's character in *Some Mothers Do 'Ave 'Em*?
16 What is the main ingredient of paella?
17 Which independent country, once part of the British Raj, is formally known as the Union of Myanmar?
18 On which river does Düsseldorf stand?
19 Which town, on Romney Marsh, is the site of London Ashford Airport?
20 Who wrote *The Day of the Jackal* (1971)?

Easy

Medium

Hard

Answers to QUIZ 111 – Pot Luck

1 India
2 Abraham
3 Reverend Wilbert Awdry
4 April 1
5 Aunt Sally
6 The Mekon
7 Isthmus
8 Sir John Major
9 Arwen
10 A lap
11 Monolith
12 Maya Angelou
13 Idle
14 Arlo
15 Lancashire
16 A loaf of bread
17 Doe
18 Mousse
19 Aga
20 *Jingle Bells*

QUIZ 114 – Musicals

ANSWERS ON PAGE 116

1 Which musical is set in Rydell High?
2 The musical *Our House* features hits from which band?
3 Which musical features Nathan Detroit and Sky Masterson?
4 Who wrote the music and lyrics for the musical *Matilda*?
5 In *The Sound of Music*, who is the eldest von Trapp daughter?
6 The song *If I Were a Rich Man* is from which musical?
7 Which 1996 film starred Antonio Banderas as Che?
8 Which musical was based on Shakespeare's *The Taming of the Shrew*?
9 Eliza Doolittle is the main character in which musical?
10 Who played Roxie Hart in the 2002 film *Chicago*?
11 Which 1999 musical set in Greece features Donna and her daughter Sophie?
12 John Travolta starred as Edna Turnblad in which 2007 film?
13 Which musical features the song *Tomorrow*?
14 *A Couple of Swells* featured in which 1948 Fred Astaire film?
15 What is the name of the 2015 musical about one of the Founding Fathers?
16 Which adjective describes the lion in *The Wizard of Oz*?
17 Who wrote the musical *Oliver!*?
18 Which musical by Andrew Lloyd Webber (Baron Lloyd-Webber) was based on a collection of poems by TS Eliot?
19 The 2017 talent show *Let it Shine* searched for the cast of a musical featuring songs by which band?
20 What is the name of the Sharks' rival gang in Leonard Bernstein's *West Side Story*?

Answers to QUIZ 112 – Technology

1 Artificial intelligence
2 YouTube™
3 Search engines
4 Twitter™
5 Steve Jobs
6 Augmented reality and virtual reality
7 Isaac Asimov
8 2010
9 Facebook™
10 1989
11 Chess
12 Turing Test
13 Global Positioning System
14 Bitcoin
15 The Large Hadron Collider
16 Drone
17 What you see is what you get
18 Ada
19 Robot
20 Hypertext Markup Language

QUIZ 115 – Pot Luck

ANSWERS ON PAGE 117

1 Daryl Hannah played a mermaid in which 1984 film?
2 Which international agency aims to improve youngsters' health and education?
3 What nationality was the poet Dylan Thomas?
4 *Vienna* was a hit for which 1980s band?
5 Who starred as Derek Zoolander in the *Zoolander* films?
6 What term is given to the frilly collar associated with the Elizabethan and Jacobean periods?
7 What flower is worn as a symbol of remembrance up to the 11th November in the UK?
8 Who wrote the 1867 work *Das Kapital* (Volume 1)?
9 King Charles is a variety of which breed of dog?
10 What collective name is used for large-calibre guns used in land warfare?
11 What is the medical name for the breastbone?
12 In bookkeeping, what is an entry in an account of a sum owing?
13 The Golden Temple is in which holy city of the Punjab?
14 Which actor starred opposite Jennifer Lawrence in the 2012 film *Silver Linings Playbook*?
15 The herb rosemary usually has what colour flowers?
16 Who played Perry Mason on TV in the 1960s and 1970s?
17 The 1869 novel *Lorna Doone* was written by which author?
18 What was the nationality at birth of Olympic gymnast Nadia Comaneci?
19 Osaka is a city in which country?
20 What is the first name of Donald Trump's eldest daughter?

Answers to QUIZ 113 – Pot Luck

1 The Trossachs
2 Johann Sebastian Bach
3 Hearst
4 Fob
5 Bird
6 Ignition
7 George Gershwin
8 Hay-on-Wye
9 Spain
10 Briton
11 *Lost*
12 Jaffa
13 Richard Gere
14 The Mad Hatter
15 Frank Spencer
16 Rice
17 Burma
18 Rhine
19 Lydd
20 Frederick Forsyth

Easy Medium Hard

1 A mule is a cross between which two animals?
2 Who wrote the music and lyrics to the musical *Kinky Boots*?
3 What name is given to the traditional wooden shoe worn in the Netherlands?
4 *The Slipper and the Rose* is a film version of which fairy tale?
5 *Pump it Up* was a 1978 single for which group?
6 Which actor came to TV fame as Eddie Shoestring in 1979?
7 What is the wooden or metal form on which a shoe is fashioned or repaired?
8 In which English city was the retail chain Boots founded?
9 Which 2005 film starred Toni Collette and Cameron Diaz as sisters?
10 A Moscow mule cocktail contains which main alcoholic ingredient?
11 Which Italian bread is so named because the shape resembles a slipper?
12 What is the part of a shoe above the sole called?
13 What is the capital city of New Zealand?
14 Which strong shoe shares its name with a description of a regional accent?
15 *These Boots Are Made for Walkin'* was a hit for which singer in 1966?
16 In which county is the town of Shoeburyness?
17 What type of flower is a lady's slipper?
18 What are soft top-stitched leather shoes worn by Native Americans called?
19 In which English city is the Pump Room restaurant?
20 Who starred in the TV series *Crocodile Shoes*?

Answers to QUIZ 114 – Musicals

1 *Grease*
2 Madness
3 *Guys and Dolls*
4 Tim Minchin
5 Liesl
6 *Fiddler on the Roof*
7 *Evita*
8 *Kiss Me Kate*
9 *My Fair Lady*
10 Renée Zellweger
11 *Mamma Mia!*
12 *Hairspray*
13 *Annie*
14 *Easter Parade*
15 *Hamilton*
16 Cowardly
17 Lionel Bart
18 *Cats*
19 Take That
20 Jets

QUIZ 117 – Pot Luck

ANSWERS ON PAGE 119

1 What kitchen measure equals ten millilitres?
2 What name is given to a ring-like coral reef?
3 The character of Wishee Washee appears in which pantomime?
4 Which group topped the UK singles chart with *Words* in 1996?
5 Which Alpine mountain range is located in north-east Italy?
6 What colours are on the flag of Argentina?
7 Who was the first person to win the jackpot on the UK's *Who Wants to Be a Millionaire?*
8 Which religion involves the quest for enlightenment?
9 What name is given to a loose Japanese robe with wide sleeves?
10 The sitcom *Goodnight Sweetheart* starred which actor?
11 Haematophobia is the fear of what?
12 Which Canadian singer/songwriter wrote *Both Sides Now*?
13 What is the unit of depth measurement equal to six feet?
14 Who won the Olympic gold medal in the men's long jump in 2012?
15 The 2005 novel *Never Let Me Go* was written by which author?
16 What is the national airline of Spain?
17 Who won a Best Actor Oscar for his role in the 2014 film *The Theory of Everything*?
18 What singing voice is highest for males and lowest for females?
19 What is the main international airport of Cyprus?
20 Kahlua and vodka are used to make which "Black" cocktail?

Easy

Medium

Hard

Answers to QUIZ 115 – Pot Luck

1 *Splash*
2 UNICEF
3 Welsh
4 Ultravox
5 Ben Stiller
6 Ruff
7 Poppy
8 Karl Marx
9 Spaniel
10 Artillery
11 The sternum
12 Debit
13 Amritsar
14 Bradley Cooper
15 Blue
16 Raymond Burr
17 RD Blackmore
18 Romanian
19 Japan
20 Ivanka

Easy

1 The 1997 film *Air Force One* starred which actor as the US President?

2 Which martial arts actor is best known for the *Rush Hour* series of films?

3 Which 2016 film featured a group of boys trying to find their way out of a labyrinth?

4 In the 1998 film *Armageddon*, what poses a threat to Earth?

5 Japan was the location for which 2003 Tom Cruise film?

6 By what nickname was Bond film producer Albert Broccoli known?

7 Which actor starred in the 1993 film *Last Action Hero*?

8 What was the subtitle of the second film in the *Pirates of the Caribbean* series?

9 Mike Myers created which spoof spy?

10 In the title of a 2009 film, which year saw John Cusack battling a series of global catastrophies?

Medium

11 Who played the original Mad Max?

12 Linda Hamilton played which character in the first two *Terminator* films?

13 What was the surname of Clint Eastwood's "Dirty Harry"?

14 Who was Sylvester Stallone's character in the 1982 film *First Blood*?

15 The African kingdom of Wakanda is the setting for which 2018 film?

16 Who directed the 2018 film *Ready Player One*?

17 Which actor starred in *The Bourne Ultimatum*?

18 In which year was *Raiders of the Lost Ark* released?

19 Bruce Willis plays which character in the *Die Hard* films?

20 What catastrophe occurs in the 1997 film *Dante's Peak*?

Hard

Answers to QUIZ 116 – Footwear

1 A (male) donkey and a (female) horse
2 Cyndi Lauper
3 Clog
4 *Cinderella*
5 Elvis Costello and the Attractions
6 Trevor Eve
7 Last
8 Nottingham
9 *In Her Shoes*
10 Vodka
11 Ciabatta
12 The upper
13 Wellington
14 Brogue
15 Nancy Sinatra
16 Essex
17 An orchid
18 Moccasins
19 Bath
20 Jimmy Nail

QUIZ 119 – Pot Luck

ANSWERS ON PAGE 121

1 What is the name of the stately home at Woodstock near Oxford?

2 *Teenage Kicks* and *My Perfect Cousin* were hits for which band?

3 Who was the "Desert Fox" of WWII?

4 Which Welsh county has the longest border with England?

5 Peter Falk played which TV detective?

6 What colour is the drink Campari®?

7 Which language is spoken in Kuwait?

8 What word links a salt container with an underground room?

9 What is the unit of speed at sea?

10 The poem *To a Skylark* was written by which English Romantic poet of the early 19th century?

11 Which actress was Oscar-nominated for her starring role in the film *Changeling*?

12 Sir Christopher Cockerell designed which vehicle that rides on a cushion of air?

13 Which fruit has varieties including Gala and Granny Smith?

14 Who created the characters of Samuel Whiskers and Squirrel Nutkin?

15 Morticia and Gomez appeared in which TV and film series?

16 What is the lowest-ranking chess piece?

17 Cerulean is a shade of which colour?

18 Which tree's leaf is depicted on the Canadian flag?

19 What is the Spanish equivalent of "mister"?

20 What word can mean a doughnut and a native of Germany's capital city?

Easy Medium Hard

Answers to QUIZ 117 – Pot Luck

1 Dessertspoonful
2 Atoll
3 *Aladdin*
4 Boyzone
5 Dolomites
6 Blue and white
7 Judith Keppel
8 Buddhism
9 Kimono
10 Nicholas Lyndhurst
11 Blood
12 Joni Mitchell
13 Fathom
14 Greg Rutherford
15 Kazuo Ishiguro
16 Iberia
17 Eddie Redmayne
18 Alto
19 Larnaca
20 Black Russian

QUIZ 120 – Europe

ANSWERS ON PAGE **122**

1 Which European city is home to NATO's HQ?
2 Transylvania is a region of which country?
3 Which is the largest of the Channel Islands?
4 On which river does the city of Cologne stand?
5 What sparkling wine is made in the Piedmont region of Italy?
6 In 1992 where were the Summer Olympic Games held?
7 Which body of water lies between Greece and Turkey?
8 What is the capital city of Iceland?
9 Which small European principality contains the district of Monte Carlo?
10 Which flower is most closely associated with the Netherlands?
11 Goulash is a traditional stew from which country?
12 Which European country saw the Solidarity movement in the early 1980s?
13 Graz and Linz are both located in which European country?
14 What is the official residence of the president of France?
15 With which country does Portugal share its only border?
16 In which German state is the city of Munich?
17 Which country lies between Estonia and Lithuania?
18 Which state within Rome contains St Peter's?
19 Europe's first Disney theme park was built near which city?
20 Which French city in Burgundy is famed for its mustard?

Answers to QUIZ 118 – Action Films

1 Harrison Ford
2 Jackie Chan
3 *The Maze Runner*
4 Asteroid
5 *The Last Samurai*
6 Cubby
7 Arnold Schwarzenegger
8 *Dead Man's Chest*
9 Austin Powers
10 2012
11 Mel Gibson
12 Sarah Connor
13 Callahan
14 Rambo
15 *Black Panther*
16 Steven Spielberg
17 Matt Damon
18 1981
19 John McClane
20 A volcanic eruption

QUIZ 121 – Pot Luck

ANSWERS ON PAGE 123

1 Which 1987 thriller starred Glenn Close and Michael Douglas?
2 In which city is Tiananmen Square found?
3 What is the medical term for lockjaw?
4 What style of canoe is used by the Inuit?
5 *Ol' Man River* is a song from which musical?
6 In which English county is the Lake District?
7 Which actor starred in the 2017 film *American Made*?
8 The famous dandies Nash and Brummell shared which nickname?
9 Who was the lead singer of the Eurythmics?
10 What word describes a lifestyle devoted to pleasure-seeking?
11 In which county is Ventnor located?
12 What was the first name of legendary Russian ballerina Miss Pavlova?
13 The TV series *Ally McBeal* starred which actress in the title role?
14 Which small guitar has a name meaning "jumping flea"?
15 What was the title of the 1970s sitcom about a self-sufficient couple in suburbia?
16 What is the use of fragrant essential oils as a treatment in alternative medicine called?
17 Ancient writers Homer and Sophocles wrote in which language?
18 Which river flows through Stockport and Warrington?
19 Which Russian seaport shares its name with a heavenly being?
20 What colour are the flowers of the herb borage?

Answers to QUIZ 119 – Pot Luck

1 Blenheim Palace
2 The Undertones
3 (Erwin) Rommel
4 Powys
5 Columbo
6 Red
7 Arabic
8 Cellar
9 Knot
10 Shelley
11 Angelina Jolie
12 Hovercraft
13 Apple
14 Beatrix Potter
15 *The Addams Family*
16 Pawn
17 Blue
18 Maple
19 Señor
20 Berliner

QUIZ 122 – Money

Easy

1 In which year was the first polymer banknote issued by the Bank of England?

2 What term is given to an investment or insurance policy that pays a fixed sum of money at regular intervals?

3 What is the old term for money or food given to the poor?

4 In which year did the UK introduce decimalisation?

5 What is a person who studies the production and consumption of wealth called?

6 Which initials describe a bank's "hole in the wall"?

7 Which US institution acts as a central bank?

8 A "grand" refers to how many pounds?

9 What name is given to a person in charge of a society's funds?

10 On which day of the week is Maundy Money traditionally given?

Medium

11 Who appeared on the £5 note before Jane Austen?

12 Who became Chancellor of the Exchequer in July 2016?

13 In which year was the £1 coin introduced?

14 What do the letters ISA stand for in a UK financial context?

15 What name is given to a situation of increased prices and a fall in the value of money?

16 NatWest became part of which banking group in 2000?

17 Which famous New York thoroughfare is the US financial centre?

18 Which pre-decimal coin was commonly known as a tanner?

19 "My Word is My Bond" is the motto of which British institution?

20 Which decimal coin was last produced in 1984?

Hard

Answers to QUIZ 120 – Europe

1 Brussels
2 Romania
3 Jersey
4 Rhine
5 Asti
6 Barcelona
7 Aegean Sea
8 Reykjavik
9 Monaco
10 Tulip
11 Hungary
12 Poland
13 Austria
14 The Élysée Palace
15 Spain
16 Bavaria
17 Latvia
18 Vatican City
19 Paris
20 Dijon

QUIZ 123 – Pot Luck

ANSWERS ON PAGE 125

1 Who wrote the award winning 1984 novel *Hotel du Lac*?

2 The 41st and 43rd US presidents of the USA shared which surname?

3 Which god is the Greek equivalent of Neptune?

4 Which is Britain's oldest cathedral?

5 What is the selection of small dishes served in a Spanish restaurant called?

6 What term is given to the widow of a peer who retains his property or title?

7 Which bulbous narrow-necked bottle is used in domestic wine-making?

8 Meg Ryan co-starred with which actor in the 1989 film *When Harry Met Sally*?

9 In which country was tennis champion Novak Djokovic born?

10 What was the name of Ross Kemp's character in *EastEnders*?

11 What term is given to the projecting part on a wheel?

12 Weymouth and Corfe Castle are found in which English county?

13 Which item, sometimes eaten for breakfast, contains pork, dried blood and suet?

14 Which ornamental fabric is a traditional hallmark of Nottingham?

15 The 2000 film *How the Grinch Stole Christmas* starred which actor?

16 Which French word is used for a funeral procession?

17 Which country is bordered by Bolivia and Paraguay to the north?

18 *Back to Black* was a 2006 album for which singer?

19 Which London street leads from Trafalgar Square to the Houses of Parliament?

20 Which 1984 sci-fi film was based on a Frank Herbert novel?

Answers to QUIZ 121 – Pot Luck

1 *Fatal Attraction*
2 Beijing
3 Tetanus
4 Kayak
5 *Show Boat*
6 Cumbria
7 Tom Cruise
8 Beau
9 Annie Lennox
10 Hedonism
11 Isle of Wight
12 Anna
13 Calista Flockhart
14 Ukulele
15 *The Good Life*
16 Aromatherapy
17 Greek
18 Mersey
19 Archangel
20 Blue

QUIZ 124 – Shades of Grey

ANSWERS ON PAGE 126

1 What flavouring is used in Earl Grey tea?

2 Which substance obtained from burning wood is used as a drawing stick?

3 Who created the character of Little Grey Rabbit?

4 Which group had a hit with *Grey Day* in 1981?

5 Pewter is an alloy of tin and which other metal?

6 Which actress played Lois Lane in the 2013 film *Man of Steel*?

7 The greyhound dog lends its name to a company specialising in long-distance travel using which vehicle?

8 In the title of the 1984 film, which fictional character was associated with the legend of Greystoke?

9 What two paint colours are mixed to make grey?

10 What was the name of Leslie Ash's character in the TV series *Men Behaving Badly*?

11 Who wrote the 2011 best-seller *Fifty Shades of Grey*?

12 Which cook and food writer wrote the 2010 autobiography *Toast*?

13 Whose debut novel was *Agnes Grey* (1847)?

14 What was the nickname of Jennifer Grey's character in the 1987 film *Dirty Dancing*?

15 Which hair colour can be described as "platinum"?

16 In greyhound racing, what colour does the dog in trap one wear?

17 Which fictional detective made great use of his "little grey cells"?

18 Who played hairdresser Truvy Jones in the 1989 film *Steel Magnolias*?

19 What title is given to a monk who is a member of an order founded by St Francis of Assisi?

20 Which South Yorkshire city is particularly associated with steel?

Answers to QUIZ 122 – Money

1 2016
2 An annuity
3 Alms
4 1971
5 An economist
6 ATM
7 Federal Reserve
8 1000
9 Treasurer
10 Thursday
11 Charles Darwin
12 Philip Hammond
13 1983
14 Individual Savings Account
15 Inflation
16 Royal Bank of Scotland
17 Wall Street
18 Sixpence
19 The Stock Exchange
20 1/2p

QUIZ 125 – Pot Luck

ANSWERS ON PAGE 127

1 How is the domestic cavy better known?

2 Which British painter (b.1922) was the grandson of Sigmund Freud?

3 From which fish is caviar obtained?

4 What type of creature is a howler?

5 Who were the founders of the city-state Tenochtitlan?

6 Which 1969 Ken Loach film centres around a boy and his pet bird?

7 Which region of France forms a peninsula between the Bay of Biscay and the English Channel?

8 *Rock the Casbah* was a 1982 single by which group?

9 Which famous piece of needlework shows the Norman Conquest?

10 Which hymn begins with the words "And did those feet in ancient time"?

11 Who was Bailey's partner in the famous American circus?

12 What was the name of Lynda Baron's character in *Open All Hours* and its sequel?

13 Who commanded China's Long March in the 1930s?

14 *Cider with Rosie* is an autobiographical novel by which author?

15 Which US state is known as the "Lone Star State"?

16 Which former US Secretary of State shared the Nobel Peace Prize in 1973?

17 Who recorded the 1976 album *Songs in the Key of Life*?

18 Acetylsalicylic acid is the scientific name for which common painkiller?

19 Which alloy is a mixture of copper and tin?

20 Which four letters indicate that a reply to a letter is required?

Answers to QUIZ 123 – Pot Luck

1 Anita Brookner
2 Bush
3 Poseidon
4 Canterbury
5 Tapas
6 Dowager
7 Demijohn
8 Billy Crystal
9 Serbia
10 Grant Mitchell
11 Cam
12 Dorset
13 Black pudding
14 Lace
15 Jim Carrey
16 Cortège
17 Argentina
18 Amy Winehouse
19 Whitehall
20 *Dune*

Easy
Medium
Hard

QUIZ 126 – Music Used in Adverts

ANSWERS ON PAGE 128

Easy

1 Which group had a hit in 2004 with *Somewhere Only We Know*?

2 Which song was the only UK no.1 hit for Babylon Zoo?

3 In which year was *Hold My Hand* a hit for Jess Glynne...?

4 ...and with whom did she feature the previous year on *Rather Be*?

5 What type of creature was seen in an advert for Cadbury's playing the drums to Phil Collins' *In The Air Tonight?*

6 In which decade did Snap! have a hit with *Rhythm is a Dancer*?

7 Ellie Goulding covered which Sir Elton John song in 2010?

8 Which group had a 1982 hit with *Living on the Ceiling*?

9 Which Rolling Stones song was used by Microsoft to advertise Windows® 95?

10 *The Impossible Dream* is a song from which 1964 musical?

Medium

11 What item of clothing did Lord David Dundas want to put on in 1977?

12 *The Final Countdown* was the only UK no.1 hit for which band?

13 Which song begins "Left a good job in the city, working for the man ev'ry night and day"?

14 The flight of which insect provided inspiration for a piece of music by Rimsky-Korsakov?

15 Who recorded 1992's *The Passenger*, minus Ricky Gardiner?

16 Dvorak's *New World Symphony* featured in a famous advert for which brand of sliced bread?

17 Who wrote Bonnie Tyler's hit *Total Eclipse of the Heart?*

Hard

18 In which year did Take That top the charts with *Shine*?

19 Which composer wrote *The Flower Duet*, used in a 1989 British Airways advert?

20 Which band had a 1989 hit with *I Want it All*?

Answers to QUIZ 124 – Shades of Grey

1 Bergamot
2 Charcoal
3 Alison Uttley
4 Madness
5 Lead
6 Amy Adams
7 Bus
8 Tarzan
9 Black and white
10 Deborah
11 EL James
12 Nigel Slater
13 Anne Brontë
14 Baby
15 Blonde
16 Red
17 Hercule Poirot
18 Dolly Parton
19 Grey Friar
20 Sheffield

QUIZ 127 – Pot Luck

ANSWERS ON PAGE 129

1 What was the nickname of Wellington, who defeated Napoleon at Waterloo in 1815?

2 What is the collective name for plants of the heather family?

3 Who, in folklore, pulled a thorn from the paw of a lion?

4 In which European country would you find the city of Bilbao?

5 What is the common name of nitrous oxide?

6 In which city can you visit *HMS Victory*?

7 Which actor starred in the 1967 film *Half a Sixpence*?

8 What is the name of the *David Copperfield* character who optimistically expects that "something will turn up"?

9 Which town in south-east England is famed for its Ford car factory?

10 What word describes a building officially designated as historically or culturally significant?

11 Which Italian city is capital of the Lombardy region?

12 What is the study of the nature of God and religion?

13 What is the term for a fear of spiders?

14 *When a Man Loves a Woman* was a hit in 1966 for which singer?

15 The Pilgrim Fathers sailed from which port in 1620?

16 Mayonnaise combined with ketchup is the basis for which sauce?

17 What term is given to a male duck?

18 What was the name of Trevor Eve's character in the TV series *Waking the Dead*?

19 Cabbage belongs to which plant genus?

20 In which US state is the region of Death Valley?

Answers to QUIZ 125 – Pot Luck

1 A guinea pig
2 Lucian Freud
3 Sturgeon
4 Monkey
5 Aztecs
6 *Kes*
7 Brittany
8 The Clash
9 Bayeux Tapestry
10 *Jerusalem*
11 Barnum
12 Gladys Emmanuel
13 Mao Zedong
14 Laurie Lee
15 Texas
16 Henry Kissinger
17 Stevie Wonder
18 Aspirin
19 Bronze
20 RSVP

QUIZ 128 – Games

Easy

1 Which game used to be known as "housey housey"?
2 The highest hand in poker is what kind of flush?
3 Which chess piece can only move diagonally?
4 Which Algarve city has the same name as a card game?
5 What is the American name for the board-game draughts?
6 How many weapons are there in Cluedo®?
7 Which game is played on a board with 24 narrow triangles?
8 A board and pegs are traditionally used to keep score in which card game?
9 Which board game takes its name from the Latin for "I play"?
10 What colour are the history questions in Trivial Pursuit™?
11 What is the cheapest property on a standard Monopoly™ board?

Medium

12 Which card game shares its name with a type of bridge?
13 Squidgers are used in which indoor game?
14 Which children's card game traditionally includes Mr Bun the Baker?
15 In solo whist, what is a call of nine tricks?
16 What is the highest-ranking suit of cards in a game of bridge?
17 Which gambling game has a French name meaning "small wheel"?
18 The Pokémon™ Pikachu is what colour?
19 In which decade was Pictionary® first published?
20 In which game do players act out the titles of films, books etc?

Hard

Answers to QUIZ 126 – Music Used in Adverts

1 Keane
2 *Spaceman*
3 2015
4 Clean Bandit
5 Gorilla
6 1990s
7 *Your Song*
8 Blancmange
9 *Start Me Up*
10 *Man of La Mancha*
11 Jeans
12 Europe
13 *Proud Mary*
14 Bumblebee
15 Iggy Pop
16 Hovis®
17 Jim Steinman
18 2006
19 Delibes
20 Queen

QUIZ 129 – Pot Luck

ANSWERS ON PAGE 131

1 Who was the first woman to fly the Atlantic solo?

2 Which singer had a hit with *On a Night Like This* in 2000?

3 Which mound-building insect is also called the white ant?

4 What type of food is focaccia?

5 Which gas makes up about 21% of the earth's atmosphere?

6 Which actor starred as James Stevens in the 1993 film *The Remains of the Day*?

7 Who wrote *Lady Chatterley's Lover*?

8 On which English river is Evesham situated?

9 Which French word is applied to the design and making of clothes to customers' requirements?

10 What name is given to a vocal piece such as *Nessun Dorma*?

11 According to legend, which lady rode naked through the streets of Coventry?

12 Which international airport has the code MIA?

13 Which wealthy industrialist was portrayed by Leonardo DiCaprio in the 2004 film *The Aviator*?

14 Which 20th-century word was coined to describe promotional copy for a book or film?

15 How many "Tribes" took Frankie Goes to Hollywood to the top of the charts in 1984?

16 Which ocean lies to the east of South Africa?

17 What was the surname of Ralph Waldo, the American philosopher and poet?

18 In which county is Weston-super-Mare?

19 Which 1970s TV series starred John Thaw and Dennis Waterman?

20 What is the common name for the tympanum?

Easy

Medium

Hard

Answers to QUIZ 127 – Pot Luck

1 The Iron Duke
2 Erica
3 Androcles
4 Spain
5 Laughing gas
6 Portsmouth
7 Tommy Steele
8 Mr Micawber
9 Dagenham
10 Listed
11 Milan
12 Theology
13 Arachnophobia
14 Percy Sledge
15 Plymouth
16 Thousand Island dressing
17 Drake
18 Peter Boyd
19 *Brassica*
20 California

QUIZ 130 – Legal Dramas

ANSWERS ON PAGE 132

1 Stephen Fry played a solicitor in which series set in the fictional town of Market Shipborough?

2 What was the first name of 1980s TV barrister Rumpole of the Bailey?

3 Which actress played Patty Hewes in the series *Damages*?

4 Which series starred Maxine Peake and Rupert Penry-Jones as barristers?

5 Who played the title role in the series *Judge John Deed*?

6 Who starred in the series *New Street Law*?

7 Which long-running US series that started in 1990 shows a crime from both the police and the court perspective...?

8 ...and in the British version, who played DS Ronnie Brooks?

9 Alicia Florrick is the title character in which series...?

10 ...and what is the title of the sequel series that began in 2017?

11 What was the name of William Shatner's character in the series *Boston Legal*?

12 In which series did Meghan Markle appear from 2011 to 2018?

13 In the ITV drama series *Eternal Law*, what type of beings were Zak and Thomas?

14 Which series featured a firm with partners Leland McKenzie and Douglas Brackman Jr?

15 Which actress starred in the sitcom *Is It Legal*?

16 What was the nickname of Andrew Lincoln's character in the 1990s series *This Life*?

17 Who played the title role in the 1980s series *Garrow's Law*?

18 Which actor starred in the series *The Irish RM*?

19 John Thaw played the title role in which 1990s series about a barrister?

20 Which former *Spooks* actress starred as a divorce lawyer in the 2018 series *The Split*?

Answers to QUIZ 128 – Games

1 Bingo
2 Royal flush
3 Bishop
4 Faro
5 Checkers
6 Six
7 Backgammon
8 Cribbage
9 Ludo
10 Yellow
11 Old Kent Road
12 Pontoon
13 Tiddlywinks
14 Happy Families
15 Abundance
16 Spades
17 Roulette
18 Yellow
19 1980s
20 Charades

QUIZ 131 – Pot Luck

ANSWERS ON PAGE 133

1 "Clap along if you feel like a room without a roof", are lyrics from which 2013 song?

2 What is the name of the former county of west Wales, abolished in 1996, which had the chief town Carmarthen?

3 Who directed the 1972 film *Cabaret*?

4 Of the four chambers of the human heart, what are the two larger, lower chambers called?

5 In which temperature scale does water boil at 212°?

6 Which religion is presided over by the Pope?

7 Danny DeVito played dispatcher Louie in which US comedy series?

8 What is the most famous feature of St Mary and All Saints Parish Church in Chesterfield?

9 What colour is carmine?

10 What mixture of sand, gravel and pitch is used for roads and roofs?

11 The TV series *Desperate Housewives* was set in which fictional road?

12 Who was the Wimbledon women's singles champion in 1977?

13 What is the surname of the Sheridan character known for her word blunders?

14 What kind of establishment is "Bart's" in London?

15 The *Famous Five* series was written by which author?

16 In terms of business, what do the initials CBI stand for?

17 What is the name of the main body of the church where the congregation sit?

18 Traditionally, Béarnaise sauce is served with what main dish?

19 What name is given to the young of an elephant?

20 Who was the lead singer of The Boomtown Rats?

Answers to QUIZ 129 – Pot Luck

1 Amelia Earhart
2 Kylie Minogue
3 Termite
4 Bread
5 Oxygen
6 Sir Anthony Hopkins
7 DH Lawrence
8 Avon
9 Couture
10 Aria
11 Godiva
12 Miami
13 Howard Hughes
14 Blurb
15 Two
16 Indian
17 Emerson
18 Somerset
19 *The Sweeney*
20 The eardrum

QUIZ 132 – Prequels and Sequels

ANSWERS ON PAGE 134

Easy

1 PD James' 2011 novel *Death Comes to Pemberley* is a sequel to which classic novel?
2 The TV series *Smallville* follows the early life of which superhero?
3 Which musical is a backstory of *The Wizard of Oz*?
4 What was the title of the sequel to Walt Disney's *Fantasia*, released 59 years after the original?
5 *Young Hyacinth* was a 2016 one-off prequel to which TV series?
6 Which actor starred in the 2005 prequel *Batman Begins*?
7 What was the sequel to *Saturday Night Fever*, directed by Sylvester Stallone?
8 What was the title of the prequel to *Only Fools and Horses...?*
9 ...and what was the title of the sequel featuring Boycie and his family?
10 What was the sequel to the 1984 film *Romancing the Stone*?

Medium

11 *Young Sheldon* is a prequel to which sitcom?
12 *Tokyo Drift* was the 2006 sequel in which film franchise?
13 Who played Stephanie in the 1982 film *Grease 2*?
14 The 2009 novel *Return to the Hundred Acre Wood* featured which children's character?
15 In the Inspector Morse prequel *Endeavour*, who plays the title role...?
16 ...and who played James Hathaway in the sequel *Lewis*?
17 The TV series *Bates Motel* is a contemporary prequel to which classic film?
18 Who provided the voice of the Fairy Godmother in the 2004 film *Shrek 2*?

Hard

19 What is the title of the sequel to *Alice's Adventures in Wonderland*?
20 Who played the title role in the 2009 film *X-Men Origins: Wolverine*?

Answers to QUIZ 130 – Legal Dramas

1 *Kingdom*
2 Horace
3 Glenn Close
4 *Silk*
5 Martin Shaw
6 John Hannah
7 *Law & Order*
8 Bradley Walsh
9 *The Good Wife*
10 *The Good Fight*
11 Denny Crane
12 *Suits*
13 Angels
14 *LA Law*
15 Imelda Staunton
16 Egg
17 Andrew Buchan
18 Peter Bowles
19 *Kavanagh QC*
20 Nicola Walker

QUIZ 133 – Pot Luck

1 *Tiger Feet* was a 1974 hit for which group?
2 Which central Asian inland sea has been shrinking since the 1960s?
3 What imperial measurement unit is equal to 0.9144 metres?
4 Which gas has the chemical symbol H?
5 Which is Africa's largest venomous snake?
6 Which brass instrument shares its name with a wild flower and a plastic bead?
7 Gary Cooper and Grace Kelly starred in which classic 1952 western?
8 How many points win championship darts games?
9 Which tennis player won the tournament at Queen's in 2018?
10 Tinseltown refers to which part of Los Angeles?
11 Which language is spoken in Prague?
12 Which former county of north-west London was abolished in 1965?
13 Which car manufacturer produced the Silver Ghost?
14 Which river flows through Manchester?
15 Which adjective refers to the nose?
16 What French term denotes a thing done, or a decision already made?
17 In the songwriting duo Burt Bacharach and Hal David, who wrote the lyrics?
18 From which language did the Romance languages derive?
19 Which fruit has a morello variety?
20 In which county is High Wycombe?

Answers to QUIZ 131 – Pot Luck

1 *Happy* (Pharrell Williams)
2 Dyfed
3 Bob Fosse
4 Ventricles (left and right)
5 Fahrenheit
6 Catholicism
7 *Taxi*
8 Crooked spire
9 Red
10 Asphalt
11 Wisteria Lane
12 Virginia Wade
13 Malaprop
14 Hospital
15 Enid Blyton
16 Confederation of British Industry
17 Nave
18 Steak
19 Calf
20 Bob Geldof

QUIZ 134 – Sweet Things

ANSWERS ON PAGE 136

Easy

1 The cake parkin is flavoured with which spice?

2 Eskimo Pie was the first type of which sweet treat?

3 What is the Italian word for "nougat"?

4 Which dessert is made with bread, jam and meringue?

5 What name is given to a sponge that has more than one colour?

6 From what are Pontefract cakes made?

7 What type of pastry is used to make a chocolate éclair?

8 What are the two main ingredients of a meringue?

9 At what time of year would a bûche de Noël be eaten?

10 Which nuts are used to make a macaroon?

11 Pectin is used in making what sweet item?

Medium

12 Which cocktail consists of white rum, sugar, lime juice, sparkling water and mint?

13 Gelato is what type of dessert?

14 Bakewell tart takes its name from a town in which county?

15 Which Scottish whisky liqueur, first produced in 1910, is sweetened with honey?

16 Tablet is a type of fudge from which country?

17 What cake is made of pink and yellow squares and covered in marzipan?

18 What name is given to the popular French dessert of upside-down apple pie?

Hard

19 Which type of bean is used as a substitute for chocolate?

20 An Eccles cake is a pastry filled with what?

Answers to QUIZ 132 – Prequels and Sequels

1 *Pride and Prejudice*
2 Superman
3 *Wicked*
4 *Fantasia 2000*
5 *Keeping Up Appearances*
6 Christian Bale
7 *Staying Alive*
8 *Rock & Chips*
9 *The Green Green Grass*
10 *The Jewel of the Nile*
11 *The Big Bang Theory*
12 *Fast and Furious*
13 Michelle Pfeiffer
14 Winnie-the-Pooh
15 Shaun Evans
16 Laurence Fox
17 *Psycho*
18 Jennifer Saunders
19 *Alice Through the Looking Glass*
20 Hugh Jackman

QUIZ 135 – Pot Luck

ANSWERS ON PAGE 137

1 Which West Indian republic has Port-au-Prince as its capital?

2 Which soft metal has the symbol Cu?

3 In which Welsh city was the TV series *Torchwood* originally set?

4 Chevre cheese is made from the milk of which animal?

5 Who directed the 2013 version of *The Great Gatsby*?

6 Which expression is used after a good fencing hit?

7 Which first name is shared by architects Gehry and Lloyd Wright?

8 What type of animal has a grizzly variety?

9 In which county is Alderley Edge?

10 Which country won the Eurovision Song Contest three years in a row from 1992?

11 Which type of hardy cabbage has a curly variety?

12 Which Irish group's debut hit was *Runaway* in 1996?

13 Which river forms much of the boundary between Devon and Cornwall?

14 Philip K Dick's short story *We Can Remember it for You Wholesale* is the basis for which sci-fi film?

15 Which symbol is given to beaches meeting stringent environmental and safety standards?

16 What was the name of the secret base in *Thunderbirds*?

17 In which year did the 50p coin first come into circulation?

18 Which of the Great Lakes of North America is not in Canada?

19 Where in London is Speakers' Corner?

20 Who had a UK hit in 1975 with *Stand By Your Man*?

Easy

Medium

Hard

Answers to QUIZ 133 – Pot Luck

1 Mud
2 Aral
3 A yard
4 Hydrogen
5 Mamba
6 Bugle
7 *High Noon*
8 501
9 Marin Čilić
10 Hollywood
11 Czech
12 Middlesex
13 Rolls Royce
14 Irwell
15 Nasal
16 *Fait accompli*
17 Hal David
18 Latin
19 Cherry
20 Buckinghamshire

QUIZ 136 – Bridges

ANSWERS ON PAGE 138

Easy

1 New York's Brooklyn Bridge connects Brooklyn to which other borough?

2 In which county is the Test cricket ground of Trent Bridge located?

3 What creature lived under the bridge in the tale of *The Three Billy Goats Gruff*?

4 Which area of Bristol is famous for its suspension bridge?

5 In which Italian city is the Ponte Vecchio?

6 Which footbridge across the Thames was briefly opened in 2000 then closed until 2002?

7 Which Scottish river, rising in the Trossachs, gives its name to a famous railway bridge?

8 Which football team plays its home games at Stamford Bridge?

9 The bridge at Kyle of Lochalsh links the Scottish mainland to which island?

10 The Golden Gate Bridge is in which American city?

11 Which Australian bridge is nicknamed "The Coathanger"?

Medium

12 In which county is Ironbridge Gorge?

13 The TV series *The Bridge*, first broadcast in 2011, is set in which two countries?

14 Where does the Oxford and Cambridge Boat Race start?

15 Which duo had a 1970 hit with *Bridge Over Troubled Water*?

16 Which walled market town on the north coast of Wales has a castle and a suspension bridge?

17 The Rialto Bridge is a famous landmark in which city?

18 What is the name of the bridge at the Dartford Crossing over the Thames?

19 Who co-starred with Meryl Streep in *The Bridges of Madison County*?

20 Who wrote the 1886 novel *The Mayor of Casterbridge*?

Hard

Answers to QUIZ 134 – Sweet Things

1 Ginger
2 Choc-ice
3 Torrone
4 Queen of Puddings
5 Marble cake
6 Liquorice
7 Choux
8 Egg whites and sugar
9 Christmas
10 Almonds
11 Jam
12 Mojito
13 Ice-cream
14 Derbyshire
15 Drambuie®
16 Scotland
17 Battenberg
18 Tarte tatin
19 Carob
20 Currants

QUIZ 137 – Pot Luck

ANSWERS ON PAGE 139

1 Who was Sooty and Sweep's panda friend in the 1960s TV puppet show?
2 In which body of water is Lundy Island?
3 "Love apple" was an old name for which food item?
4 What is the surname of the family in *The Darling Buds of May*?
5 Which actor starred in the 1990 film *Kindergarten Cop*?
6 Which sport has "lawn" and "real" versions?
7 How many finger holes are there in a tenpin bowling ball?
8 Which actor starred as Ryan Bingham in the 2009 film *Up in the Air*?
9 What term is given to a first coat of plaster applied to a wall?
10 What is the nickname for a native of Tyneside?
11 Who played Captain Salazar in the 2017 *Pirates of the Caribbean: Dead Men Tell No Tales* film?
12 What is the name given to the grounds or buildings of a college or university?
13 Split is a city in which European country?
14 Who wrote *The Hunchback of Notre-Dame* (1831)?
15 What is a male pig called?
16 Pernod® has what flavour?
17 What term is given to a mound of stones used as a memorial or landmark?
18 Who sang *Livin' La Vida Loca* in 1999?
19 The Tiber river runs through which European capital city?
20 Armando Iannucci co-wrote and directed which film released in 2017?

Answers to QUIZ 135 – Pot Luck

1 Haiti
2 Copper
3 Cardiff
4 The goat
5 Baz Luhrmann
6 Touché
7 Frank
8 Bear
9 Cheshire
10 Ireland
11 Kale
12 The Corrs
13 Tamar
14 *Total Recall*
15 Blue flag
16 Tracy Island
17 1969
18 Lake Michigan
19 Hyde Park
20 Tammy Wynette

QUIZ 138 – Architects and Architecture

ANSWERS ON PAGE 140

1 Doric, Ionian and which other style make up the three orders of Greek architecture?
2 What shape is a gable?
3 On which part of a building would you find a cupola?
4 Which cathedral sits on Ludgate Hill?
5 For what purpose did Mughal Emperor Shah Jahan build the Taj Mahal?
6 What type of feature is a transom?
7 In which city is the Bird's Nest Olympic stadium?
8 Which Hungarian architect's surname did Ian Fleming borrow for a Bond villain?
9 Which French engineer designed the internal structure of the Statue of Liberty?
10 On which type of building might you find bartizans and a portcullis?
11 Of what material is the London Shard made?
12 Who designed the Millennium Dome?
13 What shape is a rotunda?
14 Of which surprising material is the dome of the Roman Pantheon constructed?
15 For what purpose is rock wool used in a building?
16 Which Glaswegian architect and designer created several Art Nouveau buildings in his home city?
17 What term is given to a small floor built between two main floors of a building?
18 In which New Zealand city is the Cardboard Cathedral, created after a 2011 earthquake?
19 Who designed London's Cenotaph?
20 What name is given to a sun-dried building brick?

Easy

Medium

Hard

Answers to QUIZ 136 – Bridges

1 Manhattan
2 Nottinghamshire
3 Troll
4 Clifton
5 Florence
6 The Millennium Bridge
7 Forth
8 Chelsea FC
9 Skye
10 San Francisco
11 Sydney Harbour Bridge
12 Shropshire
13 Denmark and Sweden
14 Putney Bridge
15 Simon and Garfunkel
16 Conwy
17 Venice
18 Queen Elizabeth II Bridge
19 Clint Eastwood
20 Thomas Hardy

QUIZ 139 – Pot Luck

ANSWERS ON PAGE 141

1 Which gardening implement has Dutch and draw varieties?
2 *Hotel California* was a 1970s hit for which group?
3 Which French word means a very thin pancake?
4 What is the study of history through excavation?
5 Which citrus fruit takes its name from a Moroccan port?
6 Which Latin phrase means "for a specific purpose only"?
7 On *University Challenge*, which category of question is worth ten points?
8 In which county are the Lost Gardens of Heligan?
9 Peter Sellers played which military scientist in a 1964 Stanley Kubrick film?
10 What name is given to the area between about 23° north and south of the Equator?
11 What armoured vehicle was first used on the Somme in 1916?
12 Which London Underground line terminates at Elephant and Castle?
13 The agave plant is the source of which distilled Mexican spirit?
14 Which kind of state has a president rather than a monarch?
15 Which Beatles song includes the line "cos I don't care too much for money"?
16 What is the sign of BSI approval?
17 What name is given to a gathering of witches?
18 The TV series *Lovejoy* starred which actor in the title role?
19 How many lives is a cat said to have?
20 Which flower is the national emblem of Japan?

Answers to QUIZ 137 – Pot Luck

1 Soo
2 Bristol Channel
3 Tomato
4 Larkin
5 Arnold Schwarzenegger
6 Tennis
7 Three
8 George Clooney
9 Render
10 Geordie
11 Javier Bardem
12 Campus
13 Croatia
14 Victor Hugo
15 Boar
16 Aniseed
17 Cairn
18 Ricky Martin
19 Rome
20 *The Death of Stalin*

QUIZ 140 – Months

ANSWERS ON PAGE 142

Easy

1 Which two summer months were named after Roman emperors?
2 What term is used to describe a year with 29 days in February?
3 Who starred as Ron Kovic in the 1989 film *Born on the Fourth of July*?
4 Who played Betty Draper in *Mad Men*?
5 What, according to TS Eliot, is "the cruellest month"?
6 What is the state capital of Maine, USA?
7 Who sang *January February* in 1982?
8 Who played Edina's mother in *Absolutely Fabulous*?
9 *June is Bustin' Out All Over* is a song from which musical?
10 Which song was the only UK no.1 single for The Four Seasons?
11 Which "mad" animal is associated with the month of March?

Medium

12 The Oktoberfest takes place in which European city?
13 Who recorded the 1971 song *Maggie May*?
14 March is named after which Roman god?
15 Which month represents a consonant in the radio phonetic alphabet?
16 Who played April in the TV series *Parks and Recreation*?
17 What month did Earth, Wind and Fire sing about in 1978?
18 What was *Red October* in the title of a 1990 film?
19 Who won the 2005 Best Actress Oscar for her role as June Carter Cash in *Walk the Line*?
20 In which year did Theresa May become UK Prime Minister?

Hard

Answers to QUIZ 138 – Architects and Architecture

1 Corinthian
2 Triangular
3 Roof
4 St Paul's
5 As a mausoleum for his favourite wife
6 Window (or a crossbar above it)
7 Beijing
8 Goldfinger
9 Gustav Eiffel
10 Castle
11 Glass
12 Richard Rogers (Baron Rogers of Riverside)
13 Round
14 Concrete
15 Insulation
16 Charles Rennie Mackintosh
17 Mezzanine
18 Christchurch
19 Sir Edwin Lutyens
20 Adobe

QUIZ 141 – Pot Luck

ANSWERS ON PAGE 143

1 Which container port lies across the Thames Estuary from Gravesend?
2 How many crotchets are there in a semibreve?
3 *El Gordo* is the lottery in which country?
4 What is the device that controls an aircraft by instruments called?
5 Which film series starred Vanessa Hudgens and Zac Efron?
6 What title is given to the wife of an earl?
7 In which city is the Crucible, home of the world snooker tournament?
8 What was the first name of epic film director Mr B DeMille?
9 What colour is the ribbon on the Victoria Cross?
10 Who topped the charts in the 1970s with *How Can I Be Sure* and *Daydreamer*?
11 What is the reading system of raised type for blind people?
12 The active volcano Cotopaxi is in which range of mountains?
13 Which racecourse has an annual meeting called "Glorious"?
14 What are male hares called?
15 What is the title of Fleetwood Mac's eleventh album, released in 1977?
16 Chatsworth House is the ancestral home of which duke?
17 An MOT is required for cars over what age?
18 Which US city hosted the 1996 Summer Olympics?
19 In 1875 what did Captain Matthew Webb become the first person to do?
20 In which county is Frome?

Answers to QUIZ 139 – Pot Luck

1 Hoe
2 Eagles
3 Crêpe
4 Archaeology
5 Tangerine
6 Ad hoc
7 Starter question
8 Cornwall
9 Dr Strangelove
10 The Tropics
11 Tank
12 The Bakerloo line
13 Tequila
14 A republic
15 *Can't Buy Me Love*
16 Kitemark
17 Coven
18 Ian McShane
19 Nine
20 Chrysanthemum

QUIZ 142 – Italy

ANSWERS ON PAGE 144

Easy

1 What is the capital of Italy...?
2 ...and in which administrative region does it lie?
3 On which island is the Blue Grotto?
4 Which almond-flavoured liqueur is used to flavour tiramisu?
5 *The Birth of Venus* is a 15th-century work by which Italian artist?
6 Who was the leader of Italy at the outbreak of WWII?
7 What do Italians call the city of Florence?
8 *Nove* is the Italian word for which number?
9 What is the Italian name for squid?
10 An Italian autostrada has what British equivalent?
11 What was the Italian currency unit until 2002?

Medium

12 Which island lies at the "toe" of Italy?
13 Basil, oil, Parmesan and pine nuts are the usual ingredients of which green sauce?
14 Which Italian city is the centre of the fashion industry?
15 Which 19th-century Italian patriot shares his name with a currant biscuit?
16 In which Italian region is Chianti produced?
17 Frittata is an Italian version of which dish?
18 The Testarossa is a model of which Italian car?
19 Which small Italian dumplings are made from semolina or potato?
20 The name of which Italian opera house translates as "The Staircase"?

Hard

Answers to QUIZ 140 – Months

1 July and August
2 Leap year
3 Tom Cruise
4 January Jones
5 April
6 Augusta
7 Barbara Dickson
8 Dame June Whitfield
9 *Carousel*
10 *December 1963 (Oh, What a Night)*
11 Hare
12 Munich
13 Sir Rod Stewart
14 Mars
15 November
16 Aubrey Plaza
17 September
18 A submarine
19 Reese Witherspoon
20 2016

QUIZ 143 – Pot Luck

ANSWERS ON PAGE 145

1 Which town is indicated by a postcode prefix of KT?
2 Which London church is the British Catholic Church's headquarters?
3 What is the name given to the crime of deliberately setting fire to property?
4 Heriot-Watt University is in which city?
5 Which canine breed is named from the Welsh for "dwarf dog"?
6 In 2018, which TV series won the Best Drama Series BAFTA?
7 What is the art of growing miniature trees in pots?
8 In which city is Arthur's Seat?
9 What is the birth sign of someone born on New Year's Day?
10 Who starred as a psychologist in the film *The Sixth Sense*?
11 In music, what note is written on the middle line of the treble clef?
12 What is the common name of the Gravelly Hill interchange on the M6?
13 In which county is Beaulieu Motor Museum?
14 Which French dish consists of chicken cooked in red wine?
15 In which body part is the conjunctiva located?
16 Who had a hit in 1986 with *Sledgehammer*?
17 What word is applied to both a synthetic fibre used in knitwear and a type of paint?
18 From which country does Lego® originate?
19 Keswick is located on the northern shore of which lake?
20 What name is given to a lawyer who pleads a case in an English court?

Answers to QUIZ 141 – Pot Luck

1 Tilbury
2 Four
3 Spain
4 Autopilot
5 *High School Musical*
6 Countess
7 Sheffield
8 Cecil
9 Purple
10 David Cassidy
11 Braille
12 The Andes
13 Goodwood
14 Bucks
15 *Rumours*
16 Duke of Devonshire
17 Three years
18 Atlanta
19 Swim the English Channel
20 Somerset

QUIZ 144 – World History

ANSWERS ON PAGE 146

Easy

1 Which ship transported the Pilgrim Fathers to America?

2 What slab of rock was discovered in 1799 and enabled the deciphering of Egyptian hieroglyphics?

3 Which volcanic Indonesian island erupted catastrophically in 1883?

4 What was the former name of the Indian city of Chennai?

5 Which Australian state was formerly known as Van Diemen's Land?

6 What was the name given to an Australasian expeditionary soldier during WWI?

7 What was the given name of the Russian tsar known as "the Terrible"?

8 To which Roman conspirator were Julius Caesar's last words supposedly spoken?

9 Which Texas mission was famously defended by Davy Crockett and others in 1836?

10 Which people were conquered by Hernán Cortés?

Medium

11 After which Vietnamese statesman is Saigon now named?

12 Which US Civil War battle gave its name to a famous speech made in November 1863?

13 Which former structure in Germany was erected in 1961?

14 Which African country's southern part seceded in 2011?

15 The Enigma Code was cracked at which Buckinghamshire site?

16 Which Norwegian explorer was the first man to reach the South Pole?

17 What was the name given to the part of the Roman Empire now called France?

18 During which conflict did the Gallipoli campaign take place?

19 Which international news agency was founded in London in 1851?

20 On which South Atlantic island did Napoleon die?

Hard

Answers to QUIZ 142 – Italy

1 Rome
2 Lazio
3 Capri
4 Amaretto
5 Botticelli
6 Benito Mussolini
7 Firenze
8 Nine
9 Calamari
10 Motorway
11 Lira
12 Sicily
13 Pesto
14 Milan
15 Garibaldi
16 Tuscany
17 Omelette
18 Ferrari
19 Gnocchi
20 La Scala

QUIZ 145 – Pot Luck

ANSWERS ON PAGE 147

1 What is the capital of the Bahamas?
2 The Commonwealth Games took place in which British city in 2002?
3 What is the chicken filled with in the dish Chicken Kiev?
4 What was the name of the receptionist in the TV series *The Office*?
5 Which former prison was located in San Francisco Bay?
6 The winter resort of Zermatt is in which country?
7 What was the title of the England World Cup Squad's no.1 hit in 1970?
8 Which poet wrote *A Shropshire Lad*?
9 In which country was actress Salma Hayek born?
10 Which wild cat has varieties including Bengal, Siberian and Sumatran?
11 What type of entertainment is associated with Sadler's Wells?
12 What is the name of Bill Sikes' girlfriend in *Oliver Twist*?
13 Who were Cromwell's Civil War supporters?
14 What is the art of stuffing animals for preservation called?
15 The Italian-inspired village of Portmeirion is in which country?
16 Which bone connects the shoulder to the elbow?
17 Who composed the 1829 opera *William Tell*?
18 What was John Wayne's real name?
19 What is a repository of public and historical records called?
20 In which forest is Robin Hood said to have lived?

Answers to QUIZ 143 – Pot Luck

1 Kingston-upon-Thames
2 Westminster Cathedral
3 Arson
4 Edinburgh
5 Corgi
6 *Peaky Blinders*
7 Bonsai
8 Edinburgh
9 Capricorn
10 Bruce Willis
11 B
12 Spaghetti Junction
13 Hampshire
14 Coq au vin
15 Eye
16 Peter Gabriel
17 Acrylic
18 Denmark
19 Derwent Water
20 Barrister

QUIZ 146 – Television Presenters

ANSWERS ON PAGE 148

Easy

1 Who was the original host of the game show *Sale of the Century*?

2 Who replaced Fern Britton as a regular co-presenter of *This Morning*?

3 Main presenters of which series have included Percy Thrower and Toby Buckland?

4 Which *Coast* presenter also presented *A History of Celtic Britain*?

5 Which gameshow was presented by Les Dawson from 1984 to 1990?

6 Who presented all the main series of *Big Brother* when it was on Channel 4?

7 Angus Deayton presented which panel show from 1990 to 2002?

8 Who was the BBC commentator for the Eurovision Song Contest from 1980 to 2008?

9 Alan Titchmarsh presented behind-the-scenes series for Channel 5 in 2017 and 2018 about which organisation?

10 Who became the host of *Fifteen to One* in 2014?

Medium

11 Which game show did Jim Bowen host in the 1980s and 1990s?

12 Craig Charles presented which engineering competition from 1998 to 2004?

13 Who was the original presenter of *Blind Date*?

14 Who is Phil Spencer's regular property programme co-presenter?

15 Which BBC breakfast presenter took part in the 2016 series of *Strictly Come Dancing*?

16 Ruth Langsford married which other presenter in 2010?

17 In which city was Lorraine Kelly born?

18 Who was the 1983-88 female co-host of *Good Morning Britain*?

19 What is the name of Kirsty Gallacher's famous sporting father?

20 What is the name of the series that the three former *Top Gear* hosts went on to present in 2016?

Hard

Answers to QUIZ 144 – World History

1 *Mayflower*
2 The Rosetta Stone
3 Krakatoa
4 Madras
5 Tasmania
6 Anzac
7 Ivan
8 Brutus
9 The Alamo
10 The Aztecs
11 Ho Chi Minh
12 Gettysburg
13 Berlin Wall
14 Sudan
15 Bletchley Park
16 Roald Amundsen
17 Gaul
18 WWI
19 Reuters
20 St Helena

QUIZ 147 – Pot Luck

ANSWERS ON PAGE 149

1 In which TV series and film did the character of Huggy Bear appear?

2 What compound is removed during the process of desalinisation?

3 Which university in Birmingham was founded in 1966?

4 Which actor starred as CS Lewis in the 1993 film *Shadowlands*?

5 In which country is the mountainous plateau of the Massif Central?

6 *I'm in the Mood for Dancing* was a 1979 hit for which group of Irish sisters?

7 Which mythical Greek poet entered the underworld to secure release of his wife Eurydice?

8 Which fishing town in Angus is famous for its smoked haddock, known as "smokies"?

9 Grappa is a strong brandy from which country?

10 Which road tunnel is located near the Thames Barrier?

11 Who was the original host of the quiz programme *Mastermind*?

12 Which "Cross" in London refers to the junction of Strand, Whitehall and Cockspur Street?

13 What name is given to an ordained minister ranking next below a priest?

14 Oboes are part of which section of an orchestra?

15 Who preceded Justin Welby as Archbishop of Canterbury?

16 What is a novella?

17 Who was Arnold Ridley's character in *Dad's Army*?

18 What name is given to the distance across a circle, through its centre?

19 American writer Samuel Langhorne Clemens adopted which pen-name?

20 Which fictional city is associated with Batman?

Answers to QUIZ 145 – Pot Luck

1 Nassau
2 Manchester
3 Garlic butter
4 Dawn
5 Alcatraz
6 Switzerland
7 *Back Home*
8 AE Housman
9 Mexico
10 Tiger
11 Dance
12 Nancy
13 Roundheads
14 Taxidermy
15 Wales
16 Humerus
17 Rossini
18 Marion Morrison
19 Archive
20 Sherwood

QUIZ 148 – Theatre

ANSWERS ON PAGE 150

Easy

1 What term is given to an actor's unscripted lines?
2 Which of Shakespeare's plays features the character of Shylock?
3 What is the final run-through of a play before it is performed?
4 Which allergy is also the title of a play by Sir Noël Coward?
5 In theatrical terms, what do the initials ASM stand for?
6 Who wrote the play *Blood Brothers*?
7 What nationality was the playwright Henrik Ibsen?
8 Which pantomime character frees a genie from a lamp?
9 Where in a theatre would you find the wings?
10 How many people speak during a monologue?

Medium

11 Which playwright wrote *Barefoot in the Park* (1963)?
12 Who wrote the long-running play *The Mousetrap*?
13 What is the name of the thoroughfare in the heart of New York's theatreland?
14 Who wrote the 1954 two one-act plays collectively called *Separate Tables*?
15 What name is given to a film or theatre wardrobe assistant?
16 The play *Toad of Toad Hall* was based on which classic 1908 book?
17 What term is given to a public performance of a play before its official opening?
18 In which area of London is the National Theatre?
19 Which English playwright is famously associated with Scarborough?
20 What name is given to the actors' place of rest in a theatre?

Hard

Answers to QUIZ 146 – Television Presenters

1 Nicholas Parsons
2 Holly Willoughby
3 *Gardeners' World*
4 Neil Oliver
5 *Blankety Blank*
6 Davina McCall
7 *Have I Got News For You*
8 Sir Terry Wogan
9 The National Trust
10 Sandi Toksvig
11 *Bullseye*
12 *Robot Wars*
13 Cilla Black
14 Kirstie Allsopp
15 Naga Munchetty
16 Eamonn Holmes
17 Glasgow
18 Anne Diamond
19 Bernard Gallacher
20 *The Grand Tour*

QUIZ 149 – Pot Luck

ANSWERS ON PAGE **151**

1 What three colours make up the German flag?
2 On which New York thoroughfare is the Empire State Building?
3 What was the call sign of Val Kilmer's character in the 1986 film *Top Gun*?
4 Which genus of plants includes onions, leeks and garlic?
5 In which county is the town of Biggleswade?
6 Who played Maria in the 1965 film *The Sound of Music*?
7 Which nostalgic TV series took its name from a late 1950s Buddy Holly hit?
8 In Formula 1, what does a red flag mean?
9 What is the secreting structure in a plant or animal such as the thyroid called?
10 What is the Buddhist and Hindu concept of reaping what you sow?
11 The 2009 film *A Single Man* starred which actor?
12 Zucchini is the American term for which vegetable?
13 Who is Roo's mother in the *Winnie-the-Pooh* books?
14 What is the main ingredient of marshmallow?
15 What is a shorter term for adipose tissue?
16 Which classic song was the 1975 Christmas no.1?
17 In Cockney rhyming slang, what phrase is used to refer to a suit?
18 What is the first name of Ms Yousafzai, co-recipient of the 2014 Nobel Peace Prize?
19 The song *Memory* is from which musical?
20 Vienna is the capital of which European country?

Answers to QUIZ 147 – Pot Luck

1 *Starsky and Hutch*
2 Salt
3 Aston
4 Sir Anthony Hopkins
5 France
6 The Nolan Sisters
7 Orpheus
8 Arbroath
9 Italy
10 Blackwall
11 Magnus Magnusson
12 Charing
13 Deacon
14 Woodwind
15 Rowan Williams
16 A short novel
17 Private Godfrey
18 The diameter
19 Mark Twain
20 Gotham

QUIZ 150 – Kate

ANSWERS ON PAGE 152

Easy

1 Who wrote the novel *What Katy Did* (1872)?
2 Who had a 2013 hit single with *Roar*?
3 In which film did Kate Winslet play Rose DeWitt Bukater?
4 Who did Katie Derham partner in the 2015 series of *Strictly Come Dancing*...?
5 ...and which series of annual classical concerts is she associated with as a presenter?
6 Kate Ford took over the role of which *Coronation Street* character in 2002?
7 Whose first single in 2003 was *The Closest Thing to Crazy*?
8 Which former *Springwatch* presenter was a presenter on *Top Gear* in the late 1990s?
9 In 2002 who became the first female winner of *Big Brother*?
10 In which English town was model Kate Moss born?
11 Which author created the character of Jackson Brodie, played on TV by Jason Isaacs?

Medium

12 2005's *Suddenly I See* won which singer/songwriter an Ivor Novello award?
13 Kate Hudson is the daughter of which famous actress?
14 Who presented the first three series of *The X Factor*?
15 What is the name of Kate Mara's actress sister?
16 Which singer recorded *Running Up That Hill* in 1985?
17 Who won the 2015 series of *Celebrity Big Brother*...?
18 ...and who was the runner-up?
19 At which university did Prince William and Kate Middleton meet?
20 What is the first name of Mary-Kate Olsen's twin sister?

Hard

Answers to QUIZ 148 – Theatre

1 Ad-libs
2 *The Merchant of Venice*
3 Dress rehearsal
4 *Hay Fever*
5 Assistant stage manager
6 Willy Russell
7 Norwegian
8 Aladdin
9 Either side of the stage
10 One
11 Neil Simon
12 Dame Agatha Christie
13 Broadway
14 Sir Terence Rattigan
15 Dresser
16 *The Wind in the Willows*
17 Preview
18 The South Bank
19 Sir Alan Ayckbourn
20 The green room

QUIZ 151 – Pot Luck

ANSWERS ON PAGE 153

1 What name is given to a female donkey?

2 Who was the 39th President of the USA?

3 Who is the heroine of Pasternak's novel *Doctor Zhivago*?

4 The M1 motorway opened in which year?

5 Which French-speaking city in Belgium was the birthplace of writer Georges Simenon and tennis-player Justine Henin?

6 Which British athlete won a second successive Olympic gold medal in the skeleton in 2018?

7 In bingo, which number is traditionally called "Snakes Alive"?

8 What sort of animal is a Cheviot?

9 Who was the two-faced Roman god of doors?

10 What is the term for a follower of Guru Nanak?

11 What is the southernmost province of mainland Spain?

12 What name is given to a follower of St Ignatius Loyola?

13 Which plant is also known as "Adam's Needle"?

14 Ewan McGregor starred with which actress in *A Life Less Ordinary*?

15 What type of drink is amontillado?

16 Who was Rachel's biblical sister?

17 Which South Kensington museum opened in 1857?

18 Who was Poet Laureate from 1968 to 1972?

19 Which fashion designer co-presented the TV series *The Clothes Show* in the 1980s?

20 What is the currency unit of Nepal?

Easy

Medium

Hard

Answers to QUIZ 149 – Pot Luck

1 Black, yellow and red
2 Fifth Avenue
3 Iceman
4 *Allium*
5 Bedfordshire
6 Dame Julie Andrews
7 *Heartbeat*
8 The session has been stopped
9 A gland
10 Karma
11 Colin Firth
12 Courgette
13 Kanga
14 Sugar
15 Fat
16 *Bohemian Rhapsody*
17 Whistle and flute
18 Malala
19 *Cats*
20 Austria

QUIZ 152 – Television Crime Drama

ANSWERS ON PAGE 154

Easy

1 Which 1990s series starred Richard Griffiths as a policeman running a restaurant?
2 Who created the series *Line of Duty*?
3 Which novelist created the characters of Dalziel and Pascoe?
4 Who played Sarah Linden in the US remake of the Danish series *The Killing*?
5 Which US series featured brothers Don and Charlie, an FBI agent and a mathematician?
6 In which 1980s detective series did Pierce Brosnan play the lead role?
7 Which US series starred Michael Emerson as billionaire Harold Finch?
8 Which fictional detective's cases included *The Dead of Jericho* and *The Daughters of Cain*?
9 Who starred in the 1980s series *The Chinese Detective*?
10 In which series did Geraldine Somerville play DS Penhaligon?
11 What is the name of the lead character in the series *Orange is the New Black*?

Medium

12 Who played Detective Jimmy McNulty in the series *The Wire*?
13 Which series starred Anna Carteret as Inspector Kate Longton?
14 In which town is the Welsh series *Hinterland* set?
15 What was the title of the US version of *Broadchurch*?
16 Who starred in the 1970s and 80s TV series *Quincy M.E.*?
17 In which series did Detective John Munch first appear?
18 Who played Hastings to David Suchet's Hercule Poirot between 1989 and 2003?
19 Who created the series *Happy Valley*?
20 Who played Jack Malone in the series *Without a Trace*?

Hard

Answers to QUIZ 150 – Kate

1 Susan Coolidge
2 Katy Perry
3 *Titanic*
4 Anton du Beke
5 The Proms
6 Tracy Barlow
7 Katie Melua
8 Kate Humble
9 Kate Lawler
10 Croydon
11 Kate Atkinson
12 KT Tunstall
13 Goldie Hawn
14 Kate Thornton
15 Rooney Mara
16 Kate Bush
17 Katie Price
18 Katie Hopkins
19 St Andrews
20 Ashley

QUIZ 153 – Pot Luck

ANSWERS ON PAGE 155

1 The mazurka is a dance from which country?

2 Which 2007 film about a serial killer starred Jake Gyllenhaal?

3 What is the name of the imaginary kingdom in Anthony Hope's *The Prisoner of Zenda* (1894)?

4 Which Old Testament character was known for his patience?

5 Singer Robyn Fenty is better known by what stage name?

6 Who was the men's Wimbledon singles champion in 2002?

7 In computing, what does RTF stand for in relation to file types?

8 Port Said is in which country?

9 Which British general in the Crimean War gave his name to a style of sleeve?

10 Zoroastrianism is associated with which ancient kingdom?

11 Who invented the cat's eye?

12 Which Italian dessert consists of egg yolks, Marsala and sugar?

13 Who wrote the 2004 novel *My Sister's Keeper*?

14 Skye is separated from the mainland by which body of water?

15 Which flower part consists of an anther and a filament?

16 Which is Australia's largest lake?

17 Who won a National Television Award for her portrayal of Cilla Black in *Cilla*?

18 What was the name of EW Hornung's "gentleman burglar"?

19 According to Greek mythology, who was the first woman?

20 Which now obsolete profession, made famous by Chaucer, involved the selling of papal indulgences?

Answers to QUIZ 151 – Pot Luck

1 Jenny
2 Jimmy Carter
3 Lara
4 1959
5 Liège
6 Lizzy Yarnold
7 55
8 Sheep
9 Janus
10 Sikh
11 Cadiz
12 Jesuit
13 Yucca
14 Cameron Diaz
15 Sherry
16 Leah
17 Science
18 Cecil Day-Lewis
19 Jeff Banks
20 Rupee

QUIZ 154 – Sport

ANSWERS ON PAGE 156

Easy

1 In which sport do women compete for the Solheim Cup?
2 In which version of hockey would you use a bladeless stick called a caman?
3 What colour is the outermost ring on an archery target?
4 In which year did the boxing match known as "The Rumble in the Jungle" take place?
5 House, sweeping and tee are terms in which sport?
6 Who won the 2017 World Rally Championship?
7 How many gold medals did gymnast Max Whitlock win at the 2016 Rio Summer Olympics?
8 Minnesota Vikings and Detroit Lions are professional teams in which sport?
9 Spa motor racing circuit is in which country?
10 Over what distance is an Olympic steeplechase?

Medium

11 Eddy Merckx was a professional in which sport?
12 What is the highest possible score in a game of tenpin bowling?
13 What term is given to a score of three under par in golf?
14 Who captained the England women's Ashes team in 2017?
15 How many times did Stephen Hendry win the World Snooker Championship?
16 What is the name of the cricket test match ground in Brisbane?
17 Which sport other than tennis is played at the All England Club in Wimbledon?
18 How many wickets did Jim Laker take in the 1956 cricket test match against Australia?
19 Which equestrian discipline is known by the French word for "training"?
20 Which was the first club in English football to be awarded a goal by VAR (Video Assistant Referee) technology?

Hard

Answers to QUIZ 152 – Television Crime Drama

1 *Pie in the Sky*
2 Jed Mercurio
3 Reginald Hill
4 Mireille Enos
5 *Numb3rs*
6 *Remington Steele*
7 *Person of Interest*
8 Inspector Morse
9 David Yip
10 *Cracker*
11 Piper Chapman
12 Dominic West
13 *Juliet Bravo*
14 Aberystwyth
15 *Gracepoint*
16 Jack Klugman
17 *Homicide: Life on the Street*
18 Hugh Fraser
19 Sally Wainwright
20 Anthony LaPaglia

QUIZ 155 – Pot Luck

ANSWERS ON PAGE 157

1 Which comedian starred in the 1926 silent film *The General*?

2 Who was awarded the Nobel Prize in Literature in 2017?

3 In which New York borough is JFK airport?

4 What type of animal is a Mexican hairless?

5 Which singer released her debut single *Stone Cold Sober* in 2009?

6 In the Old Testament, who is the older brother of Moses?

7 Which actress starred in the 2007 film *The Brave One*?

8 What nickname was given to the 16th-century Spanish painter Domenikos Theotokopoulos?

9 Which US state is nicknamed "Old Line State"?

10 On which date is St Swithin's Day?

11 Which novelist created Doctor Finlay?

12 The Mönch and the Jungfrau form a trio along with which Swiss mountain?

13 What is the name of the Italian Grand Prix circuit near Milan, built in 1922?

14 Which Swedish pop group formed as Festfolk in 1970?

15 What Latin phrase means "with hindsight"?

16 What is October's birthstone?

17 Which long-running BBC current affairs programme launched in 1953?

18 Which Egyptian sky-god has the head of a falcon?

19 Who was the UK Prime Minister from 1908 to 1916?

20 The term "viva voce" would be applied to what type of exam?

Answers to QUIZ 153 – Pot Luck

1 Poland
2 *Zodiac*
3 Ruritania
4 Job
5 Rihanna
6 Lleyton Hewitt
7 Rich text format
8 Egypt
9 Raglan
10 Persia
11 Percy Shaw
12 Zabaglione
13 Jodi Picoult
14 Sound of Sleat
15 Stamen
16 Lake Eyre
17 Sheridan Smith
18 Raffles
19 Pandora
20 Pardoner

QUIZ 156 – 1980s Music

ANSWERS ON PAGE 158

1 Who was the keyboard player in the Communards, and is now a minister and TV presenter?

2 *A Groovy Kind of Love* by Phil Collins featured in which 1988 film?

3 Who had a 1985 hit with *Move Closer*?

4 Who played harmonica on the Eurythmics hit *There Must Be an Angel (Playing with My Heart)*?

5 From which Album was A-Ha's *The Sun Always Shines on TV* taken?

6 Who partnered Neil Tennant in The Pet Shop Boys?

7 *Rock Me Amadeus* was a 1986 hit for which singer?

8 What were the first names of music producers Stock, Aitken and Waterman?

9 Who is the lead singer with T'Pau?

10 What was Kylie Minogue's first hit single in Australia?

11 What was the title of U2's debut album?

12 Which group did Enya belong to before going solo?

13 Who duetted with Marc Almond on 1989's *Something's Gotten Hold of My Heart*?

14 Who was the lead singer with The Housemartins?

15 Eddy Grant's *I Don't Wanna Dance* topped the charts in which year?

16 Which girl group had a hit in 1988 with *Nathan Jones*?

17 Who topped the UK singles chart in 1982 with *Goody Two Shoes*?

18 On which date did the first Live Aid concert take place?

19 Which male singer featured on Cherelle's *Saturday Love* in 1985?

20 Which comedian released the 1981 single *Ullo John, Got a New Motor*?

Easy

Medium

Hard

Answers to QUIZ 154 – Sport

1 Golf
2 Shinty
3 White
4 1974
5 Curling
6 Sebastien Ogier
7 Two
8 American football
9 Belgium
10 3000m
11 Cycling
12 300
13 Albatross
14 Heather Knight
15 Seven
16 The Gabba
17 Croquet
18 19
19 Dressage
20 Leicester City

QUIZ 157 – Pot Luck

ANSWERS ON PAGE 159

1 Which tan-coloured breed of horse has a white mane and tail?
2 Who was the wife of Zeus in Greek mythology?
3 What was the name of Patrick Swayze's character in the 1987 film *Dirty Dancing*?
4 Les Paul is associated with the development of which musical instrument?
5 In which National Park are Loweswater and Wasdale Head?
6 By what name is singer Paul Hewson better known?
7 In Arthurian legend, who was the son of Lancelot?
8 Who directed the 2016 film *I, Daniel Blake*?
9 Which river of Switzerland and France flows into the Mediterranean?
10 In which year did the first Red Nose Day take place?
11 Which genus of plants includes the buttercup?
12 Who invented the flying shuttle, used in weaving?
13 In which country was philanthropist Andrew Carnegie born?
14 Who composed the operetta *The Merry Widow* (1905)?
15 In biology, which taxonomic rank comes above family and below class?
16 Which organisation awards the Dickin Medal?
17 At which golf course was the 2013 Open Championship held?
18 What is the French word for "butterfly"?
19 Which Tuscan port is the location of the Italian Naval Academy?
20 What term is given to a vein of metal ore found in rock?

Answers to QUIZ 155 – Pot Luck

1 Buster Keaton
2 Kazuo Ishiguro
3 Queens
4 A dog
5 Paloma Faith
6 Aaron
7 Jodie Foster
8 El Greco
9 Maryland
10 July 15
11 AJ Cronin
12 Eiger
13 Monza
14 ABBA
15 *A posteriori*
16 Opal
17 *Panorama*
18 Horus
19 Herbert Asquith (First Earl of Oxford and Asquith)
20 An oral exam

Easy

1 How many sides are there on an icosahedron?

2 Which gas is the main constituent of natural gas?

3 In which constellation is Betelgeuse?

4 Where in the body is the talus bone located?

5 Which American chemist is credited with the discovery of nylon?

6 What is the alternative name for potassium nitrate, a substance used in preserving meat?

7 In which year was Halley's Comet last seen from Earth?

8 *Lepidoptera* is an order of which insects?

9 Which semiconductor allows current to flow in only one direction round a circuit?

10 Which chemical element has the symbol F?

Medium

11 Which scientist developed the anti-polio vaccine?

12 What is the SI unit of illumination?

13 Who was the first American in space?

14 Which is the largest of Saturn's moons?

15 Which element has the atomic number 2?

16 Who invented the Analytical Engine (c.1833)?

17 How is riboflavin more commonly known?

18 What was the name of the spacecraft that carried the Philae lander?

19 What is the chemical symbol for platinum?

20 Which word describes angles adding up to 180 degrees?

Hard

Answers to QUIZ 156 – 1980s Music

1 Richard Coles
2 *Buster*
3 Phyllis Nelson
4 Stevie Wonder
5 *Hunting High and Low*
6 Chris Lowe
7 Falco
8 Mike, Matt and Pete
9 Carol Decker
10 *Locomotion*
11 *Boy*
12 Clannad
13 Gene Pitney
14 Paul Heaton
15 1982
16 Bananarama
17 Adam Ant
18 July 13, 1985
19 Alexander O'Neal
20 Alexei Sayle

QUIZ 159 – Pot Luck

ANSWERS ON PAGE 161

1 What is the tenth letter of the Greek alphabet?

2 AMS is the code for which airport?

3 What term is given to a bridge hand with no card higher than a nine?

4 Who invented the turbojet engine?

5 What is the Latin phrase meaning "at the last gasp"?

6 Which cathedral has the tallest spire in England?

7 What is an adult insect produced after metamorphosis?

8 Where would you find a Plimsoll line?

9 What is the Scottish term for an island or meadow beside a river?

10 By what name was Frances Ethel Gumm better known?

11 Which 2013 film directed by Ron Howard portrays the relationship between two Formula 1 drivers?

12 What was Louis Armstrong's famous seven-letter nickname?

13 Who played the title character in the 2004 comedy film *Shaun of the Dead*?

14 Which Old Testament book follows Judges?

15 Which island was formerly known as Formosa?

16 The animal *Canis lupus* is known by what common name?

17 Which poet wrote the line "No man is an island"?

18 Who is the patron saint of lost causes?

19 Who won the Brits Critics' Choice Award in 2018?

20 What is the continual past tense of a verb better known as?

Answers to QUIZ 157 – Pot Luck

1 Palomino
2 Hera
3 Johnny Castle
4 Guitar
5 Lake District
6 Bono
7 Galahad
8 Ken Loach
9 Rhône
10 1988
11 *Ranunculus*
12 John Kay
13 Scotland
14 Franz Lehár
15 Order
16 PDSA
17 Muirfield
18 Papillon
19 Livorno
20 Lode

QUIZ 160 – Dogs

ANSWERS ON PAGE **162**

Easy

1 In what year was the Dangerous Dogs Act implemented in the UK?
2 Which of these cartoon dogs was created first: Scooby Doo or Snoopy?
3 Into how many breed groups does the Kennel Club of Great Britain divide dogs?
4 Which breed of working dog is most associated with the Western Alps?
5 To which biological family do domestic dogs belong?
6 Which Wallace and Gromit animation featured a robot dog?
7 How many teeth does the average adult dog have?
8 From which country does the Akita breed originate?
9 In Charles Dickens' *Oliver Twist*, what was the name and breed of Bill Sikes' dog?
10 Where on a dog would you find the carpal pad?

Medium

11 In the *Ren and Stimpy Show*, what breed of dog is Ren?
12 In which year did Pudsey the dog win *Britain's Got Talent*?
13 Which dog gave its name to the 2003 European Space Agency Mars Lander?
14 Which desert creature is the smallest member of the dog family?
15 What is the name of the mythological three-headed dog that guarded the entrance to Hades?
16 What was the original location of Battersea Dogs & Cats Home?
17 Which breed of dog was originally bred for hauling freight?
18 The withers are the highest part of what on a dog?
19 The Lhasa Apso breed originates from which Himalayan region?

Hard

20 In which sport do teams of four dogs compete in relay over a course of hurdles to release a tennis ball?

Answers to QUIZ 158 – Science

1 20
2 Methane
3 Orion
4 Ankle
5 Wallace Carothers
6 Saltpetre
7 1986
8 Moths and butterflies
9 Diode
10 Fluorine
11 Jonas Salk
12 Lux
13 Alan Shepard (1961)
14 Titan
15 Helium
16 Charles Babbage
17 Vitamin B2
18 *Rosetta*
19 Pt
20 Supplementary

QUIZ 161 – Pot Luck

ANSWERS ON PAGE 163

1 What word describes the legal rights of the owner of land adjoining a river?

2 The maneki-neko is a Japanese figurine depicting which creature?

3 Frank Matcham was famous for designing what types of building?

4 What term describes having a lack of or reduction of pigmentation but normal eye colouring?

5 What does NGO stand for?

6 Which set of principles aims to maximise the greatest happiness of the greatest number?

7 Which is the top taxonomic classification?

8 The Commonwealth of Nations has its headquarters in which London building?

9 In 1932 a mass trespass happened at which Derbyshire location?

10 What do the letters PP stand for when seen on a plastic item?

11 In which children's TV series of the 1970s did Aswad's Brinsley Forde appear?

12 Which actress co-starred with Tom Cruise in the 1986 film *Top Gun*?

13 Thoron is a radioisotope of which gas?

14 The Hetch Hetchy Valley is in which US National Park?

15 How is Rapa Nui also known?

16 In which city is the Radcliffe Observatory?

17 Who wrote the 1859 philosophical work *On Liberty*?

18 What do the initials CHP mean in the context of energy?

19 Which role did Madonna play in the 1989 film *Dick Tracy*?

20 Which South Asian country's government is guided by the measure of the Gross National Happiness Index?

Easy

Medium

Hard

Answers to QUIZ 159 – Pot Luck

1 Kappa
2 Schiphol
3 Yarborough
4 Frank Whittle
5 *In extremis*
6 Salisbury
7 Imago
8 On the side of a ship
9 Inch
10 Judy Garland
11 *Rush*
12 Satchmo
13 Simon Pegg
14 Ruth
15 Taiwan
16 Wolf
17 John Donne
18 St Jude
19 Jorja Smith
20 Imperfect

QUIZ 162 – Loves and Fears

ANSWERS ON PAGE 164

1 What is the term for a love of anything new or novelty?
2 Which term is often used to describe a fear of clowns?
3 What is the term for someone who is attracted to foreigners?
4 What the term for a fear of flying?
5 Pogonophobia is a fear of what?
6 What is the term for someone who loves wine?
7 What is calligynephobia a fear of?
8 Stigmatophilia is a love for what?
9 What is the term for someone who loves cheese?
10 Ailurophilia is a love of what?
11 Hydrophobia is another name for which disease?
12 What is acrophobia a fear of?
13 What is the term for a fear of writing?
14 Dendrophilia is a love of what?
15 What is the term for an irrational fear of dogs?
16 What is the term for a fear of fire?
17 A thalassophile is someone who loves what?
18 What is triskaidekaphobia a fear of?
19 What is the term for someone who loves to work?
20 What is a hippophobe scared of?

Answers to QUIZ 160 – Dogs

1 1991
2 Snoopy (1950)
3 Seven
4 St Bernard
5 *Canidae*
6 *A Close Shave*
7 42
8 Japan
9 Bullseye, the bull terrier
10 On the back of each foreleg
11 Chihuahua
12 2012
13 Beagle
14 Fennec fox
15 Cerberus
16 Holloway, North London
17 Alaskan malamute
18 The shoulders
19 Tibet
20 Flyball

QUIZ 163 – Pot Luck

ANSWERS ON PAGE 165

1 Which historian presented the 1969 TV series *Civilisation*?

2 The Yas Marina Formula 1 circuit is in which country?

3 In which year did Nick Berry have a hit with *Every Loser Wins*?

4 Which word means "created by people or caused by human activity"?

5 In which year did the Peak District become a National Park?

6 What do the initials NODA stand for in relation to the performing arts?

7 Which ancient Egyptian city on the Nile is now called Luxor?

8 What prefix indicates 10^{12}?

9 Which animal has the Latin name *Rattus rattus*?

10 In a trade context, what does the "E" of OPEC stand for?

11 Which character in the TV series *Lost* was named after an English philosopher and physician?

12 Which is the most northerly of the inhabited Shetland Islands?

13 Which gem is July's birthstone?

14 Which 1980s drama series starring Larry Lamb featured the crew and passengers of a North Sea ferry?

15 Which band had a UK 1982 top ten hit with *Strange Little Girl*?

16 What is the chemical symbol for methane?

17 Who wrote the 1830 poem *Mariana*?

18 Which is the oldest university in Scandinavia?

19 What is the main alcoholic ingredient of a planter's punch?

20 Which major supermarket business was founded by Sir Jack Cohen?

Answers to QUIZ 161 – Pot Luck

1 Riparian
2 Cat
3 Theatres
4 Leucistic
5 Non-governmental organisation
6 Utilitarianism
7 Kingdom
8 Marlborough House
9 Kinder Scout
10 Polypropylene
11 *Here come the Double Deckers*
12 Kelly McGillis
13 Radon
14 Yosemite
15 Easter Island
16 Oxford
17 John Stuart Mill
18 Combined heat and power
19 Breathless Mahoney
20 Bhutan

QUIZ 164 – Classical Music

ANSWERS ON PAGE 166

1 Who composed *The Flying Dutchman* (1840)?
2 Which German composer of four symphonies died in 1897?
3 From which instrument's A note does an orchestra tune up?
4 Which 1930s choral work by Carl Orff is based on 13th-century poems?
5 What type of musical composition, associated with Bach, uses counterpoint?
6 Who was the composer of the ballet *Billy the Kid* (1938)?
7 The character of Mimi features in which opera by Puccini?
8 What is the title of John Cage's 1952 "silent" work?
9 The bassoon is a member of which woodwind family?
10 What is the title of Beethoven's only opera?
11 Who was the Russian composer of *Prince Igor* (1890)?
12 What sort of instrument is a marimba?
13 Which composer's rivalry with Mozart was the subject of the film *Amadeus*?
14 What tree extract is used for treating violin bows?
15 Which 18th-century Austrian composer wrote 108 symphonies?
16 What term is given to a group of sharps and flats at the beginning of a music score?
17 What nationality was composer Frederick Delius?
18 How should a piece of music marked "doloroso" be played?
19 What is a short musical composition, usually for piano, designed as an exercise called?
20 What do the initials "DS" stand for on a musical score?

Answers to QUIZ 162 – Loves and Fears

1 Neophilia
2 Coulrophobia
3 A xenophile
4 Aviophobia
5 Beards
6 An oenophile
7 Beautiful women
8 Body piercing or tattooing
9 A turophile
10 Cats
11 Rabies
12 Heights
13 Graphophobia
14 Trees
15 Cynophobia
16 Pyrophobia
17 Seas and sea travel
18 The number 13
19 An ergophile
20 Horses

QUIZ 165 – Pot Luck

ANSWERS ON PAGE 167

1 Who played Carson in the TV series *Downton Abbey*?
2 What ion-containing substance is found in batteries?
3 Which former British coin was worth two shillings?
4 Which ex-Spice Girl had a solo hit with *Not Such an Innocent Girl*?
5 Which Old Testament prophet was swallowed by a great fish?
6 How many grams are there in a kilogram?
7 Of which South American country is Montevideo the capital?
8 Which Ibsen play centres on the character of Helen Alving?
9 What is the title of the 1983 film directed by and starring Barbra Streisand?
10 Who composed the song *White Christmas*?
11 What name is given to the group of islands within the West Indies which includes St Lucia and Dominica?
12 What is the official language of Cambodia?
13 Ikebana is the Japanese art of what?
14 On which river does Brecon stand?
15 What fruit is also known as a Chinese gooseberry?
16 What do the letters ERNIE stand for in the Premium Bond number picker?
17 Where in the UK are the mountains known as the Cuillins?
18 Which character tells the first of Chaucer's *Canterbury Tales?*
19 Which 18th-century naturalist lived at Selborne in Hampshire?
20 What nickname was given to Edward I of England on account of his unusual height?

Easy Medium Hard

Answers to QUIZ 163 – Pot Luck

1 Kenneth Clark (Baron Clark)
2 United Arab Emirates (Abu Dhabi)
3 1986
4 Anthropogenic
5 1951
6 National Operatic and Dramatic Association
7 Thebes
8 Tera
9 Black rat
10 Exporting
11 John Locke
12 Unst
13 Ruby
14 *Triangle*
15 The Stranglers
16 CH4
17 Alfred, Lord Tennyson
18 Uppsala
19 Rum
20 Tesco

QUIZ 166 – Literature

ANSWERS ON PAGE 168

Easy

1 Which was the first novel to feature the character of Jack Reacher?

2 Who wrote the 1994 novel *Captain Corelli's Mandolin*?

3 What is the name of the police sergeant in Wilkie Collins' *The Moonstone* (1868)?

4 Which Irish poet wrote *The Lake Isle of Innisfree*?

5 Who created the character of Tudor lawyer Matthew Shardlake?

6 What was in Winston Smith's Room 101, in a classic novel of 1949?

7 Who was the Roman author of the *Aeneid*?

8 What monster is lurking under the waves in the Book of Job in the Bible?

9 In 1668, who was appointed the first official Poet Laureate?

10 Which actor's autobiography was entitled *The Moon's a Balloon* (1972)?

11 What was the dog's name in the *Famous Five* children's books?

Medium

12 Who wrote the 2003 novel *We Need to Talk About Kevin?*

13 What was the real name of the novelist who was published under the name of George Eliot?

14 The TV series *Wire in the Blood* was based on the books by which author?

15 Which Swedish detective was created by Henning Mankell?

16 What kind of animal was Grip, Barnaby Rudge's pet?

17 What is the first part of Dante's *The Divine Comedy*?

18 Who wrote the poem *The Ballad of East and West* (1889)?

19 Which author created Paddington Bear?

20 Who is the Soviet spymaster in John le Carré's Smiley novels?

Hard

Answers to QUIZ 164 – Classical Music

1 Richard Wagner
2 Johannes Brahms
3 Oboe
4 *Carmina Burana*
5 Fugue
6 Aaron Copland
7 *La bohème*
8 4'33"
9 Oboe
10 *Fidelio*
11 Alexander Borodin
12 Percussion (xylophone)
13 Antonio Salieri
14 Rosin
15 Franz Joseph Haydn
16 Key signature
17 English
18 Plaintively
19 Étude
20 Dal segno (from the sign)

QUIZ 167 – Pot Luck

ANSWERS ON PAGE 169

1 Which actress starred in the 1987 comedy film *Overboard*?
2 Which girl's name comes from the Greek word for "peace"?
3 In the Old Testament, which priest was teacher to the prophet Samuel?
4 Which part of the body is affected by Ménière's disease?
5 Which figure of Greek mythology was said to be the mother of Helen of Troy?
6 Ferdinand, King of Navarre, is the main character in which of Shakespeare's plays?
7 Which European city is nicknamed "La Serenissima"?
8 What Jane Austen novel features Jane Fairfax and a vicar named Elton?
9 Sword lilies are another name for which tall garden flowers?
10 Which Japanese city is famed for its beef?
11 Which Formula 1 team was featured in a 2017 documentary film?
12 What is the method of printing from a stone or metal plate?
13 Which famous bell can be seen at Lloyd's of London?
14 *Bitter Sweet Symphony* was a 1997 hit for which group?
15 Which rope is attached to the top of a mast?
16 Which *Torchwood* actor went on to appear as Malcolm Merlyn in the TV series *Arrow*?
17 In which National Park is Malham Tarn?
18 What is a complete circle in a fingerprint called?
19 In which country is the city of Shiraz?
20 Seymour and Audrey are the lead characters in which 1982 musical?

Answers to QUIZ 165 – Pot Luck

1 Jim Carter
2 Electrolyte
3 Florin
4 Victoria Beckham
5 Jonah
6 1000
7 Uruguay
8 *Ghosts*
9 *Yentl*
10 Irving Berlin
11 Windward Islands
12 Khmer
13 Flower arranging
14 Usk
15 Kiwi fruit
16 Electronic Random Number Indicator Equipment
17 Isle of Skye
18 Knight
19 Gilbert White
20 Longshanks

QUIZ 168 – World History

ANSWERS ON PAGE 170

Easy

1 Which country, whose seat of government is La Paz, is named after "El Libertador"?
2 How many years had Nelson Mandela spent in captivity when he was released in 1990?
3 Which city replaced Samarkand as capital of Uzbekistan in 1930?
4 Founded in 1636, which is America's oldest university?
5 Which inlet of the Tasman Sea is the site of Captain James Cook's landing in Australia?
6 In which year did Tony Blair become UK Prime Minister?
7 Which country was once ruled by the Duvaliers?
8 Which ancient North African city was the enemy of Rome in the Punic Wars?
9 On which date did Apollo 11 land on the moon?
10 In which year did the American Civil War start?
11 Who commanded the British East India Company at the Battle of Plassey in 1757?
12 Which port is the capital of the United Arab Emirates?

Medium

13 Texas was part of which North American country until 1836?
14 In which year did Martin Luther King deliver his "I have a dream" speech?
15 What was the capital of New Zealand until 1865?
16 Which Russian leader died on January 21, 1924?
17 Who became the world's first "test tube baby" in 1978?
18 Which empire ended when the Ottoman Empire conquered Constantinople in 1453?
19 Which great pharaoh had Abu Simbel constructed?
20 In which year was Pakistan established as a country?

Hard

Answers to QUIZ 166 – Literature

1 *Killing Floor*
2 Louis de Bernières
3 Sergeant Cuff
4 WB Yeats
5 CJ Sansom
6 Rats
7 Virgil
8 Leviathan
9 John Dryden
10 David Niven
11 Timmy
12 Lionel Shriver
13 Mary Ann Evans
14 Val McDermid
15 Kurt Wallander
16 Raven
17 *Inferno*
18 Rudyard Kipling
19 Michael Bond
20 Karla

QUIZ 169 – Pot Luck

ANSWERS ON PAGE 171

1 Which city is home to the Burrell Art Collection?
2 How is the plant *Hedera helix* better known?
3 Which band recorded the 1997 hit *Your Woman*?
4 Which rugby position is also known as "stand-off" or "outside half"?
5 What is the Russian coin equivalent to 100th of a rouble?
6 In which Belgian town is the Menin Gate war memorial?
7 What does a numismatist collect?
8 Which very hot, spicy curry originates from the Indian region of Goa?
9 Who wrote *Silas Marner* (1861)?
10 In chess, what term is given to a checkmate in the fewest number of moves?
11 In which country was shoe designer Jimmy Choo born?
12 Which US university is situated at New Haven, Connecticut?
13 Who invented the Spinning Jenny, patented in 1770?
14 What title does the wife of a Marquis use?
15 Which is the second god of the Hindu trinity?
16 On which London street is Madame Tussauds located?
17 Which famous train crosses Australia north to south?
18 In which month is the US remembrance holiday of Memorial Day?
19 Trowbridge is the administrative centre of which county?
20 What is the national fruit of India?

Easy

Medium

Hard

Answers to QUIZ 167 – Pot Luck

1 Goldie Hawn
2 Irene
3 Eli
4 Inner ear
5 Leda
6 *Love's Labours Lost*
7 Venice
8 *Emma*
9 Gladioli
10 Kobe
11 Williams
12 Lithography
13 Lutine Bell
14 The Verve
15 Mainstay
16 John Barrowman
17 Yorkshire Dales
18 Whorl
19 Iran
20 *Little Shop of Horrors*

QUIZ 170 – Blue

ANSWERS ON PAGE 172

Easy

1 Which English-born American poet wrote *Funeral Blues* in the late 1930s?
2 Which organisation is responsible for commemorative blue plaques on buildings in England?
3 The mineral Blue John is found in which English National Park?
4 Which TV series starred Caroline Quentin as DCI Janine Lewis?
5 In which year was ELO's *Out of the Blue* album released?
6 In which county does the Bluebell railway run?
7 Who won the Best Actress Oscar for the 2013 film *Blue Jasmine*?
8 Which US state is known as "the Bluegrass State"?
9 Who wrote the 1952 play *The Deep Blue Sea*?
10 What sort of animal is a blue-faced Leicester?

Medium

11 What was the name of the craft in which Donald Campbell set speed records?
12 In which Australian state are the Blue Mountains?
13 What was the title of the Moody Blues' first UK chart-topper?
14 Which actor starred as Michael Felgate in the 1999 film *Mickey Blue Eyes*?
15 Which blue characters were created by the Belgian comics artist Peyo?
16 What type of food is blue vinney?
17 Who played WPC Shirley Trewlove in the TV series *Endeavour*?
18 What badge is worn by members of the Order of the Garter?
19 Who co-starred with Ryan Gosling in the 2010 film *Blue Valentine*?
20 What type of animal is a Kerry Blue?

Hard

Answers to QUIZ 168 – World History

1 Bolivia (Simón Bolivar)
2 27
3 Tashkent
4 Harvard
5 Botany Bay
6 1997
7 Haiti
8 Carthage
9 July 21, 1969
10 1861
11 Robert Clive
12 Abu Dhabi
13 Mexico
14 1963
15 Auckland
16 Lenin
17 Louise Brown
18 Byzantine Empire
19 Rameses II
20 1947

QUIZ 171 – Pot Luck

ANSWERS ON PAGE 173

1 Who won the Wimbledon Ladies' Singles title in 2017?

2 What is actor David Tennant's real surname?

3 Who was the star of the 1980s TV series *The Equalizer*?

4 In which US state is Cape Canaveral?

5 Who is the mother of Uranus in Greek mythology?

6 Which former boyband member had a 2016 solo no.1 with *Pillowtalk*?

7 What Italian herb liqueur is named after a 19th-century war hero?

8 Who played the witch in the 2014 film *Into the Woods*?

9 What was the scene of the first pitched battle of the English Civil War, fought in 1642?

10 Which Red Sea Israeli resort is adjacent to the Jordanian port of Aqaba?

11 To what class of mollusc do slugs, snails, cowries and whelks belong?

12 Which US poet wrote the *Leaves of Grass* collection?

13 What type of rock is marble?

14 The Kuga is a make of car by which manufacturer?

15 Which river flows through Melbourne?

16 From which country does mariachi music originate?

17 Which actor starred as Dr Chris Kelvin in the 2002 film *Solaris*?

18 What mixture of opium and alcohol was commonly prescribed for ailments during Victorian times?

19 Who released the 1980 album *Double Fantasy*?

20 Which Irish county north of Kilkenny was formerly known as Queen's?

Answers to QUIZ 169 – Pot Luck

1 Glasgow
2 Ivy
3 White Town
4 Fly-half
5 Kopek
6 Ypres
7 Coins
8 Vindaloo
9 George Eliot
10 Fool's mate
11 Malaysia
12 Yale
13 James Hargreaves
14 Marchioness
15 Vishnu
16 Marylebone Road
17 The Ghan
18 May
19 Wiltshire
20 Mango

QUIZ 172 – Food and Drink

ANSWERS ON PAGE 174

Easy

1 How is the fruit *Rubus idaeus* more commonly known?

2 What term is given to a mixture of root vegetables used as a base for stew or sauce?

3 What is a chanterelle?

4 Asparagus is a member of which plant family?

5 What is a *jus*?

6 Jarlsberg cheese comes from which country?

7 Which cocktail is made from gin, Cointreau® and lemon juice?

8 Prunes are wrapped with what to make devils on horseback?

9 What is a mangelwurzel?

10 What is the name of the Cornish pie where fish heads show through the pastry crust?

Medium

11 The red wine Barolo is from which country?

12 Anjou and Bartlett are types of which fruit?

13 Used in Indian cooking, what is a brinjal called in the UK?

14 If an aperitif is something that precedes a meal, what term is given to something that follows it?

15 The botanical name for which spice is *Zingiber officinale*?

16 What fruit is a hybrid of a tangerine and a grapefruit?

17 Which type of beer takes its name from the German word for "store"?

18 How is the garbanzo bean better known?

19 Which English cheese is coated with nettles?

20 Orange pekoe is a variety of which drink?

Hard

Answers to QUIZ 170 – Blue

1 WH Auden
2 English Heritage
3 Peak District
4 *Blue Murder*
5 1977
6 East Sussex
7 Cate Blanchett
8 Kentucky
9 Sir Terence Rattigan
10 A sheep
11 *Bluebird*
12 New South Wales
13 *Go Now*
14 Hugh Grant
15 Smurfs
16 Cheese
17 Dakota Blue Richards
18 Blue riband
19 Michelle Williams
20 A dog (terrier)

QUIZ 173 – Pot Luck

ANSWERS ON PAGE 175

1 Who played the title role in the 2008 film *The Incredible Hulk*?
2 What is the substance in wheat that makes dough elastic?
3 What is the capital city of Belarus?
4 Which author wrote *Five Children and It* (1902)?
5 Who directed the classic 1927 film *Metropolis*?
6 Which fine-quality coffee is named after a port in Yemen?
7 Who was the mythological father of Heracles?
8 Libreville is the capital city of which African nation?
9 The 1973 film and recent TV series *Westworld* are based on a novel by which writer?
10 Stratfield Saye is the stately home of which duke?
11 What prefix indicates 10^{-6}?
12 Who was Formula 1 World Champion in 1975, 1977 and 1984?
13 What were the first names of the two "Princes in the Tower"?
14 Which call is worth more than spades in bridge?
15 What type of creature is a flying fox?
16 Which river runs through Knaresborough?
17 What was the title of Matt Cardle's 2010 chart-topping single?
18 What was the name of the caravel on which Columbus sailed back to Spain in 1492?
19 Whom did Jamie Murray partner to win the 2017 Wimbledon Mixed Doubles title?
20 "Tar Heel" is the nickname of which US state?

Easy

Medium

Hard

Answers to QUIZ 171 – Pot Luck

1 Garbiñe Muguruza
2 McDonald
3 Edward Woodward
4 Florida
5 Gaia
6 Zayn
7 Galliano
8 Meryl Streep
9 Edgehill
10 Eilat
11 Gastropoda
12 Walt Whitman
13 Metamorphic
14 Ford
15 Yarra
16 Mexico
17 George Clooney
18 Laudanum
19 John Lennon and Yoko Ono
20 Laois

QUIZ 174 – Famous Roads

ANSWERS ON PAGE 176

Easy

1 Watling Street is an example of what type of thoroughfare?
2 Which London street was the home of poet Elizabeth Barrett?
3 Which WWI French general gave his name to a Parisian avenue leading from the Arc de Triomphe?
4 Between which two US states did Route 66 run?
5 In which city is the shopping destination of Grafton Street?
6 The Via Dolorosa is in which city?
7 What is the name of the zigzag road in San Francisco which features eight hairpin bends?
8 Who designed The Circus in Bath?
9 In which English city are there alleyways known as the Lanes?

Medium

10 The famous Abbey Road pedestrian crossing is close to the junction with which other thoroughfare?
11 Which Roman street begins at the bottom of the Spanish Steps?
12 On which London thoroughfare is the Apollo theatre?
13 Who was "walking with my feet ten feet off of Beale" in a 1991 song?
14 Barcelona's La Rambla connects Plaça de Catalunya with which landmark?
15 In which borough of New York is the Bowery?
16 In which city is the shopping destination of Buchanan Street?
17 What are the names of the covered walkways in the four main streets in the city of Chester?

Hard

18 Kärntner Strasse is in which European city?
19 In which arrondissement of Paris is the Champs-Élysées?
20 What type of business is associated with London's Jermyn Street?

Answers to QUIZ 172 – Food and Drink

1 Raspberry
2 Mirepoix
3 Mushroom
4 Lily
5 A gravy or extract
6 Norway
7 White lady
8 Bacon
9 A root vegetable
10 Stargazy pie
11 Italy
12 Pear
13 Aubergine
14 A digestif
15 Ginger
16 Tangelo
17 Lager
18 Chickpea
19 Yarg
20 Tea

QUIZ 175 – Pot Luck

ANSWERS ON PAGE 177

1 The argan tree is native to which continent?

2 In which region of France was the Cabernet Sauvignon black wine grape originally grown?

3 What is the currency unit used in Kabul?

4 In which German city is the car manufacturer BMW based?

5 Which Lutyens-designed stately home near Dartmoor was the last castle to be built in England?

6 What is the drink lassi mostly made from?

7 Who, in Shakespeare's play, became king of Scotland after the death of Macbeth?

8 Which Irish port is at the mouth of the River Lee?

9 In which southern French town did Van Gogh famously paint his bedroom?

10 What is the name of the girl detective in the novels by Carolyn Keene?

11 Which island is known as Kerkyra in Greek?

12 In *The Lord of the Rings*, what sort of spirit inhabits trees?

13 Who won the Best Actress Oscar for her performance in the 1960 film *Two Women*?

14 In which state is the easternmost point of the 48 contiguous United States?

15 What name was taken by former Lord Chancellor Quintin Hogg when he became a Lord?

16 Which American silent-film star was famous for scenes involving hanging from clocks?

17 The spice cardamom is a member of which family?

18 What is New Zealand's highest mountain?

19 What was an allemande, popular in Germany in the 16th century?

20 Which poet wrote the 1818 poem *Endymion?*

Answers to QUIZ 173 – Pot Luck

1 Edward Norton
2 Gluten
3 Minsk
4 Edith Nesbit
5 Fritz Lang
6 Mocha
7 Zeus
8 Gabon
9 Michael Crichton
10 Duke of Wellington
11 Micro
12 Niki Lauda
13 Edward and Richard
14 No trumps
15 Fruit bat
16 Nidd
17 *When We Collide*
18 *Nina*
19 Martina Hingis
20 North Carolina

Easy
Medium
Hard

QUIZ 176 – Television

ANSWERS ON PAGE 178

Easy

1 Who played Izzie in the series *Grey's Anatomy*?

2 Who won the BBC Overseas Sports Personality of the Year in 2017 for a record fourth time?

3 In the series *Mad Men*, what was the name of the advertising agency?

4 Who played companion Martha Jones in *Doctor Who*?

5 Which *Pirates of the Caribbean* actor played Miles in the series *This Life*?

6 What are the two colours of a standard *Blue Peter* badge?

7 Which actress co-starred with Alexander Armstrong in the series *Life Begins*?

8 Which actor narrated *The Wombles* in the early 1970s?

9 Which 1960s western series featured the Cartwright family?

10 Vicky Pattison rose to fame on which show?

Medium

11 Who was the first questionmaster on the quiz *Eggheads*?

12 Paul Nicholas starred as Vince Pinner in which sitcom?

13 Which Dame Esther Rantzen series launched the career of singer Sheena Easton?

14 Who played Robert Catesby in the 2017 mini-series *Gunpowder*?

15 Keith Barron starred in which 1980s sitcom about a holiday in Spain?

16 Who created the animated series *Family Guy*?

17 Which actress played Sable Colby in the original series of *Dynasty*?

18 Who was the cafe owner in *Last of the Summer Wine*, played by Jane Freeman?

19 A car called KITT featured in which series?

20 Who starred as Bernard Black in the series *Black Books*?

Hard

Answers to QUIZ 174 – Famous Roads

1 Roman road
2 Wimpole
3 Foch
4 California and Illinois
5 Dublin
6 Jerusalem
7 Lombard Street
8 John Wood the Elder
9 Brighton
10 Grove End Road
11 Via Condotti
12 Shaftesbury Avenue
13 Marc Cohn (*Walking in Memphis*)
14 Columbus Monument
15 Manhattan
16 Glasgow
17 The Rows
18 Vienna
19 Eighth
20 Tailoring

QUIZ 177 – Pot Luck

ANSWERS ON PAGE 179

1 The Etruscans were an ancient race living in part of which modern country?
2 In which Irish county is the small seaside town of Bray, located south of Dublin?
3 What is a calabash?
4 Which RAF rank is equivalent to vice admiral or lieutenant general?
5 What, according to Irish author Edna O'Brien, is "a wicked month"?
6 Whom did Sienna Miller portray in the 2006 film *Factory Girl*?
7 What was the first name of the 19th-century French artist Delacroix?
8 In 2011, which country became Africa's largest, by area?
9 What is the title of the Verdi opera commissioned for the opening of the Suez Canal?
10 Camembert cheese originates from which area of France?
11 What was the real name of the prolific 20th-century author Jean Plaidy?
12 The Lancaster WWII bomber was manufactured by which company?
13 Who wrote the 1982 play *Noises Off*?
14 What device records underwater distance?
15 What was the surname of the American inventor of the safety razor?
16 The fictional band The Majestics featured in which 1987 TV series?
17 What is the two-word term given to the point of entry of the optic nerve?
18 On which day of the week does the Christian feast day Ascension always occur?
19 What is the name given to a model that depicts a scene using three-dimensional figures, often in miniature?
20 Which Portuguese town was famed for religious visions in 1917?

Answers to QUIZ 175 – Pot Luck

1 Africa
2 Bordeaux
3 Afghani
4 Munich
5 Castle Drogo
6 Yoghurt
7 Malcolm
8 Cork
9 Arles
10 Nancy Drew
11 Corfu
12 An Ent
13 Sophia Loren
14 Maine
15 Lord Hailsham
16 Harold Lloyd
17 Ginger
18 Aoraki/Mount Cook
19 A dance
20 John Keats

QUIZ 178 – Rivers

ANSWERS ON PAGE 180

Easy

1 The source of the River Thames is in which county?

2 On which river does the German shipbuilding port of Bremen stand?

3 What is the English name of the town that sits at the mouth of the River Teifi?

4 Which island is surrounded by the East, Harlem and Hudson rivers?

5 Which Spanish river flows through the Rioja wine-growing region?

6 The Three Gorges dam spans which river?

7 On which north-east river does Stockton stand?

8 In which country are the rivers Adige and Arno?

9 The West Sussex town of Lancing stands on which river?

10 On which river is the Mosul Dam?

11 Which is the longest river in Europe...?

Medium

12 ...and which is the second-longest European river?

13 What is the name of the Cumbrian river that flows into the Solway Firth?

14 Which river flows through Hamburg?

15 What is the name of the river on St David's peninsula in Wales?

16 Which seaside resort of northern Cornwall lies at the mouth of the River Neet?

17 On which river are Africa's Victoria Falls?

18 On which river did Chesley Sullenberger famously land a plane in 2009?

19 Which is the longest river in the Iberian Peninsula?

20 In which district of West Sussex, named after its river, is Littlehampton?

Hard

Answers to QUIZ 176 – Television

1 Katherine Heigl
2 Roger Federer
3 Sterling Cooper & Partners
4 Freema Agyeman
5 Jack Davenport
6 Blue and white
7 Caroline Quentin
8 Bernard Cribbins
9 *Bonanza*
10 *Geordie Shore*
11 Dermot Murnaghan
12 *Just Good Friends*
13 *The Big Time*
14 Kit Harington
15 *Duty Free*
16 Seth MacFarlane
17 Stephanie Beacham
18 Ivy
19 *Knight Rider*
20 Dylan Moran

QUIZ 179 – Pot Luck

ANSWERS ON PAGE **181**

1 By what name is grape sugar more usually called?
2 Which English essayist, along with his sister Mary, wrote *Tales from Shakespeare* (1807)?
3 What is an Indian place of retreat called?
4 In which country was the 19th-century explorer Mungo Park born?
5 In the 1966 film *The Good, the Bad and the Ugly*, who played Tuco?
6 Which Moroccan city was devastated by an earthquake in 1960?
7 Who wrote the novel *The Call of the Wild* (1903)?
8 Which English constitutional settlement was passed in 1689?
9 Which is the largest city in the US state of New Hampshire?
10 Who was the Greek goddess of war and wisdom?
11 The clothing retailer Gap was founded in which US city in 1969?
12 What is the meaning of the Latin phrase *ipso jure*?
13 To what creatures does the term "passerine" apply?
14 Which 1960s Cockney singer was backed by the Bruvvers?
15 The 1959 novel *The Tin Drum* was written by which author?
16 Which Northern Irish county has a county town of the same name on the shores of Lough Neagh?
17 What is the title of the 1987 film about the life of singer Ritchie Valens?
18 Which show involving puppets won the Best Musical at the 2004 Tony awards?
19 The investigations of unit AC-12 feature in which TV police drama?
20 Which member of Take That had solo hits with *Child* and *Clementine*?

Easy

Medium

Hard

Answers to QUIZ 177 – Pot Luck

1 Italy
2 Wicklow
3 A tree, or its fruit (a gourd)
4 Air Marshal
5 August
6 Edie Sedgwick
7 Eugène
8 Algeria
9 *Aida*
10 Normandy
11 Eleanor Hibbert
12 Avro
13 Michael Frayn
14 Echograms
15 Gillette
16 *Tutti Frutti*
17 Blind spot
18 Thursday
19 Diorama
20 Fatima

QUIZ 180 – Ball Sports

ANSWERS ON PAGE 182

Easy

1 A cricket umpire raises his index finger above his head to indicate what?

2 Arsène Wenger was manager of Arsenal FC between which years?

3 The ITTF is the governing body of which sport?

4 Korfball originated in which country?

5 Where did the Italian national rugby team play their home Six Nations games from 2000 to 2011?

6 The winners of both the men's and women's 2017 World Squash Championships were from which country?

7 Which English game, similar to cricket, has the "wicket" at head or shoulder height?

8 In which indoor game might you be a "tweener" or a "cranker"?

9 Which football club plays its home games at Home Park?

10 "Gridiron" is another term for which sport?

Medium

11 Beach volleyball became an official Olympic sport in which year?

12 What sport is played at Cowdray Park?

13 Which golf club hosted the 2016 Open Championship?

14 Which was the only grand slam tennis title that Pete Sampras did not win?

15 Who won the 2017 World Championship Snooker title?

16 In which decade did BBC Radio's *Test Match Special* begin?

17 What is the nickname of Chicago's NBA basketball team?

18 Who was the 2016 winning Ryder Cup team captain?

19 In which country was the FIFA Women's World Cup held in 2015?

Hard

20 Which future monarch took part in the Wimbledon tennis championships in 1926?

Answers to QUIZ 178 – Rivers

1 Gloucestershire
2 Weser
3 Cardigan
4 Manhattan Island, NY
5 Ebro
6 Yangtze
7 Tees
8 Italy
9 Adur
10 Tigris
11 Volga
12 Danube
13 Eden
14 Elbe
15 Alun
16 Bude
17 Zambezi
18 Hudson River
19 Tagus
20 Arun

QUIZ 181 – Pot Luck

ANSWERS ON PAGE 183

1 Which town is the administrative centre of Angus, in Scotland?

2 In which city was the 20th-century artist and sculptor Joan Miró born?

3 Who wrote the 1978 novel *The Human Factor*?

4 Which purplish colour derives its name from a northern Italian location?

5 In which Lake District town was the first pencil made?

6 In which month are the feast days of saints Bernadette and Anselm?

7 The surname of which Texas rancher is used to describe an unbranded animal and an unorthodox person?

8 Who was the first chief executive of Channel 4?

9 What is the main flavour of a ganache?

10 What type of firearm would originally have been carried by a fusilier?

11 The people of which ancient civilisation lived in the area now covered by Yucatan, Belize and northern Guatemala?

12 Which Texan city stands on the Rio Grande opposite Juárez, Mexico?

13 Which Belgian town was the scene of the first major WWI battle?

14 Who was the subject of the 1964 *Carry On* film?

15 What was the first name of the engineer who invented the Moog synthesizer?

16 Charlotte Dujardin rode which horse to double gold at the London 2012 Olympics?

17 What was the name of the fairy queen referred to in Shakespeare's *Romeo and Juliet*?

18 Which US drama starring Peter Krause was set in a funeral home?

19 What is the scientific study of solid inorganic substances?

20 Which musical term means "jokingly", or "in a playful manner"?

Easy

Medium

Hard

Answers to QUIZ 179 – Pot Luck

1 Dextrose
2 Charles Lamb
3 Ashram
4 Scotland
5 Eli Wallach
6 Agadir
7 Jack London
8 Bill of Rights
9 Manchester
10 Athena
11 San Francisco
12 "By operation of law"
13 Birds
14 Joe Brown
15 Günter Grass
16 Antrim
17 *La Bamba*
18 *Avenue Q*
19 *Line of Duty*
20 Mark Owen

QUIZ 182 – Germany

ANSWERS ON PAGE 184

Easy

1 What is the main ingredient of the dish sauerkraut?

2 How many constituent states does Germany have?

3 Which river flows through Heidelberg?

4 How is the *Schwarzwald* known in English?

5 Who preceded Angela Merkel as Chancellor of Germany?

6 The Berlin Wall was torn down in which year?

7 What is the English translation of *Rathaus*?

8 Which 18th-century monument in Berlin was built on the orders of Prussian king Frederick William II?

9 Germany shares a border with the Netherlands, Czechia (Czech Republic), Luxembourg, France, Belgium, Switzerland and which three other countries?

Medium

10 What is Germany's highest mountain?

11 In German, what is the name of Germany?

12 What form of entertainment is associated with Bayreuth?

13 Which German city is called Aix-la-Chapelle in French?

14 "The cradle of the automobile" is a name given to which city?

15 Which 20th-century art movement was founded in the city of Weimar?

16 Pumpernickel bread is made from what type of flour?

17 What is the largest lake on German territory?

18 What German word is used to describe the experience of joy from learning of the misfortune of others?

Hard

19 Germany is bordered by which two seas?

20 What is the largest city on the Rhine?

Answers to QUIZ 180 – Ball Sports

1 The batsman is out
2 1996-2018
3 Table tennis
4 The Netherlands
5 Stadio Flaminio
6 Egypt
7 Stoolball
8 Tenpin bowling
9 Plymouth Argyle
10 American Football
11 1996
12 Polo
13 Royal Troon
14 French Open
15 Mark Selby
16 1950s
17 Bulls
18 Davis Love III
19 Canada
20 George VI

QUIZ 183 – Pot Luck

ANSWERS ON PAGE 185

1 Which Italian river flows into the sea at Ostia?

2 Who played the title role in the 1966 film *Our Man Flint*?

3 Which Arab capital city was known as Philadelphia during Roman times?

4 Who wrote the 1919 novel *The Moon and Sixpence*?

5 Which musical features the song *Getting to Know You*?

6 In which London thoroughfare is Drapers' Hall?

7 Angola was formerly a colony of which European country?

8 What is the largest natural lake in Wales?

9 Which Scottish town on the River Leven shares its name with an Egyptian city?

10 *Portrait of my Love* was which British singer's 1960 debut?

11 Who co-founded Microsoft® along with Bill Gates?

12 Who won an Oscar for composing the score of the 1957 film *Bridge Over the River Kwai*?

13 Which relative of a US President took a major role in organising the 1773 Boston Tea Party?

14 Which word means "representing different Christian churches"?

15 In mythology, which maiden was loved by Eros?

16 Which US state lies north of Missouri, south of Minnesota, east of Nebraska and west of Illinois?

17 In the sitcom *Drop the Dead Donkey*, who played Dave Charnley?

18 Which Spanish poet and dramatist (b.1898) was killed in the Spanish Civil War?

19 Which boxer (b.1921) only lost once in his first 123 bouts?

20 The location of Dingley Dell features in which Charles Dickens novel?

Easy Medium Hard

Answers to QUIZ 181 – Pot Luck

1 Forfar
2 Barcelona
3 Graham Greene
4 Magenta
5 Keswick
6 April
7 Maverick
8 Sir Jeremy Isaacs
9 Chocolate
10 Musket
11 Maya
12 El Paso
13 Mons
14 Cleo
15 Robert (Moog)
16 Valegro
17 Mab
18 *Six Feet Under*
19 Mineralogy
20 Scherzando

QUIZ 184 – Planet Earth

ANSWERS ON PAGE 186

Easy

1 What is the name of the Earth's lowest layer of atmosphere?
2 Mount Fuji is situated on which island?
3 Which is the world's smallest ocean?
4 What two-word phrase is given to the upper limit of population that an area can support?
5 A caldera is found in which natural feature?
6 The Earth's crust and the upper part of the mantle are collectively described by what term?
7 What are the vast lowland plains of Argentina called?
8 What does a feature described as "fluviatile" relate to?
9 What term is given to the study of seasonal timings of events such as flowering and migration?

Medium

10 What is an area of rock underneath the ground which absorbs and holds water called?
11 The swampy coniferous forest region of Siberia is given what name?
12 Angel Falls, the world's highest waterfall, is in which country?
13 Which is the deepest lake in the world...?
14 ...and which is the world's largest lake?
15 What type of rock is formed from compacted deposits of material in air, ice or water?
16 In relation to the atmosphere, what does "ppm" stand for?
17 Which Malaysian city's name means "muddy estuary"?
18 Which is the largest natural lake in England?

Hard

19 What term is given to the proportion of sunlight that is reflected from a surface?
20 The most southerly point of Ireland is marked by which rock?

Answers to QUIZ 182 – Germany

1 Cabbage
2 16
3 Neckar
4 Black Forest
5 Gerhard Schröder
6 1989
7 Town hall
8 Brandenburg Gate
9 Denmark, Poland and Austria
10 Zugspitze
11 Deutschland
12 Opera
13 Aachen
14 Stuttgart
15 Bauhaus
16 Rye
17 Lake Constance
18 Schadenfreude
19 North Sea and Baltic Sea
20 Cologne

QUIZ 185 – Pot Luck

ANSWERS ON PAGE 187

1 Actor Chevy Chase was given what first name at birth?

2 In which city might you travel on a traghetto?

3 What was the surname of brothers Auguste and Louis, the French motion-picture pioneers?

4 Which fruit with a stone has the Latin name *Prunus domestica*?

5 Which old currency unit was worth £1.05?

6 What is a leave of absence from a boarding school?

7 What is Homer Simpson's favourite brand of beer?

8 The East Sussex house of Bateman's belonged to which author?

9 Which bank launched the UK's first credit card?

10 Which US state is nicknamed "Buckeye"?

11 Of which rock are Dartmoor's tors formed?

12 Which animal's name derives from the ancient Greek for "river horse"?

13 What was the first chart-topper for The Rubettes?

14 Which castle near Grantham is the seat of the Duke of Rutland?

15 What name is given to a steak cut between two ribs?

16 The 2017 TV series *SS-GB* was based on a book by which author?

17 What type of creature is a lamprey?

18 Who directed the 1965 film *Doctor Zhivago*?

19 Who won the 1969 Nobel Prize in Literature?

20 Who starred as Ann Darrow in the 2005 version of *King Kong*?

Answers to QUIZ 183 – Pot Luck

1 Tiber
2 James Coburn
3 Amman
4 W Somerset Maugham
5 *The King and I*
6 Throgmorton Street
7 Portugal
8 Bala
9 Alexandria
10 Matt Monro
11 Paul Allen
12 Malcolm Arnold
13 Samuel Adams
14 Ecumenical
15 Psyche
16 Iowa
17 Neil Pearson
18 Federico García Lorca
19 Sugar Ray Robinson
20 *The Pickwick Papers*

QUIZ 186 – Plays and Playwrights

ANSWERS ON PAGE 188

1 *Brighton Beach Memoirs* (1982) and *Biloxi Blues* (1984) are semi-autobiographical works by which playwright?

2 Which British author wrote the play *The Second Mrs Tanqueray* (1893)?

3 The play *Festen* (2004) is based on a film in which language?

4 What are the names of the two main characters in *Waiting for Godot*?

5 In the 1945 JB Priestly play *An Inspector Calls*, what is the name of the inspector?

6 What is the title of the Sir Tom Stoppard play about two minor characters from Shakespeare's *Hamlet*?

7 What nationality was playwright Dario Fo?

8 Who wrote the Greek tragedy *Antigone*?

9 In the 1959 play *Billy Liar*, what was Billy's surname?

10 Who wrote *Art* (1994)?

11 Which 1996 play features sisters Teresa, Mary and Catherine gathered for the funeral of their mother Vi?

12 Which play with a script by Jack Thorne won the Laurence Olivier award for Best New Play in 2017?

13 Who wrote *Murder in the Cathedral* (1935)?

14 Which playwright was awarded the Nobel Prize in Literature in 2005?

15 Which Sir Terence Rattigan play deals with the events following the theft of a five-shilling postal order?

16 Who wrote the 1960s works *After the Fall* and *The Price*?

17 John Osborne's 1956 play *Look Back in Anger* premiered at which London theatre?

18 What nationality was playwright Edward Albee?

19 What was the name of William Shakespeare's mother?

20 Who wrote *The Seagull* (1895)?

Answers to QUIZ 184 – Planet Earth

1 Troposphere
2 Honshu
3 Arctic Ocean
4 Carrying capacity
5 A volcano
6 Lithosphere
7 Pampas
8 Rivers
9 Phenology
10 Aquifer
11 Taiga
12 Venezuela
13 Lake Baikal (Russia)
14 Caspian Sea
15 Sedimentary
16 Parts per million
17 Kuala Lumpur
18 Windermere
19 Albedo
20 Fastnet

QUIZ 187 – Pot Luck

ANSWERS ON PAGE 189

1 Which bridge in the north-east of England is the world's first tilting bridge?
2 Which company was granted the first registered trademark in 1876?
3 Who flew from Newfoundland to Clifden in Ireland in 1919?
4 What was the first name of KFC founder Colonel Sanders?
5 A mash tun is used in making which drink?
6 Which bid in solo whist declares a hand that will win no tricks?
7 Which former *The X Factor* contestant won 2009's *Dancing on Ice*?
8 In which year did the Bahrain Formula 1 Grand Prix become a night race?
9 When does a noctilucent cloud appear?
10 In which country is Murlough Nature Reserve?
11 What does "gsm" stand for in relation to paper and card?
12 The Home Insurance Building in Chicago became the world's first what in 1885?
13 The International or European Article Number is a standard for what identification?
14 Which stately home on Anglesey contains a mural painted by Rex Whistler?
15 In which decade were the Blackpool Illuminations first lit?
16 Which inventor filed 1093 patents in his lifetime?
17 Who wrote *The Shell Seekers* (1987) and *September* (1990)?
18 Which medal was awarded to Tenzing Norgay?
19 What was Greta Garbo's real surname?
20 Who directed the 2015 film *The Martian*?

Answers to QUIZ 185 – Pot Luck

1 Cornelius
2 Venice
3 Lumière
4 Plum
5 Guinea
6 *Exeat*
7 Duff
8 Rudyard Kipling
9 Barclays
10 Ohio
11 Granite
12 Hippopotamus
13 *Sugar Baby Love*
14 Belvoir
15 Entrecôte
16 Len Deighton
17 Fish
18 Sir David Lean
19 Samuel Beckett
20 Naomi Watts

QUIZ 188 – Education

Easy

1 Which famous girls' school near Brighton was founded by the Lawrence sisters in 1885?

2 The TV series *Glee* was set mainly in which fictional school?

3 The London School of Economics and Political Science was founded in 1875 by members of which society?

4 Which is the world's oldest university museum?

5 What does ROSLA stand for in an academic context?

6 Which English university was founded in 1209?

7 The 1940s novels about St Clare's boarding school were written by which author?

8 What was the title of the 1970s *Please Sir!* spin-off series?

9 LLB after a name indicates that the person has graduated in what subject?

10 What is the literal English translation of the German word *Kindergarten*?

Medium

11 Which two-word Latin phrase is used to describe the university or college of a former student?

12 What is the name of the university based in Middlesbrough?

13 In which year did polytechnics in the UK become universities?

14 At which fictional school did Mr McGuffey, Mrs McClusky and Mr Bronson teach?

15 Which youth achievement award scheme was introduced in 1956 for boys and in 1958 for girls?

16 Estyn is the Welsh equivalent of which English body?

17 Which independent Berkshire boarding school was founded in 1440?

18 What do the initials UCAS stand for?

Hard

19 Which world-renowned educationist born in Italy in 1870 gives her name to a "Method" of early education?

20 In which year were GCSE exams introduced?

Answers to QUIZ 186 – Plays and Playwrights

1 Neil Simon
2 Arthur Wing Pinero
3 Danish
4 Vladimir and Estragon
5 Inspector Goole
6 *Rosencrantz and Guildenstern Are Dead*
7 Italian
8 Sophocles
9 Fisher
10 Yazmina Reza
11 *The Memory of Water* (Shelagh Stephenson)
12 *Harry Potter and the Cursed Child*
13 TS Eliot
14 Harold Pinter
15 *The Winslow Boy*
16 Arthur Miller
17 The Royal Court
18 American
19 Mary Arden
20 Anton Chekhov

QUIZ 189 – Pot Luck

ANSWERS ON PAGE 191

1 Who was the proverbially wealthy king of ancient Lydia?
2 Who presented Radio 4's *Desert Island Discs* from 1988 until 2006?
3 What was the name of the hotel in Stephen King's *The Shining* (1977)?
4 Which part of a church is named from the Latin word for "ship"?
5 Which country won the Eurovision Song Contest in 2014?
6 In Norse mythology, what was the home of the gods?
7 Which town in south-east Switzerland hosted the 1928 Winter Olympics?
8 In which Derbyshire town are the Heights of Abraham?
9 Which single did Wings release as a double A side with *Mull of Kintyre*?
10 Who wrote the 1970 best-selling novel *Love Story*?
11 Kampala is the capital of which African nation?
12 The Wraith is a model from which luxury car manufacturer?
13 Which island is linked politically with Antigua?
14 What is the more common name for the linden tree?
15 Which is the westernmost of the Balearic Islands?
16 Which pale yellow variety of crystalline quartz resembles topaz?
17 Richmond is the capital of which US state?
18 What is the more common name for urticaria?
19 What is the ancient language of the Hindu scriptures?
20 In which country did the word "bungalow" originate?

Answers to QUIZ 187 – Pot Luck

1 Gateshead Millennium bridge
2 Bass Brewery
3 Alcock and Brown
4 Harland
5 Whisky
6 Misère
7 Ray Quinn
8 2014
9 At night
10 Northern Ireland
11 Grams per square metre
12 Skyscraper
13 Barcode
14 Plas Newydd
15 1870s (1879)
16 Thomas Edison
17 Rosamunde Pilcher
18 George Medal
19 Gustafsson
20 Sir Ridley Scott

QUIZ 190 – James Bond

ANSWERS ON PAGE 192

1 Who played James Bond in the 1989 film *Licence to Kill*?
2 What was the profession of the real James Bond who lent his name to the fictional spy?
3 In which of the James Bond films did the Aston Martin DB5 first appear?
4 What was the first name of James Bond's wife, to whom he was briefly married in *On Her Majesty's Secret Service*?
5 In which 1983 Bond film did Maud Adams co-star with Sir Roger Moore?
6 Which of the Bond films shares its title with Ian Fleming's Jamaican estate?
7 Which character did Jack Lord play in *Dr No* (1962)?
8 In which of the Ian Fleming novels is Vivienne Michel the central character?
9 In which year did Sir Sean Connery star in *Never Say Never Again*?
10 In how many films did Bernard Lee play the character of "M"?
11 Who played Kara Milovy in the 1987 film *The Living Daylights*?
12 Which was the first novel to be published featuring James Bond?
13 The theme tune to which James Bond film was sung by Matt Monro?
14 Who played Blofeld in the 2015 film *Spectre*?
15 In which James Bond film is there a character called Dr Christmas Jones?
16 What is the name of the industrialist in *Moonraker*?
17 In which film did Teri Hatcher play Paris Carver?
18 In which country was Bond actor George Lazenby born?
19 Daniel Craig first played Bond on film in which year?
20 Max Zorin is the villain in which film?

Answers to QUIZ 188 – Education

1 Roedean
2 William McKinley High
3 The Fabian Society
4 Ashmolean (Oxford)
5 Raising of School Leaving Age
6 Cambridge
7 Enid Blyton
8 *The Fenn Street Gang*
9 Law
10 Garden for the children
11 *Alma mater*
12 Teesside
13 1992
14 Grange Hill
15 Duke of Edinburgh's Award
16 Ofsted
17 Eton College
18 Universities and Colleges Admissions Service
19 Maria Montessori
20 1988

QUIZ 191 – Pot Luck

ANSWERS ON PAGE 193

1 Who was the oldest man in the Bible?

2 In which country is the ski resort of Klosters?

3 Which US state is known as the "Sunflower State"?

4 In which 1975 film did Warren Beatty play a hairdresser?

5 What is the name of the character in *Macbeth* whose title is Thane of Lochaber?

6 What was the title of Spandau Ballet's first single?

7 Prawle Point is the most southerly tip of which English county?

8 How many tusks does a warthog have?

9 Carson City is the capital of which US state?

10 What is the name of the cavity containing the eyeball?

11 Which ballet features the supernatural women called the Wilis?

12 In South Africa, what is a *kraal*?

13 Which actor starred in the 2007 film *Fred Claus*?

14 Which group had a no.1 in 1971 with *Chirpy Chirpy Cheep Cheep*?

15 In mythology, what kind of animal was slain by Hercules as the first of his Twelve Labours?

16 Which is the second largest of the Orkney Islands?

17 What term is given to a crucifix set at the entrance to the chancel of a church?

18 Who wrote the 1951 novel *My Cousin Rachel*?

19 Who played Belle in the 2017 live film version of *Beauty and the Beast*?

20 In which sport are the LA Lakers a professional team?

Answers to QUIZ 189 – Pot Luck

1 Croesus
2 Sue Lawley
3 Overlook Hotel
4 Nave
5 Austria
6 Asgard
7 St Moritz
8 Matlock Bath
9 *Girls' School*
10 Erich Segal
11 Uganda
12 Rolls-Royce
13 Barbuda
14 The lime
15 Ibiza
16 Citrine
17 Virginia
18 Nettle-rash
19 Sanskrit
20 India

QUIZ 192 – Park and Ride

ANSWERS ON PAGE 194

Easy

1 In which National Park is the Snake Pass?
2 Which two actors co-starred in the 1969 film *Easy Rider*?
3 Who wrote the novel *Jurassic Park*?
4 In the rhyme *Ride a Cock Horse*, in which county would the rider be at the end of the journey?
5 The Simon Park Orchestra had a 1973 hit with *Eye Level*, the theme to which detective series?
6 Who directed the 1985 western *Pale Rider*?
7 The Formula 1 street circuit of Albert Park is in which country?
8 Which group had a 1989 no.1 record with *Ride on Time*?
9 At which tourist attraction in the UK is the roller coaster ride Colossus located?
10 Who starred in the original series of *Knight Rider*?

Medium

11 In which year of the 19th century was the Great Exhibition held in Hyde Park?
12 The 1991 album *Joyride* was recorded by which duo?
13 Which Scottish National Park was established in 2003?
14 The teenage spy character of Alex Rider was created by which author?
15 In which county is the racecourse of Fontwell Park?
16 In which year was *Riders on the Storm* a hit for the Doors?
17 The station of Holland Park is on which London Underground line?
18 What was the first name of novelist H Rider Haggard?

Hard

19 Fratton Park is the home ground of which football team?
20 Which American duo issued a cover of the Beatles' *Ticket to Ride* in 1969?

Answers to QUIZ 190 – James Bond

1 Timothy Dalton
2 Ornithologist
3 *Goldfinger*
4 Tracy
5 *Octopussy*
6 *GoldenEye*
7 Felix Leiter
8 *The Spy Who Loved Me*
9 1983
10 11
11 Maryam d'Abo
12 *Casino Royale* (1953)
13 *From Russia with Love*
14 Christoph Waltz
15 *The World is Not Enough*
16 Hugo Drax
17 *Tomorrow Never Dies*
18 Australia
19 2006
20 *A View to a Kill*

QUIZ 193 – Pot Luck

ANSWERS ON PAGE 195

1 Which US measuring unit is equivalent to eight fluid ounces or 16 tablespoons?
2 In the Battle of Bosworth Field which English king was killed?
3 Which historic Belgian city lies between Brussels and Bruges?
4 What is another name for china clay?
5 Which state of north-west Borneo became a Commonwealth member in 1984?
6 *I Can See Clearly Now* was a hit for which singer in 1972?
7 Who wrote the novel *Cold Comfort Farm*?
8 What is the name of the road bridge over the Firth of Forth opened in August 2017?
9 What was the name of the Pet Shop Boys' second chart-topper in 1987?
10 Which physics unit of matter shares its name with a soft cheese?
11 "Kernow" is the local name of which English county?
12 Who was the first woman in space?
13 What is added to icing sugar to make royal icing?
14 Atahualpa was the last leader of which empire?
15 Who was King Edward I's first queen?
16 What is the fifth book of the Old Testament?
17 In the 2016 Summer Olympics, which British track cyclist won his sixth Olympic gold medal?
18 What is the French equivalent of an Oscar?
19 What is the dome-shaped sheet of muscle that separates the chest from the abdomen called?
20 ET is the international vehicle registration for which country?

Easy

Medium

Hard

Answers to QUIZ 191 – Pot Luck

1 Methuselah
2 Switzerland
3 Kansas
4 *Shampoo*
5 Banquo
6 *To Cut a Long Story Short*
7 Devon
8 Four
9 Nevada
10 Orbit
11 *Giselle*
12 Enclosed village
13 Vince Vaughn
14 Middle of the Road
15 Lion
16 Hoy
17 Rood
18 Dame Daphne du Maurier
19 Emma Watson
20 Basketball

QUIZ 194 – XYZ

ANSWERS ON PAGE 196

Easy

1 In which city in Shaanxi Province can China's famous terracotta warriors be seen?
2 What is a yawl?
3 Which German word describes the defining mood of a particular period of history?
4 What was the subtitle of the 2016 film in the X-Men franchise?
5 Yorktown was the site of the last major battle in which war?
6 The zapateado is a dance from which country?
7 What is the phonetic alphabet code word for the letter X?
8 Captain John Yossarian is the main character in which 1961 novel?
9 Which outdoor pursuit involves rolling in a transparent sphere?
10 Which line on a graph is usually marked as the x-axis, the horizontal or vertical?
11 Yerevan is the capital city of which country?

Medium

12 Which US writer married Zelda Sayre in 1920?
13 What is the chemical symbol for xenon?
14 In which National Park is Yes Tor?
15 What type of food is ziti?
16 From which country does the language Xhosa originate?
17 In which year was *YMCA* a hit for the Village People?
18 Which country has the zloty as its currency?
19 Who played the title role in the TV series *Xena: Warrior Princess*?
20 In which county is the river Yare?

Hard

Answers to QUIZ 192 – Park and Ride

1 Peak District
2 Peter Fonda and Dennis Hopper
3 Michael Crichton
4 Oxfordshire (Banbury Cross)
5 *Van Der Valk*
6 Clint Eastwood
7 Australia (Melbourne)
8 Black Box
9 Thorpe Park
10 David Hasselhoff
11 1851
12 Roxette
13 Cairngorms
14 Anthony Horowitz
15 West Sussex
16 1971
17 Central Line
18 Henry
19 Portsmouth FC
20 The Carpenters

QUIZ 195 – Pot Luck

ANSWERS ON PAGE 197

1 The town of Duffel is in which EU country?

2 What was Japan's imperial capital until 1868?

3 Which band released an album called *The Works* in 1984?

4 The song *Good Morning Starshine* is from which musical?

5 Which volcano overlooks the city of Catania?

6 Which classic London double-decker bus, with an open platform at the rear, was launched in 1954?

7 Who wrote *The Little Paris Kitchen* cook book?

8 Which philosopher wrote *Leviathan* (1651)?

9 What slang term for England comes from a Hindi word for "foreign country"?

10 A hairstyle known as a tonsure would be sported by what type of person?

11 What is an alternative name for the snow leopard?

12 Which town, situated between Yeovil and Warminster, has a well-known racecourse?

13 The quarter-mile long building at Chatham was used to make which material?

14 Which river of South Wales flows through Pontypridd?

15 A feature of Edinburgh castle, what is "Mons Meg"?

16 Who directed the 1970s films *Mean Streets* and *Taxi Driver*?

17 In relation to nuclear power plants, what does the "W" of PWR stand for?

18 What nationality is a person from Tobruk?

19 Which seaside resort on the south coast has an airport at Hurn?

20 What is the piece of metal on a ship to which ropes are attached?

Answers to QUIZ 193 – Pot Luck

1 Cup
2 Richard III
3 Ghent
4 Kaolin
5 Brunei
6 Johnny Nash
7 Stella Gibbons
8 Queensferry Crossing
9 *It's a Sin*
10 Quark
11 Cornwall
12 Valentina Tereshkova
13 Egg white
14 Inca
15 Eleanor
16 Deuteronomy
17 Jason Kenny
18 César
19 Diaphragm
20 Egypt

QUIZ 196 – Famous Relatives

ANSWERS ON PAGE 198

Easy

1 What is the name of Julia Roberts' older brother, also an actor?

2 *Grandpa's Great Escape* is a children's novel by which comedian?

3 Which Knight of the Round Table was the nephew of King Arthur?

4 In the TV series *Brothers & Sisters*, which actress played Sally Field's daughter Kitty?

5 Who was the mother of Henry VIII?

6 In Greek mythology, who killed her two sons by husband Jason?

7 Which father and son of the same name developed the furnace manufacture of pig iron?

8 Artist Bernardo Bellotto was the nephew of which famous Italian artist?

9 Who was the youngest of Chekhov's *Three Sisters*?

10 Which singer was the father of actress Carrie Fisher?

Medium

11 What is the surname of *Cold Comfort Farm* character Aunt Ada?

12 What was the name of Charles Darwin's grandfather, a founding member of the Lunar Society?

13 In the Gilbert and Sullivan operetta, who was the son of the Mikado?

14 Which Mitford sister became the Duchess of Devonshire?

15 Which father and son appeared on TV as *The Hungry Sailors*?

16 Who was the father of Paris and Hector, in Homer's *Iliad*?

17 Which daughter of a famous poet is often regarded as the first computer programmer?

18 *Son of My Father* was a 1972 hit for which group?

19 Which village in West Yorkshire was the home of the Brontë sisters?

20 In 2005 which Hollywood actor named his son Kal-El?

Hard

Answers to QUIZ 194 – XYZ

1 Xi'an
2 A fishing boat
3 *Zeitgeist*
4 *Apocalypse*
5 American War of Independence
6 Spain
7 X-ray
8 *Catch-22*
9 Zorbing
10 Horizontal
11 Armenia
12 F Scott Fitzgerald
13 Xe
14 Dartmoor
15 Pasta
16 South Africa
17 1978
18 Poland
19 Lucy Lawless
20 Norfolk

QUIZ 197 – Pot Luck

ANSWERS ON PAGE 199

1 What was the name of the werewolf son in *The Munsters*?
2 The Bedlington terrier is named after a town in which county?
3 What is the alcoholic ingredient in a screwdriver cocktail?
4 How many pence was the old English groat worth?
5 Which venue hosted the shooting events at the 2012 London Olympics?
6 Which actress co-wrote and starred in *Bridesmaids*?
7 What forms the tectonic boundary between the Pacific Plate and the North American Plate?
8 Which North Yorkshire river near Richmond is a tributary of the Ure?
9 PitmanScript is a version of what type of system?
10 Which US state is nicknamed "the Diamond State"?
11 What is the Saudi Arabian currency unit?
12 On which hill does Jerusalem stand?
13 The Carnegie Medal is awarded in which area of literature?
14 The Cornish village of Gweek, near Helston, has a sanctuary for which type of animal?
15 Which saxophonist was nicknamed "Bird", a shortened form of "Yardbird"?
16 Who wrote the 1854 poem *The Charge of the Light Brigade*?
17 The Grace Gates form the entrance to which sports ground?
18 Which actor provided the voice of Kipper in the animated TV series?
19 How is the fictional law enforcer John Reid better known?
20 What is the capital of Macedonia?

Answers to QUIZ 195 – Pot Luck

1 Belgium
2 Kyoto
3 Queen
4 *Hair*
5 Etna
6 Routemaster
7 Rachel Khoo
8 Thomas Hobbes
9 Blighty
10 A monk
11 Ounce
12 Wincanton
13 Rope
14 Taff
15 Cannon
16 Martin Scorsese
17 Water
18 Libyan
19 Bournemouth
20 A cleat

Easy

1 In which year was Lady Jane Grey briefly Queen of England?
2 Who was Britain's first Prime Minister?
3 Who was the mother of Richard the Lionheart and King John?
4 The 1890s Klondike gold rush took place in which Canadian territory?
5 Which stamp succeeded the Penny Black?
6 The Suez Canal was nationalised by which Egyptian president?
7 Who was Queen of the Netherlands from 1980 to 2013?
8 Which Russian leader was born Vladimir Ilyich Ulyanov?
9 Who was the second president of the USA?
10 Josiah Wedgwood gave which Italian name to his Stoke-on-Trent pottery works?
11 In which Greater Manchester town was the Co-operative movement born?

Medium

12 Which monarchs jointly took over the British throne in 1689?
13 Crowned in 800, who was the first Holy Roman Emperor?
14 What was the former name of the Democratic Republic of the Congo?
15 Who formed the Society of Friends?
16 Lloyd's of London began in what type of institution?
17 In which country was Florence Nightingale born?
18 The horse Copenhagen belonged to which military figure?
19 Which architect introduced the Palladian style into England?
20 What was the Roman name for the city of York?

Hard

Answers to QUIZ 196 – Famous Relatives

1 Eric
2 David Walliams
3 Gawain
4 Calista Flockhart
5 Elizabeth of York
6 Medea
7 Abraham Darby
8 Canaletto
9 Irina
10 Eddie Fisher
11 Doom
12 Erasmus Darwin
13 Nanki-Poo
14 Deborah
15 Dick and James Strawbridge
16 Priam
17 Ada Lovelace (daughter of Byron)
18 Chicory Tip
19 Haworth
20 Nicolas Cage

QUIZ 199 – Pot Luck

ANSWERS ON PAGE **201**

1 Who co-starred with Nick Nolte in the 1991 film *The Prince of Tides*?
2 What is the capital of Liechtenstein?
3 Which early Irish saint is a patron of mariners and seafarers?
4 Who sang the theme song to the 1981 Bond film *For Your Eyes Only*?
5 Who wrote the 1818 poem *Isabella, or the Pot of Basil*?
6 What type of food is Monterey Jack?
7 St Piran's flag is flown by which county?
8 What nationality was László Bíró, inventor of the ballpoint pen?
9 Which instrument was associated with jazz musician Humphrey Lyttelton?
10 Which Midlands cathedral city was badly damaged in WWII?
11 Scott Bakula starred as Sam Beckett in which 1989-93 sci-fi series?
12 What type of animal is a Suffolk Punch?
13 Which playwright wrote *The Iceman Cometh* (1939)?
14 Who had a 1982 hit with *Happy Talk*?
15 David Cornwell is the real name of which novelist?
16 What is the name of Ilchester's river?
17 Which Belgian seaport is linked by canal with Bruges?
18 In Greek mythology, who was the daughter of Agamemnon and Clytemnestra?
19 Which plant fibre is obtained from agave?
20 The Sidlaw Hills are near which Scottish city?

Answers to QUIZ 197 – Pot Luck

1 Eddie
2 Northumberland
3 Vodka
4 Four
5 Bisley
6 Kristen Wiig
7 San Andreas Fault
8 Swale
9 Shorthand
10 Delaware
11 Riyal
12 Zion
13 Children's fiction
14 Seal
15 Charlie Parker
16 Alfred, Lord Tennyson
17 Lord's
18 Martin Clunes
19 The Lone Ranger
20 Skopje

QUIZ 200 – Television Quizzes

ANSWERS ON PAGE 202

1 Who presented the prime-time edition of *Are You Smarter than a 10 Year Old* from 2007 to 2010?

2 Which of the Eggheads won the World Quizzing Championship in 2017 for the sixth time...?

3 ...and who was the first winner of *Make Me an Egghead* in 2008, who went on to join the quiz team?

4 The 2013-14 quiz *Pressure Pad* was hosted by which actor?

5 What is the title of the *Mastermind* theme tune?

6 Who hosted *Every Second Counts* from 1986 to 1993?

7 How many contestants started each episode of *The Weakest Link*?

8 In which 2003 quiz co-hosted by Carol Vorderman did contestants each pay £1,000 to take part?

9 Which quiz programme aired as a regular series for the first time in 1970 with David Vine as host?

10 Who was the original host of *The Krypton Factor*?

11 In which year did *The Chase* first air...?

12 ...and which "Chaser" went on to host *Britain's Brightest Family*?

13 The 2017 play *Quiz* centres around an incident on which prime-time show?

14 Who hosted the first series of *The People Versus*?

15 *Sale of the Century* was originally produced by which TV company?

16 What was the name of the computer which competed on the US show *Jeopardy!* in 2011?

17 Which 2014-15 quiz split contestants into different teams in each round depending on their "Yes" or "No" answer to a question?

18 Who was the original presenter of *Going for Gold*?

19 In which sitcom did a team from Scumbag College take part in *University Challenge*?

20 What is the name of the daytime quiz hosted by Warwick Davis where contestants aim to complete lists?

Answers to QUIZ 198 – History

1 1553
2 Robert Walpole (First Earl of Orford)
3 Eleanor of Aquitaine
4 Yukon
5 Penny Red
6 Gamal Nasser
7 Beatrix
8 Lenin
9 John Adams
10 Etruria
11 Rochdale
12 William III and Mary II
13 Charlemagne
14 Zaire
15 George Fox
16 Coffee shop
17 Italy
18 Duke of Wellington
19 Inigo Jones
20 Eboracum

QUIZ 201 – Pot Luck

ANSWERS ON PAGE 203

1 Which band had 1980s hits with *Hard to Say I'm Sorry* and *Hard Habit to Break*?

2 What is the county town of Ireland's County Meath?

3 Ottawa is located in which Canadian province?

4 Polish and Czech are members of which family of languages?

5 Who was *King of the Road* at the top of the UK charts in 1965?

6 Which BBC arts series was launched in 1975?

7 Mary, Queen of Scots was executed in which castle?

8 Which record label did Jerry Dammers found in 1979?

9 In the USA, what term is used for any swampy area in Louisiana?

10 Who is the chief officer of the Royal Household?

11 Which Berkshire village was the destination for an annual CND march in the late 1950s and early 1960s?

12 The garden flower, the antirrhinum, has which common name?

13 In the 1952 children's novel *Charlotte's Web*, what is the name of the young girl?

14 What is Switzerland's largest city?

15 In the 2009 film *Julie & Julia*, which actress co-starred with Meryl Streep in a title role?

16 Which girl's name is also the botanical name for the laurel bush?

17 Who played Goldfinger in the 1964 Bond film of the same name?

18 The Guildhall School of Music and Drama is situated in which City of London arts complex?

19 Which Moroccan city is said to have the world's oldest university?

20 What was the name of the one-eyed woman in the cartoon series *Futurama*?

Easy

Medium

Hard

Answers to QUIZ 199 – Pot Luck

1 Barbra Streisand
2 Vaduz
3 Brendan
4 Sheena Easton
5 John Keats
6 Cheese
7 Cornwall
8 Hungarian
9 Trumpet
10 Coventry
11 *Quantum Leap*
12 Horse
13 Eugene O'Neill
14 Captain Sensible
15 John le Carré
16 Yeo
17 Zeebrugge
18 Electra
19 Istle
20 Dundee

Easy

Medium

Hard

QUIZ 202 – 1950s Music

ANSWERS ON PAGE 204

1 In which year were the UK charts first compiled...?
2 ...and what was the first UK no.1 single?
3 Which 1950s musician was known as "The Man with the Golden Trumpet"?
4 *Secret Love* featured in which 1953 film musical?
5 Who sang the theme song to *Three Coins in the Fountain*?
6 In which year did Connie Francis top the UK charts with *Who's Sorry Now*?
7 Who had a 1955 hit with the title song from the musical *Rose Marie*?
8 *Mary's Boy Child* was a 1957 hit for which singer?
9 Tony Bennett had a 1955 hit with which song from the musical *Kismet*?
10 Which singer was known as "The Girl with the Giggle in Her Voice?"
11 In which year did Elvis Presley have his first UK no.1?
12 What instrument was Winifred Atwell famous for playing?
13 *Thank Heaven for Little Girls* is a song from which musical?
14 Which British singer topped the charts in 1959 with *What Do You Want*?
15 Which Buddy Holly hit was the last single released in his lifetime?
16 Who had a hit with *Dream Lover* in 1959?
17 Which 1950s singer went on to play Teen Angel in the 1978 film *Grease*?
18 *This Ole House* was a 1954 hit for which singer?
19 Who was the older of the two Everly brothers?
20 Who had a 1956 no.1 UK hit with *Memories are Made of This*?

Answers to QUIZ 200 – Television Quizzes

1 Noel Edmonds
2 Kevin Ashman
3 Barry Simmons
4 John Barrowman
5 *Approaching Menace*
6 Paul Daniels
7 Nine
8 *Grand Slam*
9 *A Question of Sport*
10 Gordon Burns
11 2009
12 Anne Hegerty
13 *Who Wants to Be a Millionaire?*
14 Kirsty Young
15 Anglia
16 Watson
17 *Two Tribes*
18 Henry Kelly
19 *The Young Ones*
20 *Tenable*

QUIZ 203 – Pot Luck

ANSWERS ON PAGE 205

1 Which singer's 2011 debut single *Swagger Jagger* went straight to no.1?

2 What is the imaginary dukedom in which Shakespeare's *Twelfth Night* is set?

3 What honorary title is given to a retired professor?

4 Which island lies just north of Scotland's Isle of Arran?

5 What is the most famous feature of the Sagarmatha National Park?

6 In 1989, who became a principal dancer for The Royal Ballet at the age of 20?

7 What is the first name of Kramer in the TV series *Seinfeld*?

8 Which brothers formed the group Sparks?

9 The 2008 film *Ghost Town* starred which comedian?

10 Which taxonomic classification is immediate below "family"?

11 The anchor hallmark is applied to silver made in which British city?

12 The ABC Islands of the Lesser Antilles consist of Bonaire, Curaçao and which other territory of the Kingdom of the Netherlands?

13 Which 1995 film was based on the children's book *The Sheep-Pig*?

14 Who was Edward II's queen consort?

15 The accordion is a member of which family of musical instruments?

16 In 1955, which product was the first to be advertised on ITV?

17 Which actor starred in the 1983 film *WarGames*?

18 Who wrote the 1996 novel *Popcorn*?

19 Which famous Roman statesman and orator died in 43 BC?

20 In 1923, which Irish poet was awarded the Nobel Prize in Literature?

Easy Medium Hard

Answers to QUIZ 201 – Pot Luck

1 Chicago
2 Navan
3 Ontario
4 Slavonic
5 Roger Miller
6 *Arena*
7 Fotheringhay
8 2-Tone
9 Bayou
10 Lord Chamberlain
11 Aldermaston
12 Snapdragon
13 Fern
14 Zürich
15 Amy Adams
16 Daphne
17 Gert Fröbe
18 Barbican
19 Fez (founded 859)
20 Leela

QUIZ 204 – Films

ANSWERS ON PAGE 206

Easy

1 In which year was *Thelma & Louise* released in the cinema?
2 Who starred alongside Ben Affleck in *Gone Girl*?
3 What was the name of Sting's character in the 1979 film *Quadrophenia*?
4 Rachel Weisz won an Oscar for which 2005 film?
5 Which actor starred in the 1939 film *Goodbye, Mr Chips*?
6 In *2001: A Space Odyssey*, what was the name of the computer?
7 Which 1973 film starring Steve McQueen was set on Devil's Island?
8 Who starred in the 1951 film *The Great Caruso*?
9 Which comedian played Flash Harry in the 2007 version of *St Trinians*?
10 For which film did Denzel Washington receive his second Oscar?

Medium

11 In the 1963 film *The Pink Panther*, to what did the title refer?
12 What was the surname of silent-film "It" girl Clara?
13 For which 1981 film did Warren Beatty win the Best Director Oscar?
14 In 1993, which actor starred in the film *Six Degrees of Separation*?
15 What was the subtitle of the 1984 *Star Trek III* film?
16 Which actress starred as Maggie in the 1958 film *Cat on a Hot Tin Roof*?
17 Who directed the 1986 film *Stand By Me*?
18 In the 1998 film *Shakespeare in Love*, who played the title role?
19 For which 1996 film did Frances McDormand win the Best Actress Oscar?
20 Who played Huggy Bear in the 2004 film *Starsky & Hutch*?

Hard

Answers to QUIZ 202 – 1950s Music

1 1952
2 *Here in My Heart* (Al Martino)
3 Eddie Calvert
4 *Calamity Jane*
5 Frank Sinatra
6 1958
7 Slim Whitman
8 Harry Belafonte
9 *Stranger in Paradise*
10 Alma Cogan
11 1957 (*All Shook Up*)
12 Piano
13 *Gigi*
14 Adam Faith
15 *Heartbeat*
16 Bobby Darin
17 Frankie Avalon
18 Rosemary Clooney
19 Don
20 Dean Martin

QUIZ 205 – Pot Luck

ANSWERS ON PAGE 207

1 Through which mountains does the St Gotthard Pass run?
2 Cape Cod and Martha's Vineyard are in which US state?
3 Whose tenth album *X* was released in 2007?
4 Which letter of the Greek alphabet precedes iota?
5 What land measure is equivalent to 4840 square yards?
6 What nationality was sociologist Ulrich Beck (b.1944)?
7 Who created the *Mr Men*?
8 What is the name of the Isle of Man's main airport?
9 James IV of Scotland was killed at which 1513 battle?
10 In which European city is Wencelas Square?
11 In a standard pack of cards, what are the queens pictured holding?
12 Which actor played the *Nightmare on Elm Street* character Freddy Krueger?
13 The ancient city of Palmyra is in which present-day country?
14 Which Arabian cargo ship is distinguished by its lateen sail?
15 The Mappa Mundi is housed in which city's cathedral?
16 What term is used for members of the Egyptian Orthodox Church?
17 Richard O'Brien was the original host of which game show, revived in 2017?
18 Who played Arthur to Colin Morgan's Merlin in the TV series of that name?
19 Which is the first letter of the Hebrew alphabet?
20 In Abrahamic religions, what are angelic beings of the second order called?

Answers to QUIZ 203 – Pot Luck

1 Cher Lloyd
2 Illyria
3 Emeritus
4 Bute
5 Mount Everest
6 Dame Darcey Bussell
7 Cosmo
8 Ron and Russell Mael
9 Ricky Gervais
10 Genus
11 Birmingham
12 Aruba
13 *Babe*
14 Isabella (of France)
15 Reed organ
16 Gibbs SR toothpaste
17 Matthew Broderick
18 Ben Elton
19 Cicero
20 WB Yeats

QUIZ 206 – Diaries

ANSWERS ON PAGE 208

1 In which novel does the diary of Marian Halcombe appear?

2 Which 1953 Marilyn Monroe film is based on a fictional diary by Anita Loos?

3 Which actor's diaries formed the basis for the TV film *Fantabulosa!*?

4 The first instalment of whose diaries was entitled *Prelude to Power 1994-97*?

5 In which 1897 novel does Jonathan Harker's diary describe his encounters with a vampire?

6 Which actor and traveller's diaries give an insider's view of the Monty Python team?

7 Who wrote in his diary about the "excruciating dialogue" he had to speak in *Star Wars*?

8 Published by her father in 1947, who wrote *The Diary of a Young Girl*?

9 Which thriller author wrote three volumes of his *A Prison Diary*, entitled *Hell*, *Purgatory* and *Heaven*?

10 Based on her own diaries, who wrote the WWI memoir *Testament of Youth*?

11 Which British queen's journals totalled 122 volumes?

12 Whose fictional comic diary is loosely based on *Pride and Prejudice*?

13 Who commits *thoughtcrime* by writing "DOWN WITH BIG BROTHER" in his diary?

14 Jeff Kinney created which fictional US schoolboy's diaries?

15 Whose 1906 *Country Diary* was a publishing sensation in the late 1970s and early 1980s?

16 Which 1949 novel was narrated through the journal of Cassandra Mortmain?

17 Which long-running radio series began in 1948 and featured the journals of a doctor's wife?

18 In *Harry Potter and the Chamber of Secrets*, whose diary plays a crucial role?

19 Which politician's diaries unlocked the secrets of Baroness Margaret Thatcher's government?

20 Which revolutionary documented his youthful travels in *The Motorcycle Diaries*?

Easy

Medium

Hard

Answers to QUIZ 204 – Films

1 1991
2 Rosamund Pike
3 Ace Face
4 *The Constant Gardener*
5 Robert Donat
6 Hal (9000)
7 *Papillon*
8 Mario Lanza
9 Russell Brand
10 *Training Day*
11 A diamond
12 Bow
13 *Reds*
14 Will Smith
15 *The Search for Spock*
16 Elizabeth Taylor
17 Rob Reiner
18 Joseph Fiennes
19 *Fargo*
20 Snoop Dogg

QUIZ 207 – Pot Luck

ANSWERS ON PAGE 209

1 How are the musicians Roland Orzabal and Curt Smith as a duo known?
2 Who won the men's 800m Olympic gold medal in 2012 and 2016?
3 Who played Mrs Coulter in the 2007 film *The Golden Compass*?
4 *The Government Inspector* (1836) was written by which Russian author?
5 Which author lived at Chawton House in Hampshire?
6 What is the capital of Slovenia?
7 Which Italian port is the capital of the Apulia region?
8 Which famous drink is made in Charente, France?
9 In which 1960s children's series did the puppet Troy Tempest appear?
10 Which Roman emperor made Christianity a state religion?
11 Where in London was the US Embassy located from 1960 to 2018?
12 Which sea is between Poland and Sweden?
13 Which Latin term means "from the beginning"?
14 *New Rules* was a 2017 single by which artist?
15 What was Calder Hall the first UK example of?
16 What was the pen-name of Edith Pargeter, author of the Brother Cadfael mysteries?
17 How was the old comedy team Moe, Larry and Curly collectively known?
18 In which year was the driving test introduced in the UK?
19 Who founded the Tamla Motown record label?
20 What is the common name of the herb genus *Satureja*, which has summer and winter varieties?

Answers to QUIZ 205 – Pot Luck

1 Alps
2 Massachusetts
3 Kylie Minogue
4 Theta
5 Acre
6 German
7 Roger Hargreaves
8 Ronaldsway
9 Flodden
10 Prague
11 A flower
12 Robert Englund
13 Syria
14 Dhow
15 Hereford
16 Copts
17 *The Crystal Maze*
18 Bradley James
19 Aleph
20 Cherubim

QUIZ 208 – Pink

ANSWERS ON PAGE 210

1 Who played Inspector Clouseau in the 2006 version of *The Pink Panther*?

2 Which 1980s band covered the 1955 hit *Cherry Pink and Apple Blossom White*?

3 What type of fruit is a Pink Lady?

4 Which character is played by Jada Pinkett Smith in *The Matrix* series of films?

5 Which opera features the character Lieutenant Pinkerton?

6 Which guitarist replaced Syd Barrett in Pink Floyd in 1968?

7 In which decade was the *Financial Times* first printed on pink paper?

8 Which finger is referred to as a pinkie?

9 The winner of which national cycle race is awarded a pink jersey?

10 In business, what is a "pink slip"?

11 Which actress starred in the 1986 film *Pretty in Pink*?

12 What type of creatures are the title characters in the animated TV series *Pinky and the Brain*?

13 Who wrote the 1984 song *Pink Cadillac*...?

14 ...and who had a hit with it in 1988?

15 The flower known as the common pink belongs to which plant genus?

16 Which children's author created the character of Mr Pink-Whistle?

17 Which fashion designer popularised shocking pink?

18 What was Pink's first UK solo no.1 hit...?

19 ...and on which 2001 no.1 record did she sing?

20 What gives a Pink Lady cocktail its pink colour?

Answers to QUIZ 206 – Diaries

1 *The Woman in White* (Wilkie Collins)
2 *Gentlemen Prefer Blondes*
3 Kenneth Williams
4 Alastair Campbell
5 *Dracula*
6 Michael Palin
7 Sir Alec Guinness
8 Anne Frank
9 Jeffrey Archer
10 Vera Brittain
11 Queen Victoria
12 *Bridget Jones's Diary*
13 Winston Smith (in *Nineteen Eighty-Four*)
14 *Diary of a Wimpy Kid*
15 An Edwardian Lady (Edith Holden)
16 *I Capture the Castle* (Dodie Smith)
17 *Mrs Dale's Diary*
18 Tom Riddle
19 Alan Clark
20 Che Guevara

QUIZ 209 – Pot Luck

ANSWERS ON PAGE 211

1 Which decade saw the first FA cup final take place at the original Wembley Stadium?

2 The 1990s TV series *Peak Practice* was set in which county?

3 The title of which Samuel Butler novel is an anagram of "nowhere"?

4 Which singer had a cameo role in the first episode of the seventh series of *Game of Thrones*?

5 Which children's show featured a scientist called Dr Bunsen Honeydew?

6 What is the largest city on the Baja California peninsula in Mexico?

7 On which continent are the Carpathian Mountains located?

8 Which Portuguese explorer led the first expedition to circumnavigate the world?

9 Who was Neville Chamberlain's predecessor as Prime Minister?

10 In which 2001 film did siblings Jake and Maggie Gyllenhaal appear as brother and sister?

11 Which opera was the inspiration for the musical *Rent*?

12 In the RAF, what rank is below wing commander but above flight lieutenant?

13 Which language is spoken in the western Pyrenees?

14 Which element has the atomic number 8?

15 Who sang the theme tune to the Bond film *Spectre*?

16 London's Mount Pleasant is the location for which museum?

17 Which Greek saint gave his name to the alphabet now used in Russia and certain eastern European countries?

18 Who was Biggles' cousin in the books by WE Johns?

19 What is the other name of Rome's Leonardo da Vinci airport?

20 Which girl group had a hit with *Hole in the Head* in 2003?

Answers to QUIZ 207 – Pot Luck

1 Tears for Fears
2 David Rudisha
3 Nicole Kidman
4 Nikolai Gogol
5 Jane Austen
6 Ljubljana
7 Bari
8 Cognac
9 *Stingray*
10 Constantine
11 Grosvenor Square
12 Baltic
13 *Ab initio*
14 Dua Lipa
15 Nuclear power station
16 Ellis Peters
17 The Three Stooges
18 1935
19 Berry Gordy Jr
20 Savory

QUIZ 210 – The Olympic Games

ANSWERS ON PAGE **212**

Easy

1 Which medal did the GB women's curling team win at the 2014 Winter Games?

2 In which year were the Winter Games held in Lillehammer?

3 Who won the 800m gold medal at the 1980 Summer Games?

4 In which year did Canada first host the Winter Games?

5 Which British rower wrote the 2004 book *Four Men in a Boat* about the 2000 Olympics?

6 How many Olympic medals did swimmer Michael Phelps win in total?

7 What was the title of the official sound track to the opening ceremony of the 2012 London Summer Games...?

8 ...and who directed the ceremony?

9 Which boxer won a bronze medal at the 1996 Olympics in the featherweight division?

10 Which was the first South American country to host the Summer Games?

Medium

11 Which country won the most medals at the 2018 Winter Games?

12 The 1981 film *Chariots of Fire* features the Summer Games of which year?

13 At the 2008 Summer Games, in which administrative region of China were the equestrian events held?

14 What was the last year in which the Summer and Winter games were held in the same year?

15 Which gold-medal winning Paralympian took part in the 2017 series of *Strictly Come Dancing*?

16 Athletes from which country won the women's 100m gold medal in 2008, 2012 and 2016?

17 Which Japanese city hosted the 1998 Winter Games?

Hard

18 In which year were the first Summer Games held, following the formation of the International Olympic Committee?

19 Which country always leads the parade of participants at the Summer Games?

20 Who was the first British athlete to win Olympic gold in a throwing event?

Answers to QUIZ 208 – Pink

1 Steve Martin
2 Modern Romance
3 Apple
4 Niobe
5 *Madama Butterfly* (Puccini)
6 David Gilmour
7 1890s (1893)
8 Little finger
9 Giro d'Italia
10 Notice of redundancy
11 Molly Ringwald
12 Mice
13 Bruce Springsteen
14 Natalie Cole
15 *Dianthus*
16 Enid Blyton
17 Elsa Schiaparelli
18 *Just Like a Pill*
19 *Lady Marmalade*
20 Grenadine

QUIZ 211 – Pot Luck

ANSWERS ON PAGE 213

1 Who was David Walliams' co-star in the 2015 Agatha Christie series *Partners in Crime*?
2 Which Irish county lies north of Roscommon and east of Mayo?
3 Who was the oldest of the Marx Brothers?
4 For which 2015 film did Leonardo di Caprio win the Best Actor Oscar?
5 In which year did the Crimean War start?
6 Barbados is in which Caribbean island group?
7 Who writes the *Jack Reacher* series of books?
8 Which bay on the Isle of Wight is famous for its coloured sand?
9 Which Greek god of the arts lends his name to many theatres?
10 What type of rock is granite?
11 *Sonnets from the Portuguese* is a collection by which Victorian poetess?
12 Who shared the 2001 Nobel Peace Prize with the organisation that he led at the time?
13 Who designed the Crystal Palace for the 19th-century Great Exhibition?
14 In which sitcom did Christopher Biggins play a character nicknamed Lukewarm?
15 In which year was North Sea oil discovered?
16 Which river runs through Newton Abbot, Devon?
17 What type of construction is the Humber Bridge?
18 In which Danish port was Hans Christian Andersen born?
19 Which Greek mathematician wrote *The Elements*?
20 Singer Tom Jones had which original surname?

Answers to QUIZ 209 – Pot Luck

1 1920s
2 Derbyshire
3 *Erewhon*
4 Ed Sheeran
5 *The Muppet Show*
6 Tijuana
7 Europe
8 Ferdinand Magellan
9 Stanley Baldwin (First Earl Baldwin of Bewdley)
10 *Donnie Darko*
11 *La bohème*
12 Squadron leader
13 Basque
14 Oxygen
15 Sam Smith
16 The Postal Museum
17 Cyril
18 Algy
19 Fiumicino
20 Sugababes

QUIZ 212 – Sea Creatures

ANSWERS ON PAGE 214

Easy

1 What word describes marine life that lives in the upper waters of the open sea?
2 The adult of which large sea creature was caught on camera for the first time in 2004?
3 How many legs does a lobster have?
4 What is a female dolphin called?
5 What type of fish has a variety known as "sockeye"?
6 How is a member of the *Hippocampus* genus commonly known?
7 The name "krill" comes from the word for "young fish" in which language?
8 A loggerhead is a species of which sea creature?
9 Which is the largest living fish?
10 What common name is given to both the manatee and dugong?

Medium

11 Humboldt penguins are found in the wild on which continent?
12 "Sild" is the name given to the young of which species of fish?
13 Which edible mollusc is also called the sea-ear?
14 What name is given to a group of whales?
15 What type of invertebrate is the source of mother-of-pearl?
16 Sea otters are found in which ocean?
17 The male of which type of crab has an enlarged claw, waved for courtship and territorial display?
18 What is the common name for the group of fish which have their eyes on top of their heads?
19 The "coral" is another name for which part of a shellfish?
20 Octopuses and squid belong to which class of molluscs?

Hard

Answers to QUIZ 210 – The Olympic Games

1 Bronze
2 1994
3 Steve Ovett
4 1988 (Calgary)
5 Tim Foster
6 28
7 *Isles of Wonder*
8 Danny Boyle
9 Floyd Mayweather
10 Brazil (2016)
11 Norway (39)
12 1924
13 Hong Kong
14 1992
15 Jonnie Peacock
16 Jamaica
17 Nagano
18 1896
19 Greece
20 Tessa Sanderson

QUIZ 213 – Pot Luck

ANSWERS ON PAGE 215

1 What name was given to the cavalry troopers of Oliver Cromwell?
2 *Eye of the Tiger* was from the soundtrack of which film?
3 Wolfsbane is the alternative name of which wild flower?
4 Which major Indian language is written in the Devanagari script?
5 What is the title of the opera by Verdi set in ancient Jerusalem about a Babylonian king?
6 Which Prime Minister succeeded Sir Winston Churchill in 1945?
7 At Salt Lake City in 2002, in which sport did Great Britain win their one gold medal?
8 Which actress starred in the 2003 film *How To Lose a Guy in 10 Days*?
9 Which mythological queen of Troy was the wife of Priam?
10 Which old British coin, legal tender until 1960, was worth one quarter of a penny?
11 *The Piper at the Gates of Dawn* was the first album by which band?
12 Which Kansas city was founded in 1872 as a frontier town?
13 How is Kehlsteinhaus, Berchtesgaden better known in English?
14 Lydford Gorge is in which National Park?
15 To which Irish county does Achill Island belong?
16 Ulan Bator is the capital of which country?
17 Which month is named in honour of a major Roman goddess?
18 Which actor starred as Jack Stanton in the 1998 film *Primary Colors*?
19 *Feels Like I'm in Love* was a 1980 hit for which singer?
20 The Mariinsky Theatre is located in which Russian city?

Answers to QUIZ 211 – Pot Luck

1 Jessica Raine
2 Sligo
3 Chico
4 *The Revenant*
5 1853
6 Windward Islands (within Lesser Antilles)
7 Lee Child
8 Alum Bay
9 Apollo
10 Igneous
11 Elizabeth Barrett Browning
12 Kofi Annan (United Nations)
13 Sir Joseph Paxton
14 *Porridge*
15 1966
16 Teign
17 Cable suspension
18 Odense
19 Euclid
20 Woodward

ANSWERS ON PAGE 216

Easy

1 Who wrote the children's novel *Emil and the Detectives* (1929)?

2 Who received the 1921 Nobel Prize in Physics?

3 Who did Albert, Duke of York marry in 1923 at Westminster Abbey?

4 Which UK political party formed in 1925?

5 Howard Carter discovered the tomb of Tutankhamen in 1922 under the employment of which Earl?

6 To what did the LNER company rename the *Special Scotch Express* in 1924?

7 By what name was the Republic of Ireland known from 1921 to 1937?

8 Which style of décor first became popular in the 1920s, as seen in London's Eltham Palace?

9 To what did the Equal Franchise Act of 1928 lower the female voting age?

Medium

10 Who became Prime Minister of Italy in October 1922?

11 In which month did the General Strike of 1926 occur?

12 Which European long-distance car race was first run in 1923?

13 The Tennessee Scopes trial which took place in 1925 was dramatised in which 1960 film?

14 Which English composer was appointed Master of the King's Musick in 1924?

15 Which 1920s UK Prime Minister was born in what is now Canada?

16 In which year did women become full members of Oxford University?

17 Which mountaineer (d.1924) is reported to have said "Because it's there" in response to a question about why he wanted to climb Everest?

18 The UK 1923 Intoxicating Liquor Act prohibited the sale of alcohol to people under what age?

Hard

19 In which year did the Wall Street Crash happen?

20 In 1925 Cyril Brownlie was playing rugby for which country when he became the first person to be sent off in an international match?

Answers to QUIZ 212 – Sea Creatures

1 Pelagic
2 Giant squid
3 Ten
4 Cow
5 Salmon
6 Seahorse
7 Norwegian
8 Turtle
9 Whale shark
10 Sea cow
11 South America
12 Herring
13 Ormer (or abalone)
14 Pod
15 Molluscs
16 Pacific
17 Fiddler crab
18 Flatfish
19 Roe
20 *Cephalopoda*

QUIZ 215 – Pot Luck

ANSWERS ON PAGE 217

1 How old was John Keats when he died?

2 In which year was the Bradwell nuclear power station decommissioned?

3 Which George Michael solo song had "90" added to the title to distinguish it from a Wham! song title?

4 What name is given to surgical tongs?

5 Who sang *I Talk to the Trees* in the 1969 film *Paint Your Wagon*?

6 Which former county town in the Clyde Valley is home of the William Wallace Heritage Trust?

7 In James Joyce's *Ulysses*, what is the surname of Leopold and Molly?

8 What sits on a dolly in a television studio?

9 What was the title of Cher's 1998 no.1 hit?

10 What is a cross-like emblem used in ancient Egypt as the symbol of life?

11 Buddy Holly was born in which Texas city?

12 In which Oxfordshire town is the Williams Formula 1 team based?

13 What was an old French five-centime piece called?

14 What was Coco Chanel's real first name?

15 Haiti and the Dominican Republic make up which island?

16 Which adjective describes the family of languages which includes Hebrew and Arabic?

17 During what event would you see Baily's beads?

18 Which Skye castle is the ancestral home of the clan MacLeod?

19 *Sheezus* was a 2014 album by which singer?

20 What was the name of Captain Scott's ship on his first voyage to Antarctica?

Easy

Medium

Hard

Answers to QUIZ 213 – Pot Luck

1 Ironsides
2 *Rocky III*
3 Aconite
4 Hindi
5 *Nabucco*
6 Clement Attlee (First Earl Attlee)
7 Curling
8 Kate Hudson
9 Hecuba
10 Farthing
11 Pink Floyd
12 Dodge City
13 Eagle's Nest (Hitler's retreat)
14 Dartmoor
15 Mayo
16 Mongolia
17 June (Juno)
18 John Travolta
19 Kelly Marie
20 St Petersburg

QUIZ 216 – Days

ANSWERS ON PAGE 218

Easy

1 Who appeared as Tall Karen in the 2009 series *Monday Monday*?

2 Which author created the character of Thursday Next?

3 Who wrote *Manic Monday*, a hit for the Bangles?

4 Which TV series features Simon Bird as Adam Goodman?

5 Who was The Saturdays member Frankie Bridge paired with when she took part in *Strictly Come Dancing* in 2014?

6 Actress Tuesday Weld was given which first name at birth?

7 Which actor starred in the 1940 film *His Girl Friday*?

8 The Rolling Stones' *Ruby Tuesday* was released as a B side to which song in 1967?

9 Who wrote the 1908 novel *The Man who was Thursday*?

10 Which composer wrote the music and lyrics to *Sunday in the Park with George* (1984)?

Medium

11 Who played Wednesday in the 1991 film *The Addams Family*?

12 Which US TV show is known as *SNL*?

13 *Saturday Night and Sunday Morning* was a 1958 novel by which author...?

14 ...and who played Arthur Seaton in the 1960 film version?

15 The 2013 novels *Tuesday's Gone* and *Waiting for Wednesday* were published under the name of which author?

16 In which year did Blondie have a hit with *Sunday Girl*?

17 What was the real name of the dancer with the Happy Mondays, known as "Bez"?

18 Who wrote the 1954 novel *Sweet Thursday*?

19 *Tell Me on a Sunday* features music by Andrew Lloyd Webber (Baron Lloyd-Webber) and words by which lyricist?

Hard

20 Who sang the 1994 hit *Saturday Night*?

Answers to QUIZ 214 – 1920s

1 Erich Kästner
2 Albert Einstein
3 Lady Elizabeth Bowes-Lyon
4 Plaid Cymru
5 Lord Carnarvon
6 *Flying Scotsman*
7 Irish Free State
8 Art Deco
9 21
10 Benito Mussolini
11 May
12 24 Hours of Le Mans
13 *Inherit the Wind*
14 Sir Edward Elgar
15 Andrew Bonar Law
16 1920
17 George Mallory
18 18
19 1929
20 New Zealand

QUIZ 217 – Pot Luck

ANSWERS ON PAGE 219

1 Which African republic has Dakar as its capital?

2 What is the name of Rome's ancient seaport?

3 The song *Send in the Clowns* was written by which composer?

4 Which actor co-starred with Audrey Hepburn in the 1953 film *Roman Holiday*?

5 Which carol did Bing Crosby and David Bowie record together?

6 Which shrub, also known as the wattle, is the source of gum arabic?

7 In which southern Swedish town are the *Wallander* novels set?

8 The name of which coarse woollen fabric is now used to describe any inferior substance?

9 Who is the haughty young woman in Dickens' *Great Expectations*?

10 Which Australian actor starred in *Oklahoma!* at London's National Theatre in 1998?

11 To which bird family does the puffin belong?

12 Which German astrologer was the subject of a drama by Goethe?

13 In 2015, who replaced the Foo Fighters to headline at the Glastonbury music festival?

14 Which fragrant oil comes from the damask rose?

15 Who co-starred with Martin Shaw in the TV series *The Professionals*?

16 Which is the longest railway line in the world?

17 Which 11th-century Spanish hero was the subject of a 1961 Charlton Heston film?

18 Adolphe Sax, inventor of the saxophone, had which nationality?

19 Which Egyptian god was the father of Horus?

20 Of which mammal is the aardwolf a species?

Answers to QUIZ 215 – Pot Luck

1 25
2 2002
3 *Freedom*
4 Forceps
5 Clint Eastwood
6 Lanark
7 Bloom
8 A camera
9 *Believe*
10 Ankh
11 Lubbock
12 Didcot
13 Sou
14 Gabrielle
15 Hispaniola
16 Semitic
17 Solar eclipse
18 Dunvegan Castle
19 Lily Allen
20 *Discovery*

QUIZ 218 – Arts and Crafts

ANSWERS ON PAGE 220

Easy

1 For what purpose is a mixture of size applied to a sheet of paper?

2 Which cotton-like substance obtained from the fibrous cover of seeds is usually used to stuff soft toys?

3 What shade is the paint colour gamboge?

4 What general term is given to the components used to make jewellery, such as clasps and rings?

5 In encaustic art, how are colours transferred to the surface of an item?

6 What does the letter "H" indicate on a pencil?

7 The tile cutters used in making mosaics are given what name?

8 What term is given to opaque watercolour paint?

9 Lampwork is a technique to create items from what material?

10 In which craft are "fat quarters" used?

Medium

11 What is the hand tool called a brayer used for?

12 For what would an artist use a rigger brush?

13 Which Japanese craft translates as "folding paper"?

14 What term is given to a type of knitting where all the rows are knitted in plain stitch?

15 NAFAS is the association of clubs for which artistic pursuit?

16 In which craft would lazy daisy stitch be used?

17 What term is given to the threads passed across the warp on a weaving loom?

18 "Cloisonné" is a style of design where wire outlines are filled in with which material?

19 The name of which papercraft is derived from the French verb for "to cut"?

Hard

20 What name is given to the craft of burning designs on wood surfaces with a heated tool or flame?

Answers to QUIZ 216 – Days

1 Miranda Hart
2 Jasper Fforde
3 Prince
4 *Friday Night Dinner*
5 Kevin Clifton
6 Susan
7 Cary Grant
8 *Let's Spend the Night Together*
9 GK Chesterton
10 Stephen Sondheim
11 Christina Ricci
12 *Saturday Night Live*
13 Alan Sillitoe
14 Albert Finney
15 Nicci French
16 1979
17 Mark Berry
18 John Steinbeck
19 Don Black
20 Whigfield

QUIZ 219 – Pot Luck

ANSWERS ON PAGE 221

1 Hylda Baker and Arthur Mullard recorded a spoof version of which 1978 song?

2 Which soft fruits are a cross between blackberries and raspberries?

3 What term is used for an inhabitant of Louisiana of French descent?

4 Which company started out as the California Perfume Company?

5 The 2004 film *Man on Fire* starred which actor as John Creasy?

6 What may be classified according to the Dewey Decimal System?

7 What is a gourami?

8 What is the capital of the Balearic island of Minorca?

9 *The Outsider* is the 2013 autobiography of which tennis player?

10 Which prehistoric flying reptile's name means "winged finger"?

11 What man-made feature can be seen at Foxton in Leicestershire?

12 Octavia Hill was one of the founders of which UK organisation?

13 Which old prison on London's South Bank was destroyed during the Gordon Riots of 1780?

14 What is Uruguay's unit of currency?

15 Which female novelist's debut was *White Teeth* in 2000?

16 LPL is the code for which UK airport?

17 What material represents the 13th wedding anniversary?

18 Which Beatle had a hit in 1972 with *Back Off Boogaloo*?

19 Who was Katharine Hepburn's co-star in the 1942 film *Woman of the Year*?

20 What legal phrase means "based on the first impression"?

Answers to QUIZ 217 – Pot Luck

1 Senegal
2 Ostia
3 Stephen Sondheim
4 Gregory Peck
5 *Little Drummer Boy*
6 Acacia
7 Ystad
8 Shoddy
9 Estella
10 Hugh Jackman
11 Auk
12 Johann Faust
13 Florence and the Machine
14 Attar
15 Lewis Collins
16 Trans-Siberian Railway
17 El Cid
18 Belgian
19 Osiris
20 Hyena

Easy

1 The Fitzwilliam Museum is in which city?

2 Which river flows through Barnstaple?

3 Which hills straddle the English/Scottish border?

4 The Romans named which town Corinium?

5 What is the side of salted pork called, traditionally given to long-married couples in Dunmow, Essex?

6 Which English king was killed while hunting in the New Forest?

7 The village of Tolpuddle is in which county?

8 Which English Civil War battle took place near York in 1644?

9 Which Kent castle has been home to both the Astor family and the Boleyn family?

10 Knowsley is a district of which city?

Medium

11 Which cheese is associated with the town of Hawes?

12 Which shipping area lies between Dover and Portland?

13 William Wordsworth lived in which cottage in Grasmere?

14 What is the name of the lighthouse on Plymouth Hoe?

15 Which railway runs between Alton and Alresford in Hampshire?

16 The National Memorial Arboretum is in which county?

17 In which town was the TV series *Last of the Summer Wine* filmed?

18 Which Hertfordshire town was designated a New Town in 1946?

19 Which port on the south side of the Humber is managed jointly with Grimsby?

20 Which was the UK's City of Culture for 2017?

Hard

Answers to QUIZ 218 – Arts and Crafts

1 To seal it
2 Kapok
3 Yellow
4 Findings
5 By burning or fusing
6 Hard
7 Nippers
8 Gouache
9 Glass
10 Quilting
11 Spreading ink
12 Painting thin lines
13 Origami
14 Garter stitch
15 Flower arranging
16 Embroidery
17 Weft
18 Enamel
19 Découpage
20 Pyrography

1 Which actor starred as *Walker, Texas Ranger*?

2 Which group had a hit in 1976 with *Mississippi*?

3 What thick Scottish soup is made from smoked haddock, potato and onion?

4 A cete is a group of which type of animal?

5 Which part of a church lies at right angles to the nave?

6 Which Spanish town is associated with St Teresa?

7 In which US city is the Rock and Roll Hall of Fame?

8 Which island state is linked by a causeway to the Malay Peninsula?

9 What term is given to an assembly of cathedral canons?

10 Which river flows through Ludlow?

11 Which of the Savoy Operas is subtitled *The Peer and the Peri*?

12 On which body of water is the island of Inchmurrin?

13 In which TV series did Ricky Gervais play a retirement home worker?

14 What is the 18th letter of the Greek alphabet?

15 Who published the 1610 scientific pamphlet *The Starry Messenger*?

16 Which transport company started in Hibbing, Minnesota in 1914?

17 What word links a small flat-bottomed boat and a marine food fish?

18 In the 1994 film *Clear and Present Danger*, who starred as Jack Ryan?

19 What is the translation of the Japanese word “sudoku”?

20 What are sold at Tattersalls December Sales?

Answers to QUIZ 219 – Pot Luck

1 *You're the One That I Want*
2 Tayberries
3 Cajun
4 Avon
5 Denzel Washington
6 Library books
7 A fish
8 Mahón
9 Jimmy Connors
10 Pterodactyl
11 Canal locks
12 The National Trust
13 The Clink
14 Peso
15 Zadie Smith
16 Liverpool John Lennon
17 Lace
18 Ringo Starr (Sir Richard Starkey)
19 Spencer Tracy
20 *Prima facie*

Easy Medium Hard

ANSWERS ON PAGE 224

Easy

1 What is the SI unit of electrical force?

2 With which area of physics is Michael Faraday most associated?

3 In relation to power, what does the PV stand for in "solar PV"?

4 What is measured in becquerels?

5 How many laws of motion are attributed to Newton?

6 What is the turning effect of force on an object called?

7 What name is given to the device on which a lever turns?

8 What unit is used to measure temperature on an absolute scale?

9 By which process are electrical or magnetic properties transferred from one circuit or body to another without physical contact?

10 Which German physicist (b.1858) is considered to be the founder of quantum theory?

Medium

11 What is the science of bodies in motion?

12 In which year did British scientist Peter W Higgs share the Nobel Prize in physics?

13 What are wire coils used in electrical circuits called?

14 In the term "CMB radiation", what does "CMB" stand for?

15 The Nobel Prize in Chemistry in 1908 was won by which physicist?

16 Which of the four laws of thermodynamics states that energy cannot be created or destroyed?

17 What is the SI unit of electric current?

18 What was the first name of the inventor of the Fahrenheit temperature scale?

19 Who wrote the 2008 book *Physics of the Impossible*?

20 How is the European Organisation for Nuclear Research better known?

Hard

Answers to QUIZ 220 – England

1 Cambridge
2 Taw
3 Cheviots
4 Circencester
5 Flitch
6 William II (Rufus)
7 Dorset
8 Marston Moor
9 Hever
10 Liverpool
11 Wensleydale
12 Wight
13 Dove Cottage
14 Smeaton's Tower
15 The Watercress Line
16 Staffordshire
17 Holmfirth
18 Stevenage
19 Immingham
20 Hull

QUIZ 223 – Pot Luck

ANSWERS ON PAGE 225

1 Which lake constitutes the lowest point in Australia?

2 Which Egyptian city is located at the first cataract on the Nile?

3 The 1995 film *While You Were Sleeping* starred which actress?

4 What is the meaning of the word "germane"?

5 Who headed the late 1960s, early 1970s pop group the Family Stone?

6 Which was Britain's first Area of Outstanding Natural Beauty?

7 Who directed the 1960 film *La Dolce Vita*?

8 In poker, what is a run in sequence of five cards in the same suit?

9 What name links a series of mountain ranges on the Swiss-French border and an island of the Inner Hebrides?

10 Who was runner-up on *The X Factor* in 2009?

11 The *Helliconia* trilogy was written by which British sci-fi author?

12 Who is the Hindu creator of the Universe?

13 In carpentry, what is the piece of wood inserted into a mortise called?

14 Which old Roman road ran from Rome to Brindisi, via Capua?

15 What term is given to a male ferret?

16 *Drop Dead Gorgeous* was a 1997 hit for which band?

17 Which flag is flown by the British Merchant Navy?

18 What adjective refers to Cambridge University?

19 "Cinderella Man" was the nickname of which American boxer?

20 What was the former name of the National Theatre's Dorfman auditorium?

Answers to QUIZ 221 – Pot Luck

1 Chuck Norris
2 Pussycat
3 Cullen skink
4 Badger
5 Transept
6 Avila
7 Cleveland, Ohio
8 Singapore
9 Chapter
10 Teme
11 *Iolanthe*
12 Loch Lomond
13 *Derek*
14 Sigma
15 Galileo Galilei
16 Greyhound Lines Inc
17 Dory
18 Harrison Ford
19 Single number
20 Racehorses

Easy Medium Hard

QUIZ 224 – Andrew

ANSWERS ON PAGE 226

1 What is another name for the cross of St Andrew?
2 Who wrote the 1742 novel *The History of the Adventures of Joseph Andrews*?
3 How old was Andy Murray when he was granted a knighthood?
4 Who succeeded Andrew Jackson as US President?
5 Who was the female star of the 1966 Hitchcock thriller *Torn Curtain*?
6 The 2001 novel *Looking for Andrew McCarthy* was written by which author?
7 Who had a top 5 hit in 1978 with *Never Let Her Slip Away*?
8 In which year did Sir Andrew Motion become Poet Laureate?
9 Which British singer recorded the 1971 song *Andy Warhol*?
10 Who was Andy Hamilton's co-writer on the TV series *Outnumbered*?
11 Which long-running TV series featured the character of Andy Sipowicz?
12 Which newspaper did presenter Andrew Neil edit from 1983 to 1994?
13 How were singers LaVerne, Maxene and Patricia collectively known?
14 Which retired sportsman won the first Australian series of *I'm a Celebrity...Get Me Out of Here!*?
15 Who presented the 2009 TV series *The Making of Modern Britain*?
16 Who played Andy Dufresne in the 1994 film *The Shawshank Redemption*?
17 Which Grand Slam title did Andy Roddick win in 2003?
18 Andy Fairweather-Low was a founder and lead singer of which 1960s band?
19 Which actor played Tommy in the 2010 film *Never Let Me Go*?
20 For what type of book is Andrew Morton best known?

Answers to QUIZ 222 – Physics

1 Volt
2 Electromagnetism
3 Photovoltaic
4 Radioactivity
5 Three
6 Torque
7 Fulcrum
8 Kelvin
9 Induction
10 Max Planck
11 Kinetics
12 2013
13 Resistors
14 Cosmic Microwave Background
15 Sir Ernest Rutherford
16 First
17 Ampere
18 Daniel
19 Michio Kaku
20 CERN

QUIZ 225 – Pot Luck

ANSWERS ON PAGE 227

1 Which country is situated between Togo and Côte d'Ivoire?

2 Who had a Top Ten UK single in 1959 with *Beyond the Sea*?

3 The Royal Armouries Museum can be found in which city?

4 The 1994 Italian film *Il Postino* featured which poet as a central character?

5 What name was given to the group of three destiny-shaping goddesses of Greek mythology?

6 Who was the author of the poem *Childe Harold's Pilgrimage* (1812-18)?

7 What was found buried at Sutton Hoo in 1939?

8 What is the medical term for the bone of the upper jaw?

9 Which law of thermodynamics states that heat flows from hot to cold until equilibrium is reached?

10 What name is shared by twelve popes, three from the 20th century?

11 The TV series *Parents of the Band* starred which actor and singer?

12 What title is below an earl in the aristocratic hierarchy?

13 How many books are there in the Torah?

14 In the shipping forecast, which sea area neighbours Dogger and Fisher?

15 What branch of linguistics is concerned with the meanings of words?

16 Which port is Turkey's third-largest city?

17 In which stage musical do the audience get involved by reversing polarity?

18 Who directed and starred in the 2008 film *Gran Torino*?

19 What was the original name of an order to suppress news for reasons of national security?

20 What is the county town of Rutland?

Easy Medium Hard

Answers to QUIZ 223 – Pot Luck

1 Eyre
2 Aswan
3 Sandra Bullock
4 Relevant
5 Sly
6 Gower Peninsula
7 Federico Fellini
8 Straight flush
9 Jura
10 Olly Murs
11 Brian Aldiss
12 Brahma
13 Tenon
14 The Appian Way
15 Hob
16 Republica
17 Red Ensign
18 Cantabrigian
19 James J Braddock
20 Cottesloe

Easy

1 Who wrote the 1950 novel *The Grass Is Singing*?

2 Which Italian author created the character of Inspector Montalbano?

3 Which series of novels includes *At Lady Molly's* and *Hearing Secret Harmonies*?

4 Which poet (b.1788) had the first names George Gordon?

5 Which sorceress in Homer's *Odyssey* turned men into pigs?

6 What is the first name of Miss Varden in Dickens' *Barnaby Rudge*?

7 Who is the author of the *Eragon* series of novels?

8 In which year was Mary Shelley's *Frankenstein* first published?

9 Which 1911 Edith Wharton novel is set in the fictitious town of Starkfield, Massachusetts?

10 Which French cathedral city in Picardy is featured in Sebastian Faulks' novel *Birdsong*?

Medium

11 What is the name of the girl who joins Tom in the undersea world in *The Water-Babies* (1863)?

12 Who wrote *Memoirs of an Aesthete* (1948)?

13 Which writer (b.1883) created the character of Gregor Samsa?

14 Which Dutch Renaissance humanist and Catholic priest wrote *The Praise of Folly*?

15 What do the initials JB stand for in the name of the author JB Priestley?

16 Who wrote *The Shape of Things to Come* (1933)?

17 How many sonnets is Shakespeare known to have written?

18 Who is the Greek Muse of epic poetry?

19 Which French author wrote *Le Grand Meaulnes* (1913)?

Hard

20 *The Watsons*, published in 1871, is an unfinished novel by which author?

Answers to QUIZ 224 – Andrew

1 Saltire
2 Henry Fielding
3 29
4 Martin Van Buren
5 Dame Julie Andrews
6 Jenny Colgan
7 Andrew Gold
8 1999
9 David Bowie
10 Guy Jenkin
11 *NYPD Blue*
12 *The Sunday Times*
13 The Andrews Sisters
14 Andrew "Freddie" Flintoff
15 Andrew Marr
16 Tim Robbins
17 US Open
18 Amen Corner
19 Andrew Garfield
20 Biographies

QUIZ 227 – Pot Luck

ANSWERS ON PAGE 229

1 What is a more common word for prestidigitation?
2 Who is the eventual husband of Helena in Shakespeare's *All's Well That Ends Well*?
3 What was the real name of the WWI pilot nicknamed "The Red Baron"?
4 On which continent would you find the Drakensberg Mountains?
5 Who is the voice of Viper in the *Kung Fu Panda* films?
6 With which actress did David Essex record *True Love Ways* in 1994?
7 Which word for a colour is derived from the Persian for "dust"?
8 Which shipping forecast area off Northern Ireland is east of Rockall?
9 In which decade did the British Museum open?
10 Which girl's name means "bee" in Greek?
11 Who was the mythical king of Mycenae, killed by his wife and/or her lover?
12 Who was the heroine of Verdi's *Il Trovatore*?
13 Baharat spice is used in what style of cuisine?
14 What does the Mohs scale measure?
15 What is the capital of the Indian state of Karnataka?
16 In which weather phenomenon do warm and cold air collide?
17 For which 1938 film did Bette Davis win an Oscar?
18 In which constellation is the Boomerang, or Bow Tie nebula?
19 What is the name of Jersey's parliament?
20 Which 2015 film starred Tina Fey and Amy Poehler?

Answers to QUIZ 225 – Pot Luck

1 Ghana
2 Bobby Darin
3 Leeds
4 Pablo Neruda
5 The Fates
6 Lord Byron
7 A Saxon ship
8 Maxilla
9 Second
10 Pius
11 Jimmy Nail
12 Viscount
13 Five (Pentateuch)
14 German Bight
15 Semantics
16 Izmir
17 *Return to the Forbidden Planet*
18 Clint Eastwood
19 D-Notice
20 Oakham

QUIZ 228 – Pop Music

ANSWERS ON PAGE 230

1 Who played the bass guitar on Midge Ure's 1986 no.1 *If I Was*?

2 The Carpenters' hit *Calling Occupants of Interplanetary Craft* was originally recorded by which Canadian group?

3 What was the original name of singer Billy Ocean?

4 Which band backed Desmond Dekker?

5 *Attention* was a 2017 hit for which singer?

6 In which Irish county did Clannad form?

7 Who directed the Pet Shop Boys' video to *It's A Sin*?

8 What was the debut single by The Wanted?

9 In which year did Bono receive an honorary knighthood?

10 How is Adam Richard Wiles better known?

11 Which female singer featured on the Communards' 1986 hit *Don't Leave Me This Way*?

12 Pectoralz and Starfish are previous names for which band?

13 Which *Fame Academy* winner had a 2003 hit with *Maybe That's What it Takes*?

14 *Black Ice* was a 2008 album by which rock group?

15 Which country won the Eurovision Song Contest in 1985 with *Let It Swing*?

16 Who had her first UK no.1 single in 1997 with *All I Wanna Do*?

17 Ed Sheeran's *Castle on the Hill* was written about which town?

18 What was the name of Yazz's backing band on *The Only Way is Up*?

19 Who sang the 1960s hit *Catch the Wind*?

20 In which year did Beyoncé have a hit with *Halo*?

Answers to QUIZ 226 – Literature

1 Doris Lessing
2 Andrea Camilleri
3 *A Dance to the Music of Time*
4 Lord Byron
5 Circe
6 Dolly
7 Christopher Paolini
8 1818
9 *Ethan Frome*
10 Amiens
11 Ellie
12 Harold Acton
13 Franz Kafka
14 Erasmus
15 John Boynton
16 HG Wells
17 154
18 Calliope
19 Alain-Fournier
20 Jane Austen

QUIZ 229 – Pot Luck

ANSWERS ON PAGE 231

1 The tea clipper *Cutty Sark* was named after a character in which poem?
2 What type of weather is associated with cumulonimbus clouds?
3 Which lake forms the north-eastern border of Nigeria?
4 What is a sparable?
5 From which country does the Korat cat originate?
6 In which southern French town was the artist Toulouse-Lautrec born?
7 Which ancient Roman noblewoman was mother to emperor Tiberius?
8 What is the second highest peak in Scotland?
9 Which inflammable liquid is distilled from coal-tar?
10 Who topped the charts in 1976 with the song *No Charge*?
11 Which canal connects the North Sea with the Baltic Sea?
12 In which year was the first British Bank Holiday granted?
13 Which is the largest island of French Polynesia?
14 How is trinitrotoluene more commonly known?
15 Who wrote the novel *PS I Love You*, later filmed starring Hilary Swank?
16 What is a carbonnade?
17 In which 1990s US comedy-drama series did Adam Ant make a cameo appearance?
18 Which Toledo landmark was the scene of a Spanish Civil War siege?
19 How many symphonies did the composer Mahler complete?
20 Which Cambridge college was founded in 1441?

Answers to QUIZ 227 – Pot Luck

1 Conjuring tricks
2 Bertram
3 Manfred von Richthofen
4 Africa
5 Lucy Liu
6 Catherine Zeta-Jones
7 Khaki
8 Malin
9 1750s (1759)
10 Melissa
11 Agamemnon
12 Leonora
13 Middle Eastern
14 Mineral hardness
15 Bengaluru (or Bangalore)
16 Occluded front
17 *Jezebel*
18 Centaurus
19 States
20 *Sisters*

QUIZ 230 – History

ANSWERS ON PAGE 232

Easy

1 In which year was the National Trust founded?
2 What is the name of the ancient Roman province in what is now Romania?
3 Who was the last emperor of Russia?
4 Who was the botanist on Cook's 1768-71 expedition?
5 Which historic city was the old imperial capital of Vietnam?
6 Which Oxford college was founded in 1509?
7 Roland Berrill and Dr Lancelot Ware formed which society in 1946?
8 Who was crowned King of England as a result of the Battle of Towton?
9 Which ancient kingdom of Asia Minor, now Anatolia, had Sardis as its capital?
10 In which year did Hawaii become the 50th US state?

Medium

11 Of which country was Bernardo O'Higgins an independence leader?
12 Which seafood dish is named after the 11th month of the French revolutionary calendar?
13 Which Far Eastern former Portuguese colony was handed over to China in 1999?
14 Who ruled Scotland from 1124 to 1153?
15 Which Egyptian pharaoh was the father of Rameses II?
16 St Angela Merici founded which order of nuns at Brescia in 1535?
17 Which architect designed the Brighton Pavilion and Marble Arch?
18 Who was the king of Belgium from 1934 to 1951?
19 Which Roman emperor was Hadrian's predecessor?
20 China was ruled from 206 BC to AD 220 by which dynasty?

Hard

Answers to QUIZ 228 – Pop Music

1 Mark King
2 Klaatu
3 Leslie Charles
4 Aces
5 Charlie Puth
6 Donegal
7 Derek Jarman
8 *All Time Low*
9 2007
10 Calvin Harris
11 Sarah-Jane Morris
12 Coldplay
13 Alex Parks
14 AC/DC
15 Norway
16 Dannii Minogue
17 Framlingham
18 The Plastic Population
19 Donovan
20 2009

QUIZ 231 – Pot Luck

ANSWERS ON PAGE 233

1 Which orchestral instrument is descended from the shawm?

2 What does an irenologist study?

3 A zucchetto is an ecclesiastical skullcap named after which vegetable?

4 What term describes marine life that lives on the sea bed?

5 Battle Creek, Michigan houses the headquarters of which US company?

6 What was the name of the garden in Athens where Aristotle taught philosophy?

7 What is the currency unit of Panama?

8 *Zombie* was a 2014 hit for which singer/songwriter?

9 In which year did London's Tower Bridge come into operation?

10 Who wrote *The Swiss Family Robinson*?

11 What is the capital of Tatarstan, part of Russia?

12 Which two scientists confirmed the role of DNA in inheritance in 1952?

13 In which indoor game can the opposing player be forced to be "in zugzwang"?

14 Who wrote *The Beggar's Opera* (1728)?

15 In which Staffordshire town was Samuel Johnson born in 1709?

16 In which city is the Potala Palace?

17 Who wrote the satirical play *Volpone*?

18 What is the last book of the Old Testament?

19 Where would you find a frog on a horse?

20 Which mountain range is located at the meeting point of Russia, China, Mongolia and Kazakhstan?

Easy

Medium

Hard

Answers to QUIZ 229 – Pot Luck

1 *Tam O'Shanter*
2 Thunderstorms
3 Chad
4 Headless nail
5 Thailand
6 Albi
7 Livia
8 Ben Macdui
9 Naphtha
10 JJ Barrie
11 Kiel
12 1871
13 Tahiti
14 TNT
15 Cecelia Ahern
16 Beef stew
17 *Northern Exposure*
18 Alcázar
19 Nine
20 King's

QUIZ 232 – Science

ANSWERS ON PAGE 234

Easy

1 Which is the brightest star in the constellation Aquila?
2 What does a lithologist study?
3 In 1995 Eileen Collins became the first woman to pilot which vehicle?
4 Which part of the body is affected by Addison's disease?
5 *Sciurus vulgaris* is the Latin name for which animal?
6 Which gas used in welding is produced from calcium carbide and water?
7 What Greek letter is the scientific symbol for wavelength?
8 How many joules are there in a calorie?
9 What is the common name for the disease variola?
10 What is the second stomach of a ruminant called?

Medium

11 What term is given to an abnormally slow heart rate?
12 At which Italian university was Galileo the chair of mathematics from 1592 to 1610?
13 Which is the middle of the eye's three layers?
14 What element has the atomic number 12?
15 "Parsec" is a measurement used in which branch of science?
16 What bodily tissue is composed of cells called chondrocytes?
17 X-rays were discovered by which German physicist?
18 Which institution published Sir Isaac Newton's *Principia* in 1687?
19 What are "KW Sagittarii" and "KY Cygni"?
20 What does the body lack in the condition hypoxia?

Hard

Answers to QUIZ 230 – History

1 1895
2 Dacia
3 Nicholas II
4 Sir Joseph Banks
5 Hué
6 Brasenose
7 Mensa
8 Edward IV
9 Lydia
10 1959
11 Chile
12 Lobster Thermidor
13 Macao (or Macau)
14 David I
15 Seti I
16 Ursulines
17 John Nash
18 Leopold III
19 Trajan
20 Han

QUIZ 233 – Pot Luck

ANSWERS ON PAGE 235

1 What is the branch of philosophy that deals with the nature of being?

2 Who invented the pendulum clock?

3 The Darién Gap interrupts which road?

4 To what does the word "margaric" relate?

5 Which group released a 1979 album entitled *Spirits Having Flown*?

6 "Apple of Grenada" is an old name for which fruit?

7 Which early computer language was named after a French mathematician?

8 Who wrote the 2003 book *The Lunar Men*?

9 Who directed the 1981 film *Gallipoli*?

10 Who was world chess champion from 1975 to 1985?

11 Glen Prosen, Schönemann and Cascade Delight are varieties of which fruit?

12 Haddington Hill is the highest point in Buckinghamshire of which range of hills?

13 Which philosopher wrote the *Discourse on Method* in 1637?

14 What is the state flower of New York?

15 Which capital city is situated on the Chao Phraya River?

16 What is dupion?

17 Which British 10,000m runner competed at every Summer Olympics from 2000 to 2016?

18 Hector Hugh Munro wrote under what pseudonym?

19 What are Bernard Silver and Norman Woodland credited with inventing?

20 What is the standard monetary unit of Malaysia?

Answers to QUIZ 231 – Pot Luck

1 Oboe
2 Peace
3 Small gourd
4 Benthic
5 Kellogg's
6 Lyceum
7 Balboa
8 Jamie T
9 1894
10 Johann Wyss
11 Kazan
12 Alfred Hershey and Martha Chase
13 Chess
14 John Gay
15 Lichfield
16 Lhasa
17 Ben Jonson
18 Malachi
19 On the sole of its hoof
20 Altai Mountains

QUIZ 234 – Flags

ANSWERS ON PAGE 236

Easy

1 Which African nation's flag features two tribal spears, a staff and a shield?
2 Which Caribbean country's flag has a parrot as its centrepiece?
3 Which country's flag contains 13 horizontal stripes?
4 Which two countries' flags feature a depiction of yin and yang?
5 How many flags feature a single colour background with a flat circle of colour?
6 On which country's flag is there a map of itself?
7 Which country's flag features three green diamonds as its centrepiece?

Medium

8 What term is given to someone who studies flags?
9 Which country's flag is known as "the Flag of the Five Escutcheons"?
10 "The Sun and Stripes" is the nickname of which country's flag?
11 Which country's flag features a coat of arms containing a golden eagle devouring a rattle snake?
12 The largest religious monument in the world is depicted on the flag of which country?
13 On which country's flag would you find a Raggiana bird-of-paradise?
14 Which country's flag is known as "the Broken Trident"?
15 Which South American country's flag carries its national motto in full?
16 How many flags feature the Union Jack?
17 Which is the only country not to have a quadrilateral flag?

Hard

18 The flags of which two South American countries feature "the Sun of May"?
19 Which African country's flag is light blue with a central white star?
20 Which country's flag was a single colour between 1977 and 2011?

Answers to QUIZ 232 – Science

1 Altair
2 Rocks
3 Space shuttle
4 Adrenal glands
5 Red squirrel
6 Acetylene
7 Lambda
8 4184
9 Smallpox
10 Reticulum
11 Bradycardia
12 Padua
13 Uvea
14 Magnesium
15 Astronomy
16 Cartilage
17 Wilhelm Röntgen
18 The Royal Society
19 Stars (supergiants)
20 Oxygen

ANSWERS ON PAGE 237

1 What is the number of Shakespeare's sonnet that begins "Shall I compare thee to a summer's day?"?

2 Iqique and Cuzco are cities on which of the world's continents?

3 What is the county town of Ireland's County Kildare?

4 *Cyanistes caeruleus* is the Latin name for which common garden bird?

5 In mythology, what is the collective name for Clotho, Lachesis and Atropos?

6 Which Christian festival is held on August 6?

7 Achluophobia is a fear of what?

8 Who wrote *The Ballad of Peckham Rye*?

9 Which jockey won the Prix de l'Arc de Triomphe in three successive years, from 1996 to 1998?

10 Sir Robert Peel was born in which Greater Manchester town?

11 In 1294, Celestine V was the first pope to do what?

12 In what make of plane did Alcock and Brown make their historic flight across the Atlantic?

13 Macquarie Harbour is in which Australian state?

14 Who was Aaron's sister in the Old Testament?

15 How is American singer Peter Hernandez better known?

16 Which former coal-mining town is the administrative centre of Blaenau Gwent?

17 What word describes a chemical reaction that releases energy?

18 In which area of the arts was Rudolf Laban famous?

19 What is another name for the areca palm seed?

20 Which striped animal is native to the Democratic Republic of the Congo?

Easy

Medium

Hard

Answers to QUIZ 233 – Pot Luck

1 Ontology
2 Christiaan Huygens
3 Pan-American Highway
4 Pearl
5 Bee Gees
6 Pomegranate
7 Pascal
8 Jenny Uglow
9 Peter Weir
10 Anatoly Karpov
11 Raspberry
12 Chilterns
13 René Descartes
14 Rose
15 Bangkok
16 Silk fabric
17 Jo Pavey
18 Saki
19 Barcode
20 Ringgit

QUIZ 236 – Sailing

ANSWERS ON PAGE 238

Easy

1 In marine terms, what does RIB stand for?

2 Who was the first man to sail solo around the world…?

3 …and who was the first man to sail solo around the world non-stop?

4 Who captained *HMS Beagle* during Charles Darwin's first expedition voyage to the South Americas?

5 What was the name of the UK's first nuclear submarine?

6 How many standard miles are in a nautical mile?

7 What is the highest rank in the Royal Navy?

8 What flag is used to recall all personnel to a ship that is about to go to sea?

9 What are the ropes and lines that support a ship's mast called?

10 Following the 2016 Games, which country had won the most Olympic gold medals for sailing since the sport was introduced?

Medium

11 Where did Captain James Cook meet his death?

12 Sir Ernest Shackleton travelled on which ship during his 1908 Antarctic expedition?

13 What is the name of the knot used to form a fixed eye at the end of a rope?

14 What was the name of the UK's first aircraft carrier?

15 Who was the captain of the *Titanic*?

16 What is the upper edge of the hull, or top timber on the rail round the outer edge of the deck known as?

17 What is a windlass?

18 Who was the first woman to sail solo, non-stop and unassisted around the world?

Hard

19 In which year was the wreck of Henry VIII's flagship the *Mary Rose* raised?

20 The 470 and 49er are classes in which Olympic sailing category?

Answers to QUIZ 234 – Flags

1 Eswatini (or Swaziland)
2 Dominica
3 United States
4 Mongolia & South Korea
5 Three (Bangladesh, Japan and Palau)
6 Cyprus
7 St Vincent and the Grenadines
8 Vexillologist
9 Portugal
10 Uruguay
11 Mexico
12 Cambodia (Angkor Wat)
13 Papua New Guinea
14 Barbados
15 Brazil (*Ordem e Progresso*)
16 Five (Australia, Fiji, New Zealand, Tuvalu and UK)
17 Nepal
18 Argentina and Uruguay
19 Somalia
20 Libya (green)

QUIZ 237 – Pot Luck

ANSWERS ON PAGE 239

1 What is the name of the Hindu goddess who is the destroyer of evil forces?

2 What term is given to the statistical and sociological study of elections?

3 *Hernando's Hideaway* is a song from which musical?

4 What term is given to the oldest geological era?

5 In which branch of science did Benjamin Thompson, Count Rumford, specialise?

6 Which Old Testament book follows Ezekiel?

7 Where was the US Open golf tournament played in 2017?

8 Which tree has the Latin name *Prunus spinosa*?

9 Who wrote the 1889 book *Darwinism: An Exposition of the Theory of Natural Selection, with Some of its Applications*?

10 In which building is the Society of Antiquaries of London based?

11 *Fallen Empires* is a 2011 album by which band?

12 What name was given to the policy of non-violent resistance adopted by Mahatma Ghandi?

13 On which Caribbean island is the city of Cienfuegos?

14 Which taxonomic classification is immediately below "kingdom"?

15 With whom did Émile Gagnan invent the aqualung?

16 In which country is the Alqueva Dam?

17 Which UK ship, along with the *USS Niagara*, laid the first transatlantic cable in 1858?

18 From what is the caulking material oakum made?

19 What term is given to a round prison in which all cells are visible from the centre point?

20 What is the most northerly point of mainland Britain?

Easy Medium Hard

Answers to QUIZ 235 – Pot Luck

1 18
2 South America
3 Naas
4 Blue tit
5 The Fates
6 Transfiguration
7 Darkness
8 Dame Muriel Spark
9 Olivier Peslier
10 Bury
11 Abdicate or resign
12 Vickers Vimy
13 Tasmania
14 Miriam
15 Bruno Mars
16 Ebbw Vale
17 Exothermic
18 Dance
19 Betel nut
20 Okapi

QUIZ 238 – Film

ANSWERS ON PAGE 240

1 Which Henry Fonda 1946 western takes its name from a folk song of the gold rush?

2 In which 2016 film does Jeff Bridges play a Texas Ranger trying to solve a string of bank robberies?

3 What was the name of James Dean's character in the 1955 film *East of Eden*?

4 The 2015 film *Focus* starred which actor as Nicky?

5 Which 1972 Hitchcock film is set in and around London's Covent Garden?

6 Who played the title character in the 1980 film *Flash Gordon*?

7 In the 2010 film *How to Train Your Dragon*, what is the name of the dragon befriended by Hiccup?

8 Who won the Best Actress Oscar for the 1994 film *Blue Sky*?

9 What was Marilyn Monroe's last film?

10 Who stars as Tris Prior in the *Divergent* series of films?

11 What was the name of Billy Zane's character in the 1997 film *Titanic*?

12 The 2007 film *There Will Be Blood* is based on which Upton Sinclair novel?

13 What is the name of the human-controlled underground city in the *Matrix* films?

14 For which film did Sally Field win her first Best Actress Oscar?

15 Which actress played the title role in the 2014 film *Effie Gray*?

16 Which famous scream was believed to have been used for the first time in the 1951 film *Distant Drums*?

17 *I Got Rhythm* and *'S Wonderful* are songs from which 1951 musical film?

18 Which 1988 film received four Oscars including Best Picture?

19 In the 2003 film *Love, Actually*, which actor played the US President?

20 Which 1982 Steve Martin film was in black and white and included scenes from classic films?

Answers to QUIZ 236 – Sailing

1 Rigid-hulled Inflatable boat
2 Joshua Slocum (1895-98)
3 Sir Robin Knox-Johnston
4 Robert Fitzroy
5 *Dreadnought*
6 1.1508 miles
7 Admiral of the Fleet
8 Blue Peter
9 Shrouds
10 Great Britain
11 Hawaii
12 *Nimrod*
13 Bowline
14 *Ark Royal* (1955)
15 Edward John Smith
16 Gunwale
17 A winch used to raise heavy weights on board
18 Kay Cottee (1988)
19 1982
20 Dinghy

1 Which German city of the Ruhr is the site of the Krupp steelworks?

2 Who wrote the tale *Jack the Dullard*?

3 Which indigenous people of Borneo were once called "Sea Dayaks"?

4 Which theory explains the universe in terms of force or energy?

5 In Greek myth, who was the lover of Hippolytus?

6 Which figure of the French Revolution was assassinated in his bathtub by Charlotte Corday?

7 Who wrote the 1773 play *The Barber of Seville*?

8 From which country does the ornamental box called an "inro" originate?

9 In the TV series *Friends*, what was the name of Joey's agent?

10 Which is the only Central American country with English as an official language?

11 Which knitting technique shares its name with a medieval style of marquetry?

12 Daikon is a variety of which vegetable?

13 Who directed the 1954 film *On the Waterfront*?

14 Which monastic peninsula of northern Greece forbids entry to women?

15 What is the main island and capital of the Maldives?

16 Of what sort of unaccompanied part-songs were Gabrieli, Monteverdi and Palestrina among the classic composers?

17 What is schalstein?

18 Who was crowned King of Scotland on March 25, 1306?

19 Which large grey Australian crane is the emblem of Queensland?

20 What is the surname of Sir Jacob, the British sculptor whose piece *Rima* is displayed in Hyde Park?

Easy Medium Hard

Answers to QUIZ 237 – Pot Luck

1 Kali
2 Psephology
3 *The Pajama Game*
4 Pre-Cambrian
5 Physics
6 Daniel
7 Erin Hills, Wisconsin
8 Blackthorn
9 Alfred Russell Wallace
10 Burlington House
11 Snow Patrol
12 Satyagraha
13 Cuba
14 Phylum
15 Jacques Cousteau
16 Portugal
17 *HMS Agamemnon*
18 Rope
19 Panopticon
20 Dunnet Head

QUIZ 240 – Birds

ANSWERS ON PAGE 242

Easy

1 How many toes does a rhea have on each foot?

2 Which bird is the national bird of the Bahamas?

3 *Erithacus rubecula* is the Latin name for which European garden bird?

4 A tercel is a male of what type of bird?

5 "Mother Carey's Chicken" is an old name for which bird?

6 Which bird was reintroduced to Scotland's Black Isle in the late 1980s and early 1990s?

7 Wood grouse is an alternative name for which bird?

8 Which bird of prey has the Latin name *Bubo bubo*?

9 Gentoo and macaroni are species of which bird?

10 Which British summer visitor of the rail family is famously secretive, often only located by its distinctive rasping call?

Medium

11 What colour eggs do dunnocks lay?

12 In which decade was the collared dove introduced to Britain?

13 The call of the yellowhammer is often described as resembling which phrase?

14 Which bird of the finch family has a distinctive beak used to extract seeds from conifer cones?

15 Which bird sanctuary off the coast of North Berwick is home to thousands of seabirds?

16 Which family of birds have earned the nickname "butcher bird" due to their habit of storing prey on thorns or barbed wire?

17 What name is given to the tail of a peacock?

18 The condor is a member of which family?

Hard

19 What name is given to a puffin chick?

20 Where does a goldeneye duck build its nest?

Answers to QUIZ 238 – Film

1 *My Darling Clementine*
2 *Hell or High Water*
3 Cal (Caleb Trask)
4 Will Smith
5 *Frenzy*
6 Sam J Jones
7 Toothless
8 Jessica Lange
9 *The Misfits*
10 Shailene Woodley
11 Cal Hockley
12 *Oil!*
13 Zion
14 *Norma Rae* (1979)
15 Dakota Fanning
16 The "Wilhelm Scream"
17 *An American in Paris*
18 *Rain Man*
19 Billy Bob Thornton
20 *Dead Men Don't Wear Plaid*

QUIZ 241 – Pot Luck

ANSWERS ON PAGE 243

1 What was the name of the Australian Prime Minister who mysteriously vanished in 1967?

2 A "Lett" was a former name of a citizen of which country?

3 What is the title of the 1864 poem by Alfred, Lord Tennyson about a fisherman turned merchant sailor?

4 By what name is singer Michael Barratt (b.1948) better known?

5 An indri is a species of which animal?

6 Who was the first aviator to fly over the South Pole?

7 Who featured on Ariana Grande's top 10 hit *Side to Side*?

8 Which river runs through St Petersburg?

9 *The Outsider* and *The Plague* are 1940s novels by which French writer?

10 What is a fichu?

11 Who played the title role in the 1960s TV series *I Dream of Jeannie*?

12 In which country is the Amboseli National Park?

13 Which communication precipitated the Franco-Prussian War in 1870?

14 What does "Caer" mean in a Welsh place name?

15 Which football team won the FIFA World Cup in 1934?

16 *Extreme Ways*, used as a theme in the *Bourne* films, is by which musician?

17 Which term describes a species of plant that has its male and female reproductive organs on separate plants?

18 *The River Fragments* are musings by which ancient philosopher?

19 Which British airport was originally known as Abbotsinch?

20 Which cathedral has the longest uninterrupted vaulted ceiling in England?

Answers to QUIZ 239 – Pot Luck

1 Essen
2 Hans Christian Andersen
3 Iban
4 Dynamism
5 Phaedra
6 Jean-Paul Marat
7 Pierre Beaumarchais
8 Japan
9 Estelle
10 Belize
11 Intarsia
12 Radish
13 Elia Kazan
14 Athos
15 Malé
16 Madrigals
17 Metamorphic rock
18 Robert the Bruce
19 Brolga
20 Epstein

QUIZ 242 – Sport

Easy

1 Which rugby Premiership team play their home games at Kingsholm?
2 What was the name of the winning horse in the 2016 Epsom Derby?
3 Where did the Tour de France start in 2017?
4 Battledore was a forerunner of which indoor sport?
5 Who won the PDC World Darts Championship in 2015 and 2016?
6 How high is a basketball hoop from the ground?
7 Who was the inaugural Formula E champion?
8 In which year were medals first presented at the Olympic Games?
9 What is the German term for cross-country skiing?
10 In which sport do teams compete for the Stanley Cup trophy?

Medium

11 Which retired snooker player appeared at Glastonbury in 2016 as a DJ?
12 Which golfer won the 2003 Open in his first appearance in a major championship?
13 In 1962, who became World Heavyweight Boxing champion on beating Floyd Patterson?
14 Who won the Golden Boot at the 2006 FIFA World Cup?
15 Which TV presenter represented Wales at the 1990 Commonwealth Games in gymnastics?
16 Which area of London was home to England's first golf and hockey clubs and the oldest rugby club?
17 In which winter sport is Evgeni Plushenko a former World and Olympic champion?
18 In which event did Anita Wlodarczyk win Olympic gold medals in 2012 and 2016?
19 Who was the first player to reach 10,000 test runs?

Hard

20 Who formally started the 2018 London Marathon?

Answers to QUIZ 240 – Birds

1 Three
2 Flamingo
3 Robin
4 Hawk
5 Storm petrel
6 Red kite
7 Capercaillie
8 Eagle owl
9 Penguin
10 Corncrake
11 Greenish-blue
12 1950s
13 "A little bit of bread and no cheese"
14 Crossbill
15 Bass Rock
16 Shrikes
17 Train
18 Vultures
19 Puffling
20 In a tree

QUIZ 243 – Pot Luck

ANSWERS ON PAGE 245

1 Who was the father of David in the Old Testament?

2 Which rare bear is native to British Columbia?

3 In 1982, which was the 500th single to top the UK charts?

4 Alf Wight was the real name of which English writer?

5 What other name is given to the white poplar tree?

6 The kinetoscope was an early form of which device?

7 Who was appointed Director of the Royal Ballet in July 2012?

8 People named in the Griffin Book are barred from entering what type of establishment?

9 Which Scottish engineer improved the condensation process of the steam engine designed by Thomas Newcomen?

10 In which decade was Harrow public school founded?

11 Which artist wrote the 1979 quest book *Masquerade*?

12 On which Greek island was Odysseus said to have been born?

13 Which actor starred in the title role in the 2016 remake of *Ben-Hur*?

14 What word describes a thermodynamic reaction that takes place without loss of heat or cold?

15 Who was the Austrian composer of *Lulu* (1935)?

16 What name is given to a person who cuts, polishes and engraves stones, especially precious stones?

17 The Palaeogene period occurred during which geological era?

18 What is notable about a sentence described as "sesquipedalian"?

19 In which Kent country house was Vita Sackville-West born in 1892?

20 Who was the founder of the Christian Science movement?

Answers to QUIZ 241 – Pot Luck

1 Harold Holt
2 Latvia
3 *Enoch Arden*
4 Shakin' Stevens
5 Lemur
6 Richard Byrd (in 1929)
7 Nicki Minaj
8 Neva
9 Albert Camus
10 Shawl
11 Barbara Eden
12 Kenya
13 Ems Telegram
14 Fort
15 Italy
16 Moby
17 Dioecious
18 Heraclitus
19 Glasgow
20 Exeter

QUIZ 244 – John

ANSWERS ON PAGE 246

Easy

1 In which US state is John Wayne Airport?

2 Who wrote the 2005 book *Marley & Me*?

3 Who played John Ross Ewing in the 2012 version of *Dallas*?

4 1960s singer Johnny Kidd was backed by which group?

5 Which Venetian explorer discovered Newfoundland?

6 Sir John Chilcot conducted a seven-year enquiry into which event, the results of which were published in 2016?

7 Which 1924 tale of the building of a railroad was John Ford's first full-scale western?

8 Who wrote the 1995 book *Longitude* about clockmaker John Harrison?

9 The character of John Doggett appeared in which TV series?

10 Which old county town lies sixteen miles south of John o' Groats?

Medium

11 Poet John Donne (b.1572) became dean at which building in 1621?

12 Who directed the 1999 film *Being John Malkovich*?

13 What was the real name of the Oliver Twist character known as "the Artful Dodger"?

14 Who played the title role in the 2014 film *John Wick* and its 2017 sequel?

15 John Ridd is the central male character in which 1869 novel?

16 With which player did John McEnroe win over 50 men's doubles titles, including four Wimbledon and three US Open titles?

17 What was the first name of John Nettles' character in the TV series *The Liver Birds*?

18 John Travolta starred in which 2007 biker film?

Hard

19 What title did John Prescott adopt when he took his seat in the House of Lords?

20 John of Gaunt (b.1340) was the son of which English king?

Answers to QUIZ 242 – Sport

1 Gloucester
2 Harzand
3 Dösseldorf
4 Badminton
5 Gary Anderson
6 Ten feet
7 Nelson Piquet Jr
8 1904 (St Louis Olympics)
9 *Langlauf*
10 Ice hockey
11 Steve Davis
12 Ben Curtis
13 Sonny Liston
14 Miroslav Klose
15 Gabby Logan
16 Blackheath
17 Figure skating
18 Hammer
19 Sunil Gavaskar
20 Queen Elizabeth II

QUIZ 245 – Pot Luck

ANSWERS ON PAGE 247

1 Who played Marcus in the 2002 film *About a Boy*?
2 In the Old Testament, who was Methuselah's father?
3 Which Keats poem begins: "A thing of beauty is a joy forever"?
4 In which country is the city of Eger, famed for its castle and wines?
5 What vitamin-rich tropical fruit is also known as Barbados cherry and seriz?
6 What was the real surname of singer Marc Bolan?
7 What is the capital city of Mozambique?
8 In the TV series *The Wire*, who played Detective Lester Freamon?
9 Who wrote the song *Feeling Good*, famously covered by Michael Bublé?
10 Who wrote *Goodbye, Mr Chips* (1934)?
11 Which Greek character was punished by constant thirst?
12 A friand is what type of food?
13 Who released the 2017 album entitled *Piano Portraits*?
14 What part of Malaysia was known as Prince of Wales Island until 1867?
15 Iran ruled which sheikhdom from 1602 to 1783?
16 Who starred as Tilly Dunnage in the 2015 film *The Dressmaker*?
17 Which tennis player won the World ATP finals in November 2017 in his first appearance in the competition?
18 In heraldry, what type of symbol is a pheon?
19 In what does a mercer deal?
20 What was Arthur Wynne credited with inventing in 1913?

Answers to QUIZ 243 – Pot Luck

1 Jesse
2 Kermode bear
3 *A Little Peace* (Nicole)
4 James Herriot
5 Abele
6 Film camera
7 Kevin O'Hare
8 Casinos
9 James Watt
10 1570s (1571)
11 Kit Williams
12 Ithaca
13 Jack Huston
14 Adiabatic
15 Alban Berg
16 Lapidary
17 Cenozoic
18 It uses long words
19 Knole
20 Mary Baker Eddy

QUIZ 246 – Television

Easy

1 Which actor played Arnold Vinick in *The West Wing*?

2 Who won *The X Factor* in 2014?

3 Which broadcaster and writer appeared in the first *Celebrity MasterChef* in 2006, losing in the final to Matt Dawson?

4 In the 1990s sitcom *The Upper Hand*, who played Charlie Burrows?

5 Who created the drama series *Cold Feet*?

6 Which English actress played Margaery Tyrell in *Game of Thrones*?

7 Joseph Fiennes starred as FBI agent Mark Benford in which sci-fi TV series of 2009-10?

8 Whom did Michael Dorn play in *Star Trek: The Next Generation*?

9 The first panel on which musical programme included Alma Cogan and Susan Stranks?

Medium

10 Billy Crystal played which character in *Soap*?

11 Who began her acting career as Flick Scully in *Neighbours*?

12 Which TV family in the 1960s and 70s lived at 518 Crestview Drive, Beverly Hills?

13 What was the name of *The A-Team* character nicknamed BA?

14 In *Camberwick Green*, what was the name of the baker?

15 Who won the first series of *Fame Academy* and topped the charts with *Stop Living The Lie*?

16 Which 1989-95 series featured Dr Sheila Sabatini and Dr Jonathan Haslam?

17 How is cartoon character Dr. Robert Underdunk Terwilliger Jr better known?

18 What was the name of Penelope Pitstop's car in *Wacky Races*?

Hard

19 Who played Caroline Fairchild in the 1980s comedy series *Executive Stress*?

20 In 2016 which TV presenter and comedian released an album entitled *Upon a Different Shore*?

Answers to QUIZ 244 – John

1 California
2 John Grogan
3 Josh Henderson
4 The Pirates
5 John Cabot
6 The Iraq War
7 *The Iron Horse*
8 Dava Sobel
9 *The X-Files*
10 Wick
11 St Paul's Cathedral
12 Spike Jonze
13 "Jack" (John) Dawkins
14 Keanu Reeves
15 *Lorna Doone*
16 Peter Fleming
17 Paul
18 *Wild Hogs*
19 Baron Prescott of Kingston-upon-Hull
20 Edward III

QUIZ 247 – Pot Luck

ANSWERS ON PAGE 249

1 What was the name of the last King of Italy?

2 In 1994, *Second Coming* was the second album by which band?

3 What is the meaning of "cupidity"?

4 Which north-east Indian state has Patna as its capital?

5 Who was the second person to run a mile in under four minutes?

6 How are Rose McDowall and Jill Bryson known musically?

7 In which African country is the Dallol volcano?

8 What famous landmark can be seen at Lake Havasu in Arizona?

9 In mythology, which princess was rescued from a sea-monster by Perseus?

10 Which Scottish football team plays at Gayfield Park?

11 *"Nullius in verba"* is the motto of which institution?

12 Which city was founded by Pizarro in 1535?

13 Who directed the 1944 film *Arsenic and Old Lace*?

14 On which 1995 hit did Michael Jackson duet with his sister Janet?

15 Who wrote the *Doctor Dolittle* novels?

16 The liqueur prunelle originates from which country?

17 Which Roman philosopher and dramatist died in AD 65?

18 What chemical compound is the base of common alcohol?

19 Traps and skeets are involved in which sport?

20 Which is the "Gem State" of the USA?

Answers to QUIZ 245 – Pot Luck

1 Nicholas Hoult
2 Enoch
3 *Endymion*
4 Hungary
5 Acerola
6 Feld
7 Maputo
8 Clarke Peters
9 Anthony Newley and Leslie Bricusse
10 James Hilton
11 Tantalus
12 A small (almond) cake
13 Rick Wakeman
14 Pinang
15 Bahrain
16 Kate Winslet
17 Grigor Dimitrov
18 Arrow
19 Fabric and cloth
20 The first modern crossword

QUIZ 248 – World Politics

ANSWERS ON PAGE 250

1 Who was the first Prime Minister of Australia?
2 On what day does Brazil celebrate its Independence Day?
3 What is the official residence of the French Prime Minister?
4 Jacinda Ardern was elected prime minister of which country in October 2017?
5 Who was Hillary Clinton's running mate in the 2016 US presidential election?
6 In 1982, who succeeded Leonid Brezhnev as leader of the USSR?
7 Who was the Vice-President of the United States from 1969 to 1973?
8 Former Israeli prime ministers Olmert and Barak share which first name?
9 Who was Foreign Secretary in the 1945-51 Labour government?
10 How is the Naval Support Facility Thurmont in Maryland better known?
11 Which Russian leader had the nickname "Koba"?
12 Who founded the Fianna Fáil political party in the Republic of Ireland?
13 Which was the first country to give women the vote?
14 Iceland is generally considered to have the world's oldest parliament, dating from what year?
15 What is the name of the official Canberra home of Australia's Prime Minister?
16 In 1864, which two states went to war with Denmark?
17 What name is used for the lower chamber of the Russian parliament?
18 Who was US president from 1909 to 1913?
19 In which year was Germany first unified?
20 Shinzō Abe became Prime Minister of which country in 2012?

Answers to QUIZ 246 – Television

1 Alan Alda
2 Ben Haenow
3 Hardeep Singh Kohli
4 Joe McGann
5 Mike Bullen
6 Natalie Dormer
7 *FlashForward*
8 Worf
9 *Juke Box Jury*
10 Jodie Dallas
11 Holly Valance
12 The Clampetts (*Beverly Hillbillies*)
13 Bosco Baracus
14 Mickey Murphy
15 David Sneddon
16 *Surgical Spirit*
17 Sideshow Bob (in *The Simpsons*)
18 The Compact Pussycat
19 Dame Penelope Keith
20 Alexander Armstrong

QUIZ 249 – Pot Luck

ANSWERS ON PAGE 1

1 Of which small West African country is Lomé the capital?
2 In which year was tennis originally introduced as an Olympic sport?
3 Which French composer wrote *Daphnis et Chloë* (1912)?
4 Which is the longest river that is entirely in Switzerland?
5 The album *Roll With the Punches* was released in 2017 by which musician?
6 Which Tudor house in Derbyshire is referred to in a rhyme as "more glass than wall"?
7 What is measured by the gray SI unit?
8 Who was the Prime Minister of the UK from 1902 to 1905?
9 *Can't Feel My Face* was a 2015 hit for which band?
10 Who is the Roman god of the underworld?
11 *The Adventures of Roderick Random* (1748) was a novel by which author?
12 Which geological period followed the Jurassic Period?
13 Sheffield takes its name from which river?
14 Which Spanish region was united with Castile in 1479?
15 The *Cassini* probe explored which planet?
16 Which Old Testament book follows Joel?
17 What is the currency unit of Paraguay?
18 Which philosopher wrote *The Social Contract* in 1762?
19 In the sitcom *Waiting for God*, what was the name of the retirement home?
20 What is the name of Iago's wife in Shakespeare's *Othello*?

Answers to QUIZ 247 – Pot Luck

1 Umberto II
2 The Stone Roses
3 Greed
4 Bihar
5 John Landy
6 Strawberry Switchblade
7 Ethiopia
8 London Bridge
9 Andromeda
10 Arbroath
11 The Royal Society
12 Lima
13 Frank Capra
14 *Scream*
15 Hugh Lofting
16 France
17 Seneca
18 Ethyl
19 Clay pigeon shooting
20 Idaho

ANSWERS ON PAGE 2

QUIZ 250 – Europe

Easy

1 The German state of Rhineland-Palatinate has which city as its capital?

2 Which French-speaking Belgian city is known as Luik in Flemish?

3 Which lake near Naples was said by Virgil to be the entrance to the underworld?

4 Almada is a city in which country?

5 Between 1278 and 1993, which state was governed by the French head of state and the Spanish Bishop of Urgell?

6 *Ha en bra dag*! is Swedish for which common phrase?

7 In which European city could you visit the royal palace of Belvedere?

8 What is the chief town of County Clare?

9 In which country do 100 stotinki make up one lev?

10 Which avenue runs east from the Brandenburg Gate?

Medium

11 Until the French Revolution, which city in Provence was Papal property?

12 Which shipping forecast area, taking its name from a Norwegian island, abuts the Norwegian Sea?

13 Keflavik Airport is in which country?

14 In 1996, which Venice opera house was destroyed by fire?

15 Which Irish river flows into the Atlantic near Waterford?

16 Which Roman historian wrote a history of Rome entitled *Ab Urbe Condita*?

17 In which European capital city is the Jablonowski Palace?

18 Which channel separates Sicily from Italy?

19 In which year was the first European Cup Final played?

Hard

20 Who wrote the 1879 book *Travels with a Donkey in the Cévennes*, following a tour of Europe?

Answers to QUIZ 248 – World Politics

1 Edmund Barton
2 September 7
3 Hôtel Matignon
4 New Zealand
5 Tim Kaine
6 Yuri Andropov
7 Spiro Agnew
8 Ehud
9 Ernest Bevin
10 Camp David
11 Joseph Stalin
12 Éamon de Valera
13 New Zealand (1893)
14 930
15 The Lodge
16 Austria and Prussia
17 Duma
18 William Taft
19 1871
20 Japan

QUIZ 251 – Pot Luck

ANSWERS ON PAGE 253

1 In which 2015 film does Tom Hardy play both Ronnie and Reggie Kray?
2 Which US state has Baton Rouge as its capital?
3 The Aswan Dam was originally built in 1902 to control the flood of which river?
4 Which French philosopher is famous for his remark, "I think, therefore I am"?
5 The 1964 comedy film *A Shot in the Dark* featured which fictional inspector?
6 Laxey on the Isle of Man is famous for which large industrial structure?
7 Which country disappeared when the Berlin Wall came down?
8 *The Cat in the Hat* (1957) was written by which American author?
9 Which TV crime-fighting duo's first names were Christine and Mary Beth?
10 What is the mark signifying the soft pronunciation of the letter "c" in French?
11 Anne Sullivan first became teacher to which famous pupil in 1887?
12 Which sense is related to the olfactory organs?
13 What is the name of Winnie-the-Pooh's donkey friend?
14 In Washington DC, what does the "DC" stand for?
15 *Up the Junction* was a 1979 hit for which group?
16 What name is given to the assembly of cardinals for the election of a pope?
17 Which river flows through Leeds?
18 A caber-tossing competition would appear at what type of event?
19 Which is the USA's 49th state?
20 What name is given to a male honey-bee?

Easy

Medium

Hard

Answers to QUIZ 499 – Pot Luck

1 Darrin and Samantha Stevens (*Bewitched*)
2 Tyramine
3 *Scenes from Childhood*
4 Goombay Dance Band
5 USA
6 Quarks
7 Manfred Mann
8 Burghley House
9 Zebra
10 Sir Arthur Quiller-Couch
11 RKO
12 Margery Allingham
13 The Seekers
14 Draco
15 Silvery white
16 Pat Eddery
17 Kate Mara
18 Wayne Fontana
19 Harrow
20 John Fowles

Easy

1 What type of creature is Beatrix Potter's Jeremy Fisher?

2 What is the name of the gentleman who accepts the wager in *Around the World in Eighty Days* (1873)?

3 Who wrote the 1993 book *Bravo Two Zero*?

4 Inspector Rebus was created by which writer?

5 Who was appointed Poet Laureate in 2009?

6 Which vegetable disturbs the sleep of the princess in the Hans Christian Andersen tale?

7 Who wrote *The Murders in the Rue Morgue* (1841)?

8 In *The Jungle Book* by Rudyard Kipling, what sort of animal is Shere Khan?

9 How much are the Bells of St Martins owed in the rhyme *Oranges and Lemons*?

10 Who wrote the 1859 novel *A Tale of Two Cities*?

Medium

11 The characters of Lisbeth Salander and Mikael Blomkvist were created by which author?

12 Which fictional detective was supposedly killed at Reichenbach Falls in Switzerland?

13 Who wrote *To Kill a Mockingbird* (1960)?

14 Which Roald Dahl story features Sophie and her large companion?

15 "I'll tell thee everything I can: there's little to relate" is sung by which Lewis Carroll character?

16 What is the name of TS Eliot's *Mystery Cat*?

17 Whose autobiography was entitled *The Long Walk to Freedom*?

18 *The Handmaid's Tale* is a 1985 novel by which author?

19 Which novel was the subject of an obscenity trial in 1960?

20 Who wrote the 1819 poem *Ode to a Nightingale*?

Hard

Answers to QUIZ 500 – Science

1 Mesozoic
2 See in the dark
3 Pythagoras (Venus)
4 Edwin
5 Computed Axial Tomography
6 Collagen
7 Peta
8 Astronomy
9 B_1 (thiamin)
10 Solar plexus
11 Speed of light
12 Charles Darwin
13 Enrico Fermi
14 Pascal
15 2061
16 Escape velocity
17 Poliomyelitis
18 Brass
19 Ceres
20 Myology

QUIZ 253 – Pot Luck

ANSWERS ON PAGE 255

1 Who co-starred with Jim Carrey in *Eternal Sunshine of the Spotless Mind*?
2 What name is given to pieces of grain husk separated from flour after milling?
3 What is Sachertorte?
4 In the TV series *Life on Mars*, which actor played Sam Tyler?
5 Which group had hits in the 1980s with *System Addict* and *Rain or Shine*?
6 Conwy and Harlech are famous for what type of building?
7 What is the name of the process by which a plant makes its own food?
8 Which former empire gives its name to a low upholstered seat without back or arms?
9 In the 2007 TV talent contest *Any Dream Will Do*, who won the part of Joseph?
10 What was Calliope in Greek mythology?
11 Which city is the administrative centre of Scotland's Highland council area?
12 Which pack of cards, used for fortune telling, includes the Hierophant and the High Priestess?
13 On which London avenue is the Savoy Hotel situated?
14 In which European capital city would you find the Spanish Steps?
15 Who starred as Sweeney Todd in the 2007 film of the same name?
16 In which county is Rickmansworth?
17 Which dramatist wrote *The Birthday Party* (1957) and *The Caretaker* (1960)?
18 The WWII warden service was denoted by what initials?
19 Which shipping line operated the *QE2*?
20 The "clean and jerk" movement is used in which sports discipline?

Easy Medium Hard

Answers to QUIZ 251 – Pot Luck

1 *Legend*
2 Louisiana
3 The Nile
4 René Descartes
5 Inspector Clouseau
6 Water wheel
7 East Germany
8 Dr Seuss
9 Cagney and Lacey
10 Cedilla
11 Helen Keller
12 Smell
13 Eeyore
14 District of Columbia
15 Squeeze
16 A conclave
17 Aire
18 Highland Games
19 Alaska
20 Drone

QUIZ 254 – Oscar Winners

ANSWERS ON PAGE 256

1 For which 1998 film did Steven Spielberg win the Best Director award?

2 Which actress won an award for her role in the 1997 film *L.A. Confidential*?

3 The theme to *Skyfall* won the Best Song award for which singer?

4 Which 1939 film of a classic novel won eight Oscars, including Best Picture and Best Director?

5 Who won her first Best Actress award for *The Accused*?

6 Which 1981 film won four Oscars, prompting its writer to proclaim "The British are Coming" in his acceptance speech?

7 What was the title of the 1977 Oscar-winning film starring Diane Keaton?

8 Which 2016 musical film received 14 nominations, winning six of the categories?

9 Who won the Best Supporting Actress award for the 2017 film *I, Tonya*, on her first Oscar nomination?

10 *Dances with Wolves* (1990) won the Best Director award for which of its actors?

11 Which two-time winner of the Best Actress award in the 1970s went on to become a Labour MP from 1992-2015?

12 Who won an award for his role as Dudley Moore's butler in the 1981 film *Arthur*?

13 Who won the Best Actor award for his role in *The Godfather* but refused to attend the awards ceremony?

14 Jennifer Hudson, winner of an award for the 2006 film *Dreamgirls*, first came to fame on which talent show?

15 Who won the Best Actor Oscar for his portrayal of Sir Winston Churchill in the 2017 film *The Darkest Hour*?

16 How many Best Actress Oscars did Katharine Hepburn win?

17 Which Tom Hanks film won the Best Picture in 1994?

18 Which long-awaited 2017 sci-fi sequel won Oscars for Best Achievement in Cinematography and Best Achievement in Visual Effects?

19 Who won his second Best Actor award for the 2007 *There Will Be Blood?*

20 Which 2005 Wallace and Gromit full-length film won the Best Animated Feature award?

Easy

Medium

Hard

Answers to QUIZ 252 – Literature

1 A frog
2 Phileas Fogg
3 Andy McNab
4 Ian Rankin
5 Carol Ann Duffy
6 A pea
7 Edgar Allan Poe
8 A tiger
9 Five farthings
10 Charles Dickens
11 Stieg Larsson
12 Sherlock Holmes
13 Harper Lee
14 *The BFG*
15 The White Knight
16 Macavity
17 Nelson Mandela
18 Margaret Atwood
19 *Lady Chatterley's Lover*
20 John Keats

QUIZ 255 – Pot Luck

ANSWERS ON PAGE 257

1 Who won the 2010 Wimbledon men's singles championship?
2 What is Miss Marple's first name?
3 What was the home planet of the aliens in the classic novel *The War of the Worlds*?
4 The Isle of Wight's "Needles" are formed of which substance?
5 What was the nickname of Robbie Coltrane's character in the TV series *Cracker*?
6 Dry ice, often used in stage shows, is a solid form of which gas?
7 Which actress starred in the 1991 film *Sleeping With the Enemy*?
8 Jacqueline du Pré played which instrument?
9 Which desert is found in the north of Chile?
10 What is the capital and chief port of the Philippines?
11 A craniologist studies what part of the body?
12 What title is given to a university official or the head of a cathedral chapter?
13 Who wrote *The Last Juror* (2004)?
14 *Swear it Again* was the 1999 debut no.1 hit for which boy band?
15 Which Latin phrase means "Let the buyer beware"?
16 Which plant's flowers are used to flavour beer?
17 The flag of the Soviet Union showed which two symbols?
18 Who had hits with *Rhinestone Cowboy* and *Wichita Lineman*?
19 What name is given to the ancient frame of beads used for counting?
20 Lady Penelope and her chauffeur Parker appeared in which children's TV series?

Answers to QUIZ 253 – Pot Luck

1 Kate Winslet
2 Bran
3 Chocolate cake
4 John Simm
5 Five Star
6 Castles
7 Photosynthesis
8 Ottoman
9 Lee Mead
10 A Muse (of epic poetry)
11 Inverness
12 Tarot
13 Strand
14 Rome
15 Johnny Depp
16 Hertfordshire
17 Harold Pinter
18 ARP
19 Cunard
20 Weightlifting

Easy

1 What is an electrically charged atom called?
2 What explosive substance consists of a mixture of saltpetre, sulphur and charcoal?
3 Loss of memory has what medical term?
4 Which unit is used to measure the intensity of noise?
5 What name is given to the science of studying the stars?
6 A Surrey town gives its name to which medicinal crystals?
7 Which 3-D image is produced by laser beams?
8 Which acids combine to form proteins?
9 What is the science of the use of technology in aircraft?
10 The symbol B represents which chemical element?
11 Charcoal is a form of which element?

Medium

12 What term is given to a positive electrode?
13 A neutral pH is given which number on the pH scale?
14 What is the main artery carrying blood away from the heart?
15 The scientific names of species are in which language?
16 What does the symbol ∞ represent?
17 Of what is anthropology the study?
18 What name is given to a piece of glass that resolves light into separate colours?
19 In our solar system, what is the second-largest planet?
20 What was the surname of Edmond, the astronomer who predicted the return of a comet?

Hard

Answers to QUIZ 254 – Oscar Winners

1 *Saving Private Ryan*
2 Kim Basinger
3 Adele
4 *Gone with the Wind*
5 Jodie Foster
6 *Chariots of Fire*
7 *Annie Hall*
8 *La La Land*
9 Allison Janney
10 Kevin Costner
11 Glenda Jackson
12 Sir John Gielgud
13 Marlon Brando
14 *American Idol*
15 Gary Oldman
16 Four
17 *Forrest Gump*
18 *Blade Runner 2049*
19 Sir Daniel Day-Lewis
20 *Curse of the Were-Rabbit*

QUIZ 257 – Pot Luck

ANSWERS ON PAGE 259

1 Nile Rodgers was a founding member of which disco funk band?

2 What was the first name of David Schwimmer's character in *Friends*?

3 Which epic 1959 film won the Best Picture Oscar?

4 In the Old Testament, what was the name of the Philistine giant slain by David?

5 What is the surname of the family in *Peter Pan*?

6 Salt Lake City is the capital of which US state?

7 Who had hits in 2003 with *Cry Me a River* and *Rock Your Body*?

8 Human nails are made of which protein?

9 The city of Aleppo is in which country?

10 What is a ten-cent coin called in the USA?

11 Which nursery-rhyme girl ate curds and whey?

12 Astigmatism is a condition affecting which part of the body?

13 What is the western extremity of mainland England?

14 According to legend, what was the name of the site of King Arthur's court?

15 What is the basic unit of currency in Jordan and Bahrain?

16 What, according to the proverb, does he do "who pays the piper"?

17 Which small silvery fish are the fry of herring and sprat?

18 The *Inspector Morse* stories were written by which author?

19 How many sides has a heptagon?

20 Which Michigan port s famous for car manufacturing?

Answers to QUIZ 255 – Pot Luck

1 Rafael Nadal
2 Jane
3 Mars
4 Chalk
5 Fitz
6 Carbon dioxide
7 Julia Roberts
8 Cello
9 Atacama
10 Manila
11 The skull
12 Dean
13 John Grisham
14 Westlife
15 *Caveat emptor*
16 Hop
17 Hammer and sickle
18 Glen Campbell
19 Abacus
20 *Thunderbirds*

QUIZ 258 – Cricket

ANSWERS ON PAGE 260

Easy

1 What do the initials lbw mean to a cricketer?

2 What is the longest that a test match can last?

3 Which radio cricket commentator was known as "Johnners"?

4 What does the abbreviation "st" stand for?

5 The "Home of Cricket" is the name given to which ground?

6 The Brian Statham End and the James Anderson End are found at which Test venue?

7 Which former cricketer became a team captain on *A Question of Sport* in 2008?

8 What name is given to a batsman who bats higher up the order than normal towards the end of a day's play?

9 Who stepped down as England cricket captain in 2017 after leading England for 59 Test matches?

10 Sir Donald Bradman played for which country?

11 Which shorter form of cricket that lasts only a few hours was first played in 2003?

12 If a batsman is "out for a duck", how many runs has he or she scored?

13 Which fielding position is situated just behind the batsman?

Medium

14 On which panel game did David Gower appear as a team captain from 1995 to 2003?

15 The outer surface of a cricket ball is made from what material?

16 What umpire's decision is indicated by holding the arms out horizontally on either side of the body?

17 Which team play their home matches at the County Cricket Ground in Chelmsford?

18 Who captained the England women's team from 2006 to 2016?

19 Sir Vivian Richards played for which national side?

20 What colour-related name is cricketing clothing known by?

Hard

Answers to QUIZ 256 – Science

1 Ion
2 Gunpowder
3 Amnesia
4 Decibel (or bel)
5 Astronomy
6 Epsom salts
7 Hologram
8 Amino acids
9 Avionics
10 Boron
11 Carbon
12 Anode
13 Seven
14 Aorta
15 Latin
16 Infinity
17 Mankind
18 Prism
19 Saturn
20 Halley

QUIZ 259 – Pot Luck

ANSWERS ON PAGE 261

1 Who fronted the group Dire Straits?

2 Paul Potts was the first winner of which series?

3 Which river joins the Severn near Chepstow?

4 Who is Pinocchio's "official conscience"?

5 The forsythia plant produces what colour flowers?

6 Which Beatle was the first narrator for the TV version of *Thomas the Tank Engine*?

7 What do Americans call the boot of a car?

8 What term of address is used for an unmarried Spanish woman?

9 Red, blue and yellow make up which group of colours?

10 In which London building is the Lord Mayor's Banquet held?

11 What is the name of the punctuation mark formed by two vertical dots?

12 Which legendary markswoman was a member of Buffalo Bill's Wild West Show?

13 *Too Much Too Young* was a 1979 EP by which band?

14 Who took over from Sue Lawley as presenter of Radio 4's *Desert Island Discs*?

15 Robert Galbraith is a pen-name for which famous author?

16 What was an ancient Greek warship with three banks of oars called?

17 Which 2005 Wes Craven thriller is set on a plane?

18 What body of water lies between Britain and Ireland?

19 In which football stadium is one of the stands known as the Kop?

20 Who starred as James Bond in *Moonraker* (1979)?

Answers to QUIZ 257 – Pot Luck

1 Chic
2 Ross
3 *Ben-Hur*
4 Goliath
5 Darling
6 Utah
7 Justin Timberlake
8 Keratin
9 Syria
10 Dime
11 Little Miss Muffet
12 The eye
13 Land's End
14 Camelot
15 Dinar
16 Calls the tune
17 Whitebait
18 Colin Dexter
19 Seven
20 Detroit

QUIZ 260 – US Sitcoms

ANSWERS ON PAGE 262

Easy

1 Who starred as himself in *The Fresh Prince of Bel-Air*?

2 Which series features two physicists who work at Caltech?

3 In which series did Hollywood star Chris Pratt play Andy Dwyer?

4 The phrase "jumping the shark" originated as a result of which series?

5 The fictional show *Tool Time* featured in which series starring Tim Allen?

6 Who was "*in the Middle*" in the title of a 2000s series?

7 What was the name of the coffee shop in *Friends*?

8 Which late 1970s sitcom featured the Tates and the Campbells?

9 In the series *M*A*S*H*, what did the letters stand for?

10 What was the name of Jerry's female sidekick in *Seinfeld*?

Medium

11 The sitcom *Frasier* was a spin-off from which series?

12 Who created and starred in *Curb Your Enthusiasm*?

13 Which 1964-72 series starred Elizabeth Montgomery as Samantha, daughter of Endora?

14 In *Roseanne*, what was the family's surname?

15 Who played Dick Van Dyke's wife in *The Dick Van Dyke Show* and later starred in her own show?

16 In the series *30 Rock*, which comedienne and actress played Liz Lemon?

17 Who was the eldest sister in *The Brady Bunch*?

18 In which 2000s series did Neil Patrick Harris play Barney Stinson?

19 Who is Scratchy's cartoon "co-star" in *The Simpsons*?

20 Who was Lucy in the 1950s series *I Love Lucy*?

Hard

Answers to QUIZ 258 – Cricket

1 Leg before wicket
2 Five days
3 Brian Johnston
4 Stumped
5 Lord's
6 Old Trafford
7 Phil Tufnell
8 Nightwatchman
9 Alastair Cook
10 Australia
11 Twenty20
12 None
13 Wicketkeeper
14 *They Think It's All Over*
15 Leather
16 Wide
17 Essex
18 Charlotte Edwards
19 The West Indies
20 Whites

QUIZ 261 – Pot Luck

ANSWERS ON PAGE 263

1 The song *You'll Never Walk Alone* is from which musical?
2 Which group had hits in 1985 with *Alive and Kicking* and *Don't You (Forget About Me)*?
3 Which plant's leaves yield a reddish-orange pigment used as a hair dye?
4 *Borgen* was a TV drama about the prime minister of which country?
5 Who wrote the 2009 novel *Wolf Hall*?
6 Which New Testament apostle took his name from the Greek for "rock"?
7 In which English city is Lime Street railway station?
8 Which Peak District river flows through the Chatsworth estate?
9 The Friendly Islands is the former name of which Pacific group?
10 By what name is the fixed annual allowance to cover a monarch's household known?
11 Which successful play and 2011 film is based on a Michael Morpurgo story?
12 The character of Alan Partridge was created by which comedian?
13 *Downtown* was a 1964 hit for which singer?
14 What is the term for a Formula 1 motor race?
15 What is the American term for grilling?
16 In which Swiss city are the headquarters of the Red Cross?
17 Meryl Streep and Anne Hathaway starred in which 2006 film about the fashion industry?
18 What relation to you is your uncle's son?
19 Japan has which unit of currency?
20 What sort of creature is a lory?

Answers to QUIZ 259 – Pot Luck

1 Mark Knopfler
2 *Britain's Got Talent*
3 Wye
4 Jiminy Cricket
5 Yellow
6 Ringo Starr (Sir Richard Starkey)
7 The trunk
8 Señorita
9 Primary colours
10 Guildhall
11 Colon
12 Annie Oakley
13 Specials
14 Kirsty Young
15 JK Rowling
16 Trireme
17 *Red Eye*
18 Irish Sea
19 Anfield
20 Sir Roger Moore

QUIZ 262 – History

ANSWERS ON PAGE 264

1 Which 18th-century British admiral suffered mutiny while captaining *The Bounty*?
2 General Eisenhower was given what nickname?
3 Which empire did Catherine the Great rule?
4 Which 8th-century earthworks separated Mercia and Powys?
5 In the old Soviet Union, what was the name given to a political prison or a forced labour camp?
6 Who was the brother of aviation pioneer Orville Wright?
7 Sir Francis Drake attacked which Spanish port in 1587?
8 What name was given to the start of the Allied invasion of Europe in WWII?
9 Wyatt Earp's friend Holliday had what nickname?
10 In the Wars of the Roses, what colour was Lancaster's rose?
11 What was the name of Thor Heyerdahl's craft used for his 1947 Pacific expedition?
12 Which English historian was known as "the Venerable"?
13 In 1215, which bill of rights was signed at Runnymede?
14 The British Legion was founded by which earl?
15 Which politician was leader of the movement to abolish the slave trade?
16 Which Carthaginian general took elephants across the Alps?
17 Who led the Peasants' Revolt?
18 Mary I of England married which king of Spain in 1554?
19 Which New South Wales location was the site of the first penal colony in Australia?
20 On which part of Scotland's Western Isles was a famous collection of medieval chess pieces found?

Answers to QUIZ 260 – US Sitcoms

1 Will Smith
2 *The Big Bang Theory*
3 *Parks and Recreation*
4 *Happy Days*
5 *Home Improvement*
6 Malcolm
7 Central Perk
8 *Soap*
9 Mobile Army Surgical Hospital
10 Elaine
11 *Cheers*
12 Larry David
13 *Bewitched*
14 Conner
15 Mary Tyler Moore
16 Tina Fey
17 Marcia
18 *How I Met Your Mother*
19 Itchy
20 Lucille Ball

QUIZ 263 – Pot Luck

ANSWERS ON PAGE 265

1 What is the Fahrenheit equivalent of 0° Celsius?
2 In which year did The Buggles have a hit with *Video Killed the Radio Star*?
3 The game of *Mornington Crescent* features on which radio show?
4 Which character in *Dad's Army* had the catchphrase "Don't panic"?
5 A game of netball is made up of four quarters each lasting what length of time?
6 What would a Native American refer to as a papoose?
7 Which word can describe both a piece of wood and a group of directors?
8 In *Alice's Adventures In Wonderland*, which creature smokes a hookah?
9 In various novels by PG Wodehouse, what sort of animal is the Empress of Blandings?
10 Which building holds the US gold reserves?
11 What, according to the proverb, does every cloud have?
12 In *The Simpsons*, which character drives the school bus?
13 St Helier is the capital of which Channel Island?
14 Which US Beat Generation author wrote the 1957 novel *On the Road*?
15 What part of the body is commonly called the voice box?
16 Of which drink is lapsang souchong a variety?
17 Which pigment is responsible for tanning of the skin?
18 In which county is the town of Budleigh Salterton?
19 Which country was formerly joined with Slovakia?
20 Which star sign comes between Virgo and Scorpio?

Answers to QUIZ 261 – Pot Luck

1 *Carousel*
2 Simple Minds
3 Henna
4 Denmark
5 Dame Hilary Mantel
6 Peter
7 Liverpool
8 Derwent
9 Tonga
10 The Civil List
11 *War Horse*
12 Steve Coogan
13 Petula Clark
14 Grand Prix
15 Broiling
16 Geneva
17 *The Devil Wears Prada*
18 Cousin
19 Yen
20 A bird

QUIZ 264 – Green

ANSWERS ON PAGE 266

Easy

1 A putting green surrounds which sporting target?
2 Which actress starred in the 1990 film *Green Card*?
3 Who wrote the novel *Anne of Green Gables*?
4 Which children's programme is set in Greendale?
5 Which Teletubby is green?
6 The talent show *Opportunity Knocks* originally had which host?
7 Which long, green-skinned fruit is proverbially "cool"?
8 A greenshank is what type of creature?
9 Which green gemstone is a variety of the mineral beryl?
10 Greenland is a territory belonging to which European country?
11 Which Somerset town is also the name of a green leafy vegetable?

Medium

12 From which US state did the dessert of Key Lime Pie originate?
13 Which actor starred with Mark Benton in the TV series *City Lights*?
14 In the Edward Lear poem *The Owl and the Pussycat*, what specific colour is the boat?
15 What term is given to an area of open land around a British city?
16 A Florentine pizza features which green vegetable?
17 Who played Rachel Green in the TV series *Friends*?
18 Which Shakespearean character describes jealousy as "the green-eyed monster"?
19 Spring greens are young leaves from which vegetable?
20 "Greenback" is US slang for which banknote?

Hard

Answers to QUIZ 262 –History

1 William Bligh
2 Ike
3 The Russian Empire
4 Offa's Dyke
5 Gulag
6 Wilbur
7 Cadiz
8 D-Day
9 Doc
10 Red
11 *Kon-Tiki*
12 Bede
13 The *Magna Carta*
14 Earl Haig
15 William Wilberforce
16 Hannibal
17 Wat Tyler
18 Philip II
19 Botany Bay
20 Lewis

QUIZ 265 – Pot Luck

ANSWERS ON PAGE 267

1 By what other name is wild marjoram known?

2 Which creature frightened Little Miss Muffet?

3 Who directed the 2005 film *Brokeback Mountain*?

4 In what do lugworms live?

5 Which square in New York is a focal point for New Year's Eve celebrations?

6 What is the call given by a bugle or drum to awaken troops?

7 In *A Midsummer Night's Dream*, what is the name of the character loved by Lysander and Demetrius?

8 What is the German term of address equivalent to "Mr"?

9 Which cocktail is made from champagne and chilled stout?

10 *Upside Down* was a hit for which singer in 1980?

11 Who were William the Conqueror's people, who invaded Britain in 1066?

12 Which wide London road runs between Admiralty Arch and Buckingham Palace?

13 In *The Adventures of Priscilla, Queen of the Desert* (1994), who or what is Priscilla?

14 Which actor played Tim Canterbury in *The Office*?

15 Clove hitch, running bowline and Hunter's bend are types of what?

16 What was the surname of the brothers who made up the Bee Gees?

17 Proverbially, what is a change as good as?

18 Who created the character Emma Harte, heroine of *A Woman Of Substance*?

19 The name of which sporting discipline is often abbreviated to Super-G?

20 At the border of which two countries is the peak known as the Matterhorn?

Easy

Medium

Hard

Answers to QUIZ 263 – Pot Luck

1 32°
2 1979
3 *I'm Sorry I Haven't a Clue*
4 Corporal Jones
5 15 minutes
6 A baby
7 Board
8 The caterpillar
9 A pig
10 Fort Knox
11 A silver lining
12 Otto
13 Jersey
14 Jack Kerouac
15 Larynx
16 Tea
17 Melanin
18 Devon
19 Czechia (Czech Republic)
20 Libra

Easy

1 The poet and painter Dante Rossetti (b.1828) had what middle name?
2 What nationality was artist Édouard Manet?
3 With which Italian city was Tintoretto associated?
4 In which area of the arts was Clarice Cliff famous?
5 Who painted *The Hay Wain* (1821)?
6 What term was given to the period in the 14th-16th centuries when there was a new interest in the arts in Europe?
7 In which country was photographer Annie Leibovitz born?
8 Which artist was noted for his 1960s paintings of soup cans?
9 In which Cornish town is the Barbara Hepworth Museum and Sculpture Garden?
10 Which artist painted two series of studies of sunflowers in the 1880s?

Medium

11 René Lalique was famous for working in what medium?
12 In 1871, which US artist famously painted a picture of his mother?
13 What was the birth name of photographer Lord Snowdon?
14 A branch of which art gallery is located at Albert Dock in Liverpool?
15 Which British artist was noted for his paintings of swimming pools?
16 In which London location is the National Gallery?
17 Which artist and sculptor, famous for his statue of David, worked on the design of the dome of St Peter's in Vatican City?
18 What does the abbreviation YBA, coined in the 1990s, stand for?
19 In which area of the arts is Anish Kapoor famous?
20 Which artist gave his name to a shade of brown and a beard?

Hard

Answers to QUIZ 264 – Green

1 Golf hole
2 Andie MacDowell
3 Lucy Maud Montgomery
4 *Postman Pat*
5 Dipsy
6 Hughie Green
7 Cucumber
8 Bird
9 Emerald
10 Denmark
11 Chard
12 Florida
13 Robson Green
14 Pea-green
15 Green belt
16 Spinach
17 Jennifer Aniston
18 Iago (*Othello*)
19 Cabbage
20 Dollar

QUIZ 267 – Pot Luck

ANSWERS ON PAGE 269

1 What name is given to the River Thames at Oxford?

2 "Drink sangria in the park, And then later, When it gets dark, we go home" is a lyric from which song?

3 Which British actor plays Dr Watson to Robert Downey Jr's Sherlock Holmes?

4 According to the popular verse, Tuesday's child is what?

5 In which county is Sandwich golf course?

6 Which town in Germany, near Dresden, is famous for porcelain?

7 By what two-word title was Benito Mussolini known?

8 What canine breed is also known as a sausage dog?

9 Which actor starred as Will in the 2002 film *About a Boy*?

10 In Indian cuisine, what is the term for clarified butter?

11 What is the correct form of address to a duke?

12 What is meant by the Latin phrase *Veni, vidi, vici*?

13 Basra is in which country?

14 In which county is the racing circuit of Castle Combe?

15 What is the name of the heroine in *Gone With the Wind*?

16 A word for the land of sleep also means which gesture of agreement?

17 Which French word translates as a friendly understanding between states?

18 In what type of building are hops traditionally dried?

19 Which channel has been broadcasting since 1955?

20 Who had a 1986 hit with *A Different Corner*?

Answers to QUIZ 265 – Pot Luck

1 Oregano
2 Spider
3 Ang Lee
4 Sand or mud
5 Times Square
6 Reveille
7 Hermia
8 Herr
9 Black velvet
10 Diana Ross
11 The Normans
12 The Mall
13 A bus
14 Martin Freeman
15 Knots
16 Gibb
17 A rest
18 Barbara Taylor Bradford
19 Super giant slalom
20 Switzerland/Italy

QUIZ 268 – Classical Music

ANSWERS ON PAGE **270**

Easy

1 What Latin word is used to classify musical works in order of publication?

2 The composer Mendelssohn had what first name?

3 What is the instrumental prelude to an opera or play called?

4 How many pedals does a grand piano have?

5 Which West Yorkshire city hosts an annual International Piano Competition?

6 Who composed the *Peer Gynt* suite (1875)?

7 What device marks time for musicians by giving a regular tick?

8 At which venue has the London Symphony Orchestra been resident since 1982?

9 Which orchestral instruments are also known as timpani?

10 In Rossini's *The Barber of Seville*, what is the name of the title character?

11 What term is given to the words of an opera?

Medium

12 *The Well-Tempered Clavier* was written by which composer?

13 Which wind instrument is also the name for a champagne glass?

14 What nationality was Mozart?

15 What is a group of nine musicians called?

16 The *Enigma Variations*, from which *Nimrod* is often played on state occasions, were written by which composer?

17 What was Beethoven's first name?

18 A famous Manchester orchestra and the German city where Handel was born are linked by what name?

19 Which musical term means "very loud"?

Hard

20 What is the title of the 1887 Verdi opera based on a Shakespeare tragedy?

Answers to QUIZ 266 – The Arts

1 Gabriel
2 French
3 Venice
4 Ceramics
5 John Constable
6 Renaissance
7 USA
8 Andy Warhol
9 St Ives
10 Vincent Van Gogh
11 Glass
12 James Whistler
13 Antony Armstrong-Jones
14 Tate
15 David Hockney
16 Trafalgar Square
17 Michelangelo
18 Young British Artists
19 Sculpture
20 Sir Anthony Van Dyck

QUIZ 269 – Pot Luck

1 Matt Smith was the eleventh actor to take on the starring role in which TV series?

2 What is a person summoned for compulsory state military service called?

3 Which group topped the charts in 2006 with *I Don't Feel Like Dancin'*?

4 In which war was the comedy series M*A*S*H set?

5 *Little Lies* was a hit for which group in 1987?

6 Which Russian goldsmith was famous for his jewelled Easter eggs?

7 What name is given to a small barrel usually containing less than ten gallons?

8 Which exercise system is known by the surname of the German physical fitness specialist who devised it?

9 Stacey in *Gavin & Stacey* was played by which actress?

10 Where is the famous Greek oracle site?

11 Which Chinese dish has a name that means "mixed pieces"?

12 The 2016 film *Inferno* is based on which author's book of the same name?

13 Which term is used for the peaceful region at the centre of a hurricane?

14 Which Arabian Nights character says "Open, Sesame!"?

15 Of which English county is Ipswich the county town?

16 What unit of weight of silk yarn describes the fineness of hosiery?

17 *The Listeners* (1912) was written by which poet?

18 What was the former name of Beijing?

19 Which car manufacturer's logo is two overlapping Rs?

20 "Shanks's pony" is a term for which mode of transport?

Answers to QUIZ 267 – Pot Luck

1 Isis
2 *Perfect Day* (Lou Reed)
3 Jude Law
4 Full of grace
5 Kent
6 Meissen
7 Il Duce
8 Dachshund
9 Hugh Grant
10 Ghee
11 Your Grace
12 I came, I saw, I conquered
13 Iraq
14 Wiltshire
15 Scarlett O'Hara
16 Nod
17 Entente
18 Oast house
19 ITV
20 George Michael

QUIZ 270 – Animal World

ANSWERS ON PAGE 272

Easy

1 How many parts make up an insect's body?
2 Which large white seabird's name is also used to describe a greedy person?
3 A John Dory is what type of creature?
4 What is another name for the insect known as an emmet?
5 The male of which primate might be called a "silverback"?
6 A young beaver is given what name?
7 What type of creature is an orb weaver?
8 What term is used to describe collectively the animal life of a particular area?
9 Pecorino cheese is made from the milk of which animal?
10 What name is given to the larva of a frog?
11 What are male rabbits called?

Medium

12 A Labrador is what type of dog?
13 The largest beetle is named after which Biblical character?
14 A salmon lays what colour eggs?
15 Which animal has Arabian and Bactrian species?
16 What is the term for an animal that re-chews food brought back from a first stomach?
17 Common, pygmy and water are species of which small British mammal?
18 What type of creature would be found in an apiary?
19 The Komodo dragon is the world's largest species of what animal?
20 What is a male swan called?

Hard

Answers to QUIZ 268 – Classical Music

1 *Opus*
2 Felix
3 Overture
4 Three
5 Leeds
6 Edvard Grieg
7 Metronome
8 Barbican
9 Kettledrums
10 Figaro
11 Libretto
12 Johann Sebastian Bach
13 Flute
14 Austrian
15 Nonet
16 Sir Edward Elgar
17 Ludwig
18 Hallé
19 Fortissimo
20 *Otello*

QUIZ 271 – Pot Luck

1 What type of creature is an oryx?
2 *Free* was a hit for which singer in 1976?
3 What is the first name of Timothy Spall's actor son?
4 *Mr Tambourine Man* was written by which singer/songwriter?
5 What is the milky liquid obtained from the rubber tree called?
6 In which city is the Louvre art gallery?
7 What is the largest island in the Greek Dodecanese group?
8 Which country hosted the FIFA World Cup in 2010?
9 Who wrote "She walks in beauty, like the night"?
10 In which English county is Maidenhead?
11 What is a small piece of tortilla topped with cheese called?
12 What term is given to an administrative division of Switzerland?
13 The RHS Chelsea Flower Show is held in the grounds of which building?
14 What was the name of Lily Munster's husband in TV's *The Munsters*?
15 What baked round of batter is traditionally eaten with roast beef?
16 In which series of disciplines did Jessica Ennis-Hill win Olympic gold?
17 Sherrie and Drew are the lead characters in which 2012 film featuring 1980s music?
18 What is the area under the pastoral care of a bishop, also known as a see, called?
19 The Sellafield site in Cumbria was previously known by what name?
20 What is the French word for Christmas?

Answers to QUIZ 269 – Pot Luck

1 *Doctor Who*
2 Conscript
3 Scissor Sisters
4 Korean War
5 Fleetwood Mac
6 Fabergé
7 Keg
8 Pilates
9 Joanna Page
10 Delphi
11 Chop suey
12 Dan Brown
13 The eye
14 Ali Baba
15 Suffolk
16 Denier
17 Walter de la Mare
18 Peking
19 Rolls-Royce
20 Walking

QUIZ 272 – Vegetables

ANSWERS ON PAGE 274

Easy

1 Which vegetable did Mark Twain describe as "a cabbage with a college education"?
2 Which vegetable gives pasta verde its green colour?
3 From which country did the vegetable stew ratatouille originate?
4 Which vegetable is associated with Wales?
5 What is the common name for *Allium cepa*, a plant with a large edible bulb?
6 Which vegetable's name is often used to mean "an incentive"?
7 Which vegetable features heavily in Thanksgiving meals in the USA?
8 Into the stalk of which small vegetable might you cut a cross before cooking it?
9 On which vegetable are silk, husks and kernels found?
10 How have tempura vegetables been cooked?
11 Which vegetables are proverbially identical when in their outer casing?

Medium

12 Where would you find samphire?
13 Which vegetable's name translates as "earth-apple" in French?
14 What is another name for the yam?
15 What name is given to the pieces of raw vegetable often served with dips?
16 Butternut is a variety of which fruit that is commonly used as a vegetable?
17 Which usually dark red vegetable also has golden and candy varieties?
18 Pak choi, also known as bok choy, originates from which country?
19 What name is given to a small cucumber that has been preserved in vinegar?
20 Which variety of celery has a large root that is used as a vegetable?

Hard

Answers to QUIZ 270 – Animal World

1 Three (head, thorax and abdomen)
2 Gannet
3 Fish
4 Ant
5 Gorilla
6 A kit
7 Spider
8 Fauna
9 Sheep
10 Tadpole
11 Bucks
12 Retriever
13 Goliath
14 Orange (light to dark)
15 Camel
16 Ruminant
17 Shrew
18 Bee
19 Lizard
20 Cob

QUIZ 273 – Pot Luck

ANSWERS ON PAGE 275

1 Which traffic light follows green?
2 Austin is the capital of which US state?
3 What name was given to a member of the Royalist army during the English Civil War?
4 Which British group sang *Wild Thing* in 1966?
5 A Pomeranian is what type of creature?
6 Which type of pasta is shaped like seashells?
7 Which flower, also called the Lent lily, is an emblem of Wales?
8 Newbury is situated in which English county?
9 Whose backing group were The Mechanics?
10 How many Marx Brothers were there?
11 Which Swedish tennis player won eleven Grand Slam titles between 1974 and 1981?
12 Which comedian was famous for wearing a fez?
13 Alberta and Quebec are provinces of which country?
14 What term is given to the boundary of a circle?
15 What is the Spanish name for cold vegetable soup?
16 *Reggatta de Blanc* was a 1979 album by which band?
17 In which classic sitcom did Connie Booth play the part of Polly?
18 Moorfields hospital in London specialises in which part of the body?
19 What is the name of the former head of MI5 who, in July 2001, received permission to publish a book of memoirs?
20 Eva Peron was the First Lady of which country?

Answers to QUIZ 271 – Pot Luck

1 Antelope
2 Deniece Williams
3 Rafe
4 Bob Dylan
5 Latex
6 Paris
7 Rhodes
8 South Africa
9 Lord Byron
10 Berkshire
11 Nacho
12 Canton
13 Royal Hospital
14 Herman
15 Yorkshire Pudding
16 Heptathlon
17 *Rock of Ages*
18 Diocese
19 Windscale
20 *Noël*

QUIZ 274 – Chemistry

Easy

1 What term is given to a substance that speeds up a chemical reaction?
2 What type of substance is calcium carbonate?
3 What term is used to describe matter that is non-reactive?
4 Brimstone is an old name for which element?
5 Which Swedish chemist invented dynamite?
6 Pb is the symbol for which metal?
7 Which laboratory heat source was named after a German chemist?
8 What type of substance turns litmus paper red?
9 What is the branch of chemistry that is concerned with compounds of carbon?
10 Rust has what chemical name?

Medium

11 What is the smallest fundamental unit of a chemical compound?
12 What term is given to a metallic compound containing two or more elements?
13 Which process turns a liquid into vapour?
14 Which common compound has the formula NH_3?
15 What is the chemical symbol for iodine?
16 Which element, atomic number 88, was discovered by Marie and Pierre Curie in 1898?
17 Helium, neon, argon, krypton, xenon and radon are collectively known as what?
18 What type of glass tube is used to measure or transfer liquids?
19 The chemical symbol for silver is derived from which word, still used in heraldry?
20 Which term, also used in a weather context, is given to a solid substance separated out from gas or water?

Hard

Answers to QUIZ 272 – Vegetables

1 Cauliflower
2 Spinach
3 France
4 Leek
5 Onion
6 Carrot
7 Pumpkin
8 Brussels sprout
9 Sweetcorn
10 Deep-fried
11 Peas
12 On the coast
13 Potato (*pomme de terre*)
14 Sweet potato
15 Crudités
16 Squash
17 Beetroot
18 China
19 Gherkin
20 Celeriac

QUIZ 275 – Pot Luck

ANSWERS ON PAGE 277

1 What type of resort links Bath and Cheltenham?
2 Who had a hit with the theme from the 1976 film *A Star is Born*?
3 In which 1976 horror film did Gregory Peck and Lee Remick play adoptive parents?
4 On which island was the TV series *Bergerac* set?
5 Which French emperor was defeated at Waterloo?
6 Which is the longest river in Ireland?
7 In 2017, who replaced Mary Berry as a judge on *The Great British Bake Off*?
8 What is a baby hedgehog called?
9 In which Devon city did Sir Francis Drake famously play bowls?
10 What is a co-driver in a car rally called?
11 Which US president succeeded Richard Nixon?
12 A verger called Alice featured in which sitcom?
13 What is the county town of Cumbria?
14 What is the term given to the spouse of a reigning monarch?
15 In which country is Copacabana Beach?
16 What is the term for speed and rhythm in music?
17 The French game of pétanque has what other name?
18 In Morse Code which letter is represented by three dots?
19 What is a circular tower built for coastal defence called?
20 Which ferry terminal is situated on an island off Anglesey?

Answers to QUIZ 273 – Pot Luck

1 Amber
2 Texas
3 Cavalier
4 The Troggs
5 A dog
6 Conchiglie
7 Daffodil
8 Berkshire
9 Mike (Rutherford)
10 Five
11 Björn Borg
12 Tommy Cooper
13 Canada
14 Circumference
15 Gazpacho
16 The Police
17 *Fawlty Towers*
18 Eye
19 Stella Rimington
20 Argentina

Easy

1 What is the French word for "castle"?

2 Which Scottish castle hosts an annual Military Tattoo in August?

3 In which county is Herstmonceux Castle?

4 Kronborg Castle is immortalised as Elsinore in which of Shakespeare's plays?

5 What is the central structure of the Tower of London known as?

6 What is the typical castle entrance called, characterised by lowerable wooden decks on chains?

7 *Schloss* is the word for "castle" in which language?

8 Castle Black is the location of the Night's Watch in which TV series?

9 Which royal ceremony took place at Caernarfon Castle in 1969?

10 Peel Castle is situated on which island?

Medium

11 Robert Dudley was granted Kenilworth Castle by which queen?

12 Bamburgh Castle lies on the coast of which county?

13 Castel Gandolfo is the summer residence of which church leader?

14 The London office building opened in 2001 to provide space for Members of Parliament and their staff was named after which part of a castle?

15 Tintagel Castle in Cornwall is associated with which legendary figure?

16 Which European castle was the subject of a 1970s wartime TV series?

17 Bolsover Castle and Dover Castle are in the care of which organisation?

18 Which castle near Maidstone has a name that suggests it should be located further north?

Hard

19 Castle Stalker is in which country?

20 The local authority of which county council has the address "The Castle, Winchester"?

Answers to QUIZ 274 – Chemistry

1 Catalyst
2 Chalk
3 Inert
4 Sulphur
5 Alfred Nobel
6 Lead
7 Bunsen burner
8 Acid
9 Organic chemistry
10 Iron oxide
11 Molecule
12 Alloy
13 Evaporation
14 Ammonia
15 I
16 Radium
17 Noble gases
18 Pipette
19 Argent (Ag)
20 Precipitate

QUIZ 277 – Pot Luck

ANSWERS ON PAGE 279

1 What name is given to a native of Oxford?

2 Which group's first hit was *Seven Seas of Rhye*?

3 "All the leaves are brown and the sky is grey" are the opening words to which song?

4 What is the main ingredient of borscht?

5 *Not Waving but Drowning* was written by which poet?

6 What sort of food is Bel Paese?

7 What is a share of a company's profit paid to a shareholder called?

8 What colour is muscovado sugar?

9 What was the surname of the *My Family* clan?

10 Which film featured Ronan Keating's song *When You Say Nothing At All*?

11 In which part of the body is the sciatic nerve?

12 Who is the long-running presenter of *Flog It!*?

13 *Orinoco Flow* was which singer's debut solo hit in 1988?

14 Which French Riviera resort shares its name with a variety of biscuit?

15 What weight is equivalent to 14 pounds?

16 Who played the title role in the 1991 film *Robin Hood: Prince of Thieves*?

17 Which English racecourse lends its name to a betting card game?

18 Of which country is Bern the capital?

19 What is an alternative name for maize?

20 What is the term for a fence made from stakes?

Easy

Medium

Hard

Answers to QUIZ 275 – Pot Luck

1 Spa
2 Barbra Streisand
3 *The Omen*
4 Jersey
5 Napoleon
6 Shannon
7 Prue Leith
8 Hoglet
9 Plymouth
10 Navigator
11 Gerald Ford
12 *The Vicar of Dibley*
13 Carlisle
14 Consort
15 Brazil
16 Tempo
17 Boules
18 S
19 Martello
20 Holyhead

1 What type of food is baklava?
2 How many countries share a border with Greece?
3 With what is retsina flavoured?
4 What ancient temple on the Athenian Acropolis is dedicated to the goddess Athena?
5 Which white, crumbly cheese must be produced in Greece by law to keep its name?
6 Taramasalata is what colour?
7 What Greek letter is used in English to mean "the most dominant of a group"?
8 Before the euro, what was the currency of Greece?
9 What is the largest Greek island?
10 Is Greece ahead of or behind GMT?
11 In mythology, the Minotaur had the head of which animal?
12 What Greek city that lies along the Nedon River is renowned for its eponymous olives?
13 What is the largest lake in Greece?
14 The Greek flag has which two colours?
15 What name is given to the group composed of seven principal islands including Corfu?
16 What Greek goddess shares her name with a popular sportswear company?
17 How many letters are in the Greek alphabet?
18 Which dairy product forms the basis of tzatziki?
19 In what year did Greece join the EU?
20 What Greek dish is usually based on aubergine, tomato and minced meat?

Answers to QUIZ 276 – Castles

1 *Château*
2 Edinburgh Castle
3 East Sussex
4 *Hamlet*
5 The White Tower
6 Drawbridge
7 German
8 *Game of Thrones*
9 Investiture of the Prince of Wales
10 Isle of Man
11 Elizabeth I
12 Northumberland
13 The Pope
14 Portcullis (House)
15 King Arthur
16 Colditz
17 English Heritage
18 Leeds Castle
19 Scotland
20 Hampshire

QUIZ 279 – Pot Luck

ANSWERS ON PAGE 281

1 Who topped the charts in 1979 with *I Will Survive*?
2 Who starred alongside Bruce Willis in the TV series *Moonlighting*?
3 In which position did Peter Shilton play football for England?
4 What is the order of knights in the *Star Wars* films?
5 Which Roman landmark was made famous by the film *Three Coins in the Fountain*?
6 Which 1940 Disney cartoon film had a soundtrack of classical music?
7 Which port and resort is Israel's southernmost city?
8 In a packet of Salt 'n' Shake crisps, what colour is the salt sachet?
9 *One Day in Your Life* was a 1981 hit for which singer?
10 Which Greek letter can also be a very small amount?
11 Which large water lily was sacred in ancient Egypt?
12 What is the name of the region in the "heel" of Italy?
13 Is the town of Tenby in North Wales or South Wales?
14 Which kind of TV signal has been replaced by digital?
15 What cereal is used in making American whiskey?
16 Which holiday company is famous for its Redcoats?
17 In relation to crops and food, what do the initials GM stand for?
18 During which Apollo flight did the famous "Houston we have a problem" statement occur?
19 What colour is sulphur?
20 When Simple Simon was going to the fair in the nursery rhyme, whom did he meet?

Answers to QUIZ 277 – Pot Luck

1 Oxonian
2 Queen
3 *California Dreamin'*
4 Beetroot
5 Stevie Smith
6 Cheese
7 Dividend
8 Brown
9 Harper
10 *Notting Hill*
11 Leg
12 Paul Martin
13 Enya
14 Nice
15 Stone
16 Kevin Costner
17 Newmarket
18 Switzerland
19 Corn
20 Palisade

QUIZ 280 – Money

ANSWERS ON PAGE 282

Easy

1 Which president appears on the front of the US one-dollar bill?

2 What word follows "pound" in the official currency of the UK?

3 What is made available in a rights issue?

4 How is a teller more usually referred to in a bank?

5 Who was Chancellor of the Exchequer for ten years before becoming Prime Minister in 2007?

6 Children traditionally save money in a container resembling which animal?

7 What is the state of having been declared legally financially insolvent?

8 Known as NS&I, which organisation administers Premium Bonds?

9 What two-word term is given to a commercial treaty between two or more nations?

10 In which Scottish city was Clydesdale Bank formed in 1838?

Medium

11 Automatic enrolment in what type of financial scheme started in the UK in 2012?

12 What, from 1979 to 1999, was the precursor to the euro?

13 In which year did the National Lottery begin in the UK?

14 Which old UK coin was equivalent to 12.5 pence?

15 What is the currency unit of Sweden?

16 Where a person has an IVA with their creditors, for what does the "V" stand?

17 A "monkey" refers to what sum of money?

18 What was Spain's currency before it adopted the euro?

19 The introduction of TESSAs in 1991 was intended to encourage what?

20 What term describes a building society that is owned by its customers?

Hard

Answers to QUIZ 278 – Greece

1 A dessert pastry
2 Six
3 Pine resin
4 The Parthenon
5 Feta
6 Pink
7 Alpha
8 Drachma
9 Crete
10 Ahead
11 Bull
12 Kalamata
13 Lake Trichonida
14 Blue and white
15 Ionian Islands
16 Nike
17 24
18 Yoghurt
19 1981
20 Moussaka

QUIZ 281 – Pot Luck

ANSWERS ON PAGE 283

1 Which religion has the Star of David as its symbol?

2 What name is given to the collective states of Connecticut, Maine, Massachusetts, New Hampshire, Rhode Island and Vermont?

3 Which ancient Greek city was known for its austere lifestyle?

4 Who starred in the 1969 film *The Prime of Miss Jean Brodie*?

5 *Speed of Sound* was a hit for which band in 2005?

6 Who was Labour Minister of Health from 1945 to 1951?

7 Who played the Swedish detective Kurt Wallander in the English TV version?

8 Gorilla, gibbon and orang-utan are varieties of which type of creature?

9 Which novel features the pirate Ben Gunn?

10 Who is the central character in the Disney film *The Lion King*?

11 What proverbially, cannot be made without breaking eggs?

12 Hungarian escapologist Erik Weisz is better known by which name?

13 Which river flows through Washington DC?

14 Selhurst Park is the home ground of which football club?

15 The Bluewater shopping centre is in which county?

16 A domesticated polecat has what name?

17 What is the semicircular recess at the eastern end of a church called?

18 Which champagne cocktail is made with peach?

19 Which pantomime features a boy who trades his cow on the way to market?

20 In which county is Basingstoke?

Answers to QUIZ 279 – Pot Luck

1 Gloria Gaynor
2 Cybill Shepherd
3 Goalkeeper
4 Jedi
5 Trevi Fountain
6 *Fantasia*
7 Eilat
8 Blue
9 Michael Jackson
10 Iota
11 Lotus
12 Apulia
13 South Wales
14 Analogue
15 Rye
16 Butlin's
17 Genetically modified
18 Apollo 13
19 Yellow
20 Pieman

 ANSWERS ON PAGE 284

Easy

1 Whoopi Goldberg starred as a singing nun in which 1992 film?

2 The 1985 film *Witness* featured which religious sect?

3 In which animated film did Mel Gibson provide the voice of a rooster called Rocky?

4 Who received his first Oscar nomination for his role in the 1977 film *Saturday Night Fever*?

5 Which Disney film features the song *Breaking Free*?

6 1998's *Lock, Stock and Two Smoking Barrels* saw which former footballer make his screen debut?

7 Who played Queen Victoria in the 2017 film *Victoria and Abdul*?

8 Which actor starred as "Bandit" in the 1977 film *Smokey and the Bandit*?

9 In the 1975 film *Jaws*, what was the name of the fictional island?

Medium

10 Which early US film studio was famous for its "Kops"?

11 Which 1976 film shot Sylvester Stallone to fame?

12 Jack Black provided the voice of Po in which 2008 animated film?

13 Which 1991 comedy film was about a band trying to bring soul music to Dublin?

14 Who directed the 2009 film *Avatar*?

15 In the 1974 James Bond film *The Man with the Golden Gun*, what is the name of the villain?

16 Which actress co-starred with Richard Gere in *An Officer and a Gentleman*?

17 The 2010 film *Tangled* is based on which fairy-tale character?

18 Who plays Black Widow in the *Avengers* series of films?

Hard

19 What was the name of the lioness in the film *Born Free*?

20 Which Spanish-born actress starred in the 2008 film *Vicky Cristina Barcelona*?

Answers to QUIZ 280 – Money

1 George Washington
2 Sterling
3 Shares
4 Cashier
5 Gordon Brown
6 Pig
7 Bankruptcy
8 National Savings and Investments
9 Trade agreement
10 Glasgow
11 Occupational pensions
12 ECU (European Currency Unit)
13 1994
14 Half-crown
15 Krona
16 Voluntary
17 £500
18 Peseta
19 Saving
20 Mutual

QUIZ 283 – Pot Luck

ANSWERS ON PAGE 285

1 Who had a hit in 1974 with *The Air That I Breathe?*
2 What is the profession of the title character in the *Ace Ventura* films?
3 In a legal arrangement, which Latin term indicates a formal warning?
4 Which pop group topped the charts in 1998 with *Heartbeat/Tragedy*?
5 How many points is the blue ball worth in snooker?
6 Which people built Machu Picchu?
7 Which southern English county is divided into West and East?
8 What name is given to a Mexican cattle-farm manager or worker?
9 The Grand National horse race is run in which month?
10 Which actress played the title character in the 1989 film *Shirley Valentine*?
11 What word of naval origin describes diluted rum?
12 What name is given to a Japanese poem of seventeen syllables?
13 The state of Western Australia has which capital city?
14 Coulsdon and Purley are in which London borough?
15 Who played Tucker Jenkins in *Grange Hill* and its spin-off *Tucker's Luck*?
16 What are the saddlebags of a bicycle or motorcycle called?
17 How is an adult ovine female more commonly known?
18 What is written after a title to indicate that the author is unknown?
19 Which lake lies between Kenya, Tanzania and Uganda?
20 Guy Garvey is the frontman of which British group?

Answers to QUIZ 281 – Pot Luck

1 Judaism
2 New England
3 Sparta
4 Dame Maggie Smith
5 Coldplay
6 Aneurin Bevan
7 Sir Kenneth Branagh
8 Ape
9 *Treasure Island*
10 Simba
11 An omelette
12 Harry Houdini
13 Potomac
14 Crystal Palace
15 Kent
16 Ferret
17 Apse
18 Bellini
19 *Jack and the Beanstalk*
20 Hampshire

Easy

1 From what material is paper usually made?

2 Which father and daughter starred in the 1973 film *Paper Moon*?

3 What item is ignited by lighting a touchpaper?

4 In which 1906 novel by Edith Nesbit do the title characters observe a paper chase take place through a tunnel?

5 What term is given to the paper on which music is written?

6 *Paper Plane* was a 1972 single by which rock group?

7 Where would you find an endpaper?

8 What term is given to wallpaper that has a raised velvety surface?

9 Who wrote the 1966 song *Paperback Writer*?

10 In which country was papyrus used as an early writing material?

Medium

11 Which Scottish company, named after a historic country of the Highlands, is famous for its paperweights?

12 Rice paper is used in what activity?

13 Which US author wrote the 1888 novella *The Aspern Papers*?

14 Which two animals traditionally give their names to a paper chase?

15 A paperclip featured as the default Microsoft® Office Assistant character in software by which company?

16 What is indicated in the description of a company as a "paper tiger"?

17 What name is given to the collapsible Eastern light made of paper?

18 A paper napkin is also known by what name of French origin?

Hard

19 What was the name of the paper company in the original series of *The Office*?

20 How many quires of paper make up a ream?

Answers to QUIZ 282 – Films

1 *Sister Act*
2 Amish
3 *Chicken Run*
4 John Travolta
5 *High School Musical*
6 Vinnie Jones
7 Dame Judi Dench
8 Burt Reynolds
9 Amity
10 Keystone
11 *Rocky*
12 *Kung Fu Panda*
13 *The Commitments*
14 James Cameron
15 Scaramanga
16 Debra Winger
17 Rapunzel
18 Scarlett Johansson
19 Elsa
20 Penélope Cruz

QUIZ 285 – Pot Luck

1 Which actor played the title role in the 2000 film *Get Carter*?

2 In which Welsh city is the district called Tiger Bay?

3 Which spin-off from the original series of *Dallas* was set in a Californian cul-de-sac?

4 Tirana is the capital city of which country?

5 What two colours feature on a barber's pole?

6 Which footballer claimed the "Golden Boot" for finishing as the top scorer at the 2002 FIFA World Cup?

7 What was the forename of the character played by Lisa Kudrow in *Friends*?

8 The town of Bideford is in which county?

9 What is the name of the sauce made from melted butter, egg yolks and vinegar?

10 Which musical direction means "with brisk movement"?

11 Who produced the first pair of jeans in 1850?

12 In which body of water is the Isle of Man?

13 Which singer had hits in the 1990s with *Killer* and *Kiss from a Rose*?

14 The Mountbatten family home in Hampshire has what name?

15 What is the general name for a large blood vessel leading from the heart?

16 In the French comic strip, who is the best friend of Obelix?

17 What, in Greek mythology, is a river or spring nymph called?

18 From which London station did the first Eurostar service originally depart?

19 How many inches are there in two yards?

20 Which letter is furthest left on the bottom line of a standard keyboard?

Answers to QUIZ 283 – Pot Luck

1 The Hollies
2 Pet detective
3 *Caveat*
4 Steps
5 Five
6 The Incas
7 Sussex
8 Ranchero
9 April
10 Pauline Collins
11 Grog
12 Haiku
13 Perth
14 Croydon
15 Todd Carty
16 Panniers
17 Ewe
18 Anon
19 Lake Victoria
20 Elbow

QUIZ 286 – 1940s

Easy

1 What was the name of the 1944-45 battle also known as the Ardennes Offensive?

2 Who directed and starred in the 1941 film *Citizen Kane*?

3 The "Speedee Service System" was introduced in 1948 by which fast food company?

4 What do the initials VJ stand for in VJ Day, celebrated in 1945?

5 Who wrote the novel *Double Indemnity* (1943)?

6 First broadcast in 1946, which long-running radio programme's presenters include Jenni Murray and Jane Garvey?

7 Which US president was in office from 1945 to 1953?

8 The 1942 battle of Midway took place in which body of water?

9 Which medical organisation was founded in the UK in 1948?

10 Which was the only historic bridge in the Italian city of Florence that was not destroyed in 1944?

Medium

11 Sir Winston Churchill succeeded Neville Chamberlain as UK Prime Minister in which year?

12 In which country was Placido Domingo born in 1947?

13 Popular during this decade, what was the "jitterbug"?

14 Which 1948 film of a Shakespeare play won four Oscars, including Best Actor for Sir Laurence Olivier?

15 Where were the Summer Olympic Games held in 1948?

16 Which form of transport became fully owned by the state in the UK in 1948?

17 In which year did Queen Elizabeth II marry the Duke of Edinburgh?

Hard

18 The 1949 film *The Third Man* was set in which city?

19 What retail restriction began in the UK in January 1940?

20 To what did the Local Defence Volunteer Force change its name in 1941?

Answers to QUIZ 284 – Paper

1 Wood pulp
2 Ryan and Tatum O'Neal
3 Firework (or gunpowder)
4 *The Railway Children*
5 Manuscript paper
6 Status Quo
7 At the front or end of a book
8 Flock
9 Lennon and McCartney
10 Egypt
11 Caithness Glass
12 Cooking
13 Henry James
14 Hare and hounds
15 Microsoft
16 It is not as powerful as it seems
17 Chinese lantern
18 Serviette
19 Wernham Hogg
20 Twenty

1 What is the first name of Canadian singer Ms Lavigne?
2 What name is given to a tapering flag, particularly as used on a ship?
3 What is a waterfront promenade called in the USA?
4 *Wishing I Was Lucky* was a 1987 hit for which group?
5 On *Countdown*, how many letters are selected in each round?
6 The Pilgrims' Way runs from Winchester to which other city?
7 Which country has Tehran as its capital?
8 Retired swimmer Ian Thorpe had what nickname when he was competing?
9 Endocrinology is the study of what in the body?
10 Who played Tony Blair in the 2006 film *The Queen*?
11 Which chemical element has the symbol Sn?
12 Emma Hamilton was the mistress of which British naval hero?
13 What is the French term for dry or unsweetened sparkling wine?
14 In the British award, what does the "C" of CBE stand for?
15 *It's a Miracle* was a 1984 hit for which group?
16 Which type of drum has wires stretched across it?
17 The 2000 novel *The Amber Spyglass* was written by which author?
18 What attraction previously occupied the Legoland site in Berkshire?
19 What is the long, narrow pillow, often seen on a chaise longue, called?
20 Big Sur is a section of coast of which USA state?

Answers to QUIZ 285 – Pot Luck

1 Sylvester Stallone
2 Cardiff
3 *Knots Landing*
4 Albania
5 Red and white
6 Ronaldo
7 Phoebe
8 Devon
9 Hollandaise
10 Allegro
11 Levi Strauss
12 Irish Sea
13 Seal
14 Broadlands
15 Artery
16 Asterix
17 Naiad
18 Waterloo
19 72
20 Z

QUIZ 288 – 1960s Music

ANSWERS ON PAGE **290**

Easy

1 *Apache* was a hit for which group in 1960?
2 How were Davy Jones, Mickey Dolenz, Mike Nesmith and Peter Tork collectively known?
3 Levi Stubbs was the lead singer with which group?
4 *Little Red Rooster* was a 1964 chart-topper for which band?
5 *Pretty Flamingo* was a hit in 1966 for which group?
6 *Runaway* was a 1961 UK hit for which singer?
7 Which group had a 1964 hit with *The House of the Rising Sun*?
8 Who was the first singer to win the Eurovision Song Contest for the United Kingdom?
9 *With a Little Help from My Friends* was a 1968 chart-topper for which singer?
10 The name of which satellite gave The Tornados a 1962 UK hit?

Medium

11 What was the title of Roy Orbison's first UK hit?
12 Which group topped the charts in 1966 with *The Sun Ain't Gonna Shine Anymore*?
13 What was the title of Gerry and the Pacemaker's first UK single, which reached no.1?
14 *Cathy's Clown* was a 1960 hit for which duo?
15 What was the Beatles' second feature film?
16 Which group had a hit in 1965 with *Mr Tambourine Man*?
17 What was the subtitle of Elvis Presley's hit *It's Now or Never*?
18 *I Remember You* and *The Wayward Wind* were hits for which singer?
19 Which father and daughter topped the charts in 1967 with *Somethin' Stupid*?
20 *You Really Got Me* was a 1964 no.1 for which band?

Hard

Answers to QUIZ 286 – 1940s

1 Battle of the Bulge
2 Orson Welles
3 McDonald's
4 Victory in Japan
5 James M Cain
6 *Woman's Hour*
7 Harry S Truman
8 Pacific Ocean
9 National Health Service
10 Ponte Vecchio
11 1940
12 Spain
13 A dance
14 *Hamlet*
15 London
16 Railways
17 1947
18 Vienna
19 Food rationing
20 The Home Guard

QUIZ 289 – Pot Luck

ANSWERS ON PAGE 291

1 Which scandal featured in the film *All the President's Men*?

2 Which anniversary celebrates 60 years of marriage?

3 What is the name of Tom Hanks' character in *The Da Vinci Code* and its sequels?

4 Kid Creole was backed by which group?

5 On which racecourse is Tattenham Corner?

6 Which group topped the charts in 2003 with *Crashed the Wedding*?

7 If you were born on November 1, what would your birth sign be?

8 What is the name of the *Children in Need* bear?

9 Which strait separates Hampshire from the Isle of Wight?

10 Richmal Crompton wrote which series of books about a mischievous schoolboy?

11 In which region of France is claret wine made?

12 Which soprano was known as "the Swedish nightingale"?

13 19th-century grocer John Walker established which famous drinks brand?

14 What name is given to a stone-worker?

15 What groups of animals are described as bovine?

16 Lewis and Harris are part of which island group?

17 In geometry, what term is used for a segment of a circle?

18 Ghana has which city as its capital?

19 What was Mozart's middle name?

20 Which European capital city sits at the mouth of the river Tagus?

Answers to QUIZ 287 – Pot Luck

1 Avril
2 Pennant
3 Boardwalk
4 Wet Wet Wet
5 Nine
6 Canterbury
7 Iran
8 Thorpedo
9 Glands and hormones
10 Michael Sheen
11 Tin
12 Horatio Nelson (Viscount Nelson)
13 Brut
14 Commander
15 Culture Club
16 Snare drum
17 Philip Pullman
18 Windsor Safari Park
19 Bolster
20 California

QUIZ 290 – Sport

ANSWERS ON PAGE **292**

Easy

1 What name is given to a porter on a golf course?
2 How many players are in a basketball team?
3 What name is given to the area of the track from which the cars start a Grand Prix race?
4 What are the cross-pieces on a cricket wicket called?
5 Loose head and tight head define which position in a rugby team?
6 What is the surname of the brothers who took gold and silver in the 2016 Olympic triathlon?
7 What piece of classical music is associated with Torvill and Dean's 1984 Olympic win?
8 How many hurdles are there in a 110m hurdles race?
9 Who won the men's singles at Wimbledon in 1992?
10 In which annual event do teams take either the Middlesex station or the Surrey station?

Medium

11 What is a playing period in the game of polo called?
12 Which old name for England is associated with football team West Bromwich?
13 Where were the summer Olympic Games held in 1936?
14 Schuss and telemark are terms used in which winter sport?
15 In the Isle of Man TT races, what does "TT" stand for?
16 Which point follows deuce in a tennis match?
17 Which oriental martial art has a name meaning "empty hand"?
18 In 1981, who won the Grand National on Aldaniti?
19 In which field sport did Steve Backley compete for Great Britain?
20 Which legendary Victorian cricketer scored over 54,000 runs during his career?

Hard

Answers to QUIZ 288 – 1960s Music

1 The Shadows
2 The Monkees
3 The Four Tops
4 The Rolling Stones
5 Manfred Mann
6 Del Shannon
7 The Animals
8 Sandie Shaw (*Puppet on a String*)
9 Joe Cocker
10 Telstar
11 *Only the Lonely*
12 Walker Brothers
13 *How Do You Do It?*
14 Everly Brothers
15 *Help!*
16 The Byrds
17 *O Sole Mio*
18 Frank Ifield
19 Frank and Nancy Sinatra
20 The Kinks

QUIZ 291 – Pot Luck

ANSWERS ON PAGE 293

1 Yogi Bear lives in which fictional park?

2 What name is given to a person who searches for water with a divining rod?

3 Who had hits with *Simply the Best* and *Private Dancer*?

4 Stops, pipes and pedals appear on which instrument?

5 Which is the smallest of the four main Channel Islands?

6 The UN flag features which two colours?

7 What is the term for a US legal panel, which usually has 23 members?

8 Businessman Samuel Ryder initiated a cup in which sport?

9 What is the Scottish term for the steep slope of a hillside?

10 Which single was the 1984 festive no.1?

11 What is the area of Cambridge behind the river, which shares its name with another name for defenders?

12 Contestants must speak "without hesitation, repetition or deviation" for a fixed period of time on which radio show?

13 In which film musical did Sir Rex Harrison play Professor Henry Higgins?

14 What is the name of the vast desert situated in China and southern Mongolia?

15 Who played Lewis to John Thaw's Morse?

16 The Roman numerals VII represent which number?

17 Who played Galadriel in the *Lord of the Rings* trilogy?

18 Which Asian country was formerly known as Kampuchea?

19 An eagle's nest is given what name?

20 Which item of furniture has a French name that means "office"?

Answers to QUIZ 289 – Pot Luck

1 Watergate
2 Diamond
3 Robert Langdon
4 The Coconuts
5 Epsom
6 Busted
7 Scorpio
8 Pudsey
9 The Solent
10 *Just William*
11 Bordeaux
12 Jenny Lind
13 Johnnie Walker whisky
14 Mason
15 Cattle
16 Outer Hebrides (or Western Isles)
17 Arc
18 Accra
19 Amadeus
20 Lisbon

QUIZ 292 – Superstitions

Easy

1 How many years of bad luck are associated with breaking a mirror?

2 What is the name given to the phenomenon where a novice taking part in a new activity experiences unlikely success?

3 What item is considered unlucky to open indoors?

4 According to a well-known rhyme, what bird is considered unlucky when you view one, but lucky if you view two?

5 To break the bad luck when you spill salt, what are you required to do?

6 In which county is the village of Veryan, where a number of round houses were built so that the Devil had no corners in which to hide?

7 Which animal's foot is said to be lucky?

8 What four things are considered lucky for a bride to wear on her wedding day?

9 What item is considered lucky when nailed to a door?

Medium

10 To have good luck, what must one do when one finds a penny on the floor?

11 What chicken bone is it considered lucky to break with another?

12 It is considered unlucky to put what new items of clothing on a table?

13 Which number is generally thought to be the luckiest?

14 Which day is traditionally particularly unlucky if it falls on a Friday?

15 On a pavement, what is it considered unlucky to step on?

16 Touching an item made of which material is generally considered to bring good luck?

17 Which plant is said to be lucky when it has four leaves?

18 Which two words are often said to someone who has just sneezed?

Hard

19 In China, what colour is considered lucky?

20 What is it considered unlucky to walk beneath?

Answers to QUIZ 290 – Sport

1 Caddie
2 Five
3 The grid
4 Bails
5 Prop
6 Brownlee
7 *Bolero*
8 Ten
9 Andre Agassi
10 The Boat Race
11 Chukka
12 Albion
13 Berlin
14 Skiing
15 Tourist Trophy
16 Advantage
17 Karate
18 Bob Champion
19 Javelin
20 WG Grace

QUIZ 293 – Pot Luck

ANSWERS ON PAGE 295

1 Near which Scottish town would you find the sculptures called *The Kelpies*?
2 Which group backed Smokey Robinson?
3 In which event is "the Fosbury flop" a technique?
4 Which lough in Northern Ireland is the largest freshwater lake in the UK?
5 Pope Paul III took what action against King Henry VIII in 1538?
6 Which river flows through Durham?
7 What is the name of the Flintstones' daughter?
8 A clerical dignitary attached to a cathedral shares what name with a general rule or principle?
9 What was the title of George Michael's first solo album?
10 Which title is shared by an old TV travel show, an album by Pink Floyd and a 1987 film starring Emily Lloyd?
11 In which county is Kettering?
12 What name is given to a writer of words for a song?
13 In 1989, what word was dropped from the title of soap opera *Emmerdale*?
14 Who wrote the play *Private Lives* (1930)?
15 What was the medieval knightly system of courtesy and consideration called?
16 Porridge has what main constituent?
17 Which unwanted plant, also known as convolvulus, twines around any support?
18 Qatar has what official language?
19 What is Whitehall's war memorial called?
20 In which James Bond film did Jane Seymour play a psychic?

Answers to QUIZ 291 – Pot Luck

1 Jellystone Park
2 Dowser
3 Tina Turner
4 Organ
5 Sark
6 Blue and white
7 Grand jury
8 Golf
9 Brae
10 *Do They Know It's Christmas?*
11 Backs
12 *Just a Minute*
13 *My Fair Lady*
14 Gobi
15 Kevin Whately
16 Seven
17 Cate Blanchett
18 Cambodia
19 Eyrie
20 Bureau

QUIZ 294 – Technology

ANSWERS ON PAGE 296

Easy

1 What new product did Apple release on April 24, 2015?

2 Which website featured in the film *The Social Network*?

3 What is the biggest key on a standard keyboard?

4 In which year was Twitter founded?

5 On mobile phones with a keypad on the handset, which letters appear on the number 8 key?

6 What name is given to the pen-like device used with a touchscreen computer?

7 What word is "app" short for?

8 Jimmy Wales was a co-founder of which website that launched in 2001?

9 Which mythological creature lends its name to a person who posts offensive messages on social media sites?

10 What long-handled device enables phone users to take wider photographs with their camera?

Medium

11 Which website was launched in 2010 to provide a "virtual pinboard" for users?

12 The ZX80 and the ZX Spectrum home computers were introduced in the early 1980s by which British inventor?

13 What on-line feature for discussions takes its name from an ancient Roman meeting place?

14 The Snapchat logo features what type of spooky character?

15 Which operating system has had versions called Lollipop and Marshmallow?

16 What does RAM stand for?

17 Martha Lane Fox and Brent Hoberman founded which internet company in 1998?

18 Which fruit and mathematical symbol combine to give the name of a basic computer used in education?

Hard

19 What does the "C" of ICT stand for?

20 What is COBOL an early example of?

Answers to QUIZ 292 – Superstitions

1 Seven years
2 Beginner's luck
3 Umbrella
4 Magpie
5 Throw salt over your shoulder
6 Cornwall
7 Rabbit's foot
8 Something old, new, borrowed and blue
9 Horseshoe
10 Pick it up
11 Chicken wishbone
12 Pair of shoes
13 Seven
14 13th
15 Cracks
16 Wood
17 Clover
18 "Bless you"
19 Red
20 A ladder

QUIZ 295 – Pot Luck

ANSWERS ON PAGE 297

1 Who created the characters of Wallace and Gromit?

2 In the TV series *Father Ted*, who played Mrs Doyle?

3 Which is the longest race in the decathlon?

4 Situated on the Mississippi, what is Tennessee's largest city?

5 What was the title of the 1983 hit duet by Kenny Rogers and Dolly Parton?

6 Which town is further south, Aberystwyth or Tenby?

7 *Toy Story*'s cowboy hero has what name?

8 How many degrees are there in half a circle?

9 What is the capital of Canada?

10 The 1964 film *Mary Poppins* starred which actress in the title role?

11 Who wrote the 1791 poem *The Banks o' Doon*?

12 On a standard Monopoly™ board, which property is the same colour as Park Lane?

13 What does the "D" of MOD stand for?

14 What is the name of Prospero's slave in Shakespeare's *The Tempest*?

15 The East Anglian town of Cromer is particularly associated with which type of seafood?

16 How many points does a snowflake have?

17 Which type of dagger is the traditional ceremonial sidearm of Scottish Highland regiment officers?

18 The Grand Union Canal links London with which other city?

19 Which 1960s puppet fought the Mysterons?

20 What is the Russian term for a country house or cottage?

Answers to QUIZ 293 – Pot Luck

1 Falkirk
2 The Miracles
3 The high jump
4 Neagh
5 Excommunicated him
6 Wear
7 Pebbles
8 Canon
9 *Faith*
10 *Wish You Were Here*
11 Northamptonshire
12 Lyricist
13 *Farm*
14 Sir Noël Coward
15 Chivalry
16 Oats
17 Bindweed
18 Arabic
19 The Cenotaph
20 *Live and Let Die*

QUIZ 296 – Natural World

ANSWERS ON PAGE 298

1 Which river flows through Budapest and Belgrade?
2 What line on a map connects points of the same height?
3 What is the smallest kind of living creature?
4 In which two English counties is Romney Marsh?
5 By what other name is the great maple tree known?
6 Where would a troglodyte's home be found?
7 What large bodies of water can be Black, Red, White or Yellow?
8 Fort William is the nearest town to which Scottish mountain?
9 What name is given to the study of the earth's crust and rocks?
10 What is the largest freshwater lake in the world?
11 The area around the Pacific Ocean known for earthquakes and volcanic eruptions is given what name?
12 Which tree was famously affected by a "Dutch" disease?
13 What word is given to the point where the land and sky appear to meet?
14 Which island group lies north-west of the Shetlands?
15 Situated on the Peru/Bolivia border, which lake is the largest in South America?
16 What name is given to the hilly area of Yorkshire?
17 In which two parts of the world is the midnight sun visible in midsummer?
18 Which country has the longest coastline in the world?
19 The World Heritage Site of the Jurassic Coast lies within which two counties?
20 What is the name given to the point at which the Sun is at its highest?

Answers to QUIZ 294 – Technology

1 A watch
2 Facebook
3 Space bar
4 2006
5 TUV
6 Stylus
7 Application
8 Wikipedia
9 Troll
10 Selfie stick
11 Pinterest
12 Sir Clive Sinclair
13 Forum
14 Ghost
15 Android
16 Random access memory
17 Lastminute.com
18 Raspberry Pi
19 Communications
20 Programming language

QUIZ 297 – Pot Luck

ANSWERS ON PAGE 299

1 In which season does the vernal equinox take place?
2 Alfred the Great's kingdom had which city as its capital?
3 Which word is used for fiscal studies on a large scale?
4 What was the title of the Jam's final single?
5 Jimmy Somerville left which band to form the Communards?
6 Who was president of the USA from 1974 to 1977?
7 The 2009 film *My Sister's Keeper* starred which actress as Sara Fitzgerald?
8 Who was Tina Turner's 1960s singing partner and former husband?
9 Spain and Portugal occupy which peninsula?
10 In which athletics event did Jonathan Edwards take the Olympic gold medal in 2000?
11 Which fish is cured to make a kipper?
12 What is the name of the water vole in *The Wind in the Willows* (1908)?
13 *Perfect Moment* was a hit for which ex-*EastEnders* actress in 1999?
14 Which children's series featured a pirate ship called *The Black Pig*?
15 Which architect designed Blenheim Palace?
16 Of what are ink-caps, death caps and puffballs all types?
17 *Nevermind* is a 1991 album by which band?
18 What term is given to the hammer used by judges and auctioneers?
19 Who played Sugar Kane Kowalczyk in the 1959 film *Some Like it Hot*?
20 What is an appaloosa?

Answers to QUIZ 295 – Pot Luck

1 Nick Park
2 Pauline McLynn
3 1500m
4 Memphis
5 *Islands in the Stream*
6 Tenby
7 Woody
8 180
9 Ottawa
10 Dame Julie Andrews
11 Robert Burns
12 Mayfair
13 Defence
14 Caliban
15 Crab
16 Six
17 Dirk
18 Birmingham
19 Captain Scarlet
20 Dacha

QUIZ 298 – Modern Fiction

Easy

1 Who created the character of Bridget Jones, famous for her diary?

2 Which 1995 Nick Hornby novel's principal character was record shop owner Rob Fleming?

3 Which 2003 novel is told in a series of letters written by Eva Khatchadourian?

4 The characters of Sam Vimes and Granny Weatherwax were created by which author?

5 What type of supernatural creature was interviewed in the title of a 1994 novel by Anne Rice?

6 Emma Donoghue wrote which 2011 novel that was made into a 2015 film starring Brie Larson?

7 Which London street gave Monica Ali the title for her first novel?

8 What are the first names of the two main characters in the 2009 novel *One Day*?

9 Who wrote *The Lovely Bones*, later filmed starring Mark Wahlberg?

10 *The Postcard* (2016) and *Coming Home* (2018) are novels written by which TV presenter?

Medium

11 Whose wife is referenced in the title of a 2005 book by Audrey Niffenegger?

12 Which series of novels by George RR Martin is the basis for the TV series *Game of Thrones*?

13 Harry Bosch is the detective creation of which author?

14 Who wrote the award-winning 1995 novel *Behind the Scenes at the Museum*?

15 Which 2004 novel by David Mitchell consists of six stories which are interrupted then resumed later in the book?

Hard

16 Which of Henry VIII's wives was the subject of Philippa Gregory's 2015 novel *The Taming of the Queen*?

17 Dr Kay Scarpetta is the creation of which writer?

18 Who was the Irish writer of the 1990 novel *Circle of Friends?*

19 Which 1987 Stephen King novel featured the character of Paul Sheldon who was recovering from a car crash?

20 Khaled Hosseini's novel *The Kite Runner* features a family from which country?

Answers to QUIZ 296 – Natural World

1 Danube
2 A contour line
3 Amoeba
4 Kent and East Sussex
5 Sycamore
6 In a cave or hole in the ground
7 Seas
8 Ben Nevis
9 Geology
10 Superior
11 Ring of Fire
12 Elm
13 Horizon
14 Faroe Islands
15 Titicaca
16 The Dales
17 Arctic and Antarctic Circles
18 Canada
19 Devon and Dorset
20 Zenith

QUIZ 299 – Pot Luck

ANSWERS ON PAGE 301

1 Who was the lead singer with Roxy Music?

2 In which Wiltshire town is STEAM, the Museum of the Great Western Railway?

3 Who played Annie in the 1994 film *Speed*?

4 Lanzarote lies north-east of which of the Canary Islands?

5 What is the set of three dots indicating an omission in writing called?

6 Mr Rochester appears in which classic 1847 novel?

7 Which cartoon series featured the character of Officer Dibble?

8 The play *A Doll's House* was written by which dramatist?

9 What caused the ill-fated Titanic to sink?

10 In the 1995 film *Se7en*, who played Brad Pitt's wife?

11 Which African country is separated from Spain by the Strait of Gibraltar?

12 What was the title of the 1980s yachting-based TV series with Jan Harvey?

13 On which continent is the country of Iraq?

14 Which river in Devon gives its name to Devon's county town?

15 What sort of food is vichyssoise?

16 What, in cricket, is a run that is not credited to a batsman?

17 Which meat is obtained from deer?

18 Karl Marx is buried in which cemetery?

19 What name for the country is shown on Ireland's postage stamps?

20 Crathie Kirk is close to which royal residence?

Answers to QUIZ 297 – Pot Luck

1 Spring
2 Winchester
3 Macroeconomics
4 *Beat Surrender*
5 Bronski Beat
6 Gerald Ford
7 Cameron Diaz
8 Ike
9 Iberian
10 The triple jump
11 Herring
12 Ratty
13 Martine McCutcheon
14 *Captain Pugwash*
15 Sir John Vanbrugh
16 Fungi
17 Nirvana
18 Gavel
19 Marilyn Monroe
20 A horse

QUIZ 300 – Children's Television

ANSWERS ON PAGE 302

Easy

1 Which is the UK's longest-running children's television show?

2 Which cartoon hero has a sidekick called Penfold?

3 In *Thunderbirds*, which organisation do the Tracy family run?

4 What was the title of the series designed for hearing-impaired children, whose presenters included Tony Hart?

5 Which character wore a black suit and bowler hat when visiting a magic fancy-dress shop?

6 Which series that ran from 1965 to 1977 was based on a French stop-motion animation show?

7 The Sun Baby featured at the beginning and end of each episode in which series?

8 Which animated US series ran from 1985 to 1989 and included the characters Lion-O, Panthro and Jaga?

9 Which principal character in an animated series regularly fought the evil Skeletor?

Medium

10 What was the title of the stop-motion clay animated series which centred on a family of penguins?

11 Iggle Piggle and Upsy Daisy appeared in which series?

12 What type of animals were Pinky and Perky?

13 Which animated character was originally voiced by Neil Morrissey before the series was revamped in 2014?

14 In the series *Charlie and Lola*, what relation is Lola to Charlie?

15 Where did the Wombles carry out their litter-clearing activities?

16 Which stop-motion series was set in the fictional Welsh village of Pontypandy?

17 Which three words preceded "switch off your television set and go out and do something less boring instead" in the title of a long-running series?

Hard

18 In which series was the title pink-and-white-striped character owned by a young girl named Emily?

19 Which whistling creatures eat soup provided by the Soup Dragon?

20 Which presenter, who went on to join *Countryfile*, had a long-running *Newsround*?

Answers to QUIZ 298 – Modern Fiction

1 Helen Fielding
2 *High Fidelity*
3 *We Need to Talk about Kevin*
4 Sir Terry Pratchett
5 Vampire
6 *Room*
7 Brick Lane
8 Dexter and Emma
9 Alice Sebold
10 Fern Britton
11 *The Time Traveler's Wife*
12 *A Song of Ice and Fire*
13 Michael Connelly
14 Kate Atkinson
15 *Cloud Atlas*
16 Catherine Parr
17 Patricia Cornwell
18 Maeve Binchy
19 *Misery*
20 Afghanistan

QUIZ 301 – Pot Luck

ANSWERS ON PAGE 303

1 Which Indian resort region once belonged to Portugal?
2 To which plant genus does the daffodil belong?
3 Which comedy film starring Bill Murray was based on *A Christmas Carol*?
4 Ronnie Corbett starred as Timothy Lumsden in which sitcom?
5 Which organ is affected by hepatitis?
6 In which Surrey town is the Sandown Park racecourse located?
7 Which city has the postcode prefix CF?
8 What is the large decorated goblet used in church for holding wine called?
9 The Model T was introduced by which car manufacturer in 1908?
10 Who accompanied Billy Preston on the 1979 duet *With You I'm Born Again*?
11 Which fruit is known as a bell pepper in the US?
12 What does Arthur Dent wear throughout *The Hitchhiker's Guide To The Galaxy*?
13 According to the Bible, which kind of people will inherit the Earth?
14 Which character did Ingrid Bergman play in the film *Casablanca* (1942)?
15 Where is the Isle of Wight regatta held?
16 The TV presenter and comedian brothers Jeremy and Tim have what surname?
17 What is the anatomical name for the large bone of the upper leg?
18 What sport is played by the Miami Dolphins?
19 What part of the proboscis monkey is most prominent?
20 Oslo is the capital city of which country?

Answers to QUIZ 299 – Pot Luck

1 Bryan Ferry
2 Swindon
3 Sandra Bullock
4 Fuerteventura
5 Ellipsis
6 *Jane Eyre*
7 *Top Cat*
8 Henrik Ibsen
9 It hit an iceberg
10 Gwyneth Paltrow
11 Morocco
12 *Howards' Way*
13 Asia
14 Exe
15 Soup
16 An extra
17 Venison
18 Highgate Cemetery
19 Eire
20 Balmoral

Easy Medium Hard

QUIZ 302 – Steps

ANSWERS ON PAGE 304

Easy

1 Which singer/songwriter topped the 2000 album charts with *White Ladder*?

2 What name is given to the steps set into a fence or wall to help people climb it?

3 "Walkies!" was the catchphrase of which dog trainer who featured on TV in the 1980s?

4 Fashion models parade on which raised platform?

5 Which was the title of the 2000 chart-topping single by Steps?

6 What is the American term for a careless pedestrian?

7 In which part of the body would a pacemaker be fitted?

8 Who had a Top Ten hit in 1968 with *Step Inside Love*?

9 A ladder might appear in which item of clothing?

10 Which walker, known as AW, is particularly associated with guides to the Lake District?

Medium

11 What symbols are embedded on Hollywood's Walk of Fame to honour people in the entertainment industry?

12 In the classic board game, if ladders help you reach the finish, which creatures present obstacles?

13 *Parisienne Walkways* was a hit in both 1979 and 1993 for which guitarist?

14 The UK code for pedestrians is named after which colour and symbol?

15 Who had a hit in 1960 with *Three Steps to Heaven*?

16 Which TV series features Andrew Lincoln as Sheriff Deputy Rick Grimes?

17 Who recounted his hiking adventures in 1998's *A Walk in the Woods*...?

18 ...and who played him in the 2015 film adaptation?

Hard

19 Who fronted the 1960s pop group the Pacemakers?

20 Which actor starred in the 1935 version of *The 39 Steps*?

Answers to QUIZ 300 – Children's Television

1 *Blue Peter*
2 Danger Mouse
3 International Rescue
4 *Vision On*
5 Mr Benn
6 *The Magic Roundabout*
7 *Teletubbies*
8 *ThunderCats*
9 He-Man
10 *Pingu*
11 *In the Night Garden*
12 Pigs
13 *Bob the Builder*
14 Sister
15 Wimbledon Common
16 *Fireman Sam*
17 *Why Don't You?*
18 *Bagpuss*
19 The Clangers
20 John Craven

QUIZ 303 – Pot Luck

ANSWERS ON PAGE 305

1 The duck-billed platypus is native to which country?
2 Which actress starred in the 2009 film *An Education*?
3 What is Captain Poldark's first name?
4 In which county is Blackburn?
5 Who had a 1988 hit with *One Moment in Time*?
6 Which grinning feline did Alice meet in Wonderland?
7 "The Sunshine State" is the nickname of which US state?
8 Who played Arnold Schwarzenegger's brother in the 1988 film *Twins*?
9 Which star sign is between Capricorn and Pisces?
10 Which small Cambridgeshire city is famed for its cathedral?
11 During the Falklands War, who was the UK Prime Minister?
12 Which sport featured in the 1996 film *Tin Cup*?
13 What is the outward motion of the tide called?
14 The NEC is located in which English city?
15 What cookery measure corresponds roughly to 5 millilitres?
16 Which one of the seven deadly sins involves eating to excess?
17 In *Absolutely Fabulous*, which character was played by Jennifer Saunders?
18 On which river does the annual ceremony of Swan Upping take place?
19 What type of creature is a Swaledale?
20 Which variety of curry is named after the wide, round-bottomed metal pan in which it is served?

Answers to QUIZ 301 – Pot Luck

1 Goa
2 *Narcissus*
3 *Scrooged*
4 *Sorry!*
5 The liver
6 Esher
7 Cardiff
8 Chalice
9 Henry Ford
10 Syreeta
11 Capsicum
12 A dressing-gown
13 The Meek
14 Ilsa Lund
15 Cowes
16 Vine
17 Femur
18 American football
19 Its nose
20 Norway

QUIZ 304 – Comedians

ANSWERS ON PAGE 306

Easy

1 Who is the host of *8 Out of 10 Cats*?

2 Who is Jennifer Saunders' comedy partner?

3 What are the first names of Hale and Pace?

4 The BBC sitcom *Not Going Out* is written by and stars which comedian?

5 Which comedienne presented the Royal Variety Show in 2017, the first solo female to do so?

6 The topical show *The Last Leg* is hosted by which Australian comedian?

7 Which two comedians began presenting *The Great British Bake Off* in 2017?

8 Who are the two team captains of *Have I Got News For You*?

9 Who was Syd Little's comedy partner?

10 The series *Modern Life is Goodish* featured which comedian?

Medium

11 Who is the host of *Would I Lie to You?*

12 Richard Osman appears as a team captain against which comedian in *Insert Name Here*?

13 What is the name of Sue Perkins' long-time comedy partner?

14 Who is TV's *Chatty Man*?

15 Who co-hosted Robot Wars from 2016 to 2018?

16 In the TV series *The Young Ones*, who portrayed Rick?

17 Which comedian won *Celebrity MasterChef* in 2013?

18 Greg and Alan, the stars of *Man Down* and *Jonathan Creek* respectively, share which surname?

19 Which comedian starred in *Fresh Meat* and *Bad Education*?

20 What is the first name of Mr Hill, former host of *TV Burp*?

Hard

Answers to QUIZ 302 – Steps

1 David Gray
2 Stile
3 Barbara Woodhouse
4 Catwalk
5 *Stomp*
6 Jaywalker
7 Heart
8 Cilla Black
9 Tights or a stocking
10 Alfred Wainwright
11 Stars
12 Snakes
13 Gary Moore
14 Green cross code
15 Eddie Cochran
16 *The Walking Dead*
17 Bill Bryson
18 Robert Redford
19 Gerry Marsden
20 Robert Donat

1 Whom did Michelle Dotrice play in the TV series *Some Mothers Do 'Ave 'Em*?
2 Which dance is associated with the Moulin Rouge?
3 Who starred as John Nash in the 2001 film *A Beautiful Mind*?
4 *Love Will Tear Us Apart* was originally a hit for which band?
5 Which bodily organ was once considered the seat of melancholy?
6 What is the fruit of the wild rose called?
7 Dame Katherine Grainger won four Olympic medals for Great Britain in which sport?
8 What was the title of the 1981 Eurovision-winning song by Buck's Fizz?
9 What term is given to the release of a prisoner subject to a period of good behaviour?
10 How many blank tiles are there in a Scrabble® set?
11 In which county is Aylesbury?
12 What type of creature is an opossum?
13 The Royal Opera House is in which area of London?
14 Which Bond film features the bowler-hatted baddie Oddjob?
15 How are the US group of universities including Yale and Princeton known?
16 Which public school did actor Damian Lewis attend?
17 Who succeeded Ken Livingstone as London's mayor?
18 What is the alternate name for a castle in chess?
19 To what does the expression "the fourth estate" refer?
20 Which natural harbour of southern England contains Brownsea Island?

Answers to QUIZ 303 – Pot Luck

1 Australia
2 Carey Mulligan
3 Ross
4 Lancashire
5 Whitney Houston
6 Cheshire Cat
7 Florida
8 Danny DeVito
9 Aquarius
10 Ely
11 Margaret Thatcher (Baroness Thatcher)
12 Golf
13 Ebb
14 Birmingham
15 Teaspoonful
16 Gluttony
17 Edina Monsoon
18 Thames
19 A sheep
20 Balti

QUIZ 306 – Desserts

ANSWERS ON PAGE 308

Easy

1 *Crème pâtissière* is a thick pastry cream similar to what sweet egg-based confection?

2 What dessert is made by mixing soft cooked fruit with whipped cream or custard?

3 What Italian dessert is usually composed of sponge fingers, coffee, mascarpone and chocolate?

4 An Apfelstrudel is a pastry containing which type of fruit?

5 How is the dessert *île flottante* known in English?

6 What brand-name powdered dessert is whisked with milk to create a mousse?

7 Which traditional English dessert contains sponge fingers soaked in sherry, fruit jelly, custard and cream?

8 The term for "sweetheart" in Cockney rhyming slang references which dessert?

9 What name is given to a dessert consisting of ice cream and cake, topped with meringue and then cooked?

Medium

10 What frozen dessert is made from sweetened water with flavouring, often fruit juice?

11 Neapolitan ice cream contains which three flavours?

12 What name is given to a brownie-like dessert that substitutes vanilla for the cocoa?

13 What baked, egg-based French dish is notoriously difficult to keep risen?

14 An upside-down cake traditionally features which tropical fruit?

15 What is the English translation of the name of the Italian dessert *panna cotta*?

16 "Banoffee" is a word combining which two main ingredients of banoffee pie?

17 Often used as a dessert fruit, which plant has edible pink stems and poisonous leaves?

18 Which fruit is associated with the dessert named after opera singer Dame Nellie Melba?

Hard

19 How is fruit cooked if it is served in a "compote"?

20 What does the name of the French dessert *parfait* mean in English?

Answers to QUIZ 304 – Comedians

1 Jimmy Carr
2 Dawn French
3 Gareth and Norman
4 Lee Mack
5 Miranda Hart
6 Adam Hills
7 Sandi Toksvig and Noel Fielding
8 Paul Merton and Ian Hislop
9 Eddie Large
10 Dave Gorman
11 Rob Brydon
12 Josh Widdicombe
13 Mel Giedroyc
14 Alan Carr
15 Dara Ó Briain
16 Rik Mayall
17 Adrian Edmondson
18 Davies
19 Jack Whitehall
20 Harry

QUIZ 307 – Pot Luck

ANSWERS ON PAGE 309

1 What is the name of the Channel which forms the waterway between Wales and south-west England?

2 Which motorway is known as the London Orbital?

3 Which actor directed and starred in the 1998 film *The Horse Whisperer*?

4 In which country is the football team PSV Eindhoven based?

5 What was the name of the Beatles' record label?

6 Which film includes the song *White Christmas*?

7 What is the cube root of 1000?

8 *An Unexpected Journey* was the subtitle of which 2012 film?

9 Who wrote *How to be a Domestic Goddess?*

10 What is the meaning of the Latin phrase *ad nauseam*?

11 In the Bible, which of Jacob's sons was sold as a slave by his brothers?

12 Which trees feature in the name of the London district east of Battersea, Nine _?

13 What is a fox's tail called?

14 Who broadcast the radio series *Letter from America* from 1946 until 2004?

15 To which language family do Breton and Welsh belong?

16 Which military bugle call is played at the end of the day and during services of remembrance?

17 What is the term for a vast astronomical area containing many star systems?

18 An ibex is what type of animal?

19 Who is the trumpeter with a long hooked nose in *The Muppet Show*?

20 What is the word for pruning and sculpting of trees and shrubs into artistic shapes?

Answers to QUIZ 305 – Pot Luck

1 Betty
2 Can-can
3 Russell Crowe
4 Joy Division
5 Spleen
6 Hip
7 Rowing
8 *Making Your Mind Up*
9 Probation
10 Two
11 Buckinghamshire
12 Marsupial
13 Covent Garden
14 *Goldfinger*
15 Ivy League
16 Eton
17 Boris Johnson
18 Rook
19 The press
20 Poole

QUIZ 308 – Disney Films

ANSWERS ON PAGE 310

Easy

1 Which 1997 film was the first to be completely inspired by classical mythology rather than fairy tales?

2 The character named Mushu, voiced by Eddie Murphy, appears in which 1998 film based on a Chinese legend?

3 In which 1950 film do the stepsisters Drizella and Anastasia appear?

4 What is the title of the 1951 Disney film based on books by Lewis Carroll?

5 Which 1963 Disney film was based on the boyhood of King Arthur?

6 The song *Ev'rybody Wants to Be a Cat* features in which 1970 film?

7 What is the name of the title character from *The Hunchback of Notre Dame*?

8 Which film follows the adventures of an American cocker spaniel given by Jim Dear to his wife, Darling?

9 In *The Fox and the Hound*, is the character called Copper the fox or the hound?

Medium

10 In the 1942 film, what type of creature is Bambi?

11 What is the name of the wood-carver responsible for carving Pinocchio?

12 Who provided the voice of the genie in the 1992 film *Aladdin*?

13 Which 2017 film set in Mexico won the Best Animated Film and Best Original Song Oscars?

14 Which 1991 animated film was remade as a live-action film in 2017?

15 Based on a legendary British outlaw, which film was released in 1973 with a cartoon fox as the title character?

16 What was the name of Disney's first fully animated feature film to be released?

17 In which animated feature film does Mickey Mouse disastrously command a broom to do his chores?

Hard

18 Which was the last film to actually be produced by Walt Disney?

19 Which 1989 film based on a Danish fairytale was adapted into a musical in 2008?

20 In the 1994 film *The Lion King*, what is the name of the meerkat?

Answers to QUIZ 306 – Desserts

1 Custard
2 Fool
3 Tiramisu
4 Apple
5 Floating island
6 Angel Delight
7 Trifle
8 Treacle tart
9 Baked Alaska
10 Sorbet
11 Strawberry, chocolate and vanilla
12 Blondie
13 Soufflé
14 Pineapple
15 Cooked cream
16 Banana and toffee
17 Rhubarb
18 Peach
19 With syrup
20 Perfect

QUIZ 309 – Pot Luck

ANSWERS ON PAGE 311

1 By which abbreviated name is the central character of Dickens' *Great Expectations* known?

2 What kind of animal is a tench?

3 In human anatomy, what is the name of the tendon found down the back of the leg?

4 Which Latin word is used for an open-roofed entrance hall or central court in a building?

5 Which actor starred as Danny Trevanion in the TV series *Wild at Heart*?

6 The fermentation of sugar produces which substance found in beer and wine?

7 Which English city has Oxford Road, Victoria and Piccadilly railway stations?

8 Which Scottish loch is said to have "bonnie banks"?

9 What is the common abbreviated spelling of "boatswain"?

10 In which country did karaoke originate?

11 What is the nationality of a person from Tel Aviv?

12 Who had a hit in 1982 with *Heartbreaker*?

13 In which county is Saxmundham?

14 Which is the only surviving Wonder of the Ancient World?

15 Who played the title character in the 2001 film *Captain Corelli's Mandolin*?

16 Which football team's mascot is Stamford the Lion?

17 What does a vulcanologist study?

18 Which ancient site of a Greek sporting festival lends its name to a London exhibition hall?

19 Whose novels were set in the fictional Wessex?

20 Which country has the international car registration letter E?

Answers to QUIZ 307 – Pot Luck

1 Bristol
2 M25
3 Robert Redford
4 The Netherlands
5 Apple
6 *Holiday Inn*
7 Ten
8 *The Hobbit*
9 Nigella Lawson
10 "To the point of sickness"
11 Joseph
12 Elms (Nine Elms)
13 A brush
14 Alistair Cooke
15 Celtic
16 The Last Post
17 Galaxy
18 Goat
19 Gonzo
20 Topiary

QUIZ 310 – Up and Down

ANSWERS ON PAGE 312

Easy

1 Which London football team played home games at the Boleyn Ground at Upton Park until 2016?

2 Who became presenter of *Countdown* in 2012?

3 In which county is the town of Upton-upon-Severn?

4 Who played Lord Grantham in *Downton Abbey*?

5 Which Irish group covered Billy Joel's *Uptown Girl* in 2001?

6 A hoedown is what type of dance?

7 Which theatrical verb means to force someone else out of the limelight?

8 What betting items are said to be down at a critical moment?

9 Mark Ronson's *Uptown Funk* was the best-selling song in the UK in which year?

10 Which forest, covering both West and East Sussex, was the inspiration for the Winnie-the-Pooh stories?

Medium

11 Upsilon is a letter in which alphabet?

12 What term is given to the return of a spacecraft into the sea?

13 In the TV series *Up Pompeii!*, which comedian played Lurcio?

14 What term for a hand covering is proverbially thrown down in a challenge?

15 Which car manufacturer produces the "up!"?

16 In which two counties are the Blackdown Hills?

17 Which instrument can be upright or grand?

18 A modestly sized terraced house is often referred to as how many up and down?

19 With which bird is an early riser said to get up?

20 Which day of the week is often known as "dress-down"?

Hard

Answers to QUIZ 308 – Disney Films

1 *Hercules*
2 *Mulan*
3 *Cinderella*
4 *Alice in Wonderland*
5 *The Sword in the Stone*
6 *The Aristocats*
7 Quasimodo
8 *Lady and the Tramp*
9 Hound
10 A deer
11 Geppetto
12 Robin Williams
13 *Coco*
14 *Beauty and the Beast*
15 *Robin Hood*
16 *Snow White and the Seven Dwarfs*
17 *Fantasia*
18 *The Jungle Book*
19 *The Little Mermaid*
20 Timon

QUIZ 311 – Pot Luck

ANSWERS ON PAGE 313

1 Which chart-topping group of the mid-1970s were noted for wearing tartan?
2 The 2002 series of *Celebrity Big Brother* was won by which singer?
3 What is the name of the annual American football championship game?
4 Who, in the Bible, was Esau's brother and the son of Isaac?
5 The inside of a pistachio nut is what colour?
6 Which branch of science studies viruses, bacteria etc?
7 Who directed the 2004 film *Million Dollar Baby*?
8 Catherine Parr was which of Henry VIII's wives?
9 The Radcliffe Road End is in which cricket ground?
10 What type of soil has a pH value of less than seven?
11 What is Winnie-the-Pooh's favourite food?
12 What prefix indicates 10^6?
13 Which Elvis single reached the top of the UK charts shortly after his death in 1977?
14 A purple emperor is what type of creature?
15 What is the main alcoholic ingredient in a margarita cocktail?
16 What is the term for a call made in a game of bridge?
17 According to the proverb, where does charity begin?
18 What word meaning a snooze also refers to the raised hairs on fabric?
19 According to the nursery rhyme, which child has "far to go"?
20 Which is the second largest city in the Netherlands?

Answers to QUIZ 309 – Pot Luck

1 Pip
2 Fish
3 Hamstring
4 Atrium
5 Stephen Tompkinson
6 Alcohol
7 Manchester
8 Lomond
9 Bosun
10 Japan
11 Israeli
12 Dionne Warwick
13 Suffolk
14 The Great Pyramid of Giza
15 Nicolas Cage
16 Chelsea FC
17 Volcanoes
18 Olympia
19 Thomas Hardy
20 Spain

Easy

1 The emperors of Germany were given which title?
2 Who was President of France from 2012 to 2017?
3 What is the lower house of Parliament in the Irish Republic?
4 Which Indian leader who advocated non-violent protest was assassinated in 1948?
5 China's Communist Party was led by which chairman until his death in 1976?
6 Which US President was involved in the Watergate scandal?
7 Who was President of Russia from 1991 to 1999?
8 The Isle of Man's parliament is given what name?
9 Who was Rhodesian Prime Minister when the country declared itself independent in 1965?
10 Which former British colony was returned to China in 1997?

Medium

11 Who was the emperor of Japan from 1926 to 1989?
12 From which country did the Democratic Republic of Congo gain freedom in 1960?
13 Who was President of Zimbabwe from 1987 until he resigned in 2017?
14 "The Iron Chancellor" was the nickname of which 19th-century German statesman?
15 Who was the 42nd President of the USA?
16 In 1960 which country became the first to have a female Prime Minister?
17 Who was the Israeli Prime Minister from 1969 to 1974?
18 The upper house of the US government is given what name?
19 What is the name for the medieval citadel in Moscow which is the centre of Russia's government?

Hard

20 Who was Prime Minister of Canada from 1968 to 1979 and 1980 to 1984?

Answers to QUIZ 310 – Up and Down

1 West Ham United
2 Nick Hewer
3 Worcestershire
4 Hugh Bonneville
5 Westlife
6 Barn dance
7 Upstage
8 The chips
9 2015
10 Ashdown
11 Greek
12 Splashdown
13 Frankie Howerd
14 Gauntlet
15 Volkswagen
16 Devon and Somerset
17 Piano
18 Two up, two down
19 The lark
20 Friday

QUIZ 313 – Pot Luck

ANSWERS ON PAGE 315

1 What is the capital of Bosnia and Herzegovina?

2 Which duo sang *On Top of the World* in 1973?

3 Who sang *Going Underground* and *That's Entertainment*?

4 In what foreign country would one most likely encounter Cobra beer?

5 What is the first name of TV's Sergeant Bilko, played by Phil Silvers?

6 Which is the holiest city of Islam?

7 What was the surname of Samuel, the inventor of a famous pistol?

8 In the 1963 film *The Pink Panther*, who played Inspector Clouseau?

9 Who was in the charts in 2017 with *Human*?

10 Which small rodent appears in *Alice's Adventures in Wonderland*?

11 What was the name of Ronnie Barker's character in the TV series *Open All Hours*?

12 On a standard typewriter keyboard, which letter is to the right of H?

13 Who played Ellie Miller in the TV series *Broadchurch*?

14 King Duncan is a character in which Shakespeare play?

15 Which herb has the French name *persil*?

16 Of which Scottish islands is Kirkwall the capital?

17 Which biblical character provided a song title for Tom Jones?

18 Which character was played by Catherine Zeta-Jones in the televised adaptation of HE Bates' novel, *The Darling Buds of May*?

19 Which game show has been presented by many people over the years, including Carol Smillie and Nicky Campbell?

20 What does one proverbially wear on one's sleeve, if making one's feelings apparent?

Easy

Medium

Hard

Answers to QUIZ 311 – Pot Luck

1 Bay City Rollers
2 Mark Owen
3 Super Bowl
4 Jacob
5 Green
6 Microbiology
7 Clint Eastwood
8 Sixth
9 Trent Bridge
10 Acid
11 Honey
12 Mega
13 *Way Down*
14 Butterfly
15 Tequila
16 Bid
17 At home
18 Nap
19 Thursday's
20 Rotterdam

QUIZ 314 – Theatre

ANSWERS ON PAGE 316

Easy

1 In which city was playwright Alan Bennett born?

2 Who is responsible for scenery changes during a production?

3 In which long-running musical is Cosette a central character?

4 Which country presents the Tony Awards?

5 What name is given to the area of a theatre in which tickets are sold?

6 Which character in *The Importance of Being Earnest* utters the words "A handbag?"?

7 Dramatist Ray Cooney is associated with what type of play?

8 What is the name of the area in which musicians perform in a theatre?

9 Which London theatre has been the venue for a number of TV variety shows, hosted in 2016 by Bradley Walsh?

10 Peter Shaffer wrote a 1979 play about which composer?

Medium

11 Which backstage member of staff may be credited in the programme as "continuity"?

12 Hollywood's Dolby theatre, formerly the Kodak theatre, is the venue for which annual awards?

13 Playwright August Strindberg was born in which country?

14 Who wrote the 1949 play *Death of a Salesman*?

15 What term is given to the text of a play?

16 Which Andrew Lloyd Webber (Baron Lloyd-Webber) stage musical featured a cast on roller skates?

17 What is "rep" short for in a theatrical context?

18 In which London park is there a famous open-air theatre?

Hard

19 Which US dramatist's plays include *The Odd Couple* and *The Sunshine Boys*?

20 "If music be the food of love" is the opening line of which Shakespeare play?

Answers to QUIZ 312 – World Politics

1 Kaiser
2 François Hollande
3 Dáil
4 Mahatma Gandhi
5 Mao
6 Richard Nixon
7 Boris Yeltsin
8 Tynwald
9 Ian Smith
10 Hong Kong
11 Hirohito
12 Belgium
13 Robert Mugabe
14 (Otto von) Bismarck
15 Bill Clinton
16 Sri Lanka (as Ceylon)
17 Golda Meir
18 Senate
19 Kremlin
20 Pierre Trudeau

QUIZ 315 – Pot Luck

ANSWERS ON PAGE 317

1 According to the proverb, in what is it difficult to find a needle?
2 What are the surnames of *Grease* characters Danny and Sandy?
3 What nationality was composer Sergei Rachmaninov?
4 Which item of sporting equipment, hit with a racket, has "feathers"?
5 Which element, with the atomic number 10, is a noble gas used in fluorescent lighting?
6 Which Spanish word means an afternoon snooze?
7 What is loam?
8 What was the title of the Matt Lucas and David Walliams comedy show set in an airport?
9 What is the syrupy blackcurrant liqueur from France called?
10 Which south-east Devon village on Lyme Bay shares its name with a drink?
11 The comedian Groucho Marx had what real first name?
12 Who co-starred with Richard Briers in the TV series *The Good Life*?
13 *Genie in a Bottle* and *Beautiful* were hits for which singer?
14 What sport does Bubba Watson play?
15 Which Kent coastal town shares its name with a transaction?
16 What is the internet country code for Germany?
17 In football, which set piece may be direct or indirect?
18 Who played Hyacinth Bucket in the TV series *Keeping Up Appearances*?
19 In which country are the Preseli Hills?
20 Which actress played Rose Tyler in *Doctor Who*?

Answers to QUIZ 313 – Pot Luck

1 Sarajevo
2 Carpenters
3 The Jam
4 India
5 Ernie
6 Mecca
7 Colt
8 Peter Sellers
9 Rag'n'bone Man
10 Dormouse
11 Arkwright
12 J
13 Olivia Colman
14 *Macbeth*
15 Parsley
16 Orkneys
17 Delilah
18 Mariette Larkin
19 *Wheel of Fortune*
20 One's heart

QUIZ 316 – Languages

ANSWERS ON PAGE 318

Easy

1 What is the ancient and modern language of Judaism?
2 By native speakers, what is the most spoken language in the world?
3 What is the name of the most widely spoken constructed language?
4 The *Star Trek* series popularised what fictional language?
5 What types of languages exclusively use manual communication?
6 The fictional language Na'vi is spoken by the aliens in which sci-fi film?
7 "Aloha" means both "hello" and "goodbye" in which language?
8 How many official languages are there of the United Nations?
9 Which two languages provide most of the influence for modern English?
10 What is the study of language called?
11 Old English is also referred to as which language?

Medium

12 What is the most spoken language in Mozambique?
13 What is the most translated book?
14 In which small enclaved country can you use an ATM in Latin?
15 *Fresa, plátano* and *manzana* are fruits in which language?
16 What does "dog-and-bone" mean in Cockney rhyming slang?
17 In Scandinavian countries, which language was spoken in medieval times?
18 Which country has the most official languages with 11?
19 What do Americans call a bathroom tap?
20 What is the profession of someone who converts one language to another?

Hard

Answers to QUIZ 314 – Theatre

1 Leeds
2 Stage manager
3 *Les Misérables*
4 USA
5 Box office
6 Lady Bracknell
7 Farce
8 Orchestra pit
9 London Palladium
10 Mozart (*Amadeus*)
11 The prompt
12 Oscars
13 Sweden
14 Arthur Miller
15 Script
16 *Starlight Express*
17 Repertory
18 Regent's Park
19 Neil Simon
20 *Twelfth Night*

QUIZ 317 – Pot Luck

ANSWERS ON PAGE 319

1 Azure is a shade of which colour?

2 Which river flows through Shrewsbury?

3 Clark Gable played which character in *Gone with the Wind* (1939)?

4 In which US state is the city of Palm Springs?

5 What kind of spoon is described in Lear's *The Owl and the Pussycat*?

6 What was the first name of media mogul Baron Grade whose son Michael was Chairman of the BBC from 2004 to 2006?

7 Lancashire's council is based in which city?

8 Which city in Nevada was associated with quick divorces?

9 Frankie Goes to Hollywood and Jennifer Rush both had hits in the 1980s with which song title?

10 In Tandoori dishes, what is a tandoor?

11 Which cookery-based reality TV show has been fronted by Gordon Ramsay and Marco Pierre White, amongst others?

12 What is the international car registration letter for France?

13 Who was Nicole Kidman's co-star in *Moulin Rouge!*?

14 Which island borough contains New York's central business district?

15 K2 is in which mountain range?

16 How is the Left Bank area of Paris known in the local language?

17 In Scotland, which two teams are known as the "Old Firm"?

18 Who had a 1981 UK hit with *This Ole House*?

19 In which year did ABBA reach the top of the charts with their Eurovision Song Contest winner *Waterloo*?

20 What name is given to a ten-sided shape?

Answers to QUIZ 315 – Pot Luck

1 Haystack
2 Zuko and Olsson
3 Russian
4 A shuttlecock
5 Neon
6 *Siesta*
7 Soil mixture of clay and sand
8 *Come Fly with Me*
9 Crème de cassis
10 Beer
11 Julius
12 Felicity Kendal
13 Christina Aguilera
14 Golf
15 Deal
16 .de
17 Free kick
18 Dame Patricia Routledge
19 Wales
20 Billie Piper

QUIZ 318 – Michaels

ANSWERS ON PAGE 320

1 What is the name of the famous big-eared mascot of the Walt Disney Company?

2 As at 2018, which former boxer held the record of being the youngest heavyweight champion in history?

3 Which English actor played the lead role of Charlie Croker in the 1969 film *The Italian Job*?

4 Who is best known for playing the starring role of Dexter Morgan in the US TV series *Dexter*?

5 Which Canadian singer released a 2016 album entitled *Nobody but Me*?

6 As at 2018, which retired US athlete held the record for winning the most Olympic gold medals?

7 Who played the lead role in the 1993 film *Falling Down* and the 1989 film *Black Rain*?

8 Which Formula 1 racing driver won seven championship titles between 1994 and 2004?

9 The 2004 documentary film *Fahrenheit 9/11* was by which American film-maker?

10 Who provides the voice of the title character in the *Shrek* series of films?

11 Who portrayed the title role in the 2015 film *Macbeth*?

12 Which retired professional basketball player (b.1963) played 15 seasons in the NBA for the Chicago Bulls and the Washington Wizards?

13 In the 2008 film *Frost/Nixon*, who played Sir David Frost?

14 Which Irish-born English actor took over the role of Professor Dumbledore in the final six *Harry Potter* films?

15 The *Transformers* series of films are produced and directed by which American film-maker?

16 *How Am I Supposed to Live Without You* was a 1989 hit for which singer?

17 Who played the title role in the 1988 film *Beetlejuice* and Tim Burton's *Batman* series of films?

18 From 1980 to 1983, who was the leader of the Labour party?

19 What is the name of the American actor noted for playing the role of prison inmate John Coffey in the 1999 film *The Green Mile*?

20 Who is noted for playing Gary Windass in the TV series *Coronation Street*?

Answers to QUIZ 316 – Languages

1 Hebrew
2 Mandarin
3 Esperanto
4 Klingon
5 Sign languages
6 *Avatar*
7 Hawaiian
8 Six (Arabic, Chinese, English, French, Russian and Spanish)
9 Latin and French
10 Linguistics
11 Anglo-Saxon
12 Portuguese
13 The Bible
14 Vatican City
15 Spanish
16 Phone
17 Norse
18 South Africa
19 A faucet
20 Translator

QUIZ 319 – Pot Luck

ANSWERS ON PAGE 321

1 In which sporting event do competitors have to swim, cycle and run?

2 Which US state is bordered by Arizona to the south and Colorado to the east?

3 Which English player was Footballer of the Year in 1986 and 1992?

4 In *Little Women* (1868), what was the name of the eldest sister?

5 Which forearm bone lies parallel to the radius?

6 In the title of a play by John Webster, where was the duchess from?

7 Which ex-Neighbours actor topped the charts in 1989 with *Too Many Broken Hearts* and *Sealed with a Kiss*?

8 What is the name of the Narnia lion?

9 Which 1990s comedy drama was set in Cicely, Alaska?

10 What kind of animal gave Chas & Dave a 1981 hit?

11 Lindisfarne is off the coast of which county?

12 Whose first UK hit single was *Run To You*?

13 Which group had a hit with *Karma Chameleon* in 1983?

14 What was the title of the 1990 film featuring Johnny Depp as a fantasy hairdresser?

15 Totton is in which English county?

16 Which classic 1945 film starred Trevor Howard and Dame Celia Johnson?

17 What was the title of the 1981-83 drama series in which Wendy Craig cared for children?

18 A stonechat is what type of creature?

19 Which 1990s TV sleuth was played by Dame Patricia Routledge?

20 Which band had a no.1 hit in 1981 with *Ghost Town*?

Answers to QUIZ 317 – Pot Luck

1 Blue
2 Severn
3 Rhett Butler
4 California
5 Runcible
6 Lew
7 Preston
8 Reno
9 *The Power of Love*
10 Type of oven
11 *Hell's Kitchen*
12 F
13 Ewan McGregor
14 Manhattan
15 Himalayas
16 Rive Gauche
17 Celtic and Rangers (from Glasgow)
18 Shakin' Stevens
19 1974
20 Decagon

Easy

Medium

Hard

QUIZ 320 – Fashion

ANSWERS ON PAGE 322

Easy

1 What is the first name of fashion designer Gaultier?

2 The 2017 film *Valerian and the City of a Thousand Planets* starred which English model (b.1992)?

3 What nationality is model Gigi Hadid?

4 Which British model (b.1970) appears on the international TV show *The Face*?

5 Who wore the controversial meat dress to the 2010 MTV Video Music Awards?

6 What nickname is English model Lesley Lawson (née Hornby) more widely known by?

7 "We don't wake up for less than $10,000 a day" was famously said by which Canadian model?

8 In what decade was the miniskirt designed?

9 What is the name of the fashion company known as "D&G"?

10 What is the name of the shoe company known by its logo of a star within a circle?

Medium

11 Which fashion company is known by its back-to-back C's logo?

12 In which country was Gucci founded?

13 Which actress and model starred in the 1961 film *Breakfast at Tiffany's*?

14 The word "chic" originates from which language?

15 What is the three-letter brand name of the sheepskin footwear of Antipodean origin?

16 Which two colours were most associated with the 1960s Mod style?

17 What international fashion and lifestyle magazine first ran in the United States in 1892?

18 Formerly known as *Gentleman's Quarterly*, what is now the name of the international men's fashion and lifestyle magazine?

Hard

19 Which American model (b.1966) is a host on MTV's *House of Style*?

20 Which men's trousers, originally popular in the 1920s, were named after an English city?

Answers to QUIZ 318 – Michaels

1 Mickey Mouse
2 Mike Tyson
3 Sir Michael Caine
4 Michael C Hall
5 Michael Bublé
6 Michael Phelps
7 Michael Douglas
8 Michael Schumacher
9 Michael Moore
10 Mike Myers
11 Michael Fassbender
12 Michael Jordan
13 Michael Sheen
14 Sir Michael Gambon
15 Michael Bay
16 Michael Bolton
17 Michael Keaton
18 Michael Foot
19 Michael Clarke Duncan
20 Mikey North

QUIZ 321 – Pot Luck

ANSWERS ON PAGE 323

1 Which structure in Jerusalem is traditionally where Jews lament and pray?
2 What was Humphry Repton (b.1752) famous for creating?
3 What was the first name of 1930s Hollywood star Ms Harlow?
4 Stockard Channing played Betty Rizzo in which musical film?
5 Which member of Genesis had a solo hit with *One More Night*?
6 What term is given to a word that reads the same forwards and backwards?
7 Which of the BBC's TV channels began broadcasting in 1964?
8 In the 1973 film *Live and Let Die*, who played James Bond?
9 Which piece of cane or metal is used to produce sound from clarinets and oboes?
10 What is the name of Dame Emma Thompson's actress sister?
11 *You Wear It Well* and *Sailing* were 1970s hits for which singer?
12 What is the principal town of Portugal's Algarve?
13 What colour is saffron?
14 Which girl's name provided Barry Manilow with his debut hit?
15 A hydrangea's colour depends on what quality of the soil?
16 Which colour is that of unbleached linen?
17 Which Turkish city was formerly called Constantinople?
18 Which energy-generating machines are found in nuclear power stations?
19 The chain of small islands off the coast of South Florida are given what name?
20 In which US city is Madison Avenue, the street associated with advertising?

Answers to QUIZ 319 – Pot Luck

1 Triathlon
2 Utah
3 Gary Lineker
4 Meg
5 Ulna
6 Malfi (*The Duchess of Malfi*)
7 Jason Donovan
8 Aslan
9 *Northern Exposure*
10 Rabbit
11 Northumberland
12 Bryan Adams
13 Culture Club
14 *Edward Scissorhands*
15 Hampshire
16 *Brief Encounter*
17 *Nanny*
18 A bird
19 Hetty Wainthropp
20 The Specials

QUIZ 322 – Flowers

ANSWERS ON PAGE 324

1 Which pink or white flower, also known as the chalk plant or baby's breath, is a favourite with flower arrangers?

2 The pansy is a member of which genus that shares its name with a musical instrument?

3 Which flower can be tea or floribunda?

4 The name of which water lily is also a sitting position in yoga?

5 "No flowers bloom, No wedding Saturday within the month of June" is a lyric from which song?

6 What is the male fertilising organ of a flower called?

7 In which decade did the slogan "Flower Power" become popular?

8 Which flower is also known as the "windflower"?

9 In which Shakespeare play does a character say "A rose by any other name would smell as sweet"?

10 From which flower is the drug opium obtained?

11 Who was entreated to "Give me your answer do" in a popular song?

12 With which country is heather associated?

13 In what form are daffodils and crocuses planted?

14 Which chef has children named Poppy Honey and Petal Blossom?

15 Lily flowers can be particularly toxic to which type of animal?

16 In which area of London does the title character sell flowers in the musical *My Fair Lady*?

17 Which group recorded *Flowers in the Rain* in 1967?

18 Off which Edinburgh thoroughfare is there a famous floral clock?

19 What is the most common colour for the cornflower?

20 Which flower is associated with the month of March?

Answers to QUIZ 320 – Fashion

1 Jean-Paul
2 Cara Delevingne
3 American
4 Naomi Campbell
5 Lady Gaga
6 Twiggy
7 Linda Evangelista
8 1960s
9 Dolce & Gabbana
10 Converse
11 (Coco) Chanel
12 Italy
13 Audrey Hepburn
14 French
15 Ugg® boots
16 Black and white
17 *Vogue*
18 GQ
19 Cindy Crawford
20 Oxford bags

QUIZ 323 – Pot Luck

ANSWERS ON PAGE 325

1 Who backed the American singer Martha Reeves?
2 What is a female swan called?
3 "Mars ain't the kind of place to raise your kids" is a lyric from which song?
4 The South American agouti is related to which domestic animal?
5 Which group had a 1986 hit with *Through the Barricades*?
6 What animal group has a shorthorn variety?
7 The alligator pear is also known by what name?
8 The 1857 novel *Barchester Towers* was written by which author?
9 What is the internet country code for Switzerland?
10 Who was Shakespeare's Prince of Denmark?
11 Which English city has the postcode SO?
12 Which band had a 1981 hit with *Girls on Film*?
13 Purl, cable and rib are terms associated with which craft?
14 Which National Trust landmark is situated at Marazion in Cornwall?
15 A Gloucester Old Spot is what type of animal?
16 What is the largest county in Ireland?
17 What is the first name of the actor who played Renton in the *Trainspotting* films?
18 Which disease, once associated with sailors, is caused by vitamin C deficiency?
19 Which singer had hits with *Thank You*, *White Flag*, and *Life For Rent*?
20 Cliff Clavin and Carla Tortelli were characters in which show?

Answers to QUIZ 321 – Pot Luck

1 Wailing Wall
2 Landscape gardens
3 Jean
4 *Grease*
5 Phil Collins
6 Palindrome
7 BBC2 (now BBC Two)
8 Sir Roger Moore
9 Reed
10 Sophie
11 Sir Rod Stewart
12 Faro
13 Yellow
14 Mandy
15 Acidity
16 Ecru
17 Istanbul
18 Reactors
19 The Florida Keys
20 New York

QUIZ 324 – Pop Music

ANSWERS ON PAGE 326

Easy

1 Which city was Gene Pitney "twenty-four hours from"?

2 Which group's hits include *The Last Time* and *Honky Tonk Woman*?

3 In 1986, which song from the TV series *Spitting Image* topped the charts?

4 Who was *(Sittin' On) The Dock of the Bay* in 1968?

5 Marshall Mathers is better known by what name?

6 Which US family group sang *Love Me for a Reason* in 1974?

7 The Miami Sound Machine was the backing group for which singer?

8 Which group had a hit in 1995 with *Roll with It*?

9 Which "illness'"provided hits for Peggy Lee in 1958 and Madonna in 1993?

10 The 2002 film *Maid in Manhattan* starred which pop singer?

11 Who led Dozy, Beaky, Mick and Tich in a 1960s pop group?

Medium

12 Named after an aircraft, what was the title of the first big hit for Orchestral Manoeuvres in the Dark?

13 Which reptile is mentioned in the title of a 1956 hit by Bill Haley and the Comets?

14 Who is the lead singer with the Human League?

15 *Grace Kelly* was a 2007 hit for which singer?

16 Who had a 2006 hit with *Put Your Records On*?

17 Who had a hit in 1985 with *Everytime You Go Away*?

18 "I'm bulletproof nothing to lose, Fire away, fire away" are lyrics from which song?

19 *I Cry When I Laugh* was the 2015 debut album from which singer?

20 Who topped the UK singles charts in 2017 with *Sign of the Times*?

Hard

Answers to QUIZ 322 – Flowers

1 Gypsophila
2 *Viola*
3 Rose
4 Lotus
5 *I Just Called to Say I Love You* (Stevie Wonder)
6 Stamen
7 1960s
8 Anemone
9 *Romeo and Juliet*
10 Poppy
11 Daisy
12 Scotland
13 Bulbs
14 Jamie Oliver
15 Cats
16 Covent Garden
17 The Move
18 Princes Street
19 Blue
20 Daffodil

QUIZ 325 – Pot Luck

ANSWERS ON PAGE 327

1 Which singer had a hit with *Achy Breaky Heart* in 1992?
2 The Roman numerals XXXVIII equate to which number?
3 Next to which room in a house would you find a scullery?
4 Which actor starred in *Closer* and *Gattaca*?
5 Who played Baldrick in the TV series *Blackadder*?
6 What are male antelopes called?
7 *Band on the Run* was a 1973 hit for which band?
8 Which prehistoric animal group included the velociraptor and the triceratops?
9 What is the first name of Canadian singer Ms Furtado?
10 Tony Hancock's television place of residence was the East part of which town?
11 Which city was the capital of West Germany before reunification?
12 Robert Burns described which creature as a "Wee, sleekit, cowrin, tim'rous beastie"?
13 Which cartoon cat is Tweety Pie's arch-foe?
14 The Tintin cartoons were created by which Belgian cartoonist?
15 Which of Dexys Midnight Runners' no.1 hits in the UK was the only one to also top the US charts?
16 Which organisation was founded for those with high IQ scores?
17 If a Scottish person is "havering", what are they doing?
18 Who was the Beatles' manager until his death in 1967?
19 The rook and the raven belong to which family of birds?
20 Which actor starred as Ray Kinsella in the 1989 film *Field of Dreams*?

Answers to QUIZ 323 – Pot Luck

1 The Vandellas
2 Pen
3 *Rocket Man* (Sir Elton John)
4 Guinea pig
5 Spandau Ballet
6 Cattle
7 Avocado
8 Anthony Trollope
9 .ch
10 Hamlet
11 Southampton
12 Duran Duran
13 Knitting
14 St Michael's Mount
15 Pig
16 Cork
17 Ewan (McGregor)
18 Scurvy
19 Dido
20 *Cheers*

Easy

1 In which event did Carl Lewis win four Olympic Golds - in Los Angeles, Seoul, Barcelona and Atlanta?

2 In which country was Sir Mo Farah born?

3 In what do triple jump competitors land?

4 What are the two main categories of athletics?

5 In what event did Sally Gunnell win a gold medal at the 1992 Olympics in Barcelona?

6 Which former athlete became an MP in 1992?

7 The heptathlon is made up of how many events?

8 How many Olympic gold medals did Usain Bolt win?

9 Who won gold medals at both the 5000 metre and 10,000 metre events in the 1972 Summer Olympics?

10 With which field event was Geoff Capes particularly associated?

Medium

11 What is the nationality of athlete Donovan Bailey?

12 Who famously collided with Zola Budd in the 3000 metres in the Olympic Games in 1984?

13 Which athlete, portrayed by Ian Charleson in the film *Chariots of Fire*, refused to run on a Sunday?

14 In which year did the women's pole vault become an Olympic sport?

15 The Great North Run begins in which city?

16 Which event has an Ironman version?

17 What is the name of the stick passed between competitors in a relay race?

18 Which English female runner won the London Marathon three times from 2002 to 2005?

Hard

19 In which event did Colin Jackson specialise?

20 Which former leader of the Liberal Democrats competed at the Tokyo Olympics and was UK 100m record holder from 1967 to 1974?

Answers to QUIZ 324 – Pop Music

1 Tulsa
2 The Rolling Stones
3 *The Chicken Song*
4 Otis Redding
5 Eminem
6 Osmonds
7 Gloria Estefan
8 Oasis
9 Fever
10 Jennifer Lopez
11 Dave Dee
12 *Enola Gay*
13 Alligator (*See You Later, Alligator*)
14 Phil Oakey
15 Mika
16 Corinne Bailey Rae
17 Paul Young
18 *Titanium* (David Guetta featuring Sia)
19 Jess Glynne
20 Harry Styles

 ANSWERS ON PAGE 329

1 What is the capital of Nebraska?

2 What was the name of George Cole's character in the original TV series of *Minder*?

3 Which small snake is supposed to have killed Cleopatra?

4 Who wrote the 1912 play *Pygmalion*?

5 What breed of animal is a Munchkin?

6 Which friar was one of Robin Hood's Merry Men?

7 *Whiskey in the Jar* was a hit for which group in 1973?

8 On which day of the week was Solomon Grundy married?

9 What is the French clear meat-based soup called?

10 Leipzig and Dortmund are cities in which country?

11 Which actress was married to Tom Cruise from 2006 to 2012?

12 In Greek mythology, which Gorgon was slain by Perseus?

13 What name is given to the first four New Testament books of the Bible?

14 Which particle is formed by gaining or losing electrons?

15 Indira Gandhi International Airport is in which city?

16 Which duo had a hit with *This Town Ain't Big Enough for Both of Us* in 1974?

17 Which playwright wrote the 1891 play *Hedda Gabler*?

18 In which board game do players solve the murder of Dr Black?

19 Which notorious Russian monk was murdered in Moscow in 1916?

20 How many items are there in a brace?

Answers to QUIZ 325 – Pot Luck

1 Billy Ray Cyrus
2 38
3 The kitchen
4 Jude Law
5 Sir Tony Robinson
6 Bucks
7 Wings
8 Dinosaur
9 Nelly
10 Cheam
11 Bonn
12 A mouse
13 Sylvester
14 Hergé
15 *Come On Eileen*
16 Mensa
17 Chattering foolishly
18 Brian Epstein
19 Crows (Corvids)
20 Kevin Costner

QUIZ 328 – Stars

ANSWERS ON PAGE 330

Easy

1 Who had a hit in 2000 with *Reach*?

2 "The Stars and Stripes" is a name for the flag of which country?

3 What is the correct name for a star on a keypad and keyboard?

4 Whom did Cat Deeley replace (not in specials) as host of *Stars in Their Eyes*?

5 "Starry, starry night" are the opening words to which Don McLean song?

6 Which band released the single *A Sky Full of Stars* in 2014?

7 Who wrote the 2012 novel *The Fault in Our Stars*...?

8 ...and who provided the theme tune *All of the Stars* for the 2014 film adaptation?

9 In which decade was *Stars on 45* and its follow-up hits?

10 Who presented the TV series *Shooting Stars*?

11 Which film company claimed to have "More stars than there are in heaven"?

12 If you were seeing stars, from what would you be suffering?

13 Who had a 1978 hit with *Lucky Stars*?

14 Which 2016 film musical featured the song *City of Stars*?

15 What feature of a newspaper is often referred to as "the stars"?

16 What device is used to get a better look at the stars?

17 *Dancing with the Stars* is the US version of which UK series?

18 Who said "We are all in the gutter, but some of us are looking at the stars"?

19 The 2018 song *All the Stars* by Kendrick Lamar and SZA featured in which superhero film?

20 Which is better, a four-star or a five-star hotel?

Medium

Hard

Answers to QUIZ 326 – Athletics

1 Long jump
2 Somalia
3 Sandpit
4 Track and field
5 400m hurdles
6 Sebastian Coe (Baron Coe)
7 Seven
8 Eight
9 Lasse Viren
10 Shot put
11 Canadian
12 Mary Decker
13 Eric Liddell
14 2000
15 Newcastle-upon-Tyne
16 Triathlon
17 Baton
18 Paula Radcliffe
19 110m hurdles
20 Menzies (Ming) Campbell

QUIZ 329 – Pot Luck

ANSWERS ON PAGE 331

1 *Waterloo Sunset* reached no.2 in the charts in 1967 for which band?

2 Which actress played the Dowager Countess of Grantham in *Downton Abbey*?

3 Which word means "fear" in German, but "deep anxiety" in English?

4 What is the international car registration symbol for Brazil?

5 Camargue is a variety of which type of food?

6 If you sailed due west from Land's End, which country would you arrive at first?

7 Which revamped schoolchildren's game show was hosted by Simon Mayo in 2012?

8 Who sang the 1979 song *Brass in Pocket*?

9 What does the first "A" of ACAS stand for?

10 Which TV presenter joined *TV-am* as Scotland Correspondent in 1984?

11 *Mad World* and *Everybody Wants to Rule the World* were hits for which duo in the 1980s?

12 Which European republic may be described as Hellenic?

13 Which knighted British actor was born Maurice Micklewhite?

14 What species of camel has two humps?

15 In which town was Ricky Gervais' sitcom *The Office* set?

16 "I believe in angels, Something good in everything I see" is a lyric from which song?

17 Which city is the setting for the TV series *Hollyoaks*?

18 From which southern Rio neighbourhood was the girl in the Astrud Gilberto hit?

19 Diana Ross originally sang with which group?

20 What is the capital of Afghanistan?

Answers to QUIZ 327 – Pot Luck

1 Lincoln
2 Arthur Daley
3 Asp
4 George Bernard Shaw
5 A cat
6 Friar Tuck
7 Thin Lizzy
8 Wednesday
9 Consommé
10 Germany
11 Katie Holmes
12 Medusa
13 Gospels
14 Ion
15 Delhi
16 Sparks
17 (Henrik) Ibsen
18 Cluedo®
19 Rasputin
20 Two

Easy

1 In which 1988 comedy film did Tom Hanks star as a child trapped in an adult's body?

2 The phrase "Show me the money" featured in which 1996 Tom Cruise film?

3 What profession did Tom Hanks' character follow in the 1993 film *Philadelphia*?

4 Lestat, played by Tom Cruise in a 1994 film, was what type of supernatural creature?

5 Who played Tom Hanks' crime-fighting partner in the 1987 film *Dragnet*?

6 The 1993 Tom Cruise film *The Firm* was based on a novel by which author?

7 Which was the title of the second film starring Tom Hanks that was adapted from a Dan Brown novel?

8 Tom Cruise plays which character in the *Mission: Impossible* films?

9 What type of animal was Hooch in the 1989 film *Turner & Hooch*?

10 In which 2008 film did Tom Cruise play a German wartime officer?

Medium

11 Tom Hanks was on which "Road" in the title of a 2002 film?

12 What was Tom Cruise's call sign in the 1986 film *Top Gun*?

13 What was the name of the mermaid that Tom Hanks' character befriended in the 1984 film *Splash*?

14 The 1990 Tom Cruise film *Days of Thunder* featured which pursuit?

15 Which real-life person did Tom Hanks portray in the 2013 film *Saving Mr Banks*?

16 In which 1988 film did Tom Cruise play a bartender?

17 Which 1992 film features Tom Hanks as the manager of a baseball team?

18 Which day appears in the title of a 1989 film starring Tom Cruise as a war veteran?

Hard

19 Tom Hanks played which real-life person who was captured by pirates in a 2013 film?

20 In which 2005 film was Tom Cruise under attack by Martians?

Answers to QUIZ 328 – Stars

1 S Club 7
2 USA
3 Asterisk
4 Matthew Kelly
5 *Vincent*
6 Coldplay
7 John Green
8 Ed Sheeran
9 1980s
10 Vic Reeves and Bob Mortimer
11 MGM
12 Dizziness
13 Dean Friedman
14 *La La Land*
15 Horoscopes
16 Telescope
17 *Strictly Come Dancing*
18 Oscar Wilde
19 *Black Panther*
20 Five-star

QUIZ 331 – Pot Luck

ANSWERS ON PAGE 333

1 The festive favourite *I Wish It Could Be Christmas Everyday* was a hit for which glam rock band?

2 What term is given to a solid figure with ten faces?

3 Leaves of which plant are traditionally used to relieve nettle stings?

4 Which word meaning "a snare" means "a piece" when read backwards?

5 *Every Little Thing She Does is Magic* was a 1981 hit for which group?

6 On which front was it *All Quiet* in the title of a 1930 film?

7 Who was Britain's first female radio disc jockey?

8 Whose second solo album, released in 1983, was *Hello I Must Be Going*?

9 Which is the largest of the Shetland Islands?

10 Coins are thrown into which Rome landmark, traditionally to guarantee one's return to the city?

11 In which Cairo suburb are the Pyramids located?

12 Which limb is affected by carpal tunnel syndrome?

13 What was a mangle used for?

14 Which thoroughfare in London is associated with the medical profession?

15 What is the surname of the hero of *The Thirty-Nine Steps*?

16 On a Monopoly™ board, what colour is the Old Kent Road?

17 Which fruit are used in a traditional Black Forest gateau?

18 The Bull represents which sign of the zodiac?

19 Which former Liverpool FC player was appointed manager of Glasgow Rangers in May 2018?

20 What is the name of the code used to access a cash machine?

Easy

Medium

Hard

Answers to QUIZ 329 – Pot Luck

1 The Kinks
2 Dame Maggie Smith
3 Angst
4 BR
5 Rice
6 Canada
7 *Blockbusters*
8 The Pretenders
9 Arbitration
10 Lorraine Kelly
11 Tears for Fears
12 Greece
13 Sir Michael Caine
14 Bactrian
15 Slough
16 *I Have a Dream* (ABBA)
17 Chester
18 Ipanema
19 The Supremes
20 Kabul

QUIZ 332 – Geography

ANSWERS ON PAGE 334

Easy

1 What is the capital of Cyprus?
2 In which county is the stately home of Hatfield House?
3 Mexico shares a border with how many US states?
4 In which country is the city of Volgograd?
5 The Brazilian flag has what background colour?
6 What is the Spanish word for a public square?
7 Which town in the Netherlands gives its name to blue and white earthenware?
8 In which county is Torquay?
9 On which north-east river does Middlesbrough stand?
10 In which US state did the Mormons settle?

Medium

11 Which county lies between Northamptonshire and Nottinghamshire?
12 The Australian state of Queensland was named after which queen?
13 Which Nebraskan city gave its name to one of the D-Day beaches?
14 The Welsh "Beacons" are near which historic market town?
15 What nationality is a native of Zagreb?
16 What is the currency unit of India?
17 Which island lies off the west coast of Malta?
18 Lausanne is located on which body of water on the Swiss-French border?
19 Which famous Australian beach is named after an Aboriginal weapon?
20 In which US state is the city of Seattle?

Hard

Answers to QUIZ 330 – Tom Tom

1 *Big*
2 *Jerry Maguire*
3 Lawyer
4 Vampire
5 Dan Aykroyd
6 John Grisham
7 *Angels & Demons*
8 Ethan Hunt
9 A dog
10 Valkyrie
11 *Road to Perdition*
12 Maverick
13 Madison
14 Stock car racing
15 Walt Disney
16 *Cocktail*
17 *A League of Their Own*
18 *Born on the Fourth of July*
19 Captain Phillips
20 *War of the Worlds*

QUIZ 333 – Pot Luck

ANSWERS ON PAGE 335

1 What word meaning "genial" can also refer to a diluted fruit drink?

2 What name meaning "crown of the valley" is shared by cities in California and Texas?

3 Which English city has the postcode NR?

4 *Sweet Little Mystery* and *Sweet Surrender* were hits for which group in the 1980s?

5 An object described as "ovoid" has what shape?

6 How many metres are there in four kilometres?

7 In the TV series *Only Fools and Horses*, what was the name of Nicholas Lyndhurst's character?

8 What collective name was given to the nine goddesses of the arts in Greek mythology?

9 The Australian soap *Neighbours* is set in which fictional street?

10 Which opera is subtitled *The Lass that Loved a Sailor?*

11 Who played the title role in the TV series *McCloud*?

12 If a creature is described as "diurnal", when is it active?

13 Which New York borough lies north-east of Manhattan?

14 Which bird of the crow family is traditionally described as "thieving"?

15 Which organ of the body produces insulin?

16 Singers Kelly Clarkson and Jordin Sparks were discovered on which TV talent show?

17 How many sides does a pentagon have?

18 Who directed the 2012 film *Life of Pi*?

19 What is the collective term for a group of elephants?

20 Which Italian author wrote the 14th-century work *The Divine Comedy*?

Answers to QUIZ 331 – Pot Luck

1 Wizzard
2 Decahedron
3 Dock
4 Trap
5 The Police
6 The Western Front
7 Annie Nightingale
8 Phil Collins
9 Mainland
10 Trevi Fountain
11 Giza
12 Wrist and lower arm
13 Wringing clothes dry
14 Harley Street
15 (Richard) Hannay
16 Brown
17 Cherries
18 Taurus
19 Steven Gerrard
20 PIN

QUIZ 334 – Television

ANSWERS ON PAGE 336

1 Who plays Demelza in the revived version of Poldark?

2 What were the names of the two cartoon mice who tormented Mr Jinks?

3 Which teen idol starred in the 1970s series *The Partridge Family*?

4 Which children's character has the catchphrase "Can we fix it?"?

5 The fictional London area of Walford is the setting for which long-running drama?

6 Which comedian is known for his *Good News*?

7 Who played Inspector Jack Frost on TV?

8 What nationality is actor Nikolaj Coster-Waldau?

9 Bryan Cranston and Aaron Paul played the lead roles in which American crime drama?

10 Which 1990s sitcom was set in the offices of GlobeLink News?

11 In the TV series *Mary, Mungo and Midge,* what type of creature was Midge?

12 What was the nickname of Roger Lloyd Pack's character in *Only Fools and Horses*?

13 Who played Uther Pendragon in the 2008 TV series *Merlin*?

14 *Tricks of the Mind* and *Confessions of a Conjuror* are books by which TV illusionist?

15 Which detective has been played on TV by both John Hannah and Ken Stott?

16 In which city was the police series *Taggart* set?

17 For what is Huw Edwards best known?

18 Evan Davis is the long-running presenter of which programme involving investors?

19 *The Durrells* stars which actress as Louisa?

20 Anne Robinson, Nicky Campbell and Matt Allwright have all been presenters on which consumer affairs programme?

Answers to QUIZ 332 – Geography

1 Nicosia
2 Hertfordshire
3 Four (California, Arizona, New Mexico and Texas)
4 Russia
5 Green
6 Plaza
7 Delft
8 Devon
9 Tees
10 Utah
11 Leicestershire
12 Queen Victoria
13 Omaha
14 Brecon
15 Croat
16 Rupee
17 Gozo
18 Lake Geneva
19 Bondi
20 Washington

QUIZ 335 – Pot Luck

ANSWERS ON PAGE 337

1 What legal phrase means "done as a favour"?

2 In which country was the composer Grieg born?

3 Which group had a hit with *Le Freak* in 1978?

4 Which two words that sound the same but are spelt differently mean "to position" and "a fish"?

5 What was the name of the chief engineer in the original *Star Trek* series?

6 Madonna's *Into the Groove* featured in which 1985 film?

7 In which US city is Ghirardelli Square?

8 During which war did the Battle of Britain take place?

9 What word means "relating to the New Stone Age"?

10 Which musical instrument's name derives from the words "soft" and "loud"?

11 What is the internet country code for Portugal?

12 Which word can describe both a drinks container and an acrobat?

13 Which London financial institution is famous for its "Names"?

14 What is the first name of French actress Ms Tautou (b.1976)?

15 In equestrian terms, how many inches are measured by one hand?

16 What title was given to the heir to the French throne?

17 Which trio had their only UK chart-topper in 1974 with *When Will I See You Again*?

18 Which TV sitcom was set in a café in the French village of Nouvion?

19 In the cartoon *Tom and Jerry*, what type of creature is Jerry?

20 What is the royal house to which Queen Anne belonged?

Easy

Medium

Hard

Answers to QUIZ 333 – Pot Luck

1 Cordial
2 Pasadena
3 Norwich
4 Wet Wet Wet
5 Egg-shaped
6 4000
7 Rodney Trotter
8 Muses
9 Ramsay Street
10 *HMS Pinafore*
11 Dennis Weaver
12 During the day
13 The Bronx
14 Magpie
15 Pancreas
16 *American Idol*
17 Five
18 Ang Lee
19 Herd
20 Dante

Easy
Medium
Hard

QUIZ 336 – Little Things

ANSWERS ON PAGE 338

1 Heather Small is the lead singer with which group?
2 In what sport do children compete in the Little League in the USA?
3 Petyr "Littlefinger" Baelish is a character from which TV series?
4 What is the smallest coin in the USA?
5 What name is given to small cubes of fried bread served with soup?
6 "It's a God-awful small affair" is the opening line from which song?
7 Who played James Herriot in the TV series *All Creatures Great and Small*?
8 The Swiss Guard is employed in which tiny state?
9 Which Charles Dickens story features the character Tiny Tim?
10 How is the constellation Ursa Minor better known?
11 Which legendary outlaw was a friend of Little John?
12 The Mini has been manufactured by which company since 2000?
13 Which of the Osmond brothers was known as "Little"?
14 What name is given to the longest part of the alimentary canal?
15 The "small screen" is another name for which household item?
16 Which group had hits in the 1960s with *Itchycoo Park* and *All or Nothing*?
17 London's Little Venice is close to which mainline train station?
18 *Shout Out to My Ex* was a 2016 UK chart-topper for which band?
19 What was the land of little people in Swift's *Gulliver's Travels*?
20 What type of creature was Stuart Little in the 1999 film?

Answers to QUIZ 334 – Television

1 Eleanor Tomlinson
2 Pixie and Dixie
3 David Cassidy
4 Bob the Builder
5 *EastEnders*
6 Russell Howard
7 Sir David Jason
8 Danish
9 *Breaking Bad*
10 *Drop the Dead Donkey*
11 Mouse
12 Trigger
13 Anthony Head
14 Derren Brown
15 Rebus
16 Glasgow
17 Reading the news
18 *Dragons' Den*
19 Keeley Hawes
20 *Watchdog*

QUIZ 337 – Pot Luck

ANSWERS ON PAGE 339

1 The composer Chopin was what nationality?

2 Which two words that sound the same but are spelt differently mean "animal flesh" and "to encounter"?

3 What is the nationality of a native of Casablanca?

4 In which current-day National Park was the novel *Lorna Doone* set?

5 Who was the 40th US president?

6 Which series of films, based on a classic trilogy, starred Elijah Wood?

7 In a glacier, what name is given to a deep open split?

8 Which actress starred in the 1956 film *Bus Stop*?

9 What word can mean "concise" and "abrupt to the point of rudeness"?

10 What is the sacred river in Coleridge's poem *Kubla Khan*?

11 What name is given to the leaf of a fern?

12 Who had three top ten hits singing with Queen, Bing Crosby and Mick Jagger?

13 The liqueur Tia Maria® has what flavour?

14 Of which 1960s and 1970s group was Sheila Ferguson a member?

15 Which green plant is traditionally associated with St Patrick's Day?

16 A chalkhill blue is what type of creature?

17 What is the Latin word for "water"?

18 *Three Times a Lady* was a hit for which group in 1978?

19 Who wrote the 1968 novel *Airport*?

20 Which fish of the genus *Cyprinus* includes koi and silver varieties?

Easy

Medium

Hard

Answers to QUIZ 335 – Pot Luck

1 *Ex gratia*
2 Norway
3 Chic
4 Place and plaice
5 Scotty
6 *Desperately Seeking Susan*
7 San Francisco
8 WWII
9 Neolithic
10 Pianoforte
11 .pt
12 Tumbler
13 Lloyd's of London
14 Audrey
15 Four inches
16 Dauphin
17 Three Degrees
18 *'Allo 'Allo!*
19 A mouse
20 Stuart

QUIZ 338 – Gardening

ANSWERS ON PAGE 340

Easy

1 Which weeding implement has a long handle?
2 What general name is given to the group of plants that grow high up on mountains?
3 *Ericaceous* plants are most suited to what type of soil?
4 What term is given to the glass or clear plastic cover put over young plants to protect them from the cold?
5 What is a trug used for?
6 The layer of earth nearest the surface in a garden is given what name?
7 Scarifying does what to soil?
8 What term is given to the act of removing old flowers from a plant?
9 For what are secateurs used?
10 What was the name of the garden makeover series that originally featured Alan Titchmarsh, Charlie Dimmock and Tommy Walsh?

Medium

11 What term is given to the process of growing more plants from an original?
12 In which decade was *Gardeners' World* first broadcast on the BBC?
13 For what is a riddle used?
14 What implement with a long curved blade is traditionally used for cutting grass?
15 Which annual national gardening competition began in 1963 and is now run by the RHS?
16 What name is given to the process of leaving garden waste to decay for future use on the garden?
17 What name is given to the perforated end of a watering can?

Hard

18 The *Big Dreams, Small Spaces* makeover show is presented by which TV gardener?
19 The practice of gardening in such a way as not to deplete the earth's natural resources is given what name?
20 What name is given to a fuchsia that is on a long stem?

Answers to QUIZ 336 – Little Things

1 M People
2 Baseball
3 *Game of Thrones*
4 Cent
5 Croutons
6 *Life on Mars?* (David Bowie)
7 Christopher Timothy
8 Vatican City
9 *A Christmas Carol*
10 Little Bear
11 Robin Hood
12 BMW
13 Jimmy Osmond
14 Small intestine
15 Television
16 The Small Faces
17 Paddington
18 Little Mix
19 Lilliput
20 A mouse

QUIZ 339 – Pot Luck

ANSWERS ON PAGE 341

1 What is a firethorn?
2 What is the nickname of Batman's assistant Robin?
3 Which actress played Strawberry Fields in *Quantum of Solace*?
4 The title of which musical, based on the music of Borodin, means "destiny"?
5 Which forest features in Shakespeare's *As You Like It*?
6 The Sherlock Holmes novel *The Hound of the Baskervilles* is set in which part of Devon?
7 Which word meaning "at this moment" means "came first" when read backwards?
8 On the Crusaders' 1979 hit *Street Life*, who sang lead vocals?
9 What initials provided the late-night spin-off from the 1980s children's TV series *Tiswas*?
10 What type of creature is a blenny?
11 A bunion affects which part of the body?
12 Which group had a hit with *Automatic* in 1984?
13 What was the name of Helen Mirren's character in the TV series *Prime Suspect*?
14 Which 1980s police show starred Don Johnson as Crockett?
15 What is an amphora?
16 What is the word for a political party's statement of intent?
17 The country of Bangladesh lies in which continent?
18 What type of creature is a redstart?
19 Who painted *Rain, Steam and Speed - The Great Western Railway*?
20 What were the former divisions of Yorkshire called?

Easy Medium Hard

Answers to QUIZ 337 – Pot Luck

1 Polish
2 Meat and meet
3 Moroccan
4 Exmoor
5 Ronald Reagan
6 *The Lord of the Rings*
7 Crevasse
8 Marilyn Monroe
9 Short
10 Alph
11 A frond
12 David Bowie
13 Coffee
14 The Three Degrees
15 Shamrock
16 Butterfly
17 *Aqua*
18 Commodores
19 Arthur Hailey
20 Carp

Easy

1 Which butterfly, with "eyes" on its wings, shares its name with a long-tailed bird?

2 If a bee has a Latin name beginning *Bombus*, to what family does it belong?

3 A Silver Y is what type of insect?

4 What common term for an insect also describes a computer error?

5 A leatherjacket is the larva of which insect?

6 What is the UK's largest wasp?

7 What family of butterflies share their name with a ship's captain?

8 A common darter is what type of insect?

9 Which large ladybird shares its name with a character usually dressed in a diamond-patterned costume?

10 Which insect is associated with biblical plagues?

Medium

11 What is the more common name for the aphid?

12 Which moth, seen in the UK, has a name that features two birds?

13 The Mexican song *La Cucaracha* is about which insect?

14 Which small biting insect is particularly associated with the west coast of Scotland?

15 A very thin person may be compared to which creature?

16 Which insects are the main food of the echidna?

17 How many legs does an insect have?

18 What are an insect's antennae better known as?

19 Which insect is associated with a popular "drive", where players aim to be the first to complete a cartoon drawing of it?

Hard

20 What name is given to the study of insects?

Answers to QUIZ 338 – Gardening

1 Hoe
2 Alpines
3 Acidic
4 Cloche
5 Carrying flowers and produce (tray)
6 Topsoil
7 Breaks it up
8 Deadheading
9 Pruning
10 *Ground Force*
11 Propagating
12 1960s
13 Sifting soil
14 Scythe
15 Britain in Bloom
16 Composting
17 Rose
18 Monty Don
19 Permaculture
20 Standard

1 What is the capital of Poland?

2 In *One Foot in the Grave*, who played Victor Meldrew?

3 What is cockney rhyming slang for "stairs"?

4 Which songbird was mentioned in the title of the long-running radio sitcom about the Royal Navy?

5 What is the device producing a fine spray for inhaling a medicinal drug called?

6 The drink perry is made from which fruit?

7 What word can refer both to a piece of foliage and part of a book?

8 In which section of the orchestra would you find a xylophone?

9 What type of creature is the misnamed slow-worm?

10 Which Italian smoked raw meat is also known as prosciutto?

11 Food prepared according to Jewish law is described by which word?

12 The town of Ilminster is in which English county?

13 Which guitarist covered Bob Dylan's *All Along the Watchtower* in 1968?

14 Who discovered penicillin in 1928?

15 *So Long, Farewell* is a song from which film and show?

16 He is the chemical symbol for which element?

17 *Young Guns (Go for It)* was a 1982 hit for which duo?

18 What is the main ingredient of the Indian dish dhal?

19 How many red balls are on the table at the start of a game of snooker?

20 What is the capital of South Korea?

Easy

Medium

Hard

Answers to QUIZ 339 – Pot Luck

1 A shrub
2 Boy Wonder
3 Gemma Arterton
4 *Kismet*
5 The Forest of Arden
6 Dartmoor
7 Now
8 Randy Crawford
9 *OTT (Over the Top)*
10 Fish
11 Toe
12 Pointer Sisters
13 Jane Tennison
14 *Miami Vice*
15 A jar
16 Manifesto
17 Asia
18 A bird
19 JMW Turner
20 Ridings

QUIZ 342 – The Bible

ANSWERS ON PAGE 344

Easy

1 Who received the Ten Commandments?
2 Which version of the Bible is named after a British monarch?
3 In the New Testament story, what was turned into wine?
4 Who was the second son of Noah?
5 Which organisation, that offers a listening ear, takes its name from a helpful person in a New Testament parable?
6 According to the book of Matthew, what should you not cast before swine?
7 Which organisation is responsible for placing Bibles in hotel rooms?
8 In the New Testament gospels, how many were present at the Last Supper?
9 Which is the last book in the New Testament?
10 Which king ordered the Massacre of the Innocents?

Medium

11 In the New Testament Gospels, how many people were fed with five loaves and two fish?
12 In which country is there an area known as "the Bible belt"?
13 Which book of the Old Testament shares its name with a collection of wise sayings?
14 What term is given to a subdivision of a chapter in the Bible?
15 "The Lord is my shepherd, I shall not want" is the first line of which Psalm?
16 In the New Testament Gospels, in which river was Jesus baptised?
17 Which biblical tower was the scene of noise and confused languages?
18 What is the first book of the Old Testament?
19 Who was the wife of Abraham?
20 What term is given to the reading of a text from the Bible in church?

Hard

Answers to QUIZ 340 – Insects

1 Peacock
2 Bumble bees
3 Moth
4 Bug
5 Daddy-long-legs (Crane fly)
6 Hornet
7 Skipper
8 Dragonfly
9 Harlequin
10 Locust
11 Greenfly
12 Hummingbird hawk-moth
13 Cockroach
14 Midge
15 Stick insect
16 Ants and termites
17 Six
18 Feelers
19 Beetle
20 Entomology

QUIZ 343 – Pot Luck

ANSWERS ON PAGE 345

1 On a map, which lines connect points of equal temperature?
2 What was the first name of George Gershwin's lyricist brother?
3 What is the radio code word that alphabetically follows Yankee?
4 Which Mexican state gives its name to a red peppery sauce?
5 In Shakespeare's *Twelfth Night*, what is the surname of Sir Toby?
6 If a creature is described as "piscivorous", on what does it feed?
7 Who replaced Len Goodman as *Strictly Come Dancing*'s head judge?
8 Which family troupe starred in the films *A Night at the Opera* and *A Day at the Races*?
9 What creature lends its name to farfalle pasta?
10 In which county is the town of Weybridge?
11 Which orange-seller became the mistress of King Charles II?
12 *Down Under* was a hit for which group in 1983?
13 Which musical term applies to a note half a tone higher than standard?
14 In 1982, which group's first hit was *Do You Really Want to Hurt Me?*
15 Which word can describe both a small glass toy and a type of stone?
16 What letter is horizontally next to "A" on a standard computer keyboard?
17 *Stand and Deliver* was a hit for which group in 1981?
18 What is the world's largest rodent?
19 The Sale Sharks play which sport?
20 Yul Brynner and Deborah Kerr starred in the 1956 film of which musical?

Answers to QUIZ 341 – Pot Luck

1 Warsaw
2 Richard Wilson
3 Apples and pears
4 Lark (*The Navy Lark*)
5 Nebuliser
6 Pears
7 Leaf
8 Percussion
9 Lizard
10 Parma ham
11 Kosher
12 Somerset
13 Jimi Hendrix
14 Sir Alexander Fleming
15 *The Sound of Music*
16 Helium
17 Wham!
18 Lentils
19 15
20 Seoul

QUIZ 344 – Space

ANSWERS ON PAGE 346

Easy

1 Which astronaut wrote the 2016 book *Hello, is this Planet Earth*?

2 Which planet is eighth in distance from the Sun?

3 The brightest star in a constellation is designated by which Greek letter?

4 On which space mission did astronauts first set foot on the Moon…?

5 …and what was the name of the rocket module, famously quoted as having landed?

6 Which "ology" is the study of the origin and nature of the universe?

7 The tagline "In space no-one can hear you scream" advertised which 1979 film?

8 What term is given to an artificial object launched into space orbit, for example, to provide communications?

9 In 1961, who became the first man in space?

10 Which planet is most famous for its rings?

Medium

11 Who was the commander of the Apollo 13 mission, played by Tom Hanks in the 1995 film?

12 NASA launched the InSight probe in 2018 to gather data about which planet?

13 What name is given to a building with a large telescope which is used for star-gazing?

14 Which word meaning "small" can be applied to stars, often also described with a colour?

15 Often given airplay in December, who sang the original version of *A Spaceman Came Travelling*?

16 In which century was the astronomer Copernicus born?

17 A large piece of rock or metal that has landed from space is given what name?

18 Who was the second man to walk on the moon?

Hard

19 What word is given to the path of an object travelling round a planet?

20 Which former commander of the ISS presented the BBC TV series *Astronauts: Do You Have What it Takes*?

Answers to QUIZ 342 – The Bible

1 Moses
2 King James Version
3 Water
4 Ham
5 The Samaritans
6 Pearls
7 Gideons
8 13
9 Revelation
10 Herod
11 5,000
12 USA
13 Proverbs
14 Verse
15 23
16 Jordan
17 Babel
18 Genesis
19 Sarah
20 Lesson

QUIZ 345 – Pot Luck

ANSWERS ON PAGE 347

1 What is the name of the South Wales peninsula near Swansea?

2 Which is the most southerly state of the USA mainland?

3 Which strait of water runs through Istanbul?

4 "See the stone set in your eyes, See the thorn twist in your side" is a lyric from which song?

5 Who played Smithy in the TV series *Gavin & Stacey*?

6 What sport is played by the Chicago White Sox?

7 Which sculptor (b.1840) created the work *The Thinker*?

8 *Music*, released in 2000, was a hit album for which singer?

9 Tony Hadley and Martin Kemp were members of which New Romantic group?

10 Who composed *The Marriage of Figaro* (1786)?

11 What is Camp Coffee® flavoured with?

12 What is the instrument like a high-pitched flute, much used in military bands called?

13 In which county is Bishop's Stortford?

14 Who wrote *Moll Flanders* (1722)?

15 What was the code name for the Allied operation of which D-Day was the first phase?

16 What type of creature is a minke?

17 On which biblical character, noted for her dancing, did Oscar Wilde base a play in 1891?

18 Which word meaning "to boast" means "clothing" when read backwards?

19 What is the book of God's law in Judaism?

20 Which number is between 16 and 19 on a dartboard?

Easy

Medium

Hard

Answers to QUIZ 343 – Pot Luck

1 Isotherms
2 Ira
3 Zulu
4 Tabasco
5 Belch
6 Fish
7 Shirley Ballas
8 Marx Brothers
9 Butterfly
10 Surrey
11 Nell Gwyn
12 Men at Work
13 Sharp
14 Culture Club
15 Marble
16 S
17 Adam and the Ants
18 Capybara
19 Rugby Union
20 *The King and I*

QUIZ 346 – Sport on Wheels

ANSWERS ON PAGE 348

1 What general term is given to cycle competitions that take place outdoors?

2 Which retired English superbike racer (b.1965) is nicknamed "Foggy"?

3 Christian Horner became principal of which team in January 2005?

4 What type of cars are used in Formula E racing?

5 From which famous royal palace did the time trial cycle races start and finish at the 2012 London Olympics?

6 Which cycle race awards the "King of the Mountains" title?

7 Which Spanish rider won the MotoGP World Championship four times between 2013 and 2017...?

8 ...and which other Spanish rider won the title three times between 2010 and 2015?

9 In which country is the Nürburgring circuit?

10 Which British driver won the Formula 1 World Championship in 1996?

11 What is "cc" an abbreviation for in reference to an engine?

12 How many Olympic gold medals did cyclist Sir Chris Hoy win?

13 In which county is the circuit of Thruxton?

14 Jason Plato and Matt Neal are previous British champions in which motorsport?

15 What does a black flag indicate in Formula 1 racing?

16 For what is BMX an abbreviation in relation to cycle competitions?

17 Which form of road racing involves driving between a number of stages?

18 In which country does the Indianapolis 500 take place?

19 Which Surrey hill was the highest point of the cycle route at the 2012 London Olympics?

20 Which Australian actor played James Hunt in the 2013 film *Rush*?

Answers to QUIZ 344 – Space

1 Tim Peake
2 Neptune
3 Alpha
4 Apollo 11
5 *Eagle*
6 Cosmology
7 *Alien*
8 Satellite
9 Yuri Gagarin
10 Saturn
11 Jim Lovell
12 Mars
13 Observatory
14 Dwarf
15 Chris de Burgh
16 15th century (1473)
17 Meteorite
18 Buzz Aldrin
19 Orbit
20 Chris Hadfield

QUIZ 347 – Pot Luck

ANSWERS ON PAGE 349

1 In which county is the open-air Minack Theatre?
2 What is the word for a letter that is not a vowel?
3 Which musical direction means "softly"?
4 Zippy, George and Bungle featured in which children's TV series?
5 *Message in a Bottle* was which group's first UK no.1 hit in 1979?
6 What is the capital city of the Republic of Ireland?
7 Who owned Winnie-the-Pooh?
8 Which is the word for the loose rocks found on the side of a mountain?
9 *Because of You* and *Behind These Hazel Eyes* were hits for which US singer?
10 What term is given to a female elephant?
11 What colour fur does the mountain hare have in winter?
12 Boston is the capital of which US state?
13 Which instrument was used in a musical "duel" in the 1972 film *Deliverance*?
14 In which sport might you use a sabre or épée?
15 What is the name of the Dr Seuss character who "hears a Who"?
16 Which "Great" river flows into the Wash?
17 A gatekeeper is what type of insect?
18 What is the legal term for reported, rather than directly gathered, information?
19 Which group had hits with *Run* and *Chasing Cars*?
20 The Tour de Yorkshire features competitors in which sport?

Answers to QUIZ 345 – Pot Luck

1 Gower
2 Florida
3 Bosporus
4 *With or Without You* (U2)
5 James Corden
6 Baseball
7 Auguste Rodin
8 Madonna
9 Spandau Ballet
10 Mozart
11 Chicory
12 Fife
13 Hertfordshire
14 Daniel Defoe
15 Overlord
16 Whale
17 Salome
18 Brag
19 The Torah
20 Seven

QUIZ 348 – Musicals

ANSWERS ON PAGE 350

Easy

1 Which musical, filmed in 1955 with Frank Sinatra and Marlon Brando, is based on stories by Damon Runyon?

2 Which song from the musical *Chess* was a hit for Elaine Paige and Barbara Dickson in 1985?

3 Which 1939 musical film features the Wicked Witch of the West?

4 *Hopelessly Devoted to You* is a song from which musical?

5 Which sport features in the 1958 film *Damn Yankees*?

6 Who played the title role in the 1980 remake of *The Jazz Singer*?

7 Ren McCormack and Ariel, daughter of a local church minister, are the central characters in which 1984 film?

8 Who starred in the 1972 film *Cabaret*?

9 Which 1975 musical featured the character of scientist Dr Frank N Furter?

Medium

10 In which 1971 film did Topol play the central character Tevye?

11 Which singer provided the voice of the plant in the 1986 film *Little Shop of Horrors*?

12 In the 2012 film *Les Misérables*, who played Fantine?

13 What was the name of Richard Gere's character in the 2002 film Chicago?

14 Who danced in bad weather in the 1952 film *Singin' in the Rain...*?

15 ...and which comedy duo performed a parody of it in their 1976 Christmas show?

16 Which 1983 film featured a welder who had aspirations to be a dancer?

17 *Defying Gravity* is a song from which 2003 musical?

Hard

18 Which 1961 film starring Natalie Wood and Richard Beymer was based on *Romeo and Juliet*?

19 The character of Jud Fry appears in which 1955 musical?

20 Which 1968 Broadway musical included the song *Aquarius*?

Answers to QUIZ 346 – Sport on Wheels

1 Road races
2 Carl Fogarty
3 Red Bull
4 Electric
5 Hampton Court Palace
6 Tour de France
7 Marc Márquez
8 Jorge Lorenzo
9 Germany
10 Damon Hill
11 Cubic centimetres
12 Six
13 Hampshire
14 Touring Cars
15 Unsafe behaviour
16 Bicycle motocross
17 Rallying
18 USA
19 Box Hill
20 Chris Hemsworth

QUIZ 349 – Pot Luck

ANSWERS ON PAGE 351

1 Which member of the Addams Family is a disembodied hand?

2 In a bulb of garlic, what is an individual section called?

3 Which famous racing-car make is named after five Italian brothers?

4 Which 1980 comedy film starred Dan Aykroyd and John Belushi?

5 The Tooting Popular Front featured in which TV series?

6 What language of Belgium is almost identical to Dutch?

7 On which river is Baghdad located?

8 In which county is the town of Petersfield?

9 What type of amphibian has palmate and smooth species?

10 Which two words that sound the same but are spelt differently mean "an entrance room" and "to drag"?

11 The second and fourth of Henry VIII's six wives shared what name?

12 Krist Novoselic and Kurt Cobain formed which band in 1987?

13 Which actor starred in the 1977 film *The Deep*?

14 Who was Muttley's partner in the cartoon series *Wacky Races*?

15 What vessel is used for clearing mud from rivers?

16 By which name is the harebell more commonly known in Scotland?

17 What name is given to the branch of fiscal studies relating to individual households?

18 Which South Yorkshire city was the setting for the film *The Full Monty*?

19 Which sport was associated with the Surrey location of Brooklands?

20 Which long-running BBC feedback programme has been presented by Anne Robinson and Jeremy Vine, amongst others?

Answers to QUIZ 347 – Pot Luck

1 Cornwall
2 Consonant
3 Piano
4 *Rainbow*
5 The Police
6 Dublin
7 Christopher Robin
8 Scree
9 Kelly Clarkson
10 Cow
11 White
12 Massachusetts
13 Banjo
14 Fencing
15 Horton
16 The Great Ouse
17 Butterfly
18 Hearsay evidence
19 Snow Patrol
20 Cycling

Easy

1 Where did the first Butlin's holiday camp open in 1936?
2 In 1930, who became emperor of Ethiopia?
3 Which fictional apeman was first played by Johnny Weissmuller in the 1930s?
4 Which ship became the world's largest liner when it was launched in 1938?
5 Born in 1932, which singer was also known as "The Man in Black"?
6 Which English composer, famous for the *Pomp and Circumstance Marches*, died in 1934?
7 In which month of 1939 did WWII start?
8 Which 1930s Brazilian actress was known for her fruit-laden headgear?
9 What sort of vehicle was *Mallard*, which set a new world speed record for its type in 1938?
10 In 1936, from which Tyneside town did workers march to London to protest against unemployment and poverty?

Medium

11 What type of insurance did the Road Traffic Act of 1930 make compulsory for drivers?
12 Which royal event was broadcast for the first time in December 1932?
13 What name was given to Franklin D Roosevelt's political programme of the mid-1930s?
14 In which sport was there a dispute over the "Bodyline" tactic during 1932-33?
15 Which actress was famously pursued by King Kong in the original film?
16 What term was given to the dry weather problems that damaged the ecology and agriculture of the North American prairies in the 1930s?
17 In which year did George VI become King?
18 Who wrote *The Big Sleep*, published in 1939?
19 Which English tennis player won three consecutive Wimbledon singles titles from 1934 to 1936?

Hard

20 In 1930, which skyscraper became the world's tallest building, until it was overtaken by the Empire State Building less than a year later?

Answers to QUIZ 348 – Musicals

1 *Guys and Dolls*
2 *I Know Him So Well*
3 *The Wizard of Oz*
4 *Grease*
5 Baseball
6 Neil Diamond
7 *Footloose*
8 Liza Minnelli
9 *The Rocky Horror Picture Show*
10 *Fiddler on the Roof*
11 Levi Stubbs
12 Anne Hathaway
13 Billy Flynn
14 Gene Kelly
15 Morecambe and Wise
16 *Flashdance*
17 *Wicked*
18 *West Side Story*
19 *Oklahoma!*
20 *Hair*

QUIZ 351 – Pot Luck

ANSWERS ON PAGE 353

1 Which actress co-starred with Gerard Butler in the 2010 film *The Bounty Hunter*?

2 Who had a 1973 hit with *The Twelfth of Never*?

3 Elmer Fudd is the arch-enemy of which cartoon rabbit?

4 Who played the title role in the TV series *Buffy the Vampire Slayer*?

5 What name is given to a person who studies the environment?

6 An inhabitant of "the Granite City" is given what name?

7 What was Spandau Ballet's only no.1 hit?

8 Which Bond character was played by Donald Pleasence, amongst others?

9 What is the holy table in a church called?

10 Which group had a no.1 hit in 2007 with *Shine*?

11 What term was used to describe a group of anti-establishment writers in the 1950s, including such figures as John Osborne and Kingsley Amis?

12 What lost object did Pickles unearth in 1966?

13 Traditionally, what does a cooper make?

14 How many (including the cox) are in each boat in the annual Oxford and Cambridge Boat Race?

15 Who had a 1986 hit with *The Lady in Red*?

16 Which tree has a "wych" species?

17 What word can mean both a hanging ornament and a communications device?

18 What name is given to a male sheep?

19 The word "sinister" derives from the Latin for which side, left or right?

20 What is the name of the house in which the 1938 novel *Rebecca* is mainly set?

Answers to QUIZ 349 – Pot Luck

1 Thing
2 Clove
3 Maserati
4 *The Blues Brothers*
5 *Citizen Smith*
6 Flemish
7 The Tigris
8 Hampshire
9 Newt
10 Hall and haul
11 Anne
12 Nirvana
13 Nick Nolte
14 Dick Dastardly
15 Dredger
16 Bluebell
17 Micro-economics
18 Sheffield
19 Motor racing
20 *Points of View*

Easy
Medium
Hard

Easy

1 Which Spanish painter had a "blue period" from 1901 to 1904?

2 In which year did Spain first host the Summer Olympics?

3 Which ocean borders Spain?

4 In which city is the Sagrada Familia church?

5 Chorizo is what type of food?

6 The Vuelta a España is a race in which sport?

7 What currency is used in Spain?

8 Spain is bordered by which three European countries?

9 In which year did Spain win the FIFA World Cup for the first time?

10 What are the curved pieces of hollow wood that Spanish dancers click together to beat time to music?

Medium

11 Which Balearic island is famous for its club scene?

12 Sangria has which alcoholic drink as its basis?

13 *Jamón* is the Spanish word for which food item?

14 What is the Spanish top football division usually called?

15 What does the Spanish word *cruz* translate to in English?

16 What geographical feature is a "sierra"?

17 David Beckham played for which team from 2003 to 2007?

18 What colour are the stripes that appear on the Spanish flag?

19 Which city lends its name to a variety of bitter orange?

20 *Begin the Beguine* was a 1981 hit for which Spanish singer?

Hard

Answers to QUIZ 350 – 1930s

1 Skegness
2 Haile Selassie
3 Tarzan
4 *RMS Queen Elizabeth*
5 Johnny Cash
6 Sir Edward Elgar
7 September (3rd)
8 Carmen Miranda
9 Steam locomotive
10 Jarrow
11 Third party
12 Christmas message
13 New Deal
14 Cricket
15 Fay Wray
16 The Dust Bowl
17 1936
18 Raymond Chandler
19 Fred Perry
20 Chrysler Building

QUIZ 353 – Pot Luck

ANSWERS ON PAGE 355

1 Which religious leader has the birth name Lhamo Thondup?

2 What was the name of King Arthur's magic sword?

3 Which barbarian was played on film by Arnold Schwarzenegger in 1982?

4 Hans Christian Andersen wrote about whose "new clothes"?

5 The chart-topping album ÷ *(divide)* was released by which singer in 2017?

6 Who wrote the 1964 novel *Chitty Chitty Bang Bang*?

7 What musical was based on the life of Argentina's Mrs Peron?

8 Which word meaning "to retain" means "a quick look" when read backwards?

9 Clovelly is in which county?

10 In which county is the theme park Alton Towers?

11 Which actor starred in the 1989 film *My Left Foot*?

12 What was the first name of singer Nilsson?

13 In which Brazilian city is Sugar Loaf Mountain?

14 .no is the internet code for which country?

15 Which bird is "ascending" in the famous work by Vaughan Williams?

16 Kelp is what type of plant?

17 *Angels* and *Old Before I Die* were 1997 hits for which singer?

18 Which British fighting service was formed in 1918?

19 Which word, the Latin for "load", is used to mean the burden of responsibility?

20 In the game of chess, which is the most powerful piece?

Answers to QUIZ 351 – Pot Luck

1 Jennifer Aniston
2 Donny Osmond
3 Bugs Bunny
4 Sarah Michelle Gellar
5 Ecologist
6 Aberdonian
7 *True*
8 Ernst Blofeld
9 Altar
10 Take That
11 Angry Young Men
12 The Jules Rimet Trophy (FIFA World Cup)
13 Barrels
14 Nine
15 Chris de Burgh
16 Elm
17 Mobile
18 Ram
19 Left
20 Manderley

QUIZ 354 – Environment

ANSWERS ON PAGE 356

Easy

1 Which term describes material that can be decomposed by natural means?
2 In the initials SSSI, what does the “I” stand for?
3 What is the word for the permanent disappearance of a species?
4 In a domestic residence, where are solar panels normally installed?
5 What colour is associated with the environmental movement?
6 The measurement of an individual’s or company’s carbon usage over a certain period of time has what two-word term?
7 Which chef and TV presenter mounted a campaign against single-use coffee cups in 2016?
8 Which measuring device can be installed in the home to track energy usage?
9 Discovered in the 1980s, there is a huge “garbage patch” in which ocean?
10 How is food described that has been grown without the use of pesticides?

Medium

11 In the phrase known as the “3 Rs of recycling”, what are the first two Rs before “Recycle”?
12 Which 2017 series presented by Sir David Attenborough highlighted the problems of plastic items?
13 In which month each year does Earth Hour take place at 8.30pm local time?
14 The level of heat in a building is controlled by what device?
15 What is the controversial energy extraction method of hydraulic fracturing more commonly called?
16 What term is given to a car that combines an engine with an electric motor?
17 What function does a material such as mineral wool provide when laid in an attic?
18 The prefix “eco-” relates to which branch of science?
19 Other than black, which two colours appear on the Fairtrade logo?
20 What word describes the use of natural resources at a level that will not damage the natural environment?

Hard

Answers to QUIZ 352 – Spain

1 Pablo Picasso
2 1992 (Barcelona)
3 Atlantic Ocean
4 Barcelona
5 Sausage
6 Cycling
7 Euros
8 France, Andorra, Portugal
9 2010
10 Castanets
11 Ibiza
12 Red wine
13 Ham
14 La Liga
15 Cross
16 Mountain range
17 Real Madrid
18 Red and yellow
19 Seville
20 Julio Iglesias

QUIZ 355 – Pot Luck

ANSWERS ON PAGE 357

1 Which vegetable is the main ingredient in coleslaw?
2 Who married Henry VII?
3 What completes the title official _, the person who winds up a company?
4 The Belfry is a venue for which sport?
5 What is the capital of New Mexico?
6 Is the town of Mold in North Wales or South Wales?
7 Which group had a hit with *I Don't Like Mondays*?
8 Who wrote the novel *Sons and Lovers*?
9 In *The Lord of the Rings* films, who played Legolas?
10 Carol Kirkwood is known for presenting what on TV?
11 Which UK coin, as of 2017, has twelve sides?
12 Which English city has the postcode CA?
13 What is five cubed?
14 From which country do borzoi dogs originate?
15 Hercules was said to have slain which many-headed monster?
16 Which herb is often associated with remembrance?
17 A large Roman building such as St Peter's in Rome is given what name?
18 Which actress played Muriel in the 1994 film *Muriel's Wedding*?
19 Who wrote *The Name of the Rose* (1980)?
20 What colour is a female blackbird?

Easy Medium Hard

Answers to QUIZ 353 – Pot Luck

1 The 14th Dalai Lama
2 Excalibur
3 Conan
4 The Emperor's
5 Ed Sheeran
6 Ian Fleming
7 *Evita*
8 Keep
9 Devon
10 Staffordshire
11 Sir Daniel Day-Lewis
12 Harry
13 Rio de Janeiro
14 Norway
15 Lark
16 Seaweed
17 Robbie Williams
18 RAF
19 Onus
20 Queen

QUIZ 356 – Long-Running Television Series ANSWERS ON PAGE 358

Easy

1 Cindy Cunningham, played by Stephanie Waring, is a character from which long-running series?

2 Which programme did Geoff Hamilton present from 1979 until his death in 1996?

3 What is the name of Emilia Fox's character in *Silent Witness*?

4 In what area of England is *Emmerdale* set?

5 2017 *Strictly Come Dancing* winner Joe McFadden played Raf di Lucca in which hospital drama series?

6 Which daytime series is set in the fictional Midlands town of Letherbridge?

7 Laila Morse is best known for playing which *EastEnders* character?

8 Who was the original questionmaster on *University Challenge*?

9 Which production company makes *Coronation Street*?

Medium

10 Johnny Galecki and Jim Parsons play physicists in which US sitcom?

11 What relation is John Barnaby to John Nettles' Tom Barnaby in *Midsomer Murders*?

12 In what type of building did Jonathan Creek live in the early series?

13 What were the names of the Mitchell sisters who made their *EastEnders* debut in 2007 and exited ten years later?

14 Which US series featured the forensic anthropologist Dr Temperance Brennan?

15 In *Neighbours*, what is the name of the hotel complex?

16 In which decade was *The Antiques Roadshow* first screened?

17 Which actor is best known in the UK for the role of Alf Stewart in *Home and Away*?

18 In the name of the US series *Law & Order: SVU*, what does SVU stand for?

Hard

19 The Simpsons live in which town?

20 In which sci-fi series did a robotic dog called K9 appear?

Answers to QUIZ 354 – Environment

1 Biodegradable
2 Interest
3 Extinction
4 On the roof
5 Green
6 Carbon footprint
7 Hugh Fearnley-Whittingstall
8 Smart meter
9 Pacific Ocean
10 Organic
11 Reduce and Reuse
12 *Blue Planet II*
13 March
14 Thermostat
15 Fracking
16 Hybrid
17 Insulation
18 Ecology
19 Blue and green
20 Sustainable

QUIZ 357 – Pot Luck

ANSWERS ON PAGE 359

1 Who directed the 2015 James Bond film *Spectre?*

2 What term describes British history from 1714 to 1830?

3 On Burns Night, which dish is traditionally "addressed"?

4 Morrissey was the lead singer of which band?

5 What is the second brightest object in the night sky?

6 What is the ninth letter of the Greek alphabet?

7 The Masai Mara wildlife reserve is in which country?

8 In which town was the TV series *Fawlty Towers* set?

9 What name is given to the sum payable to authors from their book sales?

10 Which 1968 Steppenwolf single featured in the film *Easy Rider*?

11 As seen on its stamps, what is "Switzerland" in Latin?

12 Which European country is indicated by the car registration letter P?

13 Who starred in the *Bridget Jones* films?

14 What term is given to a graduate's square cup?

15 In the TV crime series *Vera*, who plays the title role?

16 In which garden feature might you find blanket weed?

17 Which river of south-east Devon flows into Seaton Bay?

18 What style of spicy cuisine comes from the Deep South of the United States, especially Louisiana?

19 Who had a hit with *The Jean Genie* in 1972?

20 Michael Stipe was the lead singer of which group?

Answers to QUIZ 355 – Pot Luck

1 Cabbage
2 Elizabeth of York
3 Receiver
4 Golf
5 Santa Fe
6 North Wales
7 Boomtown Rats
8 DH Lawrence
9 Orlando Bloom
10 Weather forecast
11 £1
12 Carlisle
13 125
14 Russia
15 Hydra
16 Rosemary
17 Basilica
18 Toni Collette
19 Umberto Eco
20 Brown

QUIZ 358 – Numbers

Easy

1 How many ounces are there in a pound?
2 What number on a dartboard is between 11 and 16?
3 What is the sum of the digits one to nine inclusive?
4 In the game of bingo, what is the highest number?
5 How many centimetres are there in seven metres?
6 How many edges does a cube have?
7 What is 1/8 expressed as a percentage?
8 If it rains on St Swithin's Day, how many more days is it supposed to rain?
9 What is the next highest prime number above 23?
10 What is the value of pi to two decimal places?

Medium

11 How many ladies were dancing in *The Twelve Days of Christmas*?
12 Which imperial measure is equal to 1/20th of a ton?
13 How many court cards are there in a standard pack?
14 What is the square root of 49?
15 How many questions were there in the title of the Radio 4 guessing game?
16 What is thirty per cent of 600?
17 How many inches are there in six feet?
18 In which sequence, named after an Italian mathematician, do the numbers equate to the sum of the previous two numbers?
19 At what age is life said to begin?
20 What name is given to a chart showing the products of pairs of numbers?

Hard

Answers to QUIZ 356 – Long-Running Television Series

1 *Hollyoaks*
2 *Gardeners' World*
3 Dr Nikki Alexander
4 Yorkshire Dales
5 *Holby City*
6 *Doctors*
7 Mo Harris
8 Bamber Gascoigne
9 Granada Television
10 *The Big Bang Theory*
11 Cousin
12 A windmill
13 Ronnie and Roxy
14 *Bones*
15 Lassiter's
16 1970s (1979)
17 Ray Meagher
18 Special Victims Unit
19 Springfield
20 *Doctor Who*

QUIZ 359 – Pot Luck

ANSWERS ON PAGE 361

1 What, in proof-reading, is an instruction to restore a correction called?

2 *Addicted To Love* was a 1986 hit for which musician?

3 What is the nautical term meaning "near or towards the stern of a boat"?

4 Which actor starred in the 1988 semi-animated film *Who Framed Roger Rabbit*?

5 Nathaniel Parker starred as which crime solver in a series beginning in 2001?

6 What is the usual form of address to an Italian man?

7 The name of which port provided a 1996 hit for the Beautiful South?

8 Brad Pitt and Orlando Bloom starred in which 2004 swords-and-sandals epic?

9 *Lucille* was a 1977 hit for which country singer?

10 The name of which public vehicle can be read backwards as the abbreviation for an underwater vessel?

11 Which city is home to the University of Strathclyde?

12 What name is given to Rome's underground cemeteries?

13 In the TV series *Doctor Who*, which actress played River Song?

14 What was the first name of *Shaft* theme music composer Hayes?

15 What is a horse's fastest pace?

16 By what name is a recently-graduated resident physician in a US hospital known?

17 What nationality is golfer Jordan Spieth?

18 Who wrote *Swallows and Amazons* (1930)?

19 How has a goujon been cooked?

20 In which county is the town of Redruth?

Answers to QUIZ 357 – Pot Luck

1 Sam Mendes
2 Georgian
3 Haggis
4 The Smiths
5 Venus
6 Iota
7 Kenya
8 Torquay
9 Royalty
10 *Born to be Wild*
11 Helvetia
12 Portugal
13 Renée Zellweger
14 Mortar-board
15 Brenda Blethyn
16 A pond
17 Axe
18 Cajun
19 David Bowie
20 REM

QUIZ 360 – Pick and Mix

ANSWERS ON PAGE 362

Easy

1 Who had hits in the 1960s with *Mustang Sally* and *In the Midnight Hour*?

2 What are dolly mixtures?

3 What type of object is a cherry picker?

4 In bingo, which number is traditionally called as Tom Mix?

5 Which *a cappella* vocal group, formed in the 1980s, took their name from the term for mobile protesters?

6 What is linctus also known as?

7 What are you said to pick up if you pay the bill in a restaurant?

8 Which 2014 sci-film featured an "Awesome Mix Tape"?

9 *Take Your Pick!* was the first British TV game show to give away what as a prize?

10 How many times did Martina Navratilova win a mixed doubles title at Wimbledon?

Medium

11 What is a winkle-picker?

12 A piece of art that uses varied materials is given which two-word term?

13 What is another name for the pick often used with a guitar?

14 Which washbasin fitting allows hot and cold water to be blended?

15 The town of Pickering is on the border of which English National Park?

16 What type of person would use a mixing desk?

17 What does the company Pickfords specialise in?

18 The Mastermixers backed which novelty pop act in the 1980s and 1990s?

19 Who issued the 2012 single *Picking Up the Pieces*?

20 Where does a mixologist work?

Hard

Answers to QUIZ 358 – Numbers

1 16
2 Eight
3 45
4 90
5 700
6 12
7 12.5
8 40
9 29
10 3.14
11 Nine
12 Hundredweight
13 12
14 Seven
15 20
16 180
17 72
18 Fibonacci sequence
19 40
20 Multiplication table

QUIZ 361 – Pot Luck

ANSWERS ON PAGE 363

1 Which super heavy-weight boxer took the gold medal in Sydney in 2000?

2 What type of entertainment was featured in the TV series *The Good Old Days*?

3 Who was Cher's 1964-75 singing partner?

4 Who co-starred with Humphrey Bogart in the 1951 film *The African Queen*?

5 In the UK, what was the former name of the World Wide Fund for Nature?

6 What name is given to a biscuit containing a motto?

7 Which successful solo artist also recorded with The Yardbirds, Cream, Blind Faith and Derek and the Dominos?

8 Amsterdam is the largest city of which European country?

9 Which was the first grand slam tournament won by Sir Andy Murray?

10 Which is the largest of the Balearic Islands?

11 In the radio phonetic alphabet, what word is between "golf" and "India"?

12 Which film monster, back in cinemas in March 2017, first appeared on screen in 1933?

13 Which former member of Hear'Say co-presented *The One Show* in 2007?

14 The Amazon Rainforest is found on which continent?

15 Which river flows through Derby?

16 The clavicle has what common name?

17 Who played Detective Ken Hutchinson in the original *Starsky and Hutch* TV series?

18 *Slave to Love* was a hit for which singer in 1985?

19 What is the title of the classic 1881 children's book by Swiss author Johanna Spyri?

20 London Zoo is located in which park?

Easy

Medium

Hard

Answers to QUIZ 359 – Pot Luck

1 Stet
2 Robert Palmer
3 Aft
4 Bob Hoskins
5 Inspector Lynley
6 Signor
7 Rotterdam
8 *Troy*
9 Kenny Rogers
10 Bus
11 Glasgow
12 Catacombs
13 Alex Kingston
14 Isaac
15 Gallop
16 Intern
17 American
18 Arthur Ransome
19 Coated in breadcrumbs and deep-fried
20 Cornwall

QUIZ 362 – Susan and Friends

ANSWERS ON PAGE 364

Easy

1 On which TV show does Susie Dent appear?

2 Susan Sulley is a singer with which group formed in the 1980s?

3 In the 2017 series of *Strictly Come Dancing*, whom did Susan Calman partner?

4 Which fictional diarist was created by author Sue Townsend?

5 Susan Dey won a Golden Globe in 1988 for her role as Grace Van Owen in which US TV series?

6 Which novel is narrated by Susie Salmon?

7 What was the name of Susan Hampshire's character in the TV series *Monarch of the Glen*?

8 What is a lazy Susan?

9 In the TV series *Neighbours*, who plays the long-running character of Susan Kennedy?

10 In the 1981 film *Thelma & Louise*, which role did Susan Sarandon play?

Medium

11 *A Question of Sport* host Sue Barker played which sport from 1973 to 1984?

12 On which TV show did singer Susan Boyle find fame?

13 What was Little Susie told to do in the title of a 1957 Everly Brothers song?

14 What is a black-eyed Susan?

15 In the 1970s, which singer had hits with *Can the Can* and *Devil Gate Drive*?

16 Which TV presenter moved from the *BBC Breakfast* show to *Good Morning Britain* in 2014?

17 In *Coronation Street*, which character is played by Sue Cleaver?

18 Who wrote the chilling tale *The Woman in Black* (1983)?

Hard

19 The TV series *What Not to Wear* was co-presented by Susannah Constantine and which other fashion adviser?

20 Who played Susan in the TV series *Desperate Housewives*?

Answers to QUIZ 360 – Pick and Mix

1 Wilson Pickett
2 Small sweets
3 A crane
4 Six
5 The Flying Pickets
6 Cough mixture
7 The tab
8 *Guardians of the Galaxy*
9 Cash
10 Four times
11 Pointed shoe or boot
12 Mixed media
13 Plectrum
14 Mixer tap
15 North York Moors
16 A sound engineer
17 Moving (house)
18 Jive Bunny
19 Paloma Faith
20 Behind a bar

QUIZ 363 – Pot Luck

ANSWERS ON PAGE 365

1 In which county is Kidderminster?
2 Which Swedish seaport faces Copenhagen?
3 Where would you find a dado rail?
4 Which nursery-rhyme shepherdess lost her sheep?
5 In the Bible, which disciple betrayed Jesus?
6 Which plant shares its name with a word meaning "to cut short"?
7 What is the watery component of blood?
8 *Oops Up Side Your Head* was a hit for which group in 1980?
9 Which 1999 film, set in London, starred Hugh Grant and Julia Roberts?
10 Which Robert directed *Gosford Park* and *Short Cuts*?
11 What is a saveloy?
12 In which city is England's National Railway Museum?
13 Which team won the women's FA Cup in 2018?
14 In 1989, which heavy metal band had a hit with *Paradise City*?
15 Who was Kim's partner in the TV series *How Clean Is Your House*?
16 Which constellation includes the Pole Star?
17 In which county is Leatherhead?
18 What is the laurel-like shrub with aromatic leaves used in cookery called?
19 New York City has what fruity nickname?
20 What is an Inuit snow house called?

Answers to QUIZ 361 – Pot Luck

1 Audley Harrison
2 Music hall
3 Sonny
4 Katharine Hepburn
5 The World Wildlife Fund
6 Fortune cookie
7 Eric Clapton
8 The Netherlands
9 US Open (2012)
10 Majorca
11 Hotel
12 King Kong
13 Myleene Klass
14 South America
15 Derwent
16 Collarbone
17 David Soul
18 Bryan Ferry
19 *Heidi*
20 Regent's Park

QUIZ 364 – Business and Commerce

ANSWERS ON PAGE 366

1 What term describes a group of companies banded together to monopolise a market?

2 In the UK, the RMT union covers workers in which sector?

3 Which colour is associated with stocks and shares that are considered to be a safe investment?

4 In a company P&L statement, what do P and L stand for?

5 Is a person who buys a franchise known as a franchisee or a franchiser?

6 What type of business is owned by the people who run it, who share its benefits and profits?

7 What name is given to the tax collected by the government on goods coming into a country?

8 The City of London is often known by what measurement?

9 A trade restriction on the quantity of goods that can be imported into a country is given what term?

10 What does the "R" stand for in the government department HMRC?

11 What was the standard VAT rate raised to in the UK in 2011?

12 The Hang Seng index relates to the stock market in which former British colony?

13 If goods are acknowledged by a Bill of Lading, on what type of transport have they travelled?

14 What type of event is an expo?

15 Which two-word term is given to an item that has been discounted to a level that will not make a profit but is intended to attract customers?

16 As from 2014, which government department has been responsible for preventing unfair business competition and consumer choice?

17 On which date does the British tax year end?

18 Which two animals are used to describe the state of the Stock Exchange market?

19 Introduced in the UK in 1999, what term is given to the lowest amount that a company can pay its workers?

20 What two-word term is given to the historical trade associations based in London?

Answers to QUIZ 362 – Susan and Friends

1 *Countdown*
2 Human League
3 Kevin Clifton
4 Adrian Mole
5 *LA Law*
6 *The Lovely Bones* (Alice Sebold)
7 Molly MacDonald
8 A revolving food tray or stand
9 Jackie Woodburne
10 Louise
11 Tennis
12 *Britain's Got Talent*
13 Wake Up
14 A flower (of the sunflower family)
15 Suzi Quatro
16 Susanna Reid
17 Eileen Grimshaw
18 Susan Hill
19 Trinny Woodall
20 Teri Hatcher

QUIZ 365 – Pot Luck

ANSWERS ON PAGE 367

1 What was the Teenage Mutant Turtles' favourite food?

2 In which city can you visit Brunel's *SS Great Britain*?

3 Which 1980 film starring Irene Cara was remade in 2009?

4 What brand-name is given to one of the pleasure boats for sightseers in France's capital?

5 Which American humorist (b.1902), was noted for his unconventionally rhyming poetry published in the *New Yorker* magazine?

6 On a standard keyboard, which letter is to the immediate left of J?

7 In which US state is Fort Lauderdale?

8 What type of institution is Wormwood Scrubs?

9 Who captained the England team at the 2018 FIFA World Cup?

10 Jennifer Lawrence stars as Katniss Everdeen in which film franchise?

11 What was the surname of Patrick Macnee's character in *The Avengers*?

12 The traditional English dish of sausages and batter has what common name?

13 Which pioneering US four-piece punk rock band was formed in New York in 1974?

14 Which architectural style is characterised by rib vaults and flying buttresses?

15 What is the gelatinous dish made with cornflour and milk called?

16 A hairstreak is what type of creature?

17 Who wrote the novel *Twenty Thousand Leagues under the Sea* (1870)?

18 In 2018, who won the snooker World Championship title?

19 Which group had a 1982 no.1 hit with *Eye of the Tiger*?

20 Which is the second-smallest continent?

Answers to QUIZ 363 – Pot Luck

1 Worcestershire
2 Malmö
3 On a wall
4 Little Bo-Peep
5 Judas Iscariot
6 Dock
7 Plasma
8 Gap Band
9 *Notting Hill*
10 Altman
11 A sausage
12 York
13 Chelsea
14 Guns N' Roses
15 Aggie
16 Ursa Minor
17 Surrey
18 Bay
19 The Big Apple
20 Igloo

QUIZ 366 – Fantasy Films

ANSWERS ON PAGE 368

1 Which actor starred as Jack in the 1985 film *Legend*?
2 *The Golden Compass* (2007) was adapted from a novel by which author?
3 Which fairy-tale was made into a 2015 live-action film starring Lily James?
4 Warwick Davis played the title character in which 1988 fantasy film?
5 Which animated film of 2013 features a snowman called Olaf?
6 David Bowie played Jareth the Goblin King in which 1986 film?
7 What profession does Bill Murray's character follow in the 1993 film *Groundhog Day*?
8 Who played the title role in the 1987 film *The Princess Bride*?
9 What was the 1984 sequel to *Conan the Barbarian*?
10 Who directed *Edward Scissorhands* (1990)?
11 In which 2016 film is Newt Scamander the main character?
12 Who played the title role in the 2014 film *Maleficent*?
13 What was the subtitle of the 2017 film in the *Jumanji* series?
14 In the second of the *Pirates of the Caribbean* films, what was the name of Bill Nighy's character?
15 Martin Freeman starred in which trilogy of fantasy films released between 2012 and 2014?
16 Which 1982 film directed by Jim Henson and Frank Oz featured a Gelfling called Jen as the main character?
17 Which 2007 fantasy film starred Claire Danes as a celestial body and Michelle Pfeiffer as a witch?
18 Who directed the 2017 film *King Arthur: Legend of the Sword*?
19 In the 2016 film *The BFG*, who provided the voice of the title character?
20 Who played Ron Weasley in the *Harry Potter* films?

Answers to QUIZ 364 – Business and Commerce

1 Cartel
2 Transport
3 Blue (chip)
4 Profit and loss
5 Franchisee
6 Cooperative
7 Tariff
8 Square Mile
9 Quota
10 Revenue
11 20%
12 Hong Kong
13 Ship
14 A trade fair
15 Loss leader
16 The Competition and Markets Authority
17 April 5
18 Bear and bull
19 Minimum wage
20 Livery companies

QUIZ 367 – Pot Luck

ANSWERS ON PAGE 369

1 What was the title of the Avengers film released in the UK in April 2018?
2 A female rabbit is known by what name?
3 What birthday is the first for a nonagenarian?
4 An area of land described as a delta has what shape?
5 In which game would you have a pitcher's mound and an outfield?
6 Which group had a hit with *Common People* in 1995?
7 What type of food is grown in paddy fields?
8 In which soap did the character of Mike Baldwin appear?
9 Which fishing port lies on the Humber, near Cleethorpes?
10 *Discotheque* was a 1997 hit for which group?
11 Which zodiac sign is represented by two fish?
12 In which European capital city is there a statue of The Little Mermaid?
13 Dame Nellie Melba sang in which vocal range?
14 Which British actress appeared in the video of *Prince Charming* with Adam and the Ants?
15 Who played the title role in the TV series *Ironside*?
16 "Old Glory" is the nickname for which country's flag?
17 Which group was *Flying Without Wings* in 1999?
18 In bridge, who is the dummy's partner?
19 What are Jersey Royals?
20 Which month of the year was named after Julius Caesar?

Answers to QUIZ 365 – Pot Luck

1 Pizza
2 Bristol
3 *Fame*
4 Bateau Mouche
5 Ogden Nash
6 H
7 Florida
8 Prison
9 Harry Kane
10 *The Hunger Games*
11 Steed (John)
12 Toad-in-the-hole
13 Ramones
14 Gothic
15 Blancmange
16 Butterfly
17 Jules Verne
18 Mark Williams
19 Survivor
20 Europe

1 What is the stage name of the lead guitarist with Guns N' Roses?

2 Who had a hit in 1983 with *Pipes of Peace*?

3 Yehudi Menuhin was associated with which instrument?

4 Which musician had a 1978 hit with an instrumental version of John Denver's *Annie's Song*?

5 Take That had a 1992 hit with a cover of which Barry Manilow song?

6 Who played Ray Charles in the 2004 film *Ray*?

7 Which supergroup was formed by Jeff Lynne, Roy Orbison, George Harrison, Tom Petty and Bob Dylan?

8 What is the home-made music of the 1950s, as played by Lonnie Donegan?

9 Which 1971 John Lennon classic song mused on a vision of an ideal world?

10 In 2006, which actress did country musician Keith Urban marry?

11 Whose released the album 25 in November 2015?

12 In which decade of the 20th century was Sir Elton John born?

13 "Slowhand" is the nickname of which guitarist?

14 Who had a 2009 hit with *Poker Face*?

15 Which musician (b.1958) changed his name to a symbol for several years during the 1990s?

16 Trumpeter Miles Davis was famous in which area of music?

17 "Flea" is the stage name of the bass guitarist with which group?

18 Which group had a 1977 hit with the instrumental *Fanfare for the Common Man*?

19 In which country was percussionist Dame Evelyn Glennie born?

20 Which name is shared by the drummers from Queen and Duran Duran?

Easy

Medium

Hard

Answers to QUIZ 366 – Fantasy Films

1 Tom Cruise
2 Philip Pullman
3 *Cinderella*
4 *Willow*
5 *Frozen*
6 *Labyrinth*
7 Weatherman
8 Robin Wright
9 *Conan the Destroyer*
10 Tim Burton
11 *Fantastic Beasts and Where to Find Them*
12 Angelina Jolie
13 *Welcome to the Jungle*
14 Davy Jones
15 *The Hobbit*
16 *The Dark Crystal*
17 *Stardust*
18 Guy Ritchie
19 Sir Mark Rylance
20 Rupert Grint

QUIZ 369 – Pot Luck

ANSWERS ON PAGE 371

1 Which English city has the postcode LN?

2 Which 20th-century author wrote the amusing autobiography *My Family and Other Animals*?

3 The winner of a British boxing title fight is awarded which belt?

4 Where was the treaty signed that established the EEC?

5 What sort of fruit is a Worcester Pearmain?

6 *You're So Vain* was a 1972 hit for which singer/songwriter?

7 Which naval officer ranking is between a rear admiral and a captain?

8 Who is Ernie's pal in the TV series *Sesame Street*?

9 Little Rock is the capital of which US state?

10 Who wrote the 19th-century novel *Vanity Fair*?

11 *The Ugly Duckling* was a tale written by which author?

12 *It Takes Two* was a 1990 hit for Sir Rod Stewart and which female singer?

13 Which actress starred in the 1990 film *Truly, Madly, Deeply*?

14 For which duke was Blenheim Palace built?

15 Which 1990 film featured the characters of Brontë and Georges?

16 In which country is the Firth of Forth?

17 What is the Chinese dish of poultry with pancakes, spring onion and hoisin sauce called?

18 The character of Uriah Heep features in which Dickens novel?

19 What is the second largest of the Balearic Islands?

20 Which word can mean both "atmosphere" and "to broadcast"?

Answers to QUIZ 367 – Pot Luck

1 *Avengers: Infinity War*
2 Doe
3 90th
4 Triangular
5 Baseball
6 Pulp
7 Rice
8 *Coronation Street*
9 Grimsby
10 U2
11 Pisces
12 Copenhagen
13 Soprano
14 Diana Dors
15 Raymond Burr
16 USA
17 Westlife
18 Declarer
19 Potatoes
20 July

Easy

Medium

Hard

QUIZ 370 – Devon

ANSWERS ON PAGE 372

1 South Wales is separated from Devon by which stretch of water?

2 Which saint features in the name of Exeter's railway station?

3 What nickname is given to the South Devon district of Torbay?

4 In which South Devon town is the Royal Naval College located?

5 What medal did Plymouth-born diver Tom Daley win in the 2012 London Olympics?

6 In which century was Sir Francis Drake born?

7 Which Devon football team are nicknamed "The Pilgrims"?

8 Which item is usually put on the scone first in a Devon cream tea, the jam or the cream?

9 Woolacombe and Croyde in North Devon are popular destinations for which ocean-based sport?

10 Which Devon-born author created Hercule Poirot?

11 What is the name of the National Park that includes areas of both Devon and Somerset?

12 The Devon-based Dartington company is famous for making what two products?

13 In which Devon seaside town did storms wash away a section of the railway track in 2014?

14 Which ornamental material is associated with the town of Honiton?

15 Newton Abbot is famous for hosting what type of sport?

16 In which market town of South Devon was the environmental Transition Network founded?

17 As well as Somerset, which two counties border Devon?

18 Which comedian who grew up in Devon appears on the TV programme *The Last Leg*?

19 What type of buildings are Berry Pomeroy and Powderham?

20 What method of transport links the villages of Lynton and Lynmouth in North Devon?

Answers to QUIZ 368 – Musicians

1 Slash
2 Sir Paul McCartney
3 Violin
4 James Galway
5 *Could It Be Magic*
6 Jamie Foxx
7 Traveling Wilburys
8 Skiffle
9 *Imagine*
10 Nicole Kidman
11 Adele
12 1940s
13 Eric Clapton
14 Lady Gaga
15 Prince
16 Jazz
17 Red Hot Chili Peppers
18 ELP (Emerson, Lake and Palmer)
19 Scotland
20 Roger Taylor

QUIZ 371 – Pot Luck

ANSWERS ON PAGE 373

1 What is the stake put up before a new deal in poker called?

2 Through which county does the River Medway run?

3 Who was the 44th president of the USA?

4 What is the capital and chief port of Wales?

5 "I made it through the wilderness, Somehow I made it through" are lyrics from which song?

6 What type of animal was TV's Skippy?

7 How is "in the year of our Lord" written in Latin?

8 What is the fatty substance found in the cavities of bones?

9 The Pentland Firth separates which group of islands from the northern tip of Scotland?

10 *Love is the Drug* was a 1975 single by which band?

11 Kathmandu is the capital of which country?

12 "Richard of York gained battles in vain" is an acronym for what?

13 Which large Mediterranean island has Cagliari as its capital?

14 Which title is given to the ruling monarch's daughter in Spain?

15 *Losing My Religion* was a 1991 hit for which rock band?

16 Which Caribbean capital lends its name to a type of cigar?

17 What do Americans call an underground railway system?

18 At which Berkshire racecourse will the Royal Enclosure be found?

19 Which North American national park is famous for its geysers?

20 Ewan McGregor and Tara Fitzgerald starred in which 1996 film about a colliery band?

Answers to QUIZ 369 – Pot Luck

1 Lincoln
2 Gerald Durrell
3 Lonsdale Belt
4 Rome (1957)
5 Apple
6 Carly Simon
7 Commodore
8 Bert
9 Arkansas
10 William Makepeace Thackeray
11 Hans Christian Andersen
12 Tina Turner
13 Juliet Stevenson
14 Duke of Marlborough
15 *Green Card*
16 Scotland
17 Peking duck
18 *David Copperfield*
19 Minorca
20 Air

Easy

1 Which king was restored to the throne in 1660 after the English Civil War?

2 Alfred the Great was king of which region?

3 Who was King of Spain from 1975 until he abdicated in 2014?

4 What nickname was given to Louis XIV of France?

5 To which queen was William of Orange married?

6 Which man's name is the Latin word for "king"?

7 Who was Britain's last Stuart monarch?

8 Carl XVI Gustaf became king of which Scandinavian country in 1973?

9 Named after William IV's wife, what is the capital city of South Australia?

10 Which king was nicknamed "Farmer George"?

Medium

11 "Gloriana" was the nickname of which monarch?

12 King Constantine II was monarch of which country from 1964 until the monarchy was abolished in 1973?

13 Which figure in American history became known in song as "The King of the Wild Frontier"?

14 To which royal house did Queen Victoria belong?

15 Which English king utters the words "Now is the winter of our discontent" in a play by William Shakespeare?

16 Willem-Alexander became King of which European country in 2013 when his mother abdicated?

17 What religion was Queen Mary I?

18 Which king was Queen Elizabeth II's grandfather?

Hard

19 Edward VI was the son of which monarch?

20 Sweyn Forkbeard was king of which country from 986 to 1014?

Answers to QUIZ 370 – Devon

1 Bristol Channel
2 St David
3 English Riviera
4 Dartmouth
5 Bronze
6 16th century (1540)
7 Plymouth Argyle
8 Cream
9 Surfing
10 Dame Agatha Christie
11 Exmoor
12 Glass and crystal
13 Dawlish
14 Lace
15 Horse racing
16 Totnes
17 Cornwall and Dorset
18 Josh Widdicombe
19 Castles
20 Cliff railway (funicular)

QUIZ 373 – Pot Luck

ANSWERS ON PAGE 375

1 Which seaport is the largest city in Alaska?
2 What was the surname of Lorenz, the lyric-writing partner of Richard Rodgers?
3 A twelve-sided solid shape is given what name?
4 Which North Wales resort is flanked by the Great and Little Orme headlands?
5 On the 1982 hit *Ebony and Ivory*, who duetted with Sir Paul McCartney?
6 What is the second letter of the Greek alphabet?
7 Which US state lies immediately north of Louisiana?
8 What is the highest volcano in Europe?
9 The Eustachian tube is between which two parts of the body?
10 Humphrey Bogart married which actress in 1945?
11 Which river joins the Trent to form the Humber Estuary?
12 What word can mean both "the underground part of a plant" and "to search"?
13 Which glam rock group had a hit in 1973 with *Blockbuster!*?
14 The animated film *Happy Feet* features which birds?
15 In cookery, what word is abbreviated to "tsp"?
16 Who was Henry VIII's second wife?
17 What is the first name of *The One Show* presenter Ms Jones?
18 In terms of a computer, what is meant by the initials ROM?
19 What condiment has cider, malt and wine varieties?
20 Which sport takes place in a velodrome?

Answers to QUIZ 371 – Pot Luck

1 Ante
2 Kent
3 Barack Obama
4 Cardiff
5 *Like a Virgin* (Madonna)
6 A kangaroo
7 *Anno Domini*
8 Marrow
9 The Orkney islands
10 Roxy Music
11 Nepal
12 The colours of the rainbow
13 Sardinia
14 Infanta
15 REM
16 Havana
17 Subway
18 Ascot
19 Yellowstone
20 *Brassed Off*

QUIZ 374 – Snacks

ANSWERS ON PAGE 376

1 Which snack food is created by heating maize grains until they burst?
2 In Germany, what is a *bratwurst*?
3 What is the crisp disc often served at the start of an Indian meal?
4 Which snack shares its name with the ritual of raising a glass at a wedding?
5 Clusters of which fruit are sometimes called a "hand"?
6 In its native language, what snack is known as *pommes de terre frites*?
7 By what other name is a Scotch pie known, referencing the meat it may contain?
8 Which popular US snack food is often shaped like a knot?
9 What part of a plant is the misnamed pine nut?
10 A raisin is a dried version of which fruit?
11 The "Salt and Lineker" crisp was a special edition by which company?
12 What type of fruit is a Cox's orange pippin?
13 Which items sold in bags have given their name to a term for a small sum of money?
14 Ardennes and Brussels are varieties of which snack food?
15 Which green or black fruits are often eaten as part of a tapas selection?
16 Made from corn, which branded snack is shaped like the foot of a large creature?
17 What do Americans call crisps?
18 In the title of a 1982 book, which snack was it claimed that real men don't eat?
19 What is the translation of the pizza variety *quattro stagioni*?
20 Rice crackers are associated with which country?

Answers to QUIZ 372 – Kings and Queens

1 Charles II
2 Wessex
3 Juan Carlos
4 The Sun King
5 Mary II
6 Rex
7 Anne
8 Sweden
9 Adelaide
10 George III
11 Queen Elizabeth I
12 Greece
13 Davy Crockett
14 Hanover
15 Richard III
16 The Netherlands
17 Catholic
18 George V
19 Henry VIII
20 Denmark

QUIZ 375 – Pot Luck

ANSWERS ON PAGE 377

1 For what man-made feature is Ribblehead most famous?

2 Which football commentator known as "Motty" retired at the end of the 2017-18 season?

3 In which county is the National Botanic Garden of Wales?

4 What was the name of the paranoid android in the cult series *The Hitch-Hiker's Guide to the Galaxy*?

5 The characters of Florence and Dougal featured in which children's TV series and film?

6 Watford Gap was the first British site of what in 1959?

7 Which Polish seaport was originally named Danzig?

8 Which Central American island was mentioned in Madonna's 1987 hit *La Isla Bonita*?

9 In the TV series *Frasier*, what was the name of Martin's dog?

10 Which state of north-east India is known for its tea production?

11 Which London art institution holds a "Summer Exhibition" every year which is open to all artists?

12 Which Oliver Stone film starred Gary Oldman as Lee Harvey Oswald?

13 On which bay is Aberystwyth located?

14 What is the common name of the shrub buddleia?

15 In 1996, *Wannabe* was the first hit for which girl group?

16 Which word can mean both "a door opener" and "crucial"?

17 Which trademarked business binder became popular in the 1980s?

18 Of all land plants, which is the fastest growing?

19 Which sport is nicknamed "the Sport of Kings"?

20 Who created the character of Mr Bean?

Easy

Medium

Hard

Answers to QUIZ 373 – Pot Luck

1 Anchorage
2 Hart
3 Dodecahedron
4 Llandudno
5 Stevie Wonder
6 Beta
7 Arkansas
8 Etna
9 Pharynx to the middle ear
10 Lauren Bacall
11 Ouse
12 Root
13 The Sweet
14 Penguins
15 Teaspoon (or teaspoonful)
16 Anne Boleyn
17 Alex
18 Read Only Memory
19 Vinegar
20 Cycling

QUIZ 376 – Pantomime

ANSWERS ON PAGE 378

Easy

1 What sort of work does Widow Twankey do?
2 If a pantomime character says "Oh no it isn't", what is the traditional response?
3 Who is Prince Charming's aide in *Cinderella*?
4 What does the goose lay in *Jack and the Beanstalk*?
5 Alphabetically, who is the first of Snow White's Seven Dwarfs?
6 What type of creature is the villain in Dick Whittington…?
7 …and what type of creature is Dick Whittington's companion?
8 How long does the title character in *Sleeping Beauty* sleep for when under a spell?
9 Which pantomime hero is a sailor from Middle Eastern tales?
10 Maid Marian features in which pantomime?
11 What name is given to the hero of a pantomime, traditionally played by a female actor?
12 Goldilocks samples what food in the bears' house?
13 Which feline in footwear appears in the title of a pantomime?
14 Who does the wolf pretend to be in *Little Red Riding Hood*?
15 How many people usually play the pantomime cow or horse?
16 Michael and John Darling appear in which pantomime?
17 Who is the villain in *Aladdin*?
18 In *Jack and the Beanstalk*, which character cries "Fee-fi-fo-fum!"?
19 What poisoned fruit does Snow White eat?
20 Which maternal character's stories and rhymes provide the basis for a pantomime?

Medium

Hard

Answers to QUIZ 374 – Snacks

1 Popcorn
2 A sausage
3 Poppadom
4 Toast
5 Bananas
6 French fries
7 Mutton pie
8 Pretzel
9 Seed
10 Grape
11 Walkers
12 Apple
13 Peanuts
14 Pâté
15 Olives
16 Monster Munch™
17 Potato chips
18 Quiche
19 Four seasons
20 Japan

1 Which superhero lives by the mantra "with great power comes great responsibility"?

2 Who starred as Rooster Cogburn in the 1969 western *True Grit*?

3 Which Russian spirit is distilled from grain or potatoes?

4 In TV's *M*A*S*H*, who played "Hot Lips" Houlihan?

5 Who had a hit in 1999 with *Man! I Feel Like a Woman*?

6 Jakarta is the capital of which country?

7 Which taxi driver famously won *Mastermind* in 1980?

8 Australian tennis champion Evonne Cawley had what maiden name?

9 Who topped the charts in 1972 with *Puppy Love*?

10 Where would you find a rhizome?

11 In which year did Frankie Goes to Hollywood top the UK charts three times?

12 "Look at the stars, Look how they shine for you" is a lyric from which song?

13 Cantaloupe and honeydew are varieties of which type of fruit?

14 Someone called "Brummie" comes from which city?

15 What was the name of Tom Barnaby's wife in *Midsomer Murders*?

16 Which Roman emperor who died in 138 AD had a wall named in his honour in Great Britain?

17 Phoenix is the capital of which US state?

18 Which Shropshire new town was named after a famous Scottish civil engineer?

19 Henry Cooper was a champion in which sport?

20 What was the first name of *Golden Girls* actress Ms Arthur?

Easy Medium Hard

Answers to QUIZ 375 – Pot Luck

1 A viaduct (railway)
2 John Motson
3 Carmarthenshire
4 Marvin
5 *The Magic Roundabout*
6 Motorway service station
7 Gdansk
8 San Pedro
9 Eddie
10 Assam
11 The Royal Academy
12 *JFK*
13 Cardigan Bay
14 Butterfly bush
15 The Spice Girls
16 Key
17 Filofax®
18 Bamboo
19 Horse racing
20 Rowan Atkinson

QUIZ 378 – Wales

ANSWERS ON PAGE 380

Easy

1 What is the Welsh name for Wales?

2 In which Welsh village was the 1960s TV series *The Prisoner* mostly filmed?

3 On which day is St David's Day celebrated?

4 Which earthwork once formed the boundary between England and Wales?

5 Who was appointed manager of the Welsh national football team in January 2018?

6 Which Welsh singer had a 2008 hit with *Mercy*?

7 The National Library of Wales in is which university town?

8 Which North Wales village, featuring the Swallow Falls, is known as the "Gateway to Snowdonia"?

9 In 2016, which comedian took over hosting duties on *The Apprentice: You're Fired!*?

10 Which South Wales town is noted for its steelworks?

Medium

11 In the 1970s, which Welsh snooker player won six World Championship titles?

12 What is the name of the coastal National Park in the south of Wales?

13 In 2012 which North Wales town was officially granted city status?

14 Which motorway links London with South Wales?

15 In 2017 who became the first Welsh golfer to be inducted into the Golf Hall of Fame?

16 What title is given to the premier political figure in Wales...?

17 ...and what name is given to the governing body of the country?

18 Which headland includes Rhossili Bay and the "Worm's Head"?

19 What is the name of the national rugby ground in the Welsh capital?

20 From which port do boats depart for the Irish port of Rosslare?

Hard

Answers to QUIZ 376 – Pantomime

1 Laundry manager
2 "Oh yes it is"
3 Dandini
4 Golden eggs
5 Bashful
6 A rat (King Rat)
7 A cat
8 100 years
9 Sinbad
10 *Robin Hood*
11 Principal boy
12 Porridge
13 *Puss in Boots*
14 Her grandmother
15 Two
16 *Peter Pan*
17 Abanazar
18 The giant (Blunderbore)
19 Apple
20 Mother Goose

QUIZ 379 – Pot Luck

ANSWERS ON PAGE 381

1 In which county is the seaside town of Southwold?

2 In the TV series *New Tricks*, who played Brian Lane?

3 What church-related nickname is given to an overnight period of employment?

4 Who was the star of the TV series *Dixon of Dock Green*?

5 What surname was adopted by author Charles Dodgson?

6 On a dartboard, which number is between 4 and 6?

7 Which actor played the title role in the original 1981 film *Arthur*?

8 In what drama series did Terence Alexander play Charlie Hungerford?

9 Which Kent spa town has the prefix "Royal" and the suffix "Wells"?

10 What is the principal religion of Indonesia?

11 Which creature was the enemy of the Three Little Pigs?

12 In which century was Isambard Kingdom Brunel born?

13 *Uptown Girl* was written by Billy Joel about which model?

14 Which scanning technique uses a magnetic field and radio waves to create detailed images of the body?

15 *Five Colours in Her Hair* was a 2004 hit for which group?

16 What term is given to the science and art of growing plants?

17 *Funky Gibbon* was a 1975 hit for which trio?

18 Known for its connections with the army, the town of Aldershot is in which county?

19 On which river are Düsseldorf, Mainz, Strasbourg and Rotterdam?

20 Which country hosted the 1998 FIFA World Cup?

Answers to QUIZ 377 – Pot Luck

1 Spider-Man
2 John Wayne
3 Vodka
4 Loretta Swit
5 Shania Twain
6 Indonesia
7 Fred Housego
8 Goolagong
9 Donny Osmond
10 On or below the earth (underground stem)
11 1984
12 *Yellow* (Coldplay)
13 Melon
14 Birmingham
15 Joyce
16 Hadrian
17 Arizona
18 Telford
19 Boxing
20 Bea

QUIZ 380 – Waterbirds

ANSWERS ON PAGE 382

Easy

1 What colour plumage do egrets usually have?

2 Which sea duck has famously downy feathers used in bed coverings?

3 A kittiwake is what type of waterbird?

4 Which English island is known as "Puffin Island"?

5 A young goose is given what name?

6 In relation to waterbirds, what do the initials WWT stand for?

7 Which pink wading bird is often seen standing on one leg?

8 A white species of domesticated duck was named after which south-east county town?

9 Which wading bird has a name indicating that its beak is shaped like a piece of cutlery?

10 In the UK, which is the most common colour for a heron?

11 Which North American wading bird has a "whooping" species?

Medium

12 Which small fish-eating bird found in the UK is famous for its bright blue and orange plumage?

13 How many swans are a-swimming in the song *The Twelve Days of Christmas*?

14 Which is the largest species of penguin?

15 A shade of greenish-blue takes its name from which small duck?

16 In Europe, which wading bird is known for nesting on cartwheels that home owners place on top of their houses?

17 Which waterbird is often mentioned when referring to baldness?

18 On what type of terrain do guillemots nest?

19 Which diving bird's species include "great crested" and "little"?

Hard

20 Avocets have what two colours as their plumage?

Answers to QUIZ 378 – Wales

1 Cymru
2 Portmeirion
3 March 1
4 Offa's Dyke
5 Ryan Giggs
6 Duffy
7 Aberystwyth
8 Betws-y-Coed
9 Rhod Gilbert
10 Port Talbot
11 Ray Reardon
12 Pembrokeshire National Park
13 St Asaph
14 M4
15 Ian Woosnam
16 First Minister
17 Welsh Assembly
18 Gower Peninsula
19 Principality Stadium
20 Fishguard

QUIZ 381 – Pot Luck

ANSWERS ON PAGE 383

1 The funnel-web spider is native to which country?

2 What is the surname of the actress Kathy who starred in the 1995 film *Dolores Claiborne*?

3 Which character lived on a dump in the 1963 children's book?

4 Which bird lays its eggs in another's nest?

5 *Knock Three Times* was a 1971 hit for which group?

6 What is the county town of Kent?

7 Which professional skateboarder has given his name to a series of video games?

8 Which 1979 film of a Thomas Hardy novel starred Nastassja Kinski in the title role?

9 The 1989 novel *The Remains of the Day* was written by which author?

10 Whose gang included Choo Choo, Spook and Benny the Ball?

11 *Coward of the County* was a 1980 hit for which singer?

12 What is the name of the very thin slices of toast named after a famous singer?

13 Which legendary poet wrote the *Iliad*?

14 Of which part of the body is nephrology a study?

15 Which band's first album *Definitely, Maybe* was released in 1994?

16 In which county is Okehampton?

17 How is Birmingham comedian Robert Davis better known?

18 Which Caribbean island has Kingston as its capital?

19 In *Gavin & Stacey*, what was the name of Rob Brydon's character?

20 What are the sweets "bootlaces" made from?

Answers to QUIZ 379 – Pot Luck

1 Suffolk
2 Alun Armstrong
3 Graveyard shift
4 Jack Warner
5 (Lewis) Carroll
6 13
7 Dudley Moore
8 *Bergerac*
9 Tunbridge
10 Islam
11 Big Bad Wolf
12 19th century (1806)
13 Christie Brinkley
14 MRI
15 McFly
16 Horticulture
17 The Goodies
18 Hampshire
19 Rhine
20 France

QUIZ 382 – Bells and Whistles

ANSWERS ON PAGE 384

1 In which country was inventor Alexander Graham Bell born?
2 Which part of a whistle shares its name with a vegetable?
3 What term is given to naval trousers that are very wide at the end?
4 The song *Give a Little Whistle* features in which Disney film?
5 How many bells tolled in the title of the 1966 Alistair MacLean novel?
6 Which kitchen appliance sometimes whistles when its job is complete?
7 Who wrote the semi-autobiographical novel entitled *The Bell Jar*?
8 What name is given to a tour involving short stops at many different places?
9 *Ring My Bell* was a 1979 hit for which singer?
10 What would you do to wet your whistle?
11 Kristen Bell voiced which character in the 2013 film *Frozen*?
12 *I Whistle a Happy Tune* is from which musical?
13 Which former reporter was MP for Tatton from 1997 to 2001?
14 What is the penny whistle or tin whistle also known as?
15 The fairy Tinker Bell appears in which story?
16 What term is given to someone who exposes a company's often illegal secrets?
17 Where would you see a bell curve?
18 In which country is the ski resort of Whistler?
19 What are the first four words in the song *Jingle Bells*?
20 The novel *Whistle Down the Wind* by was made into a film in 1961 starring which actress, a daughter of the author?

Easy

Medium

Hard

Answers to QUIZ 380 – Waterbirds

1 White
2 Eider duck
3 Gull
4 Lundy
5 Gosling
6 Wildfowl and Wetlands Trust
7 Flamingo
8 Aylesbury
9 Spoonbill
10 Grey
11 Crane
12 Kingfisher
13 Seven
14 Emperor
15 Teal
16 Stork
17 Coot
18 Cliffs
19 Grebe
20 Black and white

QUIZ 383 – Pot Luck

ANSWERS ON PAGE 385

1 Which comedian played Rufus T Firefly in the 1939 film *Duck Soup*?

2 What is the Latin for "earth"?

3 *The Radio Ham* and *The Blood Donor* were famous episodes from which show?

4 Which jazz pianist (b.1904) was nicknamed "Count"?

5 What is the metric measure of volume, equivalent to 1.76 pints?

6 In the 1970s and 1980s, which band had hits with *So You Win Again* and *It Started with a Kiss*?

7 Which highly toxic protein is derived from the castor oil plant?

8 Konungariket Sverige is the official name of which country?

9 What is the crime of having more than one spouse?

10 Which zoologist wrote the 1967 book *The Naked Ape*?

11 What fruity sauce is traditionally served with turkey?

12 On which Hawaiian island is the state capital Honolulu situated?

13 The city of Bristol stands on which river?

14 Which two words that sound the same but are spelt differently mean "to be tedious" and "a male animal"?

15 In the Disney version of *Pinocchio*, what sort of creature is Monstro?

16 What was the title of The Police's first UK hit?

17 Edinburgh doctor Joseph Bell was the inspiration for which character created by Sir Arthur Conan Doyle?

18 Which semi-precious stone is associated with Whitby?

19 Which actress duetted with Robbie Williams in 2001 on *Somethin' Stupid*?

20 Which Portuguese river is also the name of a wine region?

Easy

Medium

Hard

Answers to QUIZ 381 – Pot Luck

1 Australia
2 Bates
3 Stig
4 Cuckoo
5 Dawn
6 Maidstone
7 Tony Hawk
8 *Tess*
9 Kazuo Ishiguro
10 Top Cat
11 Kenny Rogers
12 Melba toast
13 Homer
14 The kidneys
15 Oasis
16 Devon
17 Jasper Carrott
18 Jamaica
19 Bryn
20 Liquorice

QUIZ 384 – Chefs and Cooks

ANSWERS ON PAGE 386

Easy

1 Which TV cook is also known for her involvement with Norwich City FC?

2 Which Italian chef presents the *Italian Escape* TV series?

3 Gordon Ramsay is the long-running host of which American culinary competition?

4 Who became the judges of *MasterChef* when it was revived in 2005?

5 How are TV foodies David Myers and Simon King better known?

6 Which chef, a regular on ITV's *This Morning*, married Fern Britton in 2000?

7 The *River Cottage* series was hosted by which chef?

8 Which chef launched the "Feed Me Better" campaign in 2005 to improve school dinners?

9 What is the name of Courteney Cox's chef character in *Friends*?

10 In 2015, who won the sixth series of *The Great British Bake Off* and has gone on to be a TV presenter?

Medium

11 Which gourmet and food writer is the daughter of Nigel, a former Chancellor of the Exchequer?

12 Which chef is associated with the hotel-restaurant Le Manoir aux Quat'Saisons?

13 The former host of the TV series *The Delicious Miss Dahl* has what first name?

14 Who took over from Michel Roux Jr as judge on *MasterChef: the Professionals*?

15 Which chef presented the 2018 TV series *Lose Weight for Good* after shedding 12 stone himself?

16 Which chef co-presents *Amazing Hotels: Life Beyond the Lobby* with Giles Coren?

17 In which BBC competition do professional chefs aim to cook at a banquet at the end of the series?

Hard

18 Who presented the series *Saturday Kitchen* from 2006 to 2016?

19 Which chef opened The Fat Duck restaurant in 1995?

20 What nationality is the Muppets' chef?

Answers to QUIZ 382 – Bells and Whistles

1 Scotland
2 Pea
3 Bell-bottoms
4 *Pinocchio*
5 Eight
6 Kettle
7 Sylvia Plath
8 Whistle-stop tour
9 Anita Ward
10 Have a drink
11 Anna
12 *The King and I*
13 Martin Bell
14 Flageolet
15 *Peter Pan*
16 Whistle-blower
17 On a graph
18 Canada
19 Dashing through the snow
20 Hayley Mills

QUIZ 385 – Pot Luck

ANSWERS ON PAGE 387

1 Gin and vermouth are mixed to make which cocktail?

2 What is the name of the parrot owned by Doctor Dolittle?

3 What is the tip of an ink pen called?

4 In the radio alphabet, which word lies between India and kilo?

5 Which llama-like animal is prized for its soft wool?

6 *Everybody Hurts* was a 1992 hit for which group?

7 Stefan Dennis is best known for playing which *Neighbours* character?

8 What is the fifth colour of the rainbow?

9 Who duetted with George Michael in 1991 on *Don't Let the Sun go Down on Me*?

10 With which meat is apple sauce traditionally served?

11 Which musical notes equals half a minim?

12 *First Among Equals* is a 1984 novel by which author?

13 What name is given to the cycle of four operas by Wagner?

14 Australia has which two letters as its internet country code?

15 The concluding section of a play or book is given what name?

16 What is the French word for "yes"?

17 What do Americans call a caravan site?

18 Alexandra Burke topped the charts with which classic song after winning *The X Factor*?

19 The atria are in which organ of the body?

20 Which actress starred n the 1993 film *Indecent Proposal*?

Answers to QUIZ 383 – Pot Luck

1 Groucho Marx
2 *Terra*
3 *Hancock's Half Hour*
4 William Basie
5 Litre
6 Hot Chocolate
7 Ricin
8 Sweden
9 Bigamy
10 Desmond Morris
11 Cranberry
12 Oahu
13 Avon
14 Bore and boar
15 A whale
16 *Roxanne*
17 Sherlock Holmes
18 Jet
19 Nicole Kidman
20 Douro

Easy

1 What type of drink is arabica?

2 Bob Cratchit appears in which Charles Dickens novel?

3 Which part of the body is affected by colic?

4 Which part of London is famous for its diamond trade?

5 In which country is Entebbe?

6 Which DJ (d.2006) was nicknamed "Fluff"?

7 The Oxfordshire village of Goring is on which river?

8 "Hammersmith Palais" was one of the *Reasons to be Cheerful* for which singer?

9 What does the French word *ici* mean in English?

10 In which year did Jessie J top the charts with *Price Tag* and *Domino*?

Medium

11 Which American inventor founded the Kodak camera company?

12 Limassol is a port on which Mediterranean island?

13 As what was the Millennium Dome in Greenwich renamed in 2005?

14 In which county is the town of Newlyn?

15 What type of drink is oloroso?

16 Which team won rugby's Aviva Premiership in the 2016-17 season?

17 A ringmaster presents what type of entertainment?

18 What other playground equipment is paired with "swings" to describe changes in fortune?

19 Chris Tarrant was the original host of which game show that began in 1998?

Hard

20 What is another name for the Australian landmark Uluru?

Answers to QUIZ 384 – Chefs and Cooks

1 Delia Smith
2 Gino D'Acampo
3 *Hell's Kitchen USA*
4 Gregg Wallace and John Torode
5 The Hairy Bikers
6 Phil Vickery
7 Hugh Fearnley-Whittingstall
8 Jamie Oliver
9 Monica Geller
10 Nadiya Hussain
11 Nigella Lawson
12 Raymond Blanc
13 Sophie
14 Marcus Wareing
15 Tom Kerridge
16 Monica Galetti
17 *Great British Menu*
18 James Martin
19 Heston Blumenthal
20 Swedish

1 What name is given to the mixture of butter and flour used to thicken sauces?
2 *A New Hope* is the fourth episode in which film series?
3 Who sang *Don't Go Breaking My Heart* with Sir Elton John in 1976?
4 The zodiac sign Scorpio covers which two calendar months?
5 Which biblical boat carried two of each creature?
6 What is the name of the Muslim month of fasting?
7 "What's up, Doc?" is the catchphrase of which cartoon character?
8 Which word meaning "fuming" means "a river blockage" when read backwards?
9 Michael Bolton had a 1991 no.1 record with which song?
10 Which brand-name cooker is associated with the novels of Joanna Trollope?
11 Who composed the music for the 1889 ballet *Sleeping Beauty*?
12 Since 1967, what has been the capital of Pakistan?
13 What is the name of the small, toothed whale that resembles a dolphin?
14 Which stretch of shingle off the Dorset coast is 17 miles long?
15 The Penguin is an arch-enemy of which comic-book hero?
16 What is the surname of Kirstie, who starred in *Cheers* and the *Look Who's Talking* films?
17 The personal finance programme *Money Box* appears on which radio station?
18 Who is the star of the *Johnny English* films?
19 *We Are the Champions* was a 1977 hit for which band?
20 Which knitted woollen jacket was named after an earl?

Easy Medium Hard

Answers to QUIZ 385 – Pot Luck

1 Martini
2 Polynesia
3 Nib
4 Juliet
5 Alpaca
6 REM
7 Paul Robinson
8 Blue
9 Sir Elton John
10 Pork
11 Crotchet
12 Jeffrey Archer
13 *The Ring*
14 .au
15 Epilogue
16 *Oui*
17 Trailer park
18 *Hallelujah*
19 The heart
20 Demi Moore

QUIZ 388 – Clothing

ANSWERS ON PAGE 390

1 What is the ankle-length robe worn by members of the clergy, the name of which rhymes with the word for a prayer-cushion?
2 The poncho originates from which continent?
3 What is the modern one-word term for "fancy dress"?
4 Which US state is noted for its colourful shirts?
5 What Spanish word for twilled cotton cloth is used for a style of trousers?
6 On which part of the body would a wimple be worn?
7 Which casual cotton top takes its name from a sport played on horseback?
8 What name connects a large silky-haired hound with a 1970s sheepskin coat?
9 For what activity would you wear salopettes?
10 What is the name for a man's formal outfit worn at a wedding?
11 Which style of full-gathered skirt originates from Tyrolean peasant wear?
12 Gendarmes wear what flat-topped military hat?
13 Which two colours of tie lend their names to a formal dress code?
14 The word "jodphurs" originates from which country?
15 Which warm item of clothing shares its name with a species of cow?
16 Culottes are a short pair of trousers cut to look like which other item of clothing?
17 Which Spanish dance is also the name of a jacket?
18 What material are chaps made from?
19 Popular in the 1980s, which skirt shares its name with a type of fungus?
20 What is the long white clerical robe whose name derives from the Latin word for "white"?

Answers to QUIZ 386 – First and Last

1 Coffee
2 *A Christmas Carol*
3 Abdomen
4 Hatton Garden
5 Uganda
6 Alan Freeman
7 Thames
8 Ian Dury
9 Here
10 2011
11 George Eastman
12 Cyprus
13 The O2 Arena
14 Cornwall
15 Sherry
16 Exeter Chiefs
17 Circus acts
18 Roundabouts
19 *Who Wants to Be a Millionaire?*
20 Ayers Rock

QUIZ 389 – Pot Luck

ANSWERS ON PAGE **391**

1 Who had a hit in 1978 with *MacArthur Park*?

2 Who starred as Frank Chambers in the 1981 film *The Postman Always Rings Twice*?

3 Which former British ski jumper was the subject of a 2016 film, the title of which was his nickname?

4 Matt Baker and Ellie Harrison are presenters on which BBC rural affairs programme?

5 Which city hosted the Eurovision Song Contest in 2018?

6 Rudyard Kipling wrote which "exact-sounding" stories?

7 What was the title of the 2007 film in the *Bourne* series?

8 What name was given to the three Victorian Acts that amended the system of parliamentary representation?

9 Who had a 1976 hit with *Sir Duke*?

10 What term is given to a female fox?

11 In which county are the Mendip Hills located?

12 On the Japanese flag, what colour is the large circle?

13 Which bird is also known as the green plover or peewit?

14 What is the phrase for being held in custody awaiting trial?

15 Who plays Jackie in the TV series *Friday Night Dinner*?

16 Which Hebrew prophet was delivered from the lion's den?

17 *Swan Lake* was written by which Russian composer?

18 What is the Anglican tradition resembling Catholicism?

19 What is the world's second-largest ocean?

20 Which market city is near Fountains Abbey?

Easy Medium Hard

Answers to QUIZ 387 – Pot Luck

1 Roux
2 *Star Wars*
3 Kiki Dee
4 October and November
5 Noah's Ark
6 Ramadan
7 Bugs Bunny
8 Mad
9 *When a Man Loves a Woman*
10 Aga (Aga Saga)
11 Tchaikovsky
12 Islamabad
13 Porpoise
14 Chesil Beach
15 Batman
16 Alley
17 Radio 4
18 Rowan Atkinson
19 Queen
20 Cardigan

QUIZ 390 – 1970s Television

ANSWERS ON PAGE 392

Easy

1 Which actor starred as Steve Austin in *The Six Million Dollar Man* in the 1970s?

2 For what did the letters UXB stand in *Danger UXB*?

3 Who played Ria in the TV series *Butterflies* which began in 1978?

4 Which long-running series featured the character Cliff Barnes?

5 Who was the first presenter of *Give Us A Clue*?

6 In which 1970s sitcom did Dame Penelope Keith play Margo?

7 Which 1978-88 quiz show featured Dusty Bin?

8 Who starred in the original TV series of *Police Woman*?

9 What was the name of Brian Wilde's prison officer in *Porridge*?

10 Which spin-off from *Man About the House* starred Richard O'Sullivan as a chef?

11 How were Kate Jackson, Jaclyn Smith and Farrah Fawcett collectively known in the 1970s?

Medium

12 Which US crime series featured the catchphrase "Who loves ya, baby?"?

13 In which US sitcom did Suzi Quatro appear as "Leather" Tuscadero?

14 Which singer was the star of the TV series *Budgie*?

15 John-Boy, Olivia and Jason were members of which family?

16 The main characters in *The Sweeney* worked for which branch of the Met Police?

17 Captain Dobey was the boss of which two crime-fighters?

18 Which US series featured Bo and Luke and their cousin Daisy?

19 Who played private investigator James Rockford?

20 Which duo signed off each programme with "It's goodnight from me. And it's goodnight from him"?

Hard

Answers to QUIZ 388 – Clothing

1 Cassock
2 South America
3 Cosplay
4 Hawaii
5 Chino
6 Head
7 Polo shirt
8 Afghan
9 Skiing
10 Morning dress
11 Dirndl
12 Kepi
13 Black and white
14 Indian
15 Jersey
16 Skirt
17 Bolero
18 Leather
19 Puffball
20 Alb

QUIZ 391 – Pot Luck

ANSWERS ON PAGE 393

1 What is the fifth note of the tonic sol-fa scale?

2 The Costa del Sol is in which country?

3 Which long-running Radio 4 show is "an everyday story of country folk"?

4 Prince Rainier of Monaco married which film star?

5 Which former star of *Doctor Who* also played the title role in the TV series *Worzel Gummidge*?

6 In the name of the US TV network, what do the initials HBO stand for?

7 Who played Captain Von Trapp in the 1965 film *The Sound of Music*?

8 Which animal is known for constructing dams and lodges?

9 What is the capital city of Australia?

10 What is an Aberdeen Angus?

11 The acre was replaced by which metric measurement?

12 In what year did Austria regain full independence?

13 Who composed the music for *Cats* and *Evita*?

14 What was the nationality of philosopher/mathematician René Descartes (b.1596)?

15 The town of Bicester is in which county?

16 The Swiss ski resort of Zermatt is near the foot of which mountain?

17 Which Algarve coastal town shares a name with Nigeria's largest city?

18 In which poem does the shooting of an albatross cause bad luck?

19 Who had a 1980 hit with *Brass in Pocket*?

20 Which actress starred as Becky Sharp in the 2004 film *Vanity Fair*?

Easy

Medium

Hard

Answers to QUIZ 389 – Pot Luck

1 Donna Summer
2 Jack Nicholson
3 "Eddie" Edwards (Eddie the Eagle)
4 *Countryfile*
5 Lisbon
6 *Just So*
7 *The Bourne Ultimatum*
8 Reform Acts
9 Stevie Wonder
10 Vixen
11 Somerset
12 Red
13 Lapwing
14 On remand
15 Tamsin Greig
16 Daniel
17 Tchaikovsky
18 High Church
19 Atlantic
20 Ripon

QUIZ 392 – DIY and Decorating

ANSWERS ON PAGE 394

Easy

1 What name is given to a carved or paper band high up in a room?

2 For what is a bracket used?

3 A hod is used for carrying which items?

4 What mixture is used to fill in the spaces between tiles?

5 What type of soap is used for cleaning paintwork?

6 Which preparation material shares its name with a book containing basic facts about a subject?

7 The layer of material placed between a floor and a carpet is given what term?

8 What would an interior designer use a mood board for?

9 How is paint applied if it is "stippled"?

10 What term is given to one of four vertical surfaces in a room that has been decorated in a more noticeable manner than the rest?

Medium

11 A decorative centrepiece on the upper surface of a room has what flowery name?

12 Which device is used in checking the setting of horizontal surfaces?

13 A popular neutral paint colour shares its name with which spring-flowering shrub?

14 Which wooden style of furniture with a simple design takes its name from an American religious group?

15 Pencil pleat and eyelet are types of which soft furnishing?

16 Which style of decorating is based on making the furniture look old in an attractive way?

17 What method of decorating involves applying paint to a cut-out template?

18 A piece of string with a weight on it, used to check vertical angles, has what two-word name?

Hard

19 What type of hammer is used for extracting nails?

20 Which type of paint sounds like it is a natural casing?

Answers to QUIZ 390 – 1970s Television

1 Lee Majors
2 Unexploded Bomb
3 Wendy Craig
4 *Dallas*
5 Michael Aspel
6 *The Good Life*
7 3-2-1
8 Angie Dickinson
9 Mr Barrowclough
10 *Robin's Nest*
11 Charlie's Angels
12 *Kojak*
13 *Happy Days*
14 Adam Faith
15 The Waltons
16 Flying Squad
17 Starsky and Hutch
18 *The Dukes of Hazzard*
19 James Garner
20 The Two Ronnies

QUIZ 393 – Pot Luck

ANSWERS ON PAGE 395

1 What is the surname of André, the famous Dutch violinist?

2 Toni Basil reached no.2 in the UK charts in 1982 with which song?

3 Which actress was painted gold in the 1964 film *Goldfinger*?

4 *Sound of the Underground* (2002) was the first hit for which group?

5 Which alloy of copper, tin and zinc was originally used for making firearms?

6 Oxbridge sportsmen and women are associated with which colour?

7 What is the title of the Channel 4 TV series which features people watching television?

8 The skull of Yorick features in which Shakespeare play?

9 Which group topped the UK singles chart in 1975 with *Bye Bye Baby* and *Give A Little Love*?

10 In which board game are the letters Z and Q worth ten points each?

11 With which industry is Julien MacDonald associated?

12 Which Parisian thoroughfare leads up to the Arc de Triomphe?

13 Barbara Vine was a pseudonym for which crime author?

14 Which country did Mats Wilander represent in tennis?

15 According to the song, how many trombones were there in the big parade?

16 In which county is the town of Corsham?

17 Which town near Hastings in East Sussex is the location of a famous abbey?

18 Who starred in the 1970s sitcom *Citizen Smith*?

19 Which company created the *Super Mario* series of games?

20 The Who and Sir Elton John both had hits with which song from the film *Tommy*?

Answers to QUIZ 391 – Pot Luck

1 Soh

2 Spain

3 *The Archers*

4 Grace Kelly

5 Jon Pertwee

6 Home Box Office

7 Christopher Plummer

8 A beaver

9 Canberra

10 Breed of cattle

11 Hectare

12 1955

13 Andrew Lloyd Webber (Baron Lloyd-Webber)

14 French

15 Oxfordshire

16 Matterhorn

17 Lagos

18 *The Rime of The Ancient Mariner*

19 The Pretenders

20 Reese Witherspoon

QUIZ 394 – Musical Goodbyes

ANSWERS ON PAGE 396

Easy

1 Which duo had a hit in 1982 with *Say Hello, Wave Goodbye*?

2 *Leave Right Now* was a 2003 hit for which singer?

3 *Gudbuy T'Jane* was a 1972 single by which glam rock band?

4 Which band recorded the 1982 single *See You*?

5 Who topped the UK singles charts in 2017 with *Too Good at Goodbyes*?

6 "I just can't stand the pain. Girl I'm leaving you tomorrow" is a lyric from which 1977 song?

7 1967's *Hello, Goodbye* was taken from which Beatles album?

8 How many ways did Paul Simon say there were to leave your lover?

9 *The Last Farewell* was a 1975 hit for which singer?

10 In which year did The Spice Girls top the charts with *Goodbye*?

Medium

11 *Don't Leave Me This Way* was in the charts in 1977 for both Harold Melvin and the Bluenotes and which female singer?

12 Sir Elton John said *Goodbye* to which thoroughfare in a 1973 song?

13 *Another Suitcase in Another Hall* is a song from which musical?

14 Sarah Brightman duetted with which opera singer on 1997's *Time to Say Goodbye*?

15 Who sang *Farewell My Summer Love* in 1984?

16 *Ready To Go* was a 1990s single by which English band?

17 *Too Late for Goodbyes* was a 1984 single by which singer?

18 What was the title of the band Chicago's only UK no.1 single?

19 Which heavy metal band released the 1982 single *Run to the Hills*?

20 The album *All That You Can't Leave Behind* was a chart-topper for which band?

Hard

Answers to QUIZ 392 – DIY and Decorating

1 Frieze
2 Supporting a shelf
3 Bricks
4 Grout
5 Sugar soap
6 Primer
7 Underlay
8 Displaying samples of colour and texture
9 Dabbed on
10 Feature wall
11 Ceiling rose
12 Spirit level
13 Magnolia
14 Shaker
15 Curtains
16 Shabby chic
17 Stencilling
18 Plumb line
19 Claw hammer
20 Eggshell

QUIZ 395 – Pot Luck

ANSWERS ON PAGE 397

1 Which organisation was featured in the TV series *Jam & Jerusalem*?

2 Which group had a hit in 1980 with *Super Trouper*?

3 In a four-man bobsleigh team, where does the "brakeman" sit?

4 Who was Lou Costello's comedy partner?

5 What is the most common freestyle swimming stroke?

6 The original fairy tale of *Thumbelina* was written by which author?

7 Which Asian country has over thirteen thousand equatorial islands?

8 Which English king was executed in 1649?

9 *Oh, I Wish I'd Looked After Me Teeth* is by which writer of comic verse?

10 Which singer had a hit with *Walking on Broken Glass* in 1992?

11 Which river flows through Sheffield and Rotherham?

12 What was the surname of *The Likely Lads* actor Rodney?

13 Patrick Swayze and Demi Moore starred in which romantic film of 1990?

14 Who played JR in TV's *Dallas*?

15 Which is the most northerly British town?

16 *Under Your Thumb* was a hit for which two former members of the band 10cc?

17 Who is best known for playing David Platt in *Coronation Street*?

18 The word "fritillary" can apply to a plant and to which insect?

19 Dustin Johnson (b.1984) plays which sport?

20 Where in California is the hottest part of the USA?

Answers to QUIZ 393 – Pot Luck

1 Rieu
2 *Mickey*
3 Shirley Eaton
4 Girls Aloud
5 Gunmetal
6 Blue
7 *Gogglebox*
8 *Hamlet*
9 Bay City Rollers
10 Scrabble®
11 Fashion
12 Champs-Élysées
13 Baroness Ruth Rendell
14 Sweden
15 76
16 Wiltshire
17 Battle
18 Robert Lindsay
19 Nintendo®
20 *Pinball Wizard*

QUIZ 396 – The UK

ANSWERS ON PAGE 398

1 What term is given to the upper chamber of the UK parliament?
2 In which county is Ilfracombe?
3 Which legendary British film company is famous for its horror films?
4 Which bridge on the Thames is closest to the Tower of London?
5 In which region of Scotland is Dunfermline?
6 What is the colloquial name for female members of the Royal Navy?
7 How is the Feast of St Stephen better known in the UK?
8 In which county is the Welsh town of Brecon?
9 What name links a classic Epsom horse race and a Midlands city on the River Derwent?
10 Which Upper Deeside village near Balmoral is famous for its annual Highland Games?
11 The Pennines are crossed by which motorway?
12 A parish minister of the Church of Scotland lives in what residence?
13 Which Dartmoor village is famous for a traditional ballad about its fair?
14 Who composed *Rule Britannia*?
15 Every October, which event of medieval origin takes place in Nottingham?
16 Which writer had a home at Hill Top in the Lake District?
17 In which Northern Ireland county is the Giant's Causeway?
18 Which Brixton avenue did Eddy Grant name in a 1983 hit?
19 In an English trial, how many people sit on the jury?
20 Which Dorset port and resort is famous for its Cobb?

Easy
Medium
Hard

Answers to QUIZ 394 – Musical Goodbyes

1 Soft Cell
2 Will Young
3 Slade
4 Depeche Mode
5 Sam Smith
6 *Easy* (The Commodores)
7 *Magical Mystery Tour*
8 50
9 Roger Whittaker
10 1998
11 Thelma Houston
12 Yellow Brick Road
13 *Evita*
14 Andrea Bocelli
15 Michael Jackson
16 Republica
17 Julian Lennon
18 *If You Leave Me Now*
19 Iron Maiden
20 U2

QUIZ 397 – Pot Luck

ANSWERS ON PAGE 399

1 What is the world's lowest lake?
2 Of which type of composition is Handel's *Messiah* an example?
3 Which Dutch explorer gave his name to an Australian island state?
4 Who wrote *Treasure Island* (1883)?
5 Which glam rock group sang the festive favourite *Merry Christmas Everybody*?
6 The 2008 film *Quantum of Solace* starred which actor as James Bond?
7 Which pale yellow beverage is often drunk with Chinese meals?
8 CDN is the international vehicle registration code for which country?
9 Which group had a 1979 hit with *Cool for Cats*?
10 What was the first name of the "King of Swing" jazz musician Mr Goodman?
11 The Hungarian language is known by what name in Hungarian?
12 Which gemstone is traditionally associated with the month of February?
13 What is the protective covering on the nose-cone of a spacecraft called?
14 Erinsborough is the setting for which long-running series?
15 The 1960s band the Dreamers had who as their frontman?
16 Which Chinese exercise system translates in English as "supreme ultimate"?
17 What is the reef material made by tiny aquatic animals?
18 Andy and Lance were played by Mackenzie Crook and Toby Jones in which comedy series?
19 In which county is Margate?
20 What is the American term for an overnight plane journey called?

Answers to QUIZ 395 – Pot Luck

1 Women's Institute
2 ABBA
3 At the rear
4 Bud Abbott
5 Crawl
6 Hans Christian Andersen
7 Indonesia
8 Charles I
9 Pam Ayres
10 Annie Lennox
11 Don
12 Bewes
13 *Ghost*
14 Larry Hagman
15 Lerwick (Shetland Islands)
16 Godley and Creme
17 Jack P Shepherd
18 Butterfly
19 Golf
20 Death Valley

QUIZ 398 – Co-Stars

ANSWERS ON PAGE 400

Easy

1 Who co-starred with Michael Douglas in *Romancing the Stone*?

2 Which Scottish comedian co-starred with Dame Judi Dench in the 1997 film *Mrs Brown*?

3 In the 1988 thriller *Tequila Sunrise*, which actress co-starred with Mel Gibson?

4 Rebecca De Mornay co-starred with which actor in the 1983 film *Risky Business*?

5 Which member of the cast of *Friends* starred with Bruce Willis in *The Whole Nine Yards*?

6 Who was Nicole Kidman's co-star in the 2005 film *The Interpreter*?

7 Which 1999 adventure film starred Brendan Fraser and Rachel Weisz?

8 Who were the two stars of the 2016 film *La La Land*?

9 Which 2008 film set in Tudor times starred Scarlett Johansson and Natalie Portman?

10 How many *First Dates* did Drew Barrymore and Adam Sandler have in the title of a 2004 film?

Medium

11 Who directed Tom Hanks and Meg Ryan in *You've Got Mail*?

12 Chris O'Donnell played Robin to which star's Batman in the 1997 film *Batman & Robin*?

13 Which 1994 suspense film starred Keanu Reeves and Sandra Bullock?

14 Who co-starred with Leonardo DiCaprio in *Revolutionary Road* (2008)?

15 Which 1999 film was the second to co-star Julia Roberts and Richard Gere?

16 In the 1967 film, who played Bonnie and Clyde?

17 Who co-starred with Meryl Streep in the 1985 film *Out of Africa*?

18 Which 1995 crime thriller starred Al Pacino and Robert De Niro?

19 In the 1994 film *Four Weddings and a Funeral*, who played Charles and Carrie?

Hard

20 Which famous co-stars married in 1964 and again in 1975?

Answers to QUIZ 396 – The UK

1 House of Lords
2 Devon
3 Hammer
4 Tower Bridge
5 Fife
6 Wrens
7 Boxing Day
8 Powys
9 Derby
10 Braemar
11 M62
12 A manse
13 Widecombe
14 Thomas Arne
15 Goose Fair
16 Beatrix Potter
17 Antrim
18 Electric Avenue
19 12
20 Lyme Regis

QUIZ 399 – Pot Luck

ANSWERS ON PAGE 401

1 On which Scottish island is the town of Tobermory?

2 Which Raymond presented TV's new-technology programme *Tomorrow's World* from 1965 until 1977?

3 Which part of speech is the word "under"?

4 "They think it's all over. It is now" was said by which commentator in the 1966 FIFA World Cup Final?

5 Which sinister French cardinal features in the adventures of the Three Musketeers?

6 Which town in Kent adjoins Walmer?

7 Who was the British prime minister from 1974 to 1976?

8 In *The Wizard of Oz*, which of Dorothy's companions wanted a heart?

9 Which group had a hit in 1964 with *I Get Around*?

10 What was the first name of children's book illustrator Lucie Attwell?

11 The BBC's *Later...* TV series is presented by which musician?

12 Dean Gaffney is best known for playing which character in *EastEnders*?

13 What do the initials HGV stand for?

14 According to the rhyme, what happened to Solomon Grundy on Tuesday?

15 Which city is the capital of Bangladesh?

16 In the House of Lords, what colour are the seats?

17 Which is the USA's "Beehive State"?

18 The theme to which film gave Olivia Newton-John and ELO a 1980 no.1?

19 Bombay Duck is what type of food?

20 Galatasaray football team is based in which country?

Easy

Medium

Hard

Answers to QUIZ 397 – Pot Luck

1 Dead Sea
2 Oratorio
3 Abel Tasman (Tasmania)
4 Robert Louis Stevenson
5 Slade
6 Daniel Craig
7 Jasmine tea
8 Canada
9 Squeeze
10 Benny
11 Magyar
12 Amethyst
13 Heat shield
14 *Neighbours*
15 Freddie (Garrity)
16 Tai chi
17 Coral
18 *Detectorists*
19 Kent
20 Red-eye

QUIZ 400 – Weather

ANSWERS ON PAGE 402

Easy

1 On the Beaufort Scale, what type of tropical storm has the highest-speed wind?

2 The French word *neige* indicates what type of weather?

3 In which decade was the world's first successful weather satellite launched?

4 What name is given to the warming of part of the Pacific that happens every few years and affects weather patterns?

5 Does a warm front indicate a future drop in temperature or rise in temperature?

6 Which "ology" is the study of weather?

7 In the Solar UV index, what does "UV" stand for?

8 Which device measures air pressure to show when the weather is changing?

9 What term is given to the measure of the amount of water in the air?

10 How is visibility of less than 1 km described in weather reports?

Medium

11 A severe weather warning indicating "be aware" is shown as which colour?

12 What is a dust devil?

13 What term is given to the general weather conditions of a place?

14 Exposure to sunlight produces which vitamin?

15 Which Charles Dickens character gave her name to an inelegant umbrella?

16 What type of weather is indicated by a symbol of a cloud with one raindrop and one snowflake below it?

17 Which colour comes after green in the rainbow?

18 What term is given to the central part of a storm?

19 Does a northerly wind blow from the north or towards the north?

20 If the pollen count is shown as orange, how is it described?

Hard

Answers to QUIZ 398 – Co-Stars

1 Kathleen Turner
2 Sir Billy Connolly
3 Michelle Pfeiffer
4 Tom Cruise
5 Matthew Perry
6 Sean Penn
7 *The Mummy*
8 Emma Stone and Ryan Gosling
9 *The Other Boleyn Girl*
10 50
11 Nora Ephron
12 George Clooney
13 *Speed*
14 Kate Winslet
15 *Runaway Bride*
16 Faye Dunaway and Warren Beatty
17 Robert Redford
18 *Heat*
19 Hugh Grant and Andie MacDowell
20 Elizabeth Taylor and Richard Burton

QUIZ 401 – Pot Luck

ANSWERS ON PAGE 403

1 In Europe, which era followed the Neolithic?

2 Which writers created the series *Dad's Army*?

3 Of which Gulf state is Muscat the capital?

4 What was the name of Stephen Hawking's first wife, on whose book the 2014 film *The Theory of Everything* was based?

5 Which elaborate structure did Daedalus build for King Minos of Crete?

6 *The Lion Sleeps Tonight* was a chart-topping hit for which group in 1982?

7 Which actress starred in the 2002 film *Bend it Like Beckham*?

8 What name is given to any surgical device used to tie blood vessels to stop bleeding?

9 The opera *Dido and Aeneas* (1680) was written by which English composer?

10 Which Venice landmark is known in Italian as "Ponte dei Sospiri"?

11 James Earl Jones provided the voice of which *Star Wars* character?

12 What is the title of the Fred Astaire musical which includes the song *Cheek to Cheek*?

13 What literary form does *The Pilgrim's Progress* (1678) take?

14 Which Essex town was granted city status in 2012?

15 What is the tenth letter of the Greek alphabet?

16 Declan MacManus was the original name of which singer?

17 What name is given to volcanic glass formed from lava?

18 Joseph Smith founded which religion?

19 Whose theory of the solar system was published in 1543 just before his death?

20 Which book of the Bible tells of the birth of Moses?

Answers to QUIZ 399 – Pot Luck

1 Mull
2 Baxter
3 Preposition
4 Kenneth Wolstenholme
5 Cardinal Richelieu
6 Deal
7 Harold Wilson (Baron Wilson of Rievaulx)
8 Tin Man
9 The Beach Boys
10 Mabel
11 Jools Holland
12 Robbie Jackson
13 Heavy Goods Vehicle
14 He was Christened
15 Dhaka
16 Red
17 Utah
18 *Xanadu*
19 Fish
20 Turkey

 ANSWERS ON PAGE 404

1 By what name is artist Jack Hoggan better known?
2 Which artist painted *The Garden of Earthly Delights*?
3 Which German Renaissance artist (b.1471) was famous for his woodcuts?
4 What title precedes the names of the artists Angelico and Filippo Lippi?
5 Bridget Riley is particularly known for which type of creative design?
6 Who painted *Bar at the Folies-Bergère* (1882)?
7 A picture painted on a wall before the plaster is dry is given what term?
8 Which artist was the first president of the Royal Academy?
9 In which town of Provence, in 1888, did Van Gogh share a house with Gauguin?
10 Who was Augustus John's painter sister?
11 Which British artist designed the lions in Trafalgar Square?
12 *Saturn Devouring His Son* was painted by which artist (b.1746)?
13 What were the first two names of artist LS Lowry?
14 In which city was David Hockney born?
15 Which Suffolk river provides the setting for the painting *The Hay Wain*?
16 Which Austrian painter Gustav was best known for his early 20th-century painting *The Kiss*?
17 Who created the art installation *Another Place*, featuring 100 statues?
18 In which Spanish city was Picasso born?
19 Which painter born in Latvia in 1903 was known for his large hazy rectangles of colour?
20 What is the term for a painting or design intended to deceive the eye?

Easy

Medium

Hard

Answers to QUIZ 400 – Weather

1 Hurricane
2 Snow
3 1960s
4 El Niño
5 Rise in temperature
6 Meteorology
7 Ultraviolet
8 Barometer
9 Humidity
10 Very poor
11 Yellow
12 A small whirlwind
13 Climate
14 Vitamin D
15 Mrs Gamp
16 Sleet
17 Blue
18 Eye
19 From the north
20 Moderate

QUIZ 403 – Pot Luck

ANSWERS ON PAGE 405

1 What was the nationality of the psychologist Jean Piaget?

2 On which island does the annual Battle of Flowers take place?

3 Which part of the body is affected by Crohn's Disease?

4 Which battle of 1346 between England and France involved the Black Prince?

5 On which river does Winchester stand?

6 In which year was Helen Shapiro *Walking Back to Happiness* at the top of the UK charts?

7 Which river flows through Canterbury?

8 Which French name is given to a large decorative wardrobe?

9 Which of the Haven Ports is the northernmost coastal town in Essex?

10 In literature, what was the name of adventurer Phileas Fogg's manservant?

11 Which band had a hit in 1972 with *Children of the Revolution*?

12 In which year did Sir Edmund Hillary and Tenzing Norgay become the first people to climb Mount Everest?

13 Which US comedian, born in Eltham in London, died in 2003 aged 100?

14 What was the title of the 1983 Heaven 17 hit that was also a hit when it was re-mixed and released in 1992?

15 Which actress starred in *Ninotchka* (1939)?

16 What is the second largest lake in the Lake District?

17 A Cuba libre cocktail has what type of alcohol as its basis?

18 Which group had a 1974 hit with *Teenage Rampage*?

19 Which country is home to the Korat cat?

20 In which year did banking via the Internet first become available in the UK?

Easy

Medium

Hard

Answers to QUIZ 401 – Pot Luck

1 Bronze Age
2 Jimmy Perry and David Croft
3 Oman
4 Jane
5 Labyrinth
6 Tight Fit
7 Keira Knightley
8 A ligature
9 Henry Purcell
10 Bridge of Sighs
11 Darth Vader
12 *Top Hat*
13 Allegory
14 Chelmsford
15 Kappa
16 Elvis Costello
17 Obsidian
18 Mormonism
19 Nicolaus Copernicus
20 Exodus

QUIZ 404 – Animal World

Easy

1 Gophers are native to which continent?

2 *Corvus frugilegus* is the Latin name of which bird of the crow family?

3 What term is given to a colony of baboons?

4 What secretion do honey bees produce to feed their larvae?

5 Collectively, how is a group of rhinoceroses referred to?

6 Which animal is known in America as the caribou?

7 The term "ursine" relates to which type of animal?

8 What is a baby pigeon called?

9 Which cod-like fish is also known as saithe?

10 Which part of a horse's mane falls in front between the ears?

11 How many legs does a katydid have?

Medium

12 "Forest person" is the meaning of the name of which ape found in Borneo?

13 Which is the fastest member of the animal kingdom?

14 Which river animal has been reintroduced to Knapdale in Scotland and is now a protected species?

15 "Reynard" is an old name for which animal?

16 A gadwall is what type of animal?

17 The egg-laying mammal called the spiny anteater has what other one-word name?

18 What term is given to a female badger?

19 What is the middle section of an insect?

Hard

20 The water ouzel is an alternative name for which bird?

Answers to QUIZ 402 – Art

1 Jack Vettriano
2 Hieronymus Bosch
3 Albrecht Dürer
4 Fra
5 Op art
6 Édouard Manet
7 Fresco
8 Sir Joshua Reynolds
9 Arles
10 Gwen
11 Sir Edwin Landseer
12 Francisco Goya
13 Laurence Stephen
14 Bradford
15 Stour
16 Klimt
17 Sir Antony Gormley
18 Málaga
19 Mark Rothko
20 *Trompe l'oeil*

QUIZ 405 – Pot Luck

ANSWERS ON PAGE 407

1 Which 18th-century economist wrote *The Wealth of Nations*?

2 Which museum is located at Cosford in Shropshire?

3 Often used as a thickening agent, which cereal is obtained from the root of the cassava plant?

4 Which Swiss resort lies at the northern end of Lake Maggiore?

5 Which singer's debut album *In The Lonely Hour* was released in 2014?

6 What form of Buddhism featured in the title of Robert M Pirsig's 1974 bestseller?

7 *Setting Sons* was a 1979 album by which band?

8 What is the monetary unit of Vietnam?

9 *You Make Me Feel Brand New* was a hit for which 1970s soul band?

10 Which 1987 Michael Jackson album featured the song *Man in the Mirror*?

11 Who wrote the 1939 novel *After Many a Summer*?

12 Which beverage is made from the dried leaves of *Camellia sinensis*?

13 Which legal term means "not open to appeal"?

14 On which lake does Milwaukee stand?

15 In which Suffolk location was a Viking burial ship discovered in 1939?

16 First aired in 1953, to what did the radio programme *What Do You Know?* change its name in 1967?

17 What was Pakistan's first capital city?

18 Which Irish city stands at the head of the Shannon estuary?

19 *The Last Kiss* was a 1985 single by which former teen idol?

20 Which English king died in 1087 after falling off his horse?

Answers to QUIZ 403 – Pot Luck

1 Swiss
2 Jersey
3 The intestines (especially the colon)
4 Crécy
5 Itchen
6 1961
7 Stour
8 Armoire
9 Harwich
10 Passepartout
11 T Rex
12 1953
13 Bob Hope
14 *Temptation*
15 Greta Garbo
16 Ullswater
17 Rum
18 The Sweet
19 Thailand
20 1997

QUIZ 406 – Air Travel

ANSWERS ON PAGE **408**

Easy

1 What was the surname of the French brothers who made the first piloted ascent in an air balloon in 1783?

2 Which German-born Count pioneered airship development from the late 19th century?

3 In which year did the *Hindenberg* disaster happen?

4 Who invented the modern helicopter and later designed the R-4, the world's first mass-produced helicopter?

5 What do the initials IATA stand for?

6 What is the name of Russia's national airline?

7 In which London borough is London City Airport?

8 What is the name of the English entrepreneur who completed the longest flight in a hot air-balloon, between Japan and Canada in 1991?

9 On which island is Cristiano Ronaldo Airport?

Medium

10 What is the average in-flight altitude of passenger aeroplanes?

11 CBR is the code for which international airport?

12 ESTA is a system used when travelling to which country?

13 What do the initials LAPL stand for in relation to aviation?

14 What type of vehicle is a sailplane?

15 Which airport formerly had terminals named Europa and Oceanic?

16 Which town in West Sussex hosts the International Birdman Competition?

17 The first female flight attendant was hired by which airline?

18 Which two of London's international airports are situated in Essex?

Hard

19 Which city is served by an airport located at Dyce?

20 In 2012, who jumped to Earth from a helium balloon in the stratosphere?

Answers to QUIZ 404 – Animal World

1 North America
2 Rook
3 Troop
4 Royal jelly
5 Crash
6 Reindeer
7 Bear
8 Squab
9 Coley
10 Forelock
11 Six (a cricket)
12 Orang-utan
13 Peregrine falcon
14 Beaver
15 A fox
16 A duck
17 Echidna
18 Sow
19 Thorax
20 Dipper

QUIZ 407 – Pot Luck

ANSWERS ON PAGE 409

1 On the Beatles' *White Album*, who played lead guitar on *While My Guitar Gently Weeps*?
2 What feature has a palmiped bird?
3 Michael Brandon and Glynis Barber starred in which 1980s TV police series?
4 Which English city was called Glevum by the Romans?
5 Which Coldplay album did the single *Yellow* first appear on?
6 Bright's disease affects which organ of the body?
7 Which foodstuff was known as "hokey-pokey" in the late 19th century?
8 Which amateur detective was played by Tom Bosley on TV from 1989 to 1991?
9 Turpentine is obtained from the resin of which tree?
10 What is the capital city of Ukraine?
11 What was Elvis Presley's first UK no.1?
12 *Candy Girl* was a hit for which group in 1983?
13 What was the public space for markets in ancient Greece called?
14 Which bird has the largest wingspan of any living bird?
15 An annelid is what type of creature?
16 Which poet wrote the 1919 poem *The Second Coming*?
17 What term is given to crushed stone or gravel used to make concrete?
18 From 1999 to 2003, who captained the England cricket team?
19 Who wrote the *Twilight* series of novels?
20 Who first vaccinated people and animals against rabies, in 1885?

Answers to QUIZ 405 – Pot Luck

1 Adam Smith
2 Royal Air Force Museum
3 Tapioca
4 Locarno
5 Sam Smith
6 Zen (*Zen and the Art of Motorcycle Maintenance*)
7 The Jam
8 Dong
9 Stylistics
10 *Bad*
11 Aldous Huxley
12 Tea
13 Peremptory
14 Lake Michigan
15 Sutton Hoo
16 *Brain of Britain*
17 Karachi
18 Limerick
19 David Cassidy
20 William I

QUIZ 408 – Foreign Language Television

ANSWERS ON PAGE 410

Easy

1 Who played Sarah Lund in the Danish series *The Killing*?

2 In which fictional town is *Inspector Montalbano* set?

3 What was the name of Sidse Babett Knudsen's prime minister in *Borgen*?

4 Who starred as Saga Norén in *The Bridge*?

5 What is the English title of the Swedish series centred around a guesthouse on the Åland Islands?

6 In which city is the French series *Spiral* set?

7 Krister Henriksson played which Swedish detective from 2005 to 2014?

8 Which Swedish actor starred as Christer Wijk in the *Crimes of Passion* series?

9 The thriller series *Salamander* is from which country?

10 The first series of which Danish drama series focused on the financial affairs of the fictional company Energreen?

Medium

11 Detective Sandra Winckler features in which French thriller series?

12 The series *Trapped* is set in which country?

13 What is the title of the series set in the Spanish prison called Cruz del Sur?

14 Which Danish series followed the fortunes of the Grønnegaard family?

15 The 2012-16 French series *Les Hommes de l'ombre* was broadcast in the UK under what title?

16 Foreign series are shown on Channel 4 and its related channels under what general name?

17 What is the English title of the French series *Les Revenants*?

Hard

18 What is the title of the English and French series inspired by *The Bridge*?

19 Who is Inspector Montalbano's long-suffering girlfriend?

20 Which year provided the title of a 2014 Danish drama series about a war?

Answers to QUIZ 406 – Air Travel

1 Montgolfier
2 Ferdinand von Zeppelin
3 1937
4 Igor Sikorsky
5 International Air Transport Association
6 Aeroflot
7 Newham
8 Sir Richard Branson
9 Madeira
10 35,000 feet
11 Canberra
12 USA
13 Light aircraft pilot licence
14 Glider
15 Heathrow
16 Bognor Regis
17 United Airlines
18 Stansted and Southend
19 Aberdeen
20 Felix Baumgartner

QUIZ 409 – Pot Luck

ANSWERS ON PAGE 411

1 The song *He is an Englishman* appears in which Gilbert and Sullivan opera?

2 Which Canadian province has Winnipeg as its capital?

3 Which actor starred as Klaatu in the 2008 remake of *The Day the Earth Stood Still*?

4 *Low*, *Right Round* and *Wild Ones* have been hits for whch US rapper?

5 Who invented the vacuum flask?

6 With which motor vehicle manufacturer is Elon Musk associated?

7 Grace Road is the home of which county cricket club?

8 Which quiz programme was hosted by Hughie Green from 1955 to 1968?

9 What Latin term is given to a work of art reminding people that they will die?

10 Russian and Ukrainian belong to which family of languages?

11 The name of which shrub means "rose tree" in Greek?

12 Who developed the ideas of the collective unconscious and of the archetype?

13 Which group had hits in the 1980s with *Mirror Man* and *Open Your Heart*?

14 The character of Martin Riggs was played by Mel Gibson in which series of films?

15 What type of creature is a cowrie?

16 Writers Virginia Woolf, Leonard Woolf, John Maynard Keynes, Desmond Maccarthy and others were collectively known as what?

17 Which band was formed by Paul Weller and Mick Talbot in 1983?

18 In which British city is the Sheldonian Theatre?

19 What title was inherited by Frances Hodgson Burnett's character, Cedric Errol, an American boy?

20 Which singer has released albums entitled *Alf* and *Hoodoo*?

Answers to QUIZ 407 – Pot Luck

1 Eric Clapton
2 Webbed feet
3 *Dempsey and Makepeace*
4 Gloucester
5 *Parachutes*
6 Kidneys
7 Ice cream
8 Father Dowling
9 Pine
10 Kiev
11 *All Shook Up*
12 New Edition
13 Agora
14 Wandering (or snowy) albatross
15 A worm
16 WB Yeats
17 Aggregate
18 Nasser Hussein
19 Stephenie Meyer
20 Louis Pasteur (with Émile Roux)

ANSWERS ON PAGE 412

Easy

1 Before their marriage, what relation to Prince Albert was Queen Victoria?

2 Which Greek island was the centre of the Minoan civilisation?

3 Which region of central Spain was a separate kingdom until 1479?

4 Of which historic region of Germany is Dresden the capital?

5 Who was the first Englishman to circumnavigate the world?

6 Where was the Temple of Artemis (or Diana), one of the Seven Wonders of the Ancient World, situated?

7 King Zog once ruled which country?

8 Which extinct species of early human takes its name from a valley in Germany?

9 Which cathedral city of Andalusia was the capital of Moorish Spain?

10 From where did Concorde's first test flight take off?

Medium

11 Which city was the northern capital of the historical Kingdom of the Two Sicilies?

12 Which French province was an English possession from 1154 to 1204?

13 Ragusa is the former name of which Croatian port?

14 Leonidas was king of which ancient Greek city?

15 Which crime-stopping organisation was set up in Vienna in 1923?

16 The explorer Christopher Columbus was born in which city?

17 In 1327, who became King of England?

18 Which Austrian archduke died at Mayerling in 1889?

19 Between 1871 and 1919, which region of north-east France was under German control?

20 Which city was the first capital of a unified Italy in 1861?

Hard

Answers to QUIZ 408 – Foreign Language Television

1 Sofie Gråbøl
2 Vigàta
3 Birgitte Nyborg
4 Sofia Helin
5 *Thicker Than Water*
6 Paris
7 Kurt Wallander
8 Ola Rapace
9 Belgium
10 *Follow the Money*
11 *Witnesses*
12 Iceland
13 *Locked Up*
14 *The Legacy*
15 *Spin*
16 Walter Presents
17 *The Returned*
18 *The Tunnel*
19 Livia
20 1864

QUIZ 411 – Pot Luck

ANSWERS ON PAGE 413

1 Blondie's *Call Me* was used in which 1980 film?
2 Which group topped the UK singles chart in 2003 with *Crashed the Wedding*?
3 On which sea is the city of Sevastopol?
4 In which county is the town of Kirkby Lonsdale?
5 Ramsons is a member of which plant family?
6 In which country do Kaiserslautern football team play?
7 What is the capital of Ecuador?
8 The TV series *Diagnosis: Murder* starred which actor as Dr Mark Sloan?
9 Who wrote the 1998 play *Copenhagen*?
10 What was the name of the duo formed by Siobhan Fahey and Marcella Detroit?
11 What sport is played at Walton Heath?
12 What do the "RR" of JRR Tolkien's initials stand for?
13 How many Odes did Keats write where "*Ode*" appears in the title of the poem?
14 Which famous actor was born Ramón Antonio Gerard Estévez?
15 Who played Batman in the 2008 film *The Dark Knight*?
16 Jim Kerr is the frontman for which Scottish band?
17 In which Irish county is Tralee?
18 Which was the first nation to host the FIFA World Cup for a second time?
19 Which penguin species has yellow and black plumes on its head?
20 *Party Girl* was a 2010 hit for which band?

Answers to QUIZ 409 – Pot Luck

1 *HMS Pinafore*
2 Manitoba
3 Keanu Reeves
4 Flo Rida
5 James Dewar
6 Tesla
7 Leicestershire
8 *Double Your Money*
9 *Memento mori*
10 Slavonic
11 Rhododendron
12 Carl Jung
13 Human League
14 *Lethal Weapon*
15 Mollusc
16 The Bloomsbury Group
17 The Style Council
18 Oxford
19 Lord Fauntleroy
20 Alison Moyet

QUIZ 412 – Time

ANSWERS ON PAGE 414

Easy

1 What is the name of the clock tower of the Houses of Parliament?

2 Is Uruguay ahead of or behind Greenwich Mean Time?

3 What luxury watchmaker company was founded in London in 1905?

4 Which book by George Orwell opens with a clock tolling 13 times...?

5 ...and in which children's book by Philippa Pearce does the clock strike 13 times?

6 Which English sports ground has a weather vane in the shape of Father Time?

7 In Doctor Who, what do the initials TARDIS stand for?

8 In Sir Terry Pratchett's *Discworld* novels, which character's home has a life-timer room?

9 Who played the character of Bill Nighy's son in the 2013 film *About Time*?

10 Which 2003 novel features the characters of Henry DeTamble and Clare Abshire?

11 Who had a 1986 hit with *My Favourite Waste of Time*?

Medium

12 At which British standards establishment was the first atomic clock built?

13 In which year did the Beautiful South top the charts with *A Little Time*?

14 What is the name of the underground-dwelling creatures in the 1895 novel *The Time Machine*?

15 Who wrote the 1986 book *The Blind Watchmaker*?

16 In which European capital city is there a giant sandglass known as the Timewheel?

17 Which singer starred in the 2011 film sci-fi film *In Time*?

18 Which country has three time zones, eight to ten hours ahead of GMT?

19 Before widespread adoption of alarm clocks, what profession would be responsible for waking people up in the morning?

Hard

20 In which cathedral is the large bell called "Great Tom"?

Answers to QUIZ 410 – European History

1 First cousin
2 Crete
3 Castile
4 Saxony
5 Sir Francis Drake
6 Ephesus
7 Albania
8 Neanderthal
9 Córdoba
10 Filton (near Bristol)
11 Naples
12 Anjou
13 Dubrovnik
14 Sparta
15 Interpol
16 Genoa
17 Edward III
18 Rudolf
19 Lorraine
20 Turin

QUIZ 413 – Pot Luck

ANSWERS ON PAGE 415

1 What does an ungulate animal have?

2 Which US company collapsed in a 2001 scandal?

3 Which singer/songwriter first found fame by writing *I'm a Believer* for the Monkees?

4 Who wrote the novel *A Town Like Alice* (1950)?

5 "'O where are you going?' said reader to rider" was written by which poet?

6 Which actor starred in the 2008 film *The Wrestler*?

7 In the Old Testament, who was the third son of Adam and Eve?

8 Which town is situated on County Westmeath's border with Roscommon?

9 What travels at approximately 186,000 miles per second?

10 In the game of Scrabble®, what is the points bonus for putting down all seven letters at once?

11 Which bird was considered sacred by the Incas?

12 Which central European country borders Hungary, Ukraine and Poland?

13 In the 2009 film *Avatar*, what was the name of the planet?

14 What tree of genus *Adansonia* is also known as the monkey-bread tree?

15 In which ocean is Christmas Island, now called Kiribati?

16 *Video Games* was a 2011 single for which singer?

17 Who played Captain Mainwaring in the 2016 film version of *Dad's Army*?

18 In the 1966 World Cup Final, who scored for England other than Geoff Hurst?

19 In relation to birds, what is a "lek"?

20 North Sea Gas was first produced in which year?

Easy

Medium

Hard

Answers to QUIZ 411 – Pot Luck

1 *American Gigolo*
2 Busted
3 The Black Sea
4 Cumbria
5 *Allium* (garlic)
6 Germany
7 Quito
8 Dick Van Dyke
9 Michael Frayn
10 Shakespear's Sister
11 Golf
12 Ronald Reuel
13 Five
14 Martin Sheen
15 Christian Bale
16 Simple Minds
17 Kerry
18 Mexico (1970 and 1986)
19 Macaroni
20 McFly

QUIZ 414 – Geography

ANSWERS ON PAGE 416

Easy

1 Gaborone is the capital of which African country?

2 Which landlocked country borders Georgia?

3 In which American state is Harvard University located?

4 In which Irish county is the site of Newgrange?

5 Which river flows through Berlin?

6 The island state of Nauru lies in which ocean?

7 Which is the northernmost of the Central American republics?

8 The River Tay flows into which sea?

9 Which is Japan's second-largest city?

10 In which region of France is Strasbourg located?

Medium

11 The "Medway Towns" are Gillingham, Rochester, Strood, Rainham and which other town?

12 Which river forms the border between Germany and Poland?

13 The Vale of Eden is in which county?

14 In which city is the United Nations Headquarters building located?

15 What is the capital of the Falkland Islands?

16 The ruins of ancient Persepolis are found in which country?

17 What is the unit of currency in Thailand?

18 What name is shared by a Brittany seaport and a Belarus city near the Polish border?

19 In which US state is Cincinnati?

20 Karachi is in which province of Pakistan?

Hard

Answers to QUIZ 412 – Time

1 Elizabeth Tower (Big Ben is the bell)
2 Behind
3 Rolex
4 *Nineteen Eighty-Four*
5 *Tom's Midnight Garden*
6 Lord's cricket ground
7 Time and Relative Dimension in Space
8 Death
9 Domhnall Gleeson
10 *The Time Traveler's Wife*
11 Owen Paul
12 National Physical Laboratory
13 1990
14 Morlocks
15 Richard Dawkins
16 Budapest
17 Justin Timberlake
18 Australia
19 Knocker-up
20 Lincoln Cathedral

QUIZ 415 – Pot Luck

ANSWERS ON PAGE 417

1 With which instrument was Bert Weedon associated?

2 Heraklion is the capital of which Greek island?

3 What is the more common word for the process of parturition?

4 Pendennis Castle is situated in which Cornish town?

5 What type of animal is a Dandie Dinmont?

6 Who had a hit in 1990 with *Tears on My Pillow*?

7 How is chicken shawarma cooked?

8 Who was president of the USA during the earlier years of the Great Depression, 1929-33?

9 What was the title of the USA for Africa 1985 charity record?

10 What name is given to the part of a stem at which a leaf grows?

11 In which year was the Kingdom of Great Britain formed by the Act of Union?

12 Along with potatoes, which vegetable is a key ingredient of aloo gobi?

13 Which independence leader gave his name to a landlocked South American country?

14 Baku is the capital city of which country on the Caspian Sea?

15 Which traditional board game is set in Tudor Mansions?

16 In which county is Bishop Auckland?

17 Which bird can fly backwards?

18 The Moselle joins which other river at Koblenz?

19 What was the title applied to Siddhartha Gautama, founder of a major Eastern religion?

20 Which acid is the most predominant in the stomach?

Answers to QUIZ 413 – Pot Luck

1 Hooves
2 Enron
3 Neil Diamond
4 Nevil Shute
5 WH Auden
6 Mickey Rourke
7 Seth
8 Athlone
9 Light
10 50
11 The condor
12 Slovakia
13 Pandora
14 Baobab
15 Pacific
16 Lana Del Rey
17 Toby Jones
18 Martin Peters
19 A display area
20 1967

QUIZ 416 – Film

ANSWERS ON PAGE 418

1 Who played Brian Hope in the 1990 film *Nuns on the Run*?
2 In which decade of the 20th century was Warren Beatty born?
3 How were Susan Sarandon and Goldie Hawn known in the title of a 2002 film?
4 What is the name of Andy Serkis' character in the *Planet of the Apes* series of films?
5 In which 1986 film do Tom Hanks and Shelley Long buy an ageing mansion?
6 Which Elvis Presley film features the name of a Mexican resort in its title?
7 In which 1994 film did Arnold Schwarzenegger co-star with Jamie Lee Curtis?
8 Which cult film of 1973 is set on the Scottish island of Summerisle?
9 What was the title of the first *Carry On* film, released in 1958?
10 Sigourney Weaver portrayed which real-life scientist in the 1988 film *Gorillas in the Mist*?
11 Which actress starred alongside Sir Sean Connery in the 1999 thriller *Entrapment*?
12 Which US film company has the motto *Ars gratia artis*?
13 In which 1959 film does Peter Sellers play a shop steward and Ian Carmichael a naïve worker?
14 Who was the star of the 1971 film *Fiddler on the Roof*?
15 The 2009 film *In the Loop* was based on which TV series?
16 What was the name of Scaramanga's servant in *The Man with the Golden Gun* (1974)?
17 Which actress played Melissa Lewis in the 2015 film *The Martian*?
18 Who directed the 1976 film *Bugsy Malone*?
19 The film *The Philadelphia Story* was remade as which musical?
20 Which actor starred in the 2003 film *Master and Commander*?

Answers to QUIZ 414 – Geography

1 Botswana
2 Armenia
3 Massachusetts
4 Meath
5 Spree
6 Pacific
7 Belize
8 The North Sea
9 Yokohama
10 Alsace
11 Chatham
12 Oder
13 Cumbria
14 New York
15 Port Stanley
16 Iran
17 Baht
18 Brest
19 Ohio
20 Sindh

QUIZ 417 – Pot Luck

ANSWERS ON PAGE 419

1 Which part of the calyx of a flower encloses the petals?
2 Which Spanish region includes Seville and Granada?
3 *In The Summertime* was a 1970 hit for which group?
4 Which actor starred in the 2004 remake of *The Manchurian Candidate*?
5 What name is given to a Scottish barrister?
6 *Ride a White Swan* was a 1970 hit for which group?
7 What did the chemist John Dalton define as the smallest particle of substance?
8 Of which US state is Cheyenne the capital?
9 Oberon is a moon of which planet in the solar system?
10 Who was Hero's lover, in Greek mythology?
11 Who was the first English Christian martyr?
12 Eric Hill created which cartoon dog?
13 On a fish, where is the dorsal fin?
14 What name is given to a plant growth induced by another organism, often a wasp?
15 Which are the most ancient of the sacred Hindu writings?
16 Dr Zamenhof devised which international language in 1887?
17 Which grade of army officer is next above a colonel?
18 Which naval base and dockyard lies on the north bank of the Firth of Forth?
19 What is the capital of Venezuela?
20 Sir Rod Stewart had a successful trial with which London football club?

Answers to QUIZ 415 – Pot Luck

1 Guitar
2 Crete
3 Childbirth
4 Falmouth
5 Dog (terrier)
6 Kylie Minogue
7 Grilled on a spit
8 Herbert Hoover
9 *We Are the World*
10 Node
11 1707
12 Cauliflower
13 Simón Bolivar
14 Azerbaijan
15 Cluedo®
16 County Durham
17 Hummingbird
18 Rhine
19 Buddha
20 Hydrochloric

ANSWERS ON PAGE 420

Easy

1 What is the title of the novel by HG Wells on which *Half a Sixpence* is based?

2 "The mirror crack'd from side to side" is a line from which Tennyson poem?

3 Who wrote *The Blind Assassin* (2000)?

4 Which George Eliot novel features Dorothea Brooke?

5 SJ Watson wrote which novel that was filmed in 2014 starring Nicole Kidman and Colin Firth?

6 Which war was the subject of the *Iliad*?

7 *Open the Cage, Murphy!* is a memoir by which TV presenter?

8 What was the first name of writer AA Milne?

9 According to Wordsworth, who "dwelt among the untrodden ways"?

10 In which decade was the Guinness Book of Records first published?

Medium

11 What term is given to poetry that has lines that do not rhyme?

12 Bathsheba Everdene appears in which classic novel?

13 What is didactic literature intended to do?

14 What was the name of the Brontë sisters' brother?

15 *Tarka the Otter* was set on which two Devon rivers?

16 Who wrote the poem *The Wreck of the Hesperus* (1842)?

17 Which book by Rudyard Kipling is the story of an orphaned son of a soldier stationed in India?

18 Who wrote the 1930 Sam Spade novel *The Maltese Falcon*?

19 Charles Lamb adopted what pen-name?

20 Who wrote *The Gulag Archipelago*?

Hard

Answers to QUIZ 416 – Film

1 Eric Idle
2 1930s (1937)
3 *The Banger Sisters*
4 Caesar
5 *The Money Pit*
6 *Fun in Acapulco*
7 *True Lies*
8 *The Wicker Man*
9 *Carry On Sergeant*
10 Dian Fossey
11 Catherine Zeta-Jones
12 MGM
13 *I'm All Right Jack*
14 Topol
15 *The Thick of It*
16 Nick Nack
17 Jessica Chastain
18 Alan Parker
19 *High Society*
20 Russell Crowe

QUIZ 419 – Pot Luck

ANSWERS ON PAGE 421

1 Which British swimmer won the gold medal for the 100m breaststroke at the 1988 Olympics?

2 In Egyptian mythology, who was the mother of Horus?

3 What is the name of Leonato's daughter in Shakespeare's *Much Ado about Nothing*?

4 Which southern Asian country has been a republic since 2008?

5 The 1993 film *Free Willy* featured which type of creature?

6 Which singer had a hit in 2003 with *The Voice Within*?

7 Cedar Rapids is in which US state?

8 Which London Underground line stops at Morden?

9 What is a native of the country once called Mesopotamia called?

10 The 1990s TV series *Cadfael* starred which actor in the title role?

11 Who is the patron saint of the Czechia (Czech Republic)?

12 Which actress starred as Chuck Charles in the TV series *Pushing Daisies*?

13 What style of music is associated with John Lee Hooker and Muddy Waters?

14 In which month does the London to Brighton veteran and vintage car rally take place?

15 Which French dramatist penned *Tartuffe* (1664)?

16 By which name is the plant belladonna more widely known?

17 Who wrote the *No. 1 Ladies Detective Agency* series?

18 What is the amount by which the cost of imports exceeds the value of imports called?

19 *In Three Men in a Boat (To Say Nothing of the Dog)* (1889), what is the name of the dog?

20 Which actor starred in the 1967 film *Cool Hand Luke*?

Answers to QUIZ 417 – Pot Luck

1 Sepal
2 Andalusia
3 Mungo Jerry
4 Denzel Washington
5 Advocate
6 T Rex
7 The atom
8 Wyoming
9 Uranus
10 Leander
11 St Alban
12 Spot
13 On its back
14 Gall
15 The *Veda* writings
16 Esperanto
17 Brigadier
18 Rosyth
19 Caracas
20 Brentford FC

QUIZ 420 – Food and Drink

ANSWERS ON PAGE 422

1 Which green liqueur was once made from wormwood?
2 Lumache pasta is named after which creature?
3 What is the prime cut of beef taken from the upper middle of the body called?
4 Cookery writer Mrs Beeton had what first name?
5 Which gas mark setting is the equivalent of 200 degrees Celsius?
6 Which type of restaurant takes its name from the French word for "brewery"?
7 What is the main ingredient in laver bread?
8 Duxelles is a paste made from shallots, herbs and which other foodstuff?
9 What type of food is produced from the sumac shrub?
10 The Irish dish colcannon is made from potatoes and which other vegetable?
11 Which region of Guyana gives its name to a variety of sugar?
12 A Manhattan cocktail has which spirit as its base?
13 Which small fruit has the Latin name *Prunus armeniaca*?
14 What is the scale used to measure the heat of chillies?
15 Sage Derby is what type of food?
16 Which girl's name is given to a steak dish seasoned with Worcestershire sauce?
17 What colour is a persimmon?
18 What type of fruit is an ugli fruit?
19 Traditional balsamic vinegar is made from which fruit?
20 What are you eating if you have a "Finnan Haddie"?

Answers to QUIZ 418 – Literature

1 *Kipps*
2 *The Lady of Shalott*
3 Margaret Atwood
4 *Middlemarch*
5 *Before I Go to Sleep*
6 Trojan War
7 Paul O'Grady
8 Alan
9 Lucy
10 1950s (1955)
11 Blank verse
12 *Far from the Madding Crowd* (Thomas Hardy)
13 Instruct
14 Branwell
15 Taw and Torridge
16 Henry Wadsworth Longfellow
17 *Kim*
18 Dashiel Hammett
19 Elia
20 Aleksandr Solzhenitsyn

QUIZ 421 – Pot Luck

ANSWERS ON PAGE 423

1 Which river rises in the Pennines and flows into the North Sea between Hartlepool and Redcar?

2 W is the symbol for which chemical element?

3 Father and son doctors, Toby and Tom Latimer featured in which sitcom?

4 What type of creature is an agouti?

5 Which horse colouring consists of a brown body with black legs, mane and tail?

6 In the 2007 film *Music and Lyrics*, which actress co-starred with Hugh Grant?

7 Which dramatist wrote the play *Peer Gynt*?

8 Which actor played Dr Wilbur Larch in the film *The Cider House Rules*?

9 In which year was the first Wimpy® restaurant opened?

10 Which athlete was known as "the Flying Finn"?

11 The 1999 film *The Hurricane* starred which actor?

12 What was the title of Michael Jackson's 1995 Christmas hit?

13 Which body part is swollen if a person is suffering from myelitis?

14 *Mouldy Old Dough* was a 1972 hit for which band?

15 The ancient Chinese used clove oil as a remedy for which complaint?

16 Who wrote the play *Lady Windermere's Fan* (1892)?

17 Which queen succeeded William III?

18 Car manufacturer Dacia is based in which country?

19 What is the province of Greece in which Athens is located?

20 In which country is the port of Odessa?

Answers to QUIZ 419 – Pot Luck

1 Adrian Moorhouse
2 Isis
3 Hero
4 Nepal
5 Killer whale (orca)
6 Christina Aguilera
7 Iowa
8 Northern
9 Iraqi
10 Sir Derek Jacobi
11 Wenceslas
12 Anna Friel
13 Blues
14 November
15 Molière
16 Deadly nightshade
17 Alexander McCall Smith
18 Trade gap
19 Montmorency
20 Paul Newman

QUIZ 422 – Pop Music

ANSWERS ON PAGE 424

Easy

1 James Newell Osterberg Jr is known by which stage name?

2 Who were the Four Tops telling to *Walk Away* in their 1967 hit?

3 Which group had a 1974 hit with *The Cat Crept In*?

4 Who won the Eurovision Song Contest in 1980 and 1987, and wrote the winning song in 1992?

5 *I Owe You Nothing* is the autobiography of which singer?

6 Under what name does singer Derek Dick perform?

7 The Average White Band hit *Let's Go Round Again* was also a hit for which singer in 1997?

8 *Sorry Not Sorry* was a 2017 single by which singer?

9 Who has released albums entitled *Yours Truly* and *My Everything*?

10 Which group had a hit in 1981 with *The Land of Make Believe*?

Medium

11 By what name is musician and actor Ben Drew better known?

12 Who were *Uptown Top Ranking* in 1978?

13 In which decade of the 20th century was Sir Mick Jagger born?

14 Which former *Neighbours* actress had hits with *Born to Try* and *Lost Without You*?

15 *The Long and Winding Road* appears on which Beatles album?

16 Which group had the UK Christmas no.1 in 1996, 1997 and 1998?

17 What was Blur's first Top Ten hit?

18 Which singer/songwriter had a 2005 hit with *The One I Love*?

19 How is singer Rory Charles Graham better known?

20 Who sang *Drop the Pilot* in 1983?

Hard

Answers to QUIZ 420 – Food and Drink

1 Absinthe
2 Snail
3 Sirloin
4 Isabella
5 Gas Mark 6
6 Brasserie
7 Seaweed
8 Mushrooms
9 Spice
10 Cabbage
11 Demerara
12 Whisky
13 Apricot
14 Scoville scale
15 Cheese
16 Diane
17 Orange (fruit)
18 Citrus
19 Grapes
20 Smoked haddock

QUIZ 423 – Pot Luck

ANSWERS ON PAGE 425

1 Which 2000 thriller starred Harrison Ford and Michelle Pfeiffer?
2 In which ocean is the Sargasso Sea?
3 Which French composer wrote the *Gymnopédies*?
4 What was an old measure of weight equal to a quarter of a bushel?
5 The Jerusalem artichoke is a member of which family of plants?
6 A hat called a toque would be worn by which professional?
7 Which Rodgers and Hammerstein musical was filmed in 1955?
8 Which 1999 remake of a Steve McQueen film featured Pierce Brosnan in the title role?
9 In which US state is Pittsburgh?
10 Who played speech therapist Lionel Logue in the 2010 film *The King's Speech*?
11 If something is described as "vitreous", from what is it made?
12 Who was Dr Samuel Johnson's biographer?
13 Who captained the England rugby team when they won the Grand Slam in 1980?
14 Which actor starred as William of Baskerville in the 1986 film *The Name of the Rose*?
15 Which group had a UK hit with *Leader of the Pack* in 1965, 1972 and 1976?
16 Which classic novel is narrated by Nick Carraway?
17 In which TV series did Elisabeth Moss play the character of Peggy Olson?
18 In human anatomy, what is the lowest part of the trunk?
19 Polyphemus was a member of which mythical one-eyed race of giants?
20 What is the title of the best-seller about punctuation written by Lynne Truss?

Answers to QUIZ 421 – Pot Luck

1 Tees
2 Tungsten
3 *Don't Wait Up*
4 Rodent
5 Bay
6 Drew Barrymore
7 Henrik Ibsen
8 Sir Michael Caine
9 1954
10 Paavo Nurmi
11 Denzel Washington
12 *Earth Song*
13 The spinal cord
14 Lieutenant Pigeon
15 Toothache
16 Oscar Wilde
17 Anne
18 Romania
19 Attica
20 Ukraine

QUIZ 424 – Fictional Doctors

ANSWERS ON PAGE 426

Easy

1 What is the name of Indiana Jones' father?

2 Which fictional doctor is flatmates with Dr Leonard Hofstadter in the American sitcom *The Big Bang Theory*?

3 In the *Jurassic Park* novel and films, what is the name of the geneticist responsible for the cloning of the dinosaurs?

4 Who played Dr Curt Connors in the 2012 film *The Amazing Spider-Man*?

5 Which infamous doctor does Edward Prendick meet on an island in a 1896 HG Wells sci-fi novel?

6 In which US TV series did the characters Dr Cox and Dr Kelso work at the same hospital?

7 What is the name of Lucy Liu's character in the American TV series *Elementary*?

8 What infamous fictional doctor is first introduced in the 1981 novel *Red Dragon*?

9 GPs Daniel Granger and Heston Carter appear in which TV series?

Medium

10 Who played Dr Joel Fleischman in the TV series *Northern Exposure*?

11 Which doctor practised medicine in the town of Tannochbrae?

12 In which Shakespearean play does a doctor state "What is it she does now? Look how she rubs her hands"?

13 What pen name did crime writer Arthur Sarsfield Ward use for his novels featuring Dr Fu Manchu?

14 Dr Hugo Z Hackenbush appears in which 1937 film?

15 In which TV series did Dr Sarah Tancredi appear?

16 Clare Holman played which forensic pathologist in *Inspector Morse* and *Lewis*?

17 In which remade sci-fi series was Dr Gaius Baltar a central character?

Hard

18 Who played psychiatrist Dr Ben Sobel in the 1999 film *Analyze This*?

19 Dr Henry Higgins first appeared in which 1913 play?

20 In which series of sci-fi films did the character of Dr Emmett Brown feature?

Answers to QUIZ 422 – Pop Music

1 Iggy Pop
2 Renée
3 Mud
4 Johnny Logan
5 Luke Goss (of Bros)
6 Fish
7 Louise
8 Demi Lovato
9 Ariana Grande
10 Bucks Fizz
11 Plan B
12 Althea & Donna
13 1940s (1943)
14 Delta Goodrem
15 *Let It Be*
16 The Spice Girls
17 *There's No Other Way*
18 David Gray
19 Rag'n'Bone Man
20 Joan Armatrading

QUIZ 425 – Pot Luck

ANSWERS ON PAGE 427

1 Which fictional soap opera was linked to the TV series *Moving Wallpaper*?
2 What is the Chinese geometrical puzzle of seven differently shaped pieces called?
3 Rachael Stirling is the daughter of which actress?
4 What was the title of Stephen King's first novel?
5 Which Australian train service was previously known as "The Afghan Express"?
6 On which island is Mauna Loa?
7 Who had a hit in 2006 with *Jump in My Car*?
8 Which Hampshire town lies between Portsmouth and Chichester?
9 What prefix indicates 10^9?
10 Which South American country borders Peru and Colombia?
11 What is the chemical formula for alcohol?
12 In the TV series, who is the major adversary of the *Terrahawks*?
13 What was the title of the 1975 hit single by Telly Savalas?
14 Who won the Best Actor Oscar for the 2002 film *The Pianist*?
15 What is the largest Bronze Age archaeological site on the island of Crete?
16 A "charm" is a collective noun for which birds?
17 Who might be interested in a "Cape triangular"?
18 Of which American state is Madison the capital?
19 In which city did the TV detective Piet Van der Valk operate?
20 The island of Komodo, famous for its "dragons", is in which country?

Easy Medium Hard

Answers to QUIZ 423 – Pot Luck

1 *What Lies Beneath*
2 The North Atlantic
3 Erik Satie
4 Peck
5 Sunflower
6 Chef
7 *Oklahoma!*
8 *The Thomas Crown Affair*
9 Pennsylvania
10 Geoffrey Rush
11 Glass
12 James Boswell
13 Bill Beaumont
14 Sir Sean Connery
15 Shangri-Las
16 *The Great Gatsby*
17 *Mad Men*
18 The pelvis
19 Cyclopes
20 *Eats, Shoots and Leaves*

QUIZ 426 – Sport

ANSWERS ON PAGE 428

Easy

1 The omnium is an event in which sport?
2 Which system of Japanese fighting has a name meaning "the way of gentleness"?
3 How many players are there in a baseball team?
4 Which snooker player won the World Grand Prix title in February 2017?
5 Figure skater Katarina Witt represented which country at the 1984 Winter Olympics?
6 The 2014 Ryder Cup took place on which course?
7 Which sport is played on the largest pitch?
8 In which year did Martina Navratilova win her last singles title at Wimbledon?
9 The wood of which tree is used to make bows for archery?
10 How many inches from the ground are the bails of a wicket?

Medium

11 Which sport is played by the Florida Panthers?
12 In which country is the Interlagos motor racing circuit?
13 Turf Moor is the home ground of which football team?
14 Which distance was first run by Pheidippides in 490 BC?
15 What is the name of Cambridge University's reserve rowing crew?
16 In which field event did Jesse Owens set a record that stood from 1935 to 1960?
17 The racecourse known as the Roodee is in which English city?
18 Who won the Formula 1 World Championship in 1962 and 1968?
19 What was the first name of 1950s Czechia (Czech Republic) runner Zátopek?
20 The 1952 summer Olympic Games were held in which city?

Hard

Answers to QUIZ 424 – Fictional Doctors

1 Professor Henry Jones
2 Dr Sheldon Cooper
3 Dr Henry Wu
4 Rhys Ifan
5 Dr Moreau
6 *Scrubs*
7 Dr Joan Watson
8 Dr Hannibal Lecter
9 *Doctors*
10 Rob Morrow
11 Dr Finlay
12 *Macbeth*
13 Sax Rohmer
14 *A Day at the Races*
15 *Prison Break*
16 Dr Laura Hobson
17 *Battlestar Galactica*
18 Billy Crystal
19 *Pygmalion*
20 *Back to the Future*

QUIZ 427 – Pot Luck

ANSWERS ON PAGE 429

1 The VW Beetle was designed by which sports-car manufacturer?
2 Which place of pilgrimage is in County Mayo, Ireland?
3 What was Elvis Presley's second UK no.1?
4 In Greek myth, what name is given to the blood of the gods?
5 What device is used for measuring wind speed?
6 Which artist was associated with the Catalonian town of Figueres?
7 Who wrote a *Christmas Oratorio* in 1734?
8 In the TV series *Grey's Anatomy*, who plays the title character?
9 Where in the body are the islets of Langerhans located?
10 Which bird is known as a "laughing jackass"?
11 In the title of a Dame Agatha Christie novel, what time is the train from Paddington?
12 Who wrote the novel *The Guns of Navarone*?
13 On which continent is the Tukano language spoken?
14 Which Hungarian virtuoso composer and pianist lived from 1811 to 1886?
15 What was the title of Diana Ross's first UK no.1 single?
16 Which Cumbrian river flows through Appleby and Carlisle?
17 Which is the second largest of the Shetland Islands?
18 In Shakespeare's *Twelfth Night*, what is the name of the Duke of Illyria?
19 Which English king first enclosed the New Forest as a hunting area?
20 Who wrote *The Commitments*, part of *The Barrytown Trilogy*?

Easy

Medium

Hard

Answers to QUIZ 425 – Pot Luck

1 *Echo Beach*
2 Tangram
3 Dame Diana Rigg
4 *Carrie*
5 The Ghan
6 Hawaii
7 David Hasselhoff
8 Havant
9 Giga
10 Ecuador
11 C_2H_5O
12 Zelda
13 *If*
14 Adrien Brody
15 Knossos
16 Goldfinches
17 A stamp collector
18 Wisconsin
19 Amsterdam
20 Indonesia

QUIZ 428 – Hands and Feet

ANSWERS ON PAGE 430

Easy

1 Who was the Roman goddess of handicrafts and equivalent of the Greek Athena?
2 Which *Cold Feet* actress played DI Martha Bellamy in the TV series *Suspects*?
3 How many points are there in a perfect hand at cribbage?
4 What does the Statue of Liberty wear on her feet?
5 Which Beatle played guitar left-handed?
6 How many cubic feet are there in a cubic yard?
7 At which racecourse is the Lincoln Handicap held?
8 How many toes does a camel have on each foot?
9 In which century was George Frederick Handel born?
10 What is the legendary creature Bigfoot also called in North America?
11 What is the name for someone who studies handwriting?

Medium

12 In *One Foot in the Grave*, what was the first name of Angus Deayton's character?
13 Sir Elton John had a double-A side no.1 with *Healing Hands* and which other song?
14 In which century was Harold Harefoot king of England?
15 Which king does Ned Stark become Hand of the King to in *Game of Thrones*?
16 Where in a house would you find the footings?
17 What was the nickname of the handyman in the TV programme *Changing Rooms*?
18 "Come and meet those dancing feet" is a lyric from the title song to which musical?
19 In which sport is it forbidden for anyone to play left-handed?
20 Who co-starred with Humphrey Bogart in the 1954 film *The Barefoot Contessa*?

Hard

Answers to QUIZ 426 – Sport

1 Track cycling
2 Judo
3 Nine
4 Barry Hawkins
5 East Germany
6 Gleneagles
7 Polo (275m x 145m)
8 1990
9 Yew
10 28
11 Ice hockey
12 Brazil
13 Burnley
14 Marathon
15 Goldie
16 Long jump
17 Chester
18 Graham Hill
19 Emil
20 Helsinki

QUIZ 429 – Pot Luck

ANSWERS ON PAGE 431

1 Of what is hypnophobia a fear?

2 What is the name of the princess in the ballet *Swan Lake*?

3 Who wrote *The Fall of the House of Usher* (1839)?

4 What type of institution is run by Mrs Clonkers in Roald Dahl's *The BFG?*

5 Castlebar is the main town in which Irish county?

6 Who wrote the 1970 chart-topper *Woodstock*?

7 Which country forms the southern border of Tajikistan?

8 *Virginia Plain* was a 1972 hit for which group?

9 For which professional football team was chef Gordon Ramsay an apprentice?

10 What was the Rolling Stones' first UK no.1 single?

11 The freesia is a member of which family?

12 The musical *Sunshine on Leith* features the songs of which duo?

13 Ailsa Craig granite is used to make which sporting items?

14 Which fruit is the base for slivovitz?

15 Who won the Best Actress Oscar for the 2009 film *The Blind Side*?

16 How many points are awarded for a touchdown in American football?

17 Which group had a 1993 hit with *One Night in Heaven*?

18 What type of creature is a ruby tiger?

19 The sika deer is native to which continent?

20 From what is the Indonesian dish tempeh made?

Easy

Medium

Hard

Answers to QUIZ 427 – Pot Luck

1 Ferdinand Porsche
2 Knock
3 *Jailhouse Rock*
4 Ichor
5 Anemometer
6 Salvador Dali
7 JS Bach
8 Ellen Pompeo
9 The pancreas
10 Kookaburra
11 4:50
12 Alistair MacLean
13 South America
14 Franz Liszt
15 *I'm Still Waiting*
16 Eden
17 Yell
18 Orsino
19 William I (the Conqueror)
20 Roddy Doyle

QUIZ 430 – Ballet

ANSWERS ON PAGE 432

Easy

1 What was the former name of the English National Ballet?

2 What French word, from ballet terminology, is given to a triple-step dance step?

3 How was the English ballerina Margaret Hookham better known?

4 Which ballet includes the characters Lescaut and Des Grieux?

5 In which city is the Northern Ballet company based?

6 Sir Matthew Bourne's ballet *The Car Man* was inspired by which opera and ballet?

7 In which country was ballerina Marianela Núñez born?

8 Who composed the original music for the ballet *Giselle*?

9 Who played the title role in the 2010 film *The Black Swan*?

10 Which horse, winner of the Derby in 1970, was named after a dancer and choreographer?

Medium

11 In which decade did Rudolf Nureyev defect from the Soviet Union?

12 What is the term given to the ballet position of supporting the weight on the toes?

13 In *The Nutcracker*, what is the name of Clara's godfather?

14 Who was the principal choreographer of the Royal Ballet from 1977 to 1992?

15 Who painted *Dancing Class* (1871) and *Ballet Rehearsal* (1873)?

16 What is the title of the three-act ballet by George Balanchine that was inspired by gemstones?

17 In which city is the Ballet Rambert based?

18 Who starred in the 1948 film *The Red Shoes*?

19 What is the French term for a ballerina's knee-bend?

Hard

20 Which former ballet dancer appeared in the 2018 series of *Celebrity Big Brother*?

Answers to QUIZ 428 – Hands and Feet

1 Minerva
2 Fay Ripley
3 29
4 Sandals
5 Sir Paul McCartney
6 27
7 Doncaster
8 Two
9 17th century (1685)
10 Sasquatch
11 Graphologist
12 Patrick (Trench)
13 *Sacrifice*
14 11th century (1035-40)
15 Robert Baratheon
16 In the foundations
17 Handy Andy
18 *42nd Street*
19 Polo
20 Ava Gardner

QUIZ 431 – Pot Luck

ANSWERS ON PAGE 433

1 Which Egyptian god had the head of a jackal?

2 What was the name of Schumann's wife, a fellow pianist and composer?

3 Who was the hero of the 1960s puppet series *Stingray*?

4 *Ode on a Grecian Urn* (1819) was written by which English poet?

5 Which US group released the 1976 single *More Than a Feeling*?

6 Which Old Testament book precedes Job?

7 The name of which US city gave Scott McKenzie a 1967 UK no.1?

8 How are beetles of the family *Coccinellidae* better known?

9 Filbert and cobnut are alternative names for the fruit of which tree?

10 Which celebrity won the 2010 series of *Strictly Come Dancing*?

11 In April 2004, who became only the second person ever to score two triple centuries in Test cricket?

12 Which 1955 Dirk Bogarde comedy was based on a ship?

13 What was the middle name of Russian composer Tchaikovsky?

14 In the game of 8-ball pool, what is the colour of the last ball to be pocketed?

15 What is the cartel operated by oil-producing nations called?

16 Which flower gets its name from the Turkish word for "turban"?

17 Betsey Trotwood and Edward Murdstone feature in which Dickens novel?

18 Which author wrote the 1962 futuristic novel *A Clockwork Orange*?

19 Janus is a moon of which planet in the solar system?

20 What is the name for the left side of the tennis court for each player?

Answers to QUIZ 429 – Pot Luck

1 Sleep
2 Odette
3 Edgar Allan Poe
4 Orphanage
5 Mayo
6 Joni Mitchell
7 Afghanistan
8 Roxy Music
9 Glasgow Rangers
10 *It's All Over Now*
11 Iridaceae (Iris)
12 The Proclaimers
13 Curling stones
14 Plum
15 Sandra Bullock
16 Six
17 M People
18 A moth
19 Asia
20 Soya beans

QUIZ 432 – Cats

ANSWERS ON PAGE 434

Easy

1 Cat breeds called "Rex" are associated with which two English counties?

2 In which city was the first official cat show held in 1791?

3 What is notable about the Sphynx cat?

4 Jon Arbuckle owns which fictional cat?

5 Which cat became chief mouser to 10 Downing Street in 2011?

6 What colour was Custard the cat in the animated series *Roobarb and Custard*?

7 By what name is the tortoiseshell cat known in America?

8 The snow leopard is native to which continent?

9 Which author (b.1899) was noted for keeping cats at his Florida home?

10 From which country does the Ocicat originate?

11 Which breed is nicknamed "the swimming cat"?

Medium

12 Which cat, named after a US state, is one of the largest domesticated cats?

13 A cat's vibrissae are more commonly referred to by what name?

14 Which cat breed takes its name from characters in *The Wizard of Oz*?

15 Which artist and inventor (b.1452) said "The smallest feline is a masterpiece"?

16 In a series of children's books by Kathleen Hale, what was the name of the "marmalade cat"?

17 Which Monopoly™ token was replaced by a cat in 2013?

18 Bastet the cat goddess features in which mythology?

19 Who starred as the cat in the 2003 film *The Cat in the Hat*?

20 What is the gestation period of a domestic cat?

Hard

Answers to QUIZ 430 – Ballet

1 Festival Ballet
2 Chassé
3 Dame Margot Fonteyn
4 *Manon*
5 Leeds
6 *Carmen*
7 Argentina
8 Adolphe Adam
9 Mila Kunis
10 Nijinsky
11 1960s (1961)
12 *En pointe*
13 Drosselmeyer
14 Sir Kenneth MacMillan
15 Edgar Degas
16 *Jewels*
17 London
18 Moira Shearer
19 Plié
20 Wayne Sleep

QUIZ 433 – Pot Luck

ANSWERS ON PAGE 435

1 Which band's first UK hit was *Black Night*?

2 What is purslane?

3 Who starred as Jim Hacker in the TV series *Yes, Minister* and *Yes, Prime Minister*?

4 Oolong is what type of drink?

5 What is the county town of East Sussex?

6 In which US state is the Petrified Forest National Park?

7 Which dance shares its name with the state capital of West Virginia?

8 *Maid of Orleans* was a 1982 hit for which duo?

9 Which actor played Aragorn in *The Lord of the Rings* trilogy?

10 "Land of Enchantment" is the nickname for which US state?

11 Who had a 1981 no.1 with *Being with You*?

12 What term did WWII Allied pilots give to UFOs?

13 Banjul is the capital of which West African republic?

14 Who directed the 2016 film *Hacksaw Ridge*?

15 Which small Derbyshire settlement is known as "the plague village"?

16 Formerly known as Salisbury, what is the capital of Zimbabwe?

17 Who wrote "There shall be In that rich earth a richer dust concealed"?

18 Who topped the charts in 1975 with *January*?

19 The Mexican fir tree *Abies religiosa* is the preferred overwintering ground of which creature?

20 Rita Tushingham starred in which 1961 film set in Salford?

Answers to QUIZ 431 – Pot Luck

1 Anubis
2 Clara
3 Troy Tempest
4 Keats
5 Boston
6 Esther
7 San Francisco
8 Ladybirds
9 The hazel
10 Kara Tointon
11 Brian Lara
12 *Doctor at Sea*
13 Ilyich
14 Black
15 OPEC
16 Tulip
17 *David Copperfield*
18 Anthony Burgess
19 Saturn
20 The ad (advantage) court

QUIZ 434 – Science

ANSWERS ON PAGE 436

Easy

1 Who invented the mercury thermometer?

2 The process of evaporation of water from a plant is known by what name?

3 Which colourless, odourless, inert gas found in the Earth's atmosphere has the atomic number 18?

4 The European Space Agency has its headquarters in which capital city?

5 Where in the body would you find the malleus?

6 Which layer of the Earth lies between the crust and the core?

7 Which unit of power is equivalent to one joule per second?

8 Who was the founder of modern systematic botany and zoology?

9 In hexadecimal, what number does the letter D represent?

10 Which synthetic pain relief compound was introduced by Bayer in 1899?

Medium

11 What is the ring of light around the Sun called?

12 What is the science of the measuring of the intensity of earthquakes called?

13 In the human body, what system includes all the glands and the hormones they produce?

14 What name is given to the clockwork model of the solar system devised in the early 18th century?

15 Amoxicillin is a type of what medicine?

16 Which layer of the Earth's atmosphere lies between 10km and 50km above the planet?

17 Iron pyrites is known by what common name?

18 Which essential nutrient is also known as retinol?

Hard

19 In which year was the first manned space flight?

20 Which is the lowest taxonomic classification?

Answers to QUIZ 432 – Cats

1 Devon and Cornwall
2 London
3 It has no hair
4 Garfield
5 Larry
6 Pink
7 Calico cat
8 Asia
9 Ernest Hemingway
10 USA
11 Turkish Van
12 Maine Coon
13 Whiskers
14 Munchkin
15 Leonardo da Vinci
16 Orlando
17 An iron
18 Egyptian
19 Mike Myers
20 $8^1/_2$ to $9^1/_2$ weeks

QUIZ 435 – Pot Luck

ANSWERS ON PAGE 437

1 Who recorded the 2008 album *I Am...Sasha Fierce*?
2 The Arctic char is a member of which family of fish?
3 Who was the first chair of Radio 4's *The News Quiz* in 1977?
4 Which is the oldest Cambridge college?
5 Which mammals belong to the genus *ovis*?
6 From which country does the word "gymkhana" originate?
7 Which 1958 musical starring Leslie Caron and Maurice Chevalier won nine Oscars?
8 Who directed the 1990s films *Total Recall* and *Starship Troopers*?
9 Which shipping area lies south of Fastnet and Shannon?
10 Dudley Moore starred as an elf called Patch in which 1985 film?
11 Who wrote the plays *Loot* and *What the Butler Saw*?
12 Author Margaret Atwood was born in which country?
13 Which actress starred with Bing Crosby and Bob Hope in the *Road* films?
14 What was the name of Billy J Kramer's backing group?
15 Which country beat West Germany to win the 1982 FIFA World Cup?
16 In which English county is the feature known as the Hog's Back?
17 Who was the ancient Greek god of war?
18 How many vertebrae are there in a giraffe's neck?
19 Who co-starred with Dame Judi Dench in the film *Notes on a Scandal*?
20 Which river flows from the Cambrian Mountains and has tributaries called the Vernwy, Teme and Leadon?

Answers to QUIZ 433 – Pot Luck

1 Deep Purple
2 A plant (in marshy regions)
3 Paul Eddington
4 Tea
5 Lewes
6 Arizona
7 Charleston
8 Orchestral Manoeuvres in the Dark (OMD)
9 Viggo Mortensen
10 New Mexico
11 Smokey Robinson
12 Foo fighters
13 Gambia
14 Mel Gibson
15 Eyam
16 Harare
17 Rupert Brooke (*The Soldier*)
18 Pilot
19 Monarch butterfly
20 *A Taste Of Honey*

QUIZ 436 – Television

ANSWERS ON PAGE 438

Easy

1 What was the name of the character played by Jack Lord in the original series of *Hawaii Five-0*?

2 *A Moment Like This* was the first chart-topper for which winner of *The X Factor*?

3 Which 1960s animated character chewed oxygum?

4 Who narrated the 1999 TV series *Walking with Dinosaurs*?

5 In the series *Z Cars*, who played DCI Charlie Barlow?

6 Which of the Monkees featured in *Coronation Street* as the grandson of Ena Sharples?

7 Who created the series *In the Club* and *Fat Friends*?

8 In the series *Dad's Army*, what was Private Pike's first name?

9 Which TV presenter and traveller (b.1972) has presented the series *Tropic of Cancer* and *Tropic of Capricorn*?

Medium

10 What was the name of the character played by Bruce Willis in *Moonlighting*?

11 Which "superhero" lives at 29 Acacia Road?

12 In the TV series *Waking the Dead*, who played Grace Foley?

13 What was the name of Jim Caviezel's character in the series *Person of Interest*?

14 In which decade of the 20th century was Joanna Lumley born?

15 Who was the first presenter of *Celebrity Squares*?

16 In the TV series *Glee*, which actress played Sue Sylvester?

17 Which *Friends* star appeared in the mini-series *Band of Brothers*?

18 Who plays the title role in the *Strike* series?

19 Spotty Dog featured in which children's puppet show?

Hard

20 What is the make and model of the car used since 2017 in the *Top Gear* segment *Star in a Reasonably Fast Car*?

Answers to QUIZ 434 – Science

1 (Daniel) Fahrenheit
2 Transpiration
3 Argon
4 Paris
5 (Middle) ear
6 Mantle
7 Watt
8 Carl Linnaeus
9 13
10 Aspirin
11 Corona
12 Seismography
13 Endocrine system
14 Orrery
15 Antibiotic
16 Stratosphere
17 Fool's gold
18 Vitamin A (Vitamin A_1)
19 1961
20 Species

QUIZ 437 – Pot Luck

ANSWERS ON PAGE 439

1 Which politician was awarded the Nobel Peace Prize in 2009?

2 In the *UFO* TV series, which secret organisation defended the Earth?

3 Which of these ranks is the highest: brigadier in the army, group captain in the RAF or commander in the Navy?

4 What were the first two names of poet WH Auden?

5 The staff from Grace Brothers (*Are You Being Served?*) went on to run a country hotel in which series?

6 Which African country north-east of Botswana was formerly called Rhodesia?

7 Which organism is composed of both a fungi and an alga?

8 In the 1945 novel *Animal Farm*, what is the name of the industrious horse?

9 Which South African seaport and resort was previously called Port Natal?

10 How many pairs of walking legs has a sea spider?

11 Who was the lead vocalist with the 1970s group Dawn?

12 Weasels and stoats belong to which family of creatures?

13 Which one of these Republic of Ireland counties has a different name to its county town: Kildare, Kilkenny, Wexford or Wicklow?

14 A fashionable country club in a park in New York gave its name to which item of men's clothing?

15 Who co-starred with John Candy in the 1987 film *Planes, Trains & Automobiles*?

16 The wine-producing district of Médoc is in which region of France?

17 Who starred in the 1947 version of *The Secret Life of Walter Mitty*?

18 Which vegetable is known as the oyster plant?

19 What term is given to the young of a dragonfly after it hatches from the egg?

20 How was 1980s singer Chris Hamill better known?

Easy Medium Hard

Answers to QUIZ 435 – Pot Luck

1 Beyoncé
2 Salmon
3 Barry Norman
4 Peterhouse (founded in 1284)
5 Sheep
6 India
7 *Gigi*
8 Paul Verhoeven
9 Sole
10 *Santa Claus*
11 Joe Orton
12 Canada
13 Dorothy Lamour
14 The Dakotas
15 Italy
16 Surrey
17 Ares
18 Seven (same as humans!)
19 Cate Blanchett
20 The Severn

QUIZ 438 – History

ANSWERS ON PAGE 440

Easy

1 The 1645 English Civil War battle of Naseby took place in which county?
2 What was a commoner of ancient Rome called?
3 In which year was the Festival of Britain held?
4 Which Scandinavian capital was formerly known as Christiania?
5 Verulamium was the Roman name for which English city?
6 In which month did the Great Fire of London break out in 1666?
7 In 1911, which London Underground station was the first to have an escalator installed?
8 In which month did the Boston Tea Party take place?
9 Who was Edward VII's queen consort?
10 Which Greek city fought Athens in the Peloponnesian War?
11 Who became president of the Soviet Union in 1977?

Medium

12 In 1883, which New York bridge became the first example of a steel wire suspension bridge?
13 Which religion was founded by L Ron Hubbard?
14 In which year did the *Amoco Cadiz* run aground off Brittany?
15 In which country did the Boxer Rebellion take place?
16 Which African country was formerly known as Northern Rhodesia?
17 What was the name of the ship that rescued survivors from the *Titanic*?
18 In 1996, which Welsh county was replaced by Denbighshire and Flintshire and became a "preserved" county?
19 What nationality was Pope Adrian IV?

Hard

20 Which English king was also known as Henry Bolingbroke?

Answers to QUIZ 436 – Television

1 (Detective) Steve McGarrett
2 Leona Lewis
3 Marine Boy
4 Sir Kenneth Branagh
5 Stratford Johns
6 Davy Jones
7 Kay Mellor
8 Frank
9 Simon Reeve
10 David Addison
11 Bananaman
12 Sue Johnston
13 John Reese
14 1940s (1946)
15 Bob Monkhouse
16 Jane Lynch
17 David Schwimmer
18 Tom Burke
19 *The Woodentops*
20 Toyota GT86

QUIZ 439 – Pot Luck

ANSWERS ON PAGE 441

1 In which year did Bill Haley release *Rock Around the Clock*?

2 Which oil-bearing Moroccan tree is often climbed by goats?

3 Which radio show featured characters including Julian and Sandy and Rambling Syd Rumpo?

4 On which Eminem hit, released in December 2000, did Dido sing?

5 Which author wrote the novels *Flaubert's Parrot* and *The Noise of Time*?

6 What was the nickname of the racehorse Corbiere?

7 Which country lies north of Israel?

8 *I Will Never Let You Down* was a no.1 for which singer in 2014?

9 To which family of plants does kale belong?

10 What is the legal term for an obligation to corroborate allegations?

11 Who starred as Alex in the 1983 film *Flashdance*?

12 In which county is the town of Rothbury?

13 Which African country lies west of Botswana?

14 Which actor played Roux in the 2000 film *Chocolat*?

15 In which Lakeland village is William Wordsworth buried?

16 Which Shakespearean character is the son of Queen Gertrude?

17 In 2001, New Orleans International Airport was re-named after which musician?

18 What is the currency unit of Pakistan?

19 Which creature has species including Daubenton's and serotine?

20 In which country are the cities of Harbin, Wuhan and Shenyang?

Easy

Medium

Hard

Answers to QUIZ 437 – Pot Luck

1 Barack Obama
2 SHADO
3 Brigadier
4 Wystan Hugh
5 *Grace & Favour*
6 Zimbabwe
7 Lichen
8 Boxer
9 Durban
10 Eight
11 Tony Orlando
12 Mustelids
13 Kildare (Naas)
14 The Tuxedo
15 Steve Martin
16 Bordeaux
17 Danny Kaye
18 Salsify (the root)
19 Nymph
20 Limahl

QUIZ 440 – Technology

ANSWERS ON PAGE 442

Easy

1 What does DMA stand for in computing?

2 The letter M is on which row of a computer keyboard?

3 Which version of the Windows® operating system was released in 2007?

4 "Wi-fi" is a combination of which two words?

5 What type of online resource is DuckDuckGo?

6 What name was given to the forerunner of the emoji, used in texts and emails?

7 The logo of which on-line company consists of a globe of jigsaw pieces containing characters?

8 What is the full name of the company usually referred to as HP?

9 What term is given to code or software that anyone may modify?

10 In a computing context, what is LISP?

Medium

11 Which English mathematician is widely considered to be "the father of modern computer science"?

12 In which year was the first *Halo* video game released?

13 What does the "s" stand for in "laser"?

14 At which location did the English National Museum of Computing open in 2007?

15 In the name of the Intel Corporation, for which two words does "Intel" stand?

16 Which microblogging site was founded by David Karp in 2007?

17 What does USB stand for?

18 In which country is the Baidu technology company based?

19 Which computer, sold from 1998 to 2003, was available in a range of colours including blueberry, strawberry and grape?

20 What phrase applies to graphics programs which interact with people?

Hard

Answers to QUIZ 438 – History

1 Northamptonshire
2 Plebeian
3 1951
4 Oslo
5 St Albans
6 September
7 Earl's Court
8 December
9 Alexandra (of Denmark)
10 Sparta
11 Leonid Brezhnev
12 Brooklyn Bridge
13 Church of Scientology
14 1978
15 China
16 Zambia
17 *Carpathia*
18 Clwyd
19 English
20 Henry IV

QUIZ 441 – Pot Luck

ANSWERS ON PAGE 443

1 Who was Stefanie Powers' co-star in the TV series *Hart to Hart*?

2 Who was the first person to be buried at Poets' Corner in Westminster Abbey?

3 Brasenose College is part of which university?

4 What is a flock of partridges called?

5 Who was the first person to win European Footballer of the Year in three successive years?

6 In which novel by Charles Dickens was Dick Swiveller a clerk to Sampson Brass?

7 Which fruit can be found on the top of the trophy for the men's singles title at Wimbledon?

8 In the novel *Treasure Island*, what is the name of Long John Silver's parrot?

9 Which singer starred in the 1986 film *Shanghai Surprise*?

10 Who was the first ever Formula 1 World Champion?

11 Which Northern Ireland county is the only one not to adjoin Lough Neagh?

12 As well as scales, what does the blindfolded figure of Justice carry?

13 *In the Hall of the Mountain King* is a piece from which classical suite?

14 Who co-starred with Dawn French in the TV series *Roger & Val Have Just Got In*?

15 On which British island is Fingal's Cave?

16 Who discovered the planet Uranus?

17 What is a more common name for coquille Saint-Jacques?

18 Thornton Wilder's play *The Matchmaker* was the basis for which musical?

19 Which herb has the Latin name *Salvia officinalis*?

20 What is the cold winter wind that blows down from the mountains onto the eastern Adriatic coast?

Easy

Medium

Hard

Answers to QUIZ 439 – Pot Luck

1 1954
2 Argan
3 *Round the Horne*
4 *Stan*
5 Julian Barnes
6 Corky
7 Lebanon
8 Rita Ora
9 Brassica
10 Burden of proof
11 Jennifer Beals
12 Northumberland
13 Namibia
14 Johnny Depp
15 Grasmere
16 Hamlet
17 Louis Armstrong
18 Pakistani rupee
19 Bat
20 China

QUIZ 442 – Peter

ANSWERS ON PAGE 444

Easy

1 What was the name of St Petersburg from 1914 to 1924?

2 Who created the character of Lord Peter Wimsey?

3 Which constituency did Baron Peter Mandelson represent from 1992 to 2004?

4 By what other name are "St Peter's fish" known, so-called because of the black spot on each side, said to be St Peter's thumbprints?

5 In which 1959 film did Peter Sellers play three roles?

6 By what name is London's Collegiate Church of St Peter better known?

7 The song *Puff the Magic Dragon* was originally performed by which group?

8 Which 1964 film about a jewel robbery featured Peter Ustinov?

9 Which TV series initially starred Stephen Tompkinson as Father Peter Clifford?

10 Peter Sallis voiced which animated character up until 2010?

Medium

11 In which London borough is Petersham?

12 Peter Davison played which incarnation of the Doctor in *Doctor Who*?

13 Who directed the *Lord of the Rings* and the *Hobbit* trilogies?

14 Which football team did Peter Crouch play for from 1998 to 2000 and 2009 to 2011?

15 In which sci-fi series did Milo Ventimiglia play Peter Petrelli?

16 Peter Griffin is the main character in which animated series?

17 In which county is Peterborough?

18 Which duo topped the charts in 1973 with *Welcome Home*?

19 Which National Hunt jockey retired in 1993, setting a then all-time record for the most number of wins?

20 Who played Peter in the 1992 British comedy *Peter's Friends*?

Hard

Answers to QUIZ 440 – Technology

1 Direct memory access
2 Bottom
3 Windows Vista®
4 Wireless Fidelity
5 Search engine
6 Emoticon
7 Wikipedia®
8 Hewlett-Packard
9 Open source
10 Programming language
11 Alan Turing
12 2001
13 Stimulated
14 Bletchley Park
15 Intelligent Electronics
16 Tumblr
17 Universal Serial Bus
18 China
19 iMac G3
20 Virtual reality

QUIZ 443 – Pot Luck

1 Which American paediatrician wrote the 1946 *Common Sense Book of Baby and Child Care*?

2 What do the letters HDPE stand for when seen on a plastic item?

3 What is the smallest species of British deer?

4 In which country is the wine-growing Barossa Valley?

5 In which US state is Newark the largest city?

6 What term is given to the study of fish?

7 In which city did Shakespeare set *Measure for Measure*?

8 Which coastal footpath links Amroth to St Dogmaels?

9 What is the name of the oldest bridge in Britain?

10 King Power Stadium is the home ground for which football club?

11 The moons called Phobos and Deimos belong to which planet of our solar system?

12 Which group topped the charts in 1974 with *Billy Don't Be a Hero*?

13 Which country is landlocked between China, Vietnam, Cambodia, Thailand and Burma?

14 Brent Spiner played which android character in *Star Trek: The Next Generation*?

15 By what title was the fictional character Michael Henchard known?

16 What type of creature is a bullhead?

17 In Formula 1, what does KERS stand for?

18 Which vitamin is found in milk, wheatgerm and meat?

19 The 1930s documentary film *Night Mail* featured which form of transport?

20 Which 1990s comedy drama series featured a Canadian Mountie in the USA?

Answers to QUIZ 441 – Pot Luck

1 Robert Wagner
2 Geoffrey Chaucer
3 Oxford
4 A covey
5 Michel Platini (1983-85)
6 *The Old Curiosity Shop*
7 Pineapple
8 Captain Flint
9 Madonna
10 Nino Farina (1950)
11 Fermanagh
12 A sword
13 *Peer Gynt* (Suite no.1)
14 Alfred Molina
15 Staffa
16 William Herschel
17 Scallops
18 *Hello, Dolly!*
19 Sage
20 Bora

QUIZ 444 – Africa

ANSWERS ON PAGE 446

1 What covers 85% of Algeria?

2 The Victoria Falls is on the border of which two countries?

3 Under what pen name did Karen Blixen write *Out of Africa*?

4 Which is Africa's third longest river?

5 Timbuktu is in which country?

6 To what was the Republic of Upper Volta renamed in 1984?

7 The Serengeti National Park is in which country?

8 Which country used to be known as the Gold Coast?

9 Which Nigerian city became the country's capital in 1991?

10 Who won a Best Actor Oscar for his role in *The African Queen* (1951)?

11 Who became President of South Africa in February 2018?

12 Eritrea, Ethiopia and Somalia border which small republic?

13 What is the former name of the South African province prefixed with "KwaZulu" in 1994?

14 In which country are the ruins of ancient Carthage?

15 The Mediterranean and the Red Sea are linked by which waterway of 100 miles?

16 What does ANC stand for?

17 Which African desert is home to the bushmen?

18 Situated off the coast of south-east Africa, which island provided the title for a 2005 animated film?

19 What is the capital of Rwanda?

20 What was Ethiopia's former name?

Answers to QUIZ 442 – Peter

1 Petrograd
2 Dorothy L Sayers
3 Hartlepool
4 John Dory
5 *The Mouse That Roared*
6 Westminster Abbey
7 Peter, Paul and Mary
8 *Topkapi*
9 *Ballykissangel*
10 Wallace
11 Richmond upon Thames
12 Fifth
13 Peter Jackson
14 Tottenham Hotspur
15 *Heroes*
16 *Family Guy*
17 Cambridgeshire
18 Peters and Lee
19 Peter Scudamore
20 Stephen Fry

QUIZ 445 – Pot Luck

ANSWERS ON PAGE 447

1 What colour are the flowers of the mock orange, *Philadelphus*?
2 In mythology, who was the lover of the Carthaginian queen Dido?
3 Who co-starred with Ben Stiller in the 2004 film *Along Came Polly*?
4 Which river runs through Leicester?
5 Who was the French composer of the music for the ballet *Coppélia*?
6 Which country singer had a 1961 hit with *Crazy*?
7 The TV series *Detectorists* was set in which fictional village?
8 What do the initials FIA stand for in the context of motor sport?
9 What is the name of the Middle Eastern waters between Iran and Saudi Arabia?
10 Zeno of Citium founded which ancient Greek school of philosophy?
11 What is the name of Bob the Builder's cat?
12 What is Israel's chief seaport?
13 In the TV series *The Golden Girls*, who played Sophia?
14 What gives English mustard its colour?
15 Which sea separates Scandinavia from Germany?
16 Zennor Head is found in which English county?
17 Who wrote the 1759 novel *Tristram Shandy*?
18 Psittacosis is a disease found in which animals?
19 Which Spanish airport is indicated by the code ALC?
20 How is the gooney bird better known?

Answers to QUIZ 443 – Pot Luck

1 Dr Benjamin Spock
2 High Density Polyethylene
3 Muntjac
4 Australia
5 New Jersey
6 Ichthyology
7 Vienna
8 Pembrokeshire
9 Tarr Steps
10 Leicester City
11 Mars
12 Paper Lace
13 Laos
14 Data
15 The Mayor of Casterbridge
16 Fish
17 Kinetic Energy Recovery System
18 Niacin
19 Train
20 *Due South*

QUIZ 446 – Numbers

ANSWERS ON PAGE 448

Easy

1 What is the square root of 256?

2 How many pounds are there in a hundredweight?

3 Moving anticlockwise on a dartboard, which number is next to 9?

4 How many sides has a trapezium?

5 In geometry, how many minutes are there in a degree?

6 How many hours are there in April?

7 In imperial measurement, how many yards are in a chain?

8 How many old pence were there in £1?

9 A regular tetrahedron has how many faces?

10 What is the number on the black ball in a game of pool?

11 Which number is traditionally called as "The Brighton Line" in bingo?

Medium

12 Which number is *undici* in Italian?

13 An emerald anniversary celebrates how many years of marriage?

14 How many number slots, including 0, are there on a UK roulette wheel?

15 What is the next highest prime number above 53?

16 How many ounces are there in a stone?

17 If a billion is written in digits, how many zeros are there?

18 How many yards are there in a furlong?

19 In a quarter of an hour, how many seconds are there?

20 How many acres are there in a square mile?

Hard

Answers to QUIZ 444 – Africa

1 The Sahara Desert
2 Zambia and Zimbabwe
3 Isak Dinesen
4 Niger
5 Mali
6 Burkina Faso
7 Tanzania
8 Ghana
9 Abuja
10 Humphrey Bogart
11 Cyril Ramaphosa
12 Djibouti
13 Natal
14 Tunisia
15 Suez Canal
16 African National Congress
17 The Kalahari
18 Madagascar
19 Kigali
20 Abyssinia

QUIZ 447 – Pot Luck

ANSWERS ON PAGE 449

1 What is the SI unit of force?
2 In 2000, which former Spice Girl had a solo hit with *I Turn To You*?
3 What is the third book of the Old Testament?
4 Which canal was opened in 1869?
5 Who recorded the 1976 disco hit *More More More*?
6 Periwinkle is the name of both a flower and which type of creature?
7 What is the shipping forecast area north-west of Dogger?
8 How many eyes has a bee?
9 Who had a hit in 2001 with *Fallin'*?
10 Which poem begins "The curfew tolls the knell of parting day"?
11 What is the county town of Fermanagh?
12 Dr Samuel Johnson was famous for compiling what sort of book?
13 In which year did Premium Bonds first go on sale?
14 Which is the largest species of crocodile?
15 Which group of islands was formerly known as the Sandwich Islands?
16 What was the British Royal Family's house before it adopted the name Windsor in 1917?
17 Dr Cockroach, Insectosaurus and Missing Link all feature in which 2009 animated sci-fi film?
18 In which country is Cape Wrath?
19 Which actor starred in the 2012 film *Arbitrage*?
20 With which band was Roland Gift the lead vocalist in the mid-1980s?

Easy

Medium

Hard

Answers to QUIZ 445 – Pot Luck

1 White
2 Aeneas
3 Jennifer Aniston
4 Soar
5 Delibes
6 Patsy Cline
7 Danebury
8 Fédération Internationale de l'Automobile
9 The Gulf (also known as the Persian Gulf or the Arabian Gulf)
10 Stoicism
11 Pilchard
12 Haifa
13 Estelle Getty
14 Turmeric
15 Baltic
16 Cornwall
17 Laurence Sterne
18 Birds (communicable from parrots)
19 Alicante-Elche Airport
20 Albatross

QUIZ 448 – Lakes and Lochs

ANSWERS ON PAGE 450

1 What is the former name of Lake Malawi?
2 Which river lies between lakes Erie and Ontario?
3 Which series of films centres around Camp Crystal Lake?
4 In which Scottish region is Loch Fyne?
5 How long is Lake Windermere, in miles?
6 Drumnadrochit is on the shore of which loch?
7 Where were the Winter Olympics held in 1980?
8 What term is given to a small curved lake that lies on the flood plain of a river?
9 Which small lake is situated close to Grasmere in the Lake District?
10 What is unusual about the Scottish body of water on which Port of Menteith is situated?
11 The lake Königssee is in which region of Germany?
12 Lake Tahoe is on the border of which two US states?
13 The lochs of Coriusk and Snizort are on which Scottish island?
14 Which is Africa's longest lake?
15 What Spanish word for "beach" also denotes a dry lake bed in an arid region?
16 The *Salzkammergut* is known as the Lake District of which country?
17 Which French lakeside town is referred to as "the Venice of the Alps"?
18 In which country does the Euphrates river flow through Lake Assad?
19 Which is Africa's largest lake?
20 Montreux is located on which lake?

Answers to QUIZ 446 – Numbers

1 16
2 112
3 14
4 Four
5 60
6 720
7 22
8 240
9 Four (three sides and a triangular base)
10 Eight
11 59
12 11
13 55
14 37
15 59
16 224
17 Nine
18 220
19 900
20 640

QUIZ 449 – Pot Luck

ANSWERS ON PAGE 451

1 Who starred alongside Cher in the 1983 film *Silkwood*?

2 What sort of food is Neufchâtel?

3 Which horse breed was formerly reared to pull carriages?

4 Who was the front man with 1970s band Sweet?

5 In pre-decimal currency, which coin was worth the equivalent of 25p?

6 Which California town at the foot of Mount Wilson features in the title of a 1948 Humphrey Bogart film?

7 What is the capital city of Colombia?

8 Mary, Queen of Scots was born in which palace?

9 In which county are the Bedruthan Steps?

10 From which English city would you catch a ferry to Le Havre?

11 What was the name of the horse on which Lester Piggott first won the Derby?

12 Who composed *Finlandia* (1899)?

13 In Marvel's *Iron Man* films, what is the name of Tony Stark's personal AI system?

14 A person suffering from pruritus has an overwhelming urge to do what?

15 Singer Engelbert Humperdinck had what original name?

16 Which actor starred in the 2008 film *The Curious Case of Benjamin Button*?

17 Who was the British Prime Minister during the short reign of Edward VIII?

18 Which lake is known to the French as Lac Leman?

19 How many symphonies did the composer Beethoven complete?

20 Where did General Montgomery defeat General Rommel?

Answers to QUIZ 447 – Pot Luck

1 Newton
2 Melanie Chisholm (Mel C)
3 Leviticus
4 Suez
5 Andrea True Connection
6 Mollusc
7 Forth
8 Five
9 Alicia Keys
10 Thomas Gray's *Elegy*
11 Enniskillen
12 English dictionary
13 1956
14 Saltwater crocodile
15 Hawaii
16 Saxe-Coburg-Gotha
17 *Monsters vs. Aliens*
18 Scotland
19 Richard Gere
20 Fine Young Cannibals

QUIZ 450 – Water Sports

ANSWERS ON PAGE 452

1 In a game of water polo, what is the colour of the cap worn by the goalkeeper?

2 Which round-the-world yachtsman was rescued after four days upside down in his boat in 1996?

3 The bucket turn is used to change to breaststroke from which other swimming stroke?

4 In 2017, who was appointed chair of UK Sport?

5 The four shapes used in diving competitions are free, straight, pike and which other?

6 In which country was swimmer Hannah Miley born?

7 Which former British swimmer-turned-commentator appeared in the sixth series of *Strictly Come Dancing*?

8 Which relatively new watersport was added to the Olympics in 1984?

9 How many oars does each rower have in a sweep boat?

10 What is the highest height of a diving board used in competition?

11 At the 2012 Olympics, in which body of water did the open water swimming competitions take place?

12 In which year did Sir Matthew Pinsent win his fourth Olympic gold medal?

13 What term is used in rowing to describe older competitors?

14 In which discipline did Ed McKeever win an Olympic gold medal in 2012?

15 How long does each quarter of a water polo match usually last?

16 The Dorney Lake rowing lake, owned by Eton College, is in which county?

17 What is the name of Oxford University's reserve rowing team?

18 Women were first allowed to swim in the Olympics in which decade?

19 How long is the Oxford-Cambridge Boat Race in miles?

20 Which Scottish swimmer won the 200m breaststroke gold medal at the 1976 summer Olympic Games?

Answers to QUIZ 448 – Lakes and Lochs

1 Nyasa
2 Niagara
3 *Friday the 13th*
4 Argyll and Bute
5 11
6 Loch Ness
7 Lake Placid
8 Oxbow lake
9 Rydal Water
10 It is called a lake rather than a loch
11 Bavaria
12 California and Nevada
13 Skye
14 Lake Tanganyika
15 Playa
16 Austria
17 Annecy
18 Syria
19 Lake Victoria
20 Lake Geneva

QUIZ 451 – Pot Luck

ANSWERS ON PAGE 453

1 Which 2001 crime thriller starred Gene Hackman and Danny DeVito?
2 The song *On the Street Where You Live* features in which musical?
3 Which band had albums entitled *The Great Escape* and *Modern Life Is Rubbish*?
4 Which amount is equivalent to the pre-1971 shilling?
5 What is the literal meaning of "Algarve"?
6 The Victoria Jubilee Bridge in Canada spans which river?
7 On the Beaufort Scale, what is Force 8 called?
8 Which actress starred in the 1989 film *Dead Calm*?
9 Who designed the Lloyd's building in London?
10 How are Jake, Milo, Bella and Fizz known collectively?
11 Which port is part of the city of Edinburgh?
12 What is the capital of the US state of Delaware?
13 A chemical reaction that absorbs heat is described by what word?
14 How is the bell tower in the Piazza dei Miracoli famously known?
15 Which city was the birthplace of Dylan Thomas?
16 What is the animal symbol for Scotland?
17 Which West Indian island has Bridgetown as its capital?
18 The Kennet and Avon canal links which city and town?
19 In September 1996, which jockey won all seven races in one day at Ascot?
20 At which Channel port does the Sussex Ouse flow into the English Channel?

Answers to QUIZ 449 – Pot Luck

1 Meryl Streep
2 Cheese
3 Hackney
4 Brian Connolly
5 Crown
6 Sierra Madre
7 Bogotá
8 Linlithgow Palace
9 Cornwall
10 Portsmouth
11 Never Say Die
12 Jean Sibelius
13 JARVIS
14 Scratch
15 Arnold Dorsey
16 Brad Pitt
17 Stanley Baldwin
18 Lake Geneva
19 Nine
20 El Alamein

QUIZ 452 – Red

ANSWERS ON PAGE 454

Easy

1 In which county is the racecourse of Redcar?

2 What was the surname of the baroness who wrote *The Scarlet Pimpernel*?

3 What was the title of the first single released by Simply Red?

4 Whom did Amanda Redman play in the TV series *New Tricks*?

5 In which Olympic Games did Sir Steve Redgrave win his fifth consecutive gold medal?

6 What is a red-hot poker, if it is not a fire implement?

7 Which actress starred in the 2018 film *Red Sparrow*?

8 In US voting, a "red state" is one where people predominately voted for which party?

9 What is the setting for the 1995 film *Crimson Tide*?

10 What did the *Red Light* spell in the title of a 1977 hit for Billy Ocean?

11 Which actress starred in the 1985 film *Red Sonja*?

Medium

12 After which US state is a "red" breed of chicken named?

13 What is the name of Danny John-Jules' character in the TV series *Red Dwarf*?

14 What type of creature is a redpoll?

15 Which Irish province has the Red Hand as its symbol?

16 How many times did Sebastian Vettel win the Formula 1 World Championship with the Red Bull team?

17 Which strait separates Egypt and Saudi Arabia?

18 Which Neil Diamond song was a no.1 for UB40?

19 Who wrote the 1847 poem *Now Sleeps the Crimson Petal*?

20 Who trained the Grand National winner Red Rum?

Hard

Answers to QUIZ 450 – Water Sports

1 Red
2 Tony Bullimore
3 Backstroke
4 Dame Katherine Grainger
5 Tuck
6 Scotland
7 Mark Foster
8 Synchronised swimming
9 One
10 10m
11 Serpentine
12 2004
13 Masters
14 Kayaking
15 Eight minutes
16 Buckinghamshire
17 Isis
18 1910s (1912)
19 Just under 4.25 miles
20 David Wilkie

QUIZ 453 – Pot Luck

ANSWERS ON PAGE 456

1 Which coast runs from Salerno to Sorrento?
2 Which is the largest country in Central America?
3 By which more common name is the plant of the genus *Aquilegia* known?
4 Which member of Humble Pie had a solo hit with *Show Me the Way* in 1975?
5 Which dry white Italian wine is from the area near Verona?
6 Who had a hit in 1987 with the record *Nothing's Gonna Stop Us Now*?
7 *Express Yourself* and *Dear Jessie* are tracks on which Madonna album?
8 In which city was Sir Andy Murray born?
9 The song *Wand'rin' Star* is from which musical?
10 In the US National Football League, The Bears are a team from which city?
11 On which island was retired footballer Matt Le Tissier born?
12 A funambulist is more usually referred to by what two-word name?
13 What is the name of the lough in County Fermanagh with Enniskillen on its shore?
14 Who wrote the 1991 novel *The Famished Road*?
15 Which word meaning "therefore" spells out a fairy-tale character when read backwards?
16 A frugivorous animal eats what as the main part of its diet?
17 The Erskine Bridge spans which river?
18 A googol is the number one followed by how many zeros?
19 What is the capital of the Canadian province of New Brunswick?
20 Who wrote the 1990 novel *Possession*?

Easy Medium Hard

Answers to QUIZ 451 – Pot Luck

1 *Heist*
2 *My Fair Lady*
3 Blur
4 Five pence
5 The West
6 St Lawrence
7 Gale
8 Nicole Kidman
9 Richard Rogers (Baron Rogers of Riverside)
10 The Tweenies
11 Leith
12 Dover
13 Endothermic
14 Leaning Tower of Pisa
15 Swansea
16 Unicorn
17 Barbados
18 Bristol and Reading
19 Frankie Dettori
20 Newhaven

QUIZ 454 – Talent Shows

ANSWERS ON PAGE 456

Easy

1 The first series of *Strictly Come Dancing* was won by which professional dancer?

2 Who was the original host of *Stars in Their Eyes*?

3 Who was the first dancer to win *Britain's Got Talent*?

4 The series *America's Next Top Model* was created by which former model?

5 What was the title of the 2008 show that was searching for a Nancy for *Oliver!*?

6 Who was the original presenter of the talent show *Fame Academy*?

7 Davina McCall hosted which dance show from 2009 to 2014?

8 Which rock star was on the *American Idol* judging panel from 2011 to 2012?

9 Which act was the runner-up in the first series of *The X Factor*?

10 Which talent show gave Showaddywaddy their big break?

Medium

11 How many people were on the judging panel for the 2018 talent show *All Together Now*?

12 Who won the second series of *The Voice UK*?

13 Which group won the 2015 *a cappella* competition *The Naked Choir*?

14 What was the name of the short-lived boy band created as a result of *Popstars: the Rivals*?

15 Who won the second series of *Pop Idol*?

16 The 1999 BBC talent show *Get Your Act Together* was hosted by which singer?

17 Edd Kimber won the first series of which competition?

18 Bonnie Langford first found fame on which talent show?

19 With which winning dance troupe is Ashley Banjo associated?

20 For how many years did *Strictly Come Dancing* former winner Alesha Dixon appear on the judging panel?

Hard

Answers to QUIZ 452 – Red

1 North Yorkshire
2 Orczy
3 *Money's Too Tight (to Mention)*
4 Sandra Pullman
5 2000 (Sydney)
6 A flower
7 Jennifer Lawrence
8 Republicans
9 Nuclear submarine
10 *Danger*
11 Brigitte Nielsen
12 Rhode Island
13 The Cat
14 Bird
15 Ulster
16 Four
17 The Red Sea
18 *Red Red Wine*
19 Alfred, Lord Tennyson
20 Ginger McCain

QUIZ 455 – Pot Luck

ANSWERS ON PAGE 457

1 In which US city is the Liberty Bell located?

2 Who won the BBC Overseas Sports Personality of the Year in 2016?

3 The theme song from the TV series *Boon* was a 1986 hit for which singer?

4 Who starred with Sandra Bullock in the 2006 film *The Lake House*?

5 Spain and France are bordered by which Atlantic bay?

6 Which of the Apollo 11 astronauts did not walk on the moon?

7 Who is the third god of the Hindu trinity?

8 Which UK shipping area lies directly south of Viking?

9 *The Darkling Thrush* is a 1900 poem by which writer?

10 Who wrote the 1944 play *The Glass Menagerie*?

11 In 1961, the Nobel Peace Prize was awarded to which secretary-general of the United Nations?

12 Who wrote the 1816 poem *On First Looking into Chapman's Homer*"?

13 In which year did the UK introduce self-adhesive stamps?

14 Calico cloth originated in which country?

15 How did the TV characters the *Tomorrow People* refer to teleportation?

16 What title was given to a magistrate ranking next after a consul in Ancient Rome?

17 What name was given to the series of 1970s space probes that provided pictures of Jupiter and Saturn?

18 In which year did Eurostar first run a service from London?

19 Which novelist created the character of Jason Bourne?

20 At which English racecourse are the Coventry Stakes run?

Answers to QUIZ 453 – Pot Luck

1 Amalfi Coast
2 Nicaragua
3 Columbine
4 Peter Frampton
5 Soave
6 Starship
7 *Like A Prayer*
8 Glasgow
9 *Paint Your Wagon*
10 Chicago
11 Guernsey
12 Tightrope walker
13 Erne
14 Ben Okri
15 Ergo
16 Fruit
17 Clyde
18 100
19 Fredericton
20 AS Byatt

Easy

Medium

Hard

QUIZ 456 – Classical Music

ANSWERS ON PAGE 458

Easy

1 In which century was Chopin born?

2 Benjamin Britten (Baron Britten) and Sir Peter Pears established which annual Suffolk music festival?

3 What was the first name of the composer Rimsky-Korsakov?

4 What does *Lieder Ohne Worte* mean?

5 Who composed *The Rite of Spring* (1913)?

6 In a standard modern symphony orchestra which two brass instruments are in the back row?

7 King Ludwig II of Bavaria was the patron of which German composer?

8 Who wrote two operas based on the Shakespeare plays *Macbeth* and *Othello*, and another on the Shakespearean character Falstaff?

9 How is *The Marriage of Figaro* known in Italian?

Medium

10 Which conductor became Music Director of the London Symphony Orchestra in 2017?

11 Which instrument usually has 47 strings?

12 Anne-Sophie Mutter is associated with which instrument?

13 Which Beethoven piece is the anthem of the European Union and Council of Europe?

14 In which city is the opera *Carmen* set?

15 Which three-act Puccini opera was first performed in 1900?

16 What was the nationality of composer Jean Sibelius?

17 Which two conductors founded the London Philharmonic Orchestra?

18 *The Bartered Bride* was written by which Czech composer?

Hard

19 In which London street would you find the Royal Opera House?

20 How many *Brandenburg Concertos* did Bach compose?

Answers to QUIZ 454 – Talent Shows

1 Brendan Cole
2 Leslie Crowther
3 George Sampson
4 Tyra Banks
5 *I'd Do Anything*
6 Patrick Kielty
7 *Got to Dance*
8 Steven Tyler
9 G4
10 *New Faces*
11 100
12 Andrea Begley
13 The Sons of Pitches
14 One True Voice
15 Michelle McManus
16 Ronan Keating
17 *The Great British Bake Off*
18 *Opportunity Knocks*
19 Diversity
20 Three

ANSWERS ON PAGE 459

1 Who performed the title track to the sitcom *The Royle Family*?

2 What is the capital of the Democratic Republic of the Congo?

3 What old horse-drawn cab was named after its architect inventor?

4 Miss Moneypenny was first played by which actress in the 1995 film Bond film *GoldenEye*?

5 Which 2007 animated film featured the voices of Jerry Seinfeld and Renée Zellweger?

6 Who won a diving gold medal at the 1988 Olympics, despite hitting his head on the board performing a reverse 2½ pike?

7 What word is used in Buddhism to indicate the ideal truth as set forth by Buddha?

8 The former EU scheme of "set aside" applied to which type of business?

9 Who was Mike Chapman's most famous co-producer on many 1970s records?

10 The Cape Verde islands are in which ocean?

11 "Hoosier State" is the nickname of which US state?

12 *Love Letters in the Sand* was a 1957 hit for which singer?

13 What name is given to biblical writings that are not part of the accepted Scriptures?

14 What does the expression *Ecce homo* mean?

15 In the TV series *The Avengers*, who played Emma Peel?

16 Which country has "Suomi" on its coins and stamps?

17 In which US state is Lake Placid?

18 Which Lerner and Loewe musical is based on a novel by Colette?

19 Which actor's first name means "cool breeze over the mountains" in Hawaiian?

20 How many hearts has an octopus?

Easy Medium Hard

Answers to QUIZ 455 – Pot Luck

1 Philadelphia
2 Simone Biles
3 Jim Diamond
4 Keanu Reeves
5 Biscay
6 Michael Collins
7 Shiva
8 Forties
9 Thomas Hardy
10 Tennessee Williams
11 Dag Hammarskjöld
12 Keats
13 1993
14 India
15 Jaunting
16 Praetor
17 *Pioneer*
18 1994
19 Robert Ludlum
20 Ascot

QUIZ 458 – Royalty

ANSWERS ON PAGE 460

1 In the 12th century Blondel was the legendary minstrel of which king?
2 What was the profession of Queen Elizabeth II's cousin Lord Lichfield?
3 Of which country was King Farouk the leader from 1936 to 1952?
4 Which English monarch married Eleanor of Aquitaine?
5 In 1831, Leopold I became the first monarch of which country?
6 Madame de Pompadour was a mistress to which French king?
7 Margaret of Anjou was the wife of which English king?
8 Which plot led to the execution of Mary, Queen of Scots?
9 Windsor Castle was built by which English king?
10 In which year did the royal yacht *Britannia* make her final voyage?
11 Sir Anthony Van Dyck was court painter to which English king?
12 In which European city is the royal palace of Belvedere?
13 Which law excluded women from succeeding to the throne of some European countries?
14 The Palace of Versailles gardens were designed at the behest of which 17th-century monarch?
15 Geoffrey Plantagenet, Count of Anjou (b.1113) was the father of which English king?
16 Which English monarch reputedly lost some of the Crown Jewels in The Wash?
17 Who was the last Queen of France before the revolution?
18 The House of Grimaldi is associated with which European principality?
19 Who was the last ruler of the House of Plantagenet?
20 Kenneth I and Kenneth II were kings of which country?

Answers to QUIZ 456 – Classical Music

1 19th century (1810)
2 Aldeburgh
3 Nikolai
4 Song without words
5 Igor Stravinsky
6 Trombones and tubas
7 Richard Wagner
8 Verdi
9 *Le Nozze di Figaro*
10 Sir Simon Rattle
11 Harp
12 Violin
13 *Ode to Joy*
14 Seville
15 *Tosca*
16 Finnish
17 Sir Thomas Beecham and Sir Malcolm Sargent
18 Bedřich Smetana
19 Bow Street
20 Six

QUIZ 459 – Pot Luck

ANSWERS ON PAGE 461

1 Which group had a hit record in 1969 with *Bad Moon Rising*?
2 Which 1960s TV series starred Sir Roger Moore as Simon Templar?
3 What type of creature is a noctule?
4 Rose Byrne played Ellen Parsons in which legal drama series?
5 Which Portuguese archipelago lies 600 miles north-west of Madeira?
6 In which country would you find Mount Logan?
7 The Den is the home ground of which football team?
8 What is the capital of the Australian state of Victoria?
9 In the original TV series *Thunderbirds*, who provided the voice of Lady Penelope?
10 Who played Eric's sister in the TV series *Sykes*?
11 Which are the two Outer Hebridean islands separated by Benbecula?
12 In which Scottish town is McCaig's Tower?
13 Coir is a natural fibre from which plant?
14 Who represented the UK in the 1992 Eurovision Song Contest with *One Step Out of Time?*
15 What is the study of birds' eggs called?
16 *Girl on Fire* was a single in September 2012 for which singer?
17 In which country is Isfahan?
18 What name is given to the region to the east of the Mediterranean Sea?
19 Which stringed instrument features prominently in Dixieland and bluegrass music?
20 In which year was the debit card launched in the UK?

Answers to QUIZ 457 – Pot Luck

1 Oasis
2 Kinshasa
3 Hansom
4 Samantha Bond
5 *Bee Movie*
6 Greg Louganis
7 Dharma
8 Agriculture
9 Nicky Chinn
10 Atlantic
11 Indiana
12 Pat Boone
13 Apocrypha
14 Behold the man
15 Dame Diana Rigg
16 Finland
17 New York
18 *Gigi*
19 Keanu Reeves
20 Three

QUIZ 460 – Scandinavia

ANSWERS ON PAGE 462

1 What is the name of the most famous geothermal spa in Iceland?

2 In which decade was IKEA founded?

3 In which year did Denmark win the European Football championships after initially failing to qualify?

4 Which capital city is the most populated city in Scandinavia...?

5 ...and what is the most populated Scandinavian country?

6 Which two colours appear on the flag of Denmark?

7 The Faroe Islands are situated about halfway between which two countries?

8 What is the international car registration code for Sweden?

9 In which ocean is the Norwegian archipelago of Svalbard?

10 What were Scandinavian pirates more commonly known as?

11 In which city is the Tivoli amusement park?

12 Sonja Henie was a Norwegian Olympic champion in which sport?

13 What is the airport code for Copenhagen?

14 The Danish pastry was introduced to Denmark by bakers from which country?

15 Which two sports do Nordic Combined competitors take part in?

16 By which country was Finland governed from the 17th to the 19th century?

17 In local usage, which three countries does "Scandinavia" usually refer to?

18 Which masked Finnish rock group won the Eurovision Song Contest in 2006?

19 In which decade of the 20th century was Björn Borg born?

20 Which Scandinavian country was the setting for Disney's *Frozen*?

Easy Medium Hard

Answers to QUIZ 458 – Royalty

1 Richard I (The Lionheart)
2 Photographer
3 Egypt
4 Henry II
5 Belgium
6 Louis XV
7 Henry VI
8 The Babington Plot
9 William the Conqueror
10 1997
11 Charles I
12 Vienna
13 Salic law
14 Louis XIV
15 Henry II
16 King John
17 Marie Antoinette
18 Monaco
19 Richard III
20 Scotland

QUIZ 461 – Pot Luck

ANSWERS ON PAGE 463

1 Retired racing driver Nelson Piquet was born in which country?

2 What is another name for the honey badger?

3 Which actress starred in the film *The Piano*?

4 Which fruit flavours the Belgian beer *Kriek lambic*?

5 The novelty record *Shaddup You Face* kept which single from reaching the top of the charts in 1981?

6 "Anything can happen in the next half hour" was the announcement at the start of which popular children's TV series?

7 Radicchio is a variety of which salad plant?

8 Which African country between Nigeria and Gabon has Yaoundé as its capital?

9 What is the term used for a wide railway track?

10 In which area of Russia is Lake Baikal?

11 What type of bridge is the Forth Railway Bridge?

12 Rothesay is the main town on which Scottish island?

13 Which Dame Daphne Du Maurier novel was filmed by Sir Alfred Hitchcock in 1940?

14 Who wrote the collection of poems entitled *Songs of Innocence and of Experience?*

15 Which group recorded the 1987 album *Tango in the Night*?

16 In which branch of the arts was Sir Frederick Ashton famous?

17 Which Asian river forms much of the border between Laos and Thailand?

18 What name is given to the vertical divide on a window?

19 The 1976 book *The Selfish Gene* was written by which author?

20 Which Greek philosopher was a student of Plato and taught Alexander the Great?

Easy

Medium

Hard

Answers to QUIZ 459 – Pot Luck

1 Credence Clearwater Revival
2 *The Saint*
3 Bat
4 *Damages*
5 Azores
6 Canada
7 Millwall FC
8 Melbourne
9 Sylvia Anderson
10 Hattie Jacques
11 North Uist and South Uist
12 Oban
13 Coconut
14 Michael Ball
15 Oology
16 Alicia Keys
17 Iran
18 Levant
19 Banjo
20 1987

QUIZ 462 – Glass

ANSWERS ON PAGE 464

Easy

1 In which year was *Heart of Glass* the first UK no.1 hit for Blondie?
2 What, in military parlance, is a "glasshouse"?
3 What eye condition is indicated if a prescription for glasses includes numbers relating to "spherical", "cylinder" and "axis"?
4 Who wrote the 1994 novel *The Glass Lake*?
5 How many 250ml glasses are there in a jeroboam?
6 Who released the 1980 song *We are Glass*?
7 What is the title of the 1972 sequel to *Charlie and the Chocolate Factory*?
8 What is the name of the small magnifying glass used by jewellers?
9 The 1965 spy novel *The Looking Glass War* was written by which author?
10 Noted for its stained glass, in which area of Paris is Sainte-Chapelle?

Medium

11 Which Italian island is famous for its glass-making?
12 Under what name did Baroness Ruth Rendell write the 1990 novel *Gallowglass*?
13 Glass noodles originate from which continent?
14 What two-word term is given to a product such as Google Glass?
15 Singer Bono wears his trademark sunglasses due to having which eye condition?
16 Who played the title role in the 2016 film *Alice Through the Looking Glass*?
17 Which glass-making company has its headquarters in St Helens?
18 In which country was the composer Philip Glass born?
19 In which year was the Kirk Douglas version of the film *The Glass Menagerie* released?
20 Who had a 1978 hit with *I Love the Sound of Breaking Glass*?

Hard

Answers to QUIZ 460 – Scandinavia

1 Blue Lagoon
2 1940s (1943)
3 1992
4 Stockholm
5 Sweden
6 Red and white
7 Norway and Iceland
8 S
9 Arctic Ocean
10 Vikings
11 Copenhagen
12 Figure skating
13 CPH
14 Austria
15 Cross-country skiing and ski jumping
16 Sweden
17 Denmark, Norway and Sweden
18 Lordi
19 1950s (1956)
20 Norway

QUIZ 463 – Pot Luck

ANSWERS ON PAGE 465

1 What is the literal meaning of "spaghetti"?

2 Which is Turkey's second-largest city?

3 What was the name of the first manned spacecraft to orbit the Moon?

4 *Working My Way Back to You* was a hit for which group in 1980?

5 What did the initials UNCLE stand for in The *Man from UNCLE?*

6 Tulsa is in which US state?

7 Who was leader of the Labour Party when it adopted the Red Rose as its emblem?

8 Which comedy series featured the Brockman family?

9 Movable metal type was invented by which German printer of bibles?

10 What is the fifth letter of the Greek alphabet?

11 What is the study of the flight of projectiles?

12 Which English city traditionally holds a Miners' Gala every July?

13 Bangladesh has which official language?

14 Which former *Blue Peter* presenter was appointed Chief Scout in 2004?

15 Which celebrated mystic published his *Les Prophéties* in 1555?

16 In the 1990s, which comedian wrote the novels *Blast From the Past* and *Inconceivable*?

17 Which Germanic people invaded the Roman Empire between the third and fifth centuries?

18 In 1988, who achieved a "Golden Slam" by winning all four Grand Slam titles plus the Olympic Gold?

19 In which year were contactless payments introduced in the UK?

20 What behaviour characterises somebody named as a *flâneur*?

Easy

Medium

Hard

Answers to QUIZ 461 – Pot Luck

1 Brazil
2 Ratel
3 Holly Hunter
4 Cherry
5 *Vienna* (by Ultravox)
6 *Stingray*
7 Chicory
8 Cameroon
9 Broad gauge
10 Siberia
11 Cantilever
12 Bute
13 *Rebecca*
14 William Blake
15 Fleetwood Mac
16 Dance (choreography)
17 Mekong
18 Mullion
19 Richard Dawkins
20 Aristotle

QUIZ 464 – Golf

ANSWERS ON PAGE 466

Easy

1 Hoylake is the home of which golf club?
2 Who won the US Masters tournament in 2018?
3 In the 2014 BBC Sports Personality of the Year Award, which golfer was runner-up?
4 What nationality is Rickie Fowler?
5 Which Spanish course hosted the first Ryder Cup in mainland Europe in 1997?
6 In which month is The Open championship played?
7 What is the real first name of Fuzzy Zoeller?
8 On which course is the hole known as "the Postage Stamp"?
9 Which golf club was used to hit the three golf balls on the Moon?
10 Which of the four major tournaments is the only one to be held at the same location each year?

Medium

11 What are the first names of the two Molinari brothers?
12 What is the maximum number of clubs that a golfer is permitted to carry at any one time?
13 In which year did the "Miracle at Medinah" mark Europe's comeback in the Ryder Cup?
14 The Royal Lytham & St Anne's golf club is in which county?
15 Anchoring strokes using which long-handled club was banned at the start of 2016?
16 Which Spanish golfer (b.1964) is noted for his love of cigars?
17 What nationality is Inbee Park?
18 In 1990, who became the first international player to be named PGA of America Player of the Year?

Hard

19 How long can a golfer look for a ball before it is deemed to be lost?
20 Which golfer won The Open in 2017?

Answers to QUIZ 462 – Glass

1 1979
2 Military prison
3 Astigmatism
4 Maeve Binchy
5 12
6 Gary Numan
7 *Charlie and the Great Glass Elevator*
8 Loupe
9 John le Carré
10 Île de la Cité
11 Murano
12 Barbara Vine
13 Asia
14 Smart glasses
15 Glaucoma
16 Mia Wasikowska
17 Pilkington
18 USA
19 1950
20 Nick Lowe

QUIZ 465 – Pot Luck

ANSWERS ON PAGE 467

1 What is the Chinese *Book of Changes* more usually called?
2 In the TV series *Ever Decreasing Circles*, who played Martin's wife?
3 What is the name for a mixture of beer and cider?
4 Who was Formula 1 World Champion in 1998, 1990 and 1991?
5 In which year was Catherine the Great born?
6 Which type of insect has a "peppered" variety?
7 Which actress won an Oscar for her portrayal of a woman with Alzheimer's disease in *Still Alice* (2014)?
8 What is the name of the pub in the radio series *The Archers*?
9 Who played Mr Gruber in the 2017 film *Paddington 2*?
10 The 1975 film *Picnic at Hanging Rock* is set in which country?
11 Baron Greenback is an adversary of which TV character?
12 Which sea lies to the east of Italy?
13 Who starred as Jack Harper in the 2013 film *Oblivion*?
14 Which river of Switzerland and France flows into the Camargue delta?
15 In Greek mythology, who was the mother of Eros?
16 Who was the lead singer with the band Bread?
17 Boston crab is a term used in which sport?
18 Which term refers to waves of a frequency below the range of human hearing?
19 Who captained the 2016 European Ryder Cup team?
20 In which UK city is Queen Street station?

Easy
Medium
Hard

Answers to QUIZ 463 – Pot Luck

1 LIttle strings
2 Ankara
3 Apollo 8
4 The Detroit Spinners
5 United Network Command for Law Enforcement
6 Oklahoma
7 Neil Kinnock (Baron Kinnock)
8 *Outnumbered*
9 Gutenberg
10 Epsilon
11 Ballistics
12 Durham
13 Bengali
14 Peter Duncan
15 Nostradamus
16 Ben Elton
17 Goths
18 Steffi Graf
19 2007
20 Idleness

QUIZ 466 – Biopics

Easy

1 Benedict Cumberbatch portrayed which mathematician in the 2014 film *The Imitation Game*?

2 Who directed the 1982 film *Gandhi*?

3 Which 2015 film featuring Jake Gyllenhaal portrayed members of an ill-fated 1996 expedition?

4 Which singer did Sissy Spacek play in the 1980 film *Coal Miner's Daughter*?

5 *Amazing Grace* (2006) featured which actor as William Wilberforce?

6 Who starred in the 1953 film *Calamity Jane*?

7 Kurt Russell and Kevin Costner both portrayed which lawman in the mid-1990s?

8 Which Tudor figure is the main character in *A Man For All Seasons* (1966)?

9 Sir Daniel Day-Lewis won his first Oscar for portraying which artist in 1989?

10 In the 1994 film *Ed Wood*, who played the title role?

Medium

11 Who played the title role in the 1952 film *Hans Christian Andersen*?

12 *The Spirit of St Louis* (1957) told the story of which aviator?

13 Who played figure skater Tonya Harding in the 2017 film *I, Tonya*?

14 Which 2013 film tells the story of Solomon Northup?

15 Which of Henry VIII's wives was featured in a 1969 film?

16 In the 2011 film *My Week with Marilyn*, who played Marilyn Monroe?

17 Who was the *Funny Girl* in the title of the 1968 musical film?

18 Bushranger Ned Kelly was played by which singer in a 1970 film?

19 Which Irish singer was the subject of the 1991 film *Hear My Song*?

20 Who played George Adamson in the 1966 film *Born Free*?

Hard

Answers to QUIZ 464 – Golf

1 Royal Liverpool
2 Patrick Reed
3 Rory McIlroy
4 American
5 Valderrama
6 July
7 Frank
8 Royal Troon
9 Six iron
10 The Masters (Augusta)
11 Edoardo and Francesco
12 14
13 2012
14 Lancashire
15 Belly putter
16 Miguel Ángel Jiménez
17 South Korean
18 Nick Faldo
19 Five minutes
20 Jordan Spieth

QUIZ 467 – Pot Luck

ANSWERS ON PAGE 469

1 Who was the lead singer with Led Zeppelin?

2 Who played Julius Caesar in *Carry on Cleo* and Judge Burke in *Carry on Cowboy*?

3 Who won the Best Supporting Actor Oscar for his role in the 1993 film *The Fugitive*?

4 Retired American footballer William Perry had what nickname when he was playing?

5 *I Want Your Love* and *Baby I Don't Care* were 1980s hits for which group?

6 Which programme has been presented at different times by Anne, Kenneth, Robert and Tony Robinson?

7 *I've Never Been to Me* was a hit for which singer in 1982?

8 Who wrote *The Invisible Man* (1897)?

9 Which white wine grape variety is most widely planted in California?

10 What is the title of the 1981 Stephen King novel about a killer dog?

11 The Sperrin Mountains are in which country?

12 Who is the Greek goddess of hunting?

13 What was Frank Sinatra's middle name?

14 Who was King of Macedonia from 336 to 323 BC?

15 Which white cheese is named after a South Wales town?

16 What is the seventh letter of the Greek alphabet?

17 Hamilton is the capital of which British dependency in the western Atlantic?

18 What name is given to a triangle with all sides unequal?

19 *He's So Fine* was a US no.1 hit for which group?

20 Which city was Australia's capital from 1901 to 1927?

Answers to QUIZ 465 – Pot Luck

1 *I Ching*
2 Dame Penelope Wilton
3 Snakebite
4 Ayrton Senna
5 1729
6 Moth
7 Julianne Moore
8 The Bull
9 Jim Broadbent
10 Australia
11 Danger Mouse
12 Adriatic
13 Tom Cruise
14 Rhône
15 Aphrodite
16 David Gates
17 Wrestling
18 Infrasonic or subsonic
19 Darren Clarke
20 Glasgow

Easy

1 What is the literal meaning of "karaoke"?

2 Which prefix indicates 10^{-9}?

3 From which language is the word "ghetto" derived?

4 Bathophobia is a fear of what?

5 What name is used in Britain for the vegetable that Americans called rutabaga?

6 What is the meaning of the word "grockle"?

7 Which two words that sound the same but are spelt differently mean "a car make" and "to grade"?

8 The French word *cheveux* has what English translation?

9 Which Latin phrase means "genuine" or "in good faith"?

10 What in animal terms, is a bellwether?

Medium

11 The Spanish word *manzana* refers to which fruit?

12 What word can refer to both a bird and a frilly collar?

13 Of what is speleology the study?

14 What is a peruke?

15 If someone is described as "bibulous", what do they like to do?

16 What word meaning "to steal" means "a piece of equipment" when read backwards?

17 Which card game derives its name from the Spanish word for basket?

18 The American word "bullhorn" has what British equivalent?

19 From which language does the word "smithereens" originate?

20 What is the term for words that mean the opposite of each other?

Hard

Answers to QUIZ 466 – Biopics

1 Alan Turing
2 Sir Richard Attenborough
3 *Everest*
4 Loretta Lynn
5 Ioan Gruffudd
6 Doris Day
7 Wyatt Earp
8 Sir Thomas More
9 Christy Brown (in *My Left Foot*)
10 Johnny Depp
11 Danny Kaye
12 Charles Lindbergh
13 Margot Robbie
14 *12 Years a Slave*
15 Anne Boleyn (*Anne of a Thousand Days*)
16 Michelle Williams
17 Fanny Brice (played by Barbra Streisand)
18 Sir Mick Jagger
19 Josef Locke
20 Bill Travers

QUIZ 469 – Pot Luck

ANSWERS ON PAGE 471

1 Which German dramatist wrote *The Caucasian Chalk Circle* (1948)?
2 Peter Noone was the lead singer with which group?
3 Which TV series starring Neil Pearson and Sarah Lancashire featured two rival choirs?
4 Lyn Paul and Eve Graham were members of which 1970s group?
5 What type of animal is a macaque?
6 Which musical includes the song *Happy Talk*?
7 In which county is the town of Cricklade?
8 *Say You Won't Let Go* was a 2016 hit for which singer?
9 Which character in ancient myth was visited by Zeus in the form of a swan?
10 Which US state lies to the south of the Beaufort Sea?
11 How many rounds are there in a woman's Olympic boxing match?
12 What type of creature is a gurnard?
13 "The Baggies" is the nickname of which football team?
14 Which fabric did chemist Joseph Shivers invent in 1958?
15 2240lb is the same as which imperial weight?
16 What type of rock is created by a structural change from pressure or heat?
17 Who starred in the 1970s TV series *Cannon*?
18 The juice of which fruit is used in a whiskey sling?
19 Who played the young Han Solo in the film *Solo: A Star Wars Story*?
20 Which country both hosted and won the first ever football World Cup in 1930?

Answers to QUIZ 467 – Pot Luck

1 Robert Plant
2 Kenneth Williams
3 Tommy Lee Jones
4 The Fridge
5 Transvision Vamp
6 *Points of View*
7 Charlene
8 HG Wells
9 Chardonnay
10 *Cujo*
11 Northern Ireland
12 Artemis
13 Albert
14 Alexander the Great
15 Caerphilly
16 Eta
17 Bermuda
18 Scalene
19 The Chiffons
20 Melbourne

ANSWERS ON PAGE 472

QUIZ 470 – Human Biology

Easy

1 Where in the human body is the plantar fascia?
2 Referred to as "good cholesterol", what do the initials HDL stand for?
3 In which part of the body would you find the pineal gland?
4 Who developed a vaccine against smallpox in 1796?
5 What is the largest organ of the human body?
6 How many milk teeth do humans normally develop?
7 What is the more common name of the disease pertussis?
8 Where in the body is the incus?
9 Which part of the body is affected by osteomyelitis?
10 What is the third portion of the small intestine?
11 Where would you find something that is said to be subcutaneous?

Medium

12 Episcleritis affects which part of the body?
13 What term is given to a tube inserted into the body for the delivery or removal of fluid?
14 William Harvey was the first person to describe what body process in detail?
15 What name is given to the fused vertebrae at the base of the spinal column?
16 The ethmoid, vomer and zygomatic bones can all be found in which part of the body?
17 Which bony tissue forms the bulk of a tooth?
18 How many pairs of ribs does an adult normally have?
19 Which glands are found immediately above the kidneys in the human body?
20 Where in the human body would you find metacarpal bones?

Hard

Answers to QUIZ 468 – Words

1 Empty orchestra
2 Nano
3 Italian
4 Depth
5 Swede
6 Tourist (in Devon or Cornwall)
7 Marque and mark
8 Hair
9 *Bona fide*
10 A sheep that leads the flock
11 Apple
12 Ruff
13 Caves
14 (Old style) wig
15 Drink (alcohol)
16 Loot
17 Canasta
18 Loudhailer or megaphone
19 Irish Gaelic
20 Antonyms

QUIZ 471 – Pot Luck

ANSWERS ON PAGE 473

1 In which county is the National Trust stately home of Wallington?
2 What is the capital of Lithuania?
3 Which wind instrument was played by jazz musician Benny Goodman?
4 Gilbert O'Sullivan had a 1972 hit with which girl's name?
5 Which actor starred in the 1984 thriller *Tightrope*?
6 Who is the Earl of Gloucester's son in Shakespeare's *King Lear*?
7 In the *X-Men* series of films, who starred as Mystique?
8 Which strait separates Alaska from Russia?
9 Who was the first person to fly around the world solo?
10 The Black Country museum is in which town?
11 Which actress played the title role in the 1998 film *Little Voice*?
12 Originally a hit for Dusty Springfield, what was the title of the last UK top 10 hit for the Bay City Rollers?
13 Which industrial city of north-east Mexico lies at the foothills of the Sierra Madre Oriental mountains?
14 Which was the title of the Beatles' debut studio album?
15 Who had a 1983 hit with *Give It Up*?
16 San Juan is the capital of which Caribbean island?
17 How long does each round of men's boxing last at the Olympics?
18 Which 1990s sitcom about an airline crew starred Alan Cumming?
19 Which French artist, first name Henri, died in 1954?
20 The Eurovision Song Contest was won for the first time by which country in 2017?

Easy
Medium
Hard

Answers to QUIZ 469 – Pot Luck

1 Bertolt Brecht
2 Herman's Hermits
3 *All the Small Things*
4 The New Seekers
5 Monkey
6 *South Pacific*
7 Wiltshire
8 James Arthur
9 Leda
10 Alaska
11 Four
12 Fish
13 West Bromwich Albion
14 Lycra
15 Ton
16 Metamorphic
17 William Conrad
18 Lemon
19 Alden Ehrenreich
20 Uruguay

QUIZ 472 – World Politics

Easy

1 Who was President of South Africa before FW de Klerk?
2 Which US President declared that "The ballot is stronger than the bullet"?
3 In elections, for what do the letters STV stand?
4 Who was British Prime Minister four times between 1868 and 1894?
5 In which decade of the 20th century was Bill Clinton born?
6 The famous concert pianist Ignace Paderewski became Prime Minister of which country in 1919?
7 Where exactly would one find the Resolute desk?
8 Who was the first Labour Party Prime Minister?
9 In which year did minister John Profumo resign, admitting that he had misled the House of Commons regarding his relationship with Christine Keeler?
10 Robert Menzies was twice the Prime Minister of which country?

Medium

11 Which public school did Sir Winston Churchill attend from 1888 to 1892?
12 Who was the first Egyptian leader to visit Israel and to address the Knesset (parliament) there?
13 In which year was the minimum voting age in the UK lowered from 21 to 18 years of age?
14 Of which country was Hosni Mubarak the president from 1981 until 2011?
15 In 1959, who deposed dictator Fulgencio Batista?
16 What does the Serjeant at Arms carry into and out of the debating chamber of the House of Commons each day?
17 Which party did Robert Mugabe represent when he became Zimbabwe's first executive president?
18 Who was the first Prime Minister to make use of Chequers?
19 Of which country was Nawaz Sharif the Prime Minister from 1990 to 1999 and 2013 to 2017?
20 The Cortes is the parliament of which country?

Hard

Answers to QUIZ 470 – Human Biology

1 The foot (band of tissue)
2 High-density lipoprotein
3 In the brain
4 Edward Jenner
5 Skin
6 20
7 Whooping cough
8 Ear (middle ear bone)
9 Bones
10 Ileum
11 Under the skin
12 Eye
13 Cannula
14 The circulation of the blood
15 The coccyx
16 The skull
17 Dentine
18 12
19 Adrenal glands
20 Hand

QUIZ 473 – Pot Luck

ANSWERS ON PAGE 475

1 In which county is the Forestry Commission site of Westonbirt?
2 The Annapurna ridge is in which mountain range?
3 What is the name of the square cap worn by the Catholic clergy?
4 Jenever is a drink from which country?
5 The late 14th-century soldier Sir Henry Percy had what nickname?
6 What were the first names of author DH Lawrence?
7 The Savill garden is part of which park?
8 Which number is next to 5 reading anticlockwise on a dartboard?
9 Who played Lt Daniel Kaffee in the 1992 film *A Few Good Men*?
10 The Monach Isles belong to which country?
11 In and around which town does the action of the 1977 film *A Bridge Too Far* take place?
12 Which actor starred in the 1996 fim *Broken Arrow*?
13 The ski resort of Verbier is in which country?
14 The radio station Classic FM launched in which year?
15 Who had a hit in 1999 with *Beautiful Stranger*?
16 Which US state lies immediately south of Iowa?
17 In the TV series *Jemima Shore Investigates*, which actress played the title role?
18 Which group had hits in the 1990s with *Fall at Your Feet* and *Weather with You*?
19 Furze and whin are other names for which shrub?
20 Who is the Roman goddess of agriculture?

Easy

Medium

Hard

Answers to QUIZ 471 – Pot Luck

1 Northumberland (near Morpeth)
2 Vilnius
3 Clarinet
4 Clair
5 Clint Eastwood
6 Edgar
7 Jennifer Lawrence
8 The Bering Strait
9 Wiley Post (in 1933)
10 Dudley
11 Jane Horrocks
12 *I Only Want to Be With You*
13 Monterrey
14 *Please, Please Me*
15 KC and the Sunshine Band
16 Puerto Rico
17 Two minutes
18 *The High Life*
19 Matisse
20 Portugal

QUIZ 474 – The UK

ANSWERS ON PAGE 476

Easy

1 What is the highest rank in the British Army?

2 In pre-decimal currency, what was one-fortieth of a pound?

3 Which is the second-largest island of the Inner Hebrides?

4 Which vegetable's UK season officially runs from 23rd April to Midsummer's Day?

5 In which year was the London Marathon first run?

6 The highest point of which range of hills is at Cross Fell?

7 In which year did the Church of England's parliament vote by a narrow margin to allow women to be ordained as priests?

8 Which company developed the pottery called Jasperware?

9 Which city is served by an airport located at Ringway?

10 What is the Welsh word for "valley"?

Medium

11 A famous oyster festival takes place in which Essex town?

12 What title is given to the head of a Scottish municipal corporation?

13 What is the county town of Somerset?

14 Who laid the foundation stone at Coventry Cathedral in 1956?

15 The ship "Cutty Sark" carried what as its cargo?

16 Which is London's oldest theatre site?

17 In which year was the bimetallic £2 coin first issued into general circulation?

18 What does it mean if the Union Jack is flown upside down from a ship?

19 The first Chelsea Flower Show was held in which decade?

20 Which two rivers flow through Aberdeen?

Hard

Answers to QUIZ 472 – World Politics

1 PW Botha
2 Abraham Lincoln
3 Single Transferable Vote
4 William Gladstone
5 1940s (1946)
6 Poland
7 The Oval Office
8 Ramsay MacDonald
9 1963
10 Australia
11 Harrow
12 Anwar Sadat
13 1969
14 Egypt
15 Fidel Castro
16 The mace
17 ZANU
18 David Lloyd George (First Earl Lloyd-George of Dwyfor)
19 Pakistan
20 Spain

QUIZ 475 – Pot Luck

ANSWERS ON PAGE 477

1 Jeremy Bentham was associated with which set of principles?
2 Which word for a mischievous person is derived from the Old French word for "rabble"?
3 In which year did the Beatles disband?
4 The plant *Myosotis* is better known by what name?
5 Which river runs through the centre of Warsaw?
6 Who had a hit with *Your Game* in 2004?
7 The *kabuki* style of drama is associated with which country?
8 Tiffi and Mr Yeti are characters from which game?
9 Who played Edward Cullen in the *Twilight* films?
10 Which Catholic organisation is mentioned in the novel *The Da Vinci Code*?
11 In which 2002 biopic did Salma Hayek play a Mexican artist?
12 *Sad Sweet Dreamer* was a 1974 hit for which group?
13 Who played Reggie Perrin's wife in the 2009 remake of the classic series?
14 What is the state capital of South Dakota?
15 Which fruit has a variety called Ellison's orange?
16 Which author lived at Abbotsford House near Melrose?
17 Who sang *One Man Band* in 1974?
18 What is the chief port of Senegal?
19 Los Barcos was the setting for which 1990s soap?
20 A bundt cake is baked in a mould of what shape?

Answers to QUIZ 473 – Pot Luck

1 Gloucestershire
2 Himalayas
3 Biretta
4 The Netherlands
5 Hotspur
6 David Herbert
7 Windsor Great Park
8 12
9 Tom Cruise
10 Scotland
11 Arnhem
12 John Travolta
13 Switzerland
14 1992
15 Madonna
16 Missouri
17 Patricia Hodge
18 Crowded House
19 Gorse
20 Ceres

QUIZ 476 – Football

ANSWERS ON PAGE 478

Easy

1 What was notable about a football game played at Bramall Lane on October 14, 1878?

2 The Golden Cage is a goalkeeping award in which European country?

3 Who won the BBC Women's Footballer of the Year 2017?

4 In the 1956 FA Cup Final, which goalkeeper played the end of the match with a broken neck?

5 Who was the first goalkeeper to captain a FIFA World Cup winning team?

6 Which was the first team to be managed by Brian Clough?

7 Who captained Tottenham Hotspur FC during the double-winning season of 1961?

8 Beating Inter Milan 2-1 in Lisbon, in which year did Celtic become the first British football club to win the European Cup?

9 On retiring from playing football, which team did Peter Shilton manage from 1992 to 1995?

Medium

10 In which country do the teams Omonia, Enosis and Anorthosis play?

11 In 1957, who became the first player to twice be named the Football Writers' Association Footballer of the Year?

12 Which major UK football club was founded as Dial Square?

13 Against which team did Archie Gemmill score his famous goal at the 1978 FIFA World Cup?

14 In which decade did Everton FC play their first game at Goodison Park?

15 Who won English football's Premier League Golden Boot award in 2010?

16 Which was the first purpose-built all-seater football stadium in Scotland?

17 How old was Pelé when he won his first World Cup?

Hard

18 Northern Ireland lost out to which country in the 2018 World Cup play-offs?

19 Billy Bremner and Graeme Souness both received how many caps for Scotland?

20 Which was Luis Figo's last club before retiring from playing football in 2009?

Answers to QUIZ 474 – The UK

1 Field marshal
2 Sixpence
3 Mull
4 Asparagus
5 1981
6 Pennines
7 1992
8 Wedgwood
9 Manchester
10 Cwm
11 Colchester
12 Lord Provost
13 Taunton
14 Queen Elizabeth II
15 Tea
16 Theatre Royal, Drury Lane
17 1998
18 A distress signal
19 1910s (1912)
20 The Dee and the Don

QUIZ 477 – Pot Luck

ANSWERS ON PAGE 479

1 Which Hollywood actor changed his name from Eric Bishop?
2 Which authoress challenged the traditional roles of women in the book *The Second Sex*?
3 The Sutherland Falls lie between Lake Quill and Arthur River in which country?
4 What was the theme song to the TV series *Boon*?
5 What is King Alfred's Cake?
6 *Have I the Right* was a 1964 hit for which group?
7 Which poet (d.1529) wrote the work *Phillip Sparrow*?
8 Skokholm island lies off the coast of which country?
9 What is the capital of Qatar?
10 Who wrote the 1791 book *The Rights of Man*?
11 *Nights in the Gardens of Spain* (1916) was written by which composer?
12 For what is an Aldis lamp used?
13 Who was the Greek Muse of love poetry?
14 Manama is the capital of which Gulf state?
15 Of what is anuptaphobia a fear?
16 What trade does Omar Khayyam's surname imply?
17 Which Normandy city is the burial place of William the Conqueror?
18 In John le Carre's book, what was the name of the *Spy Who Came in From the Cold*?
19 Which football team plays at Oakwell?
20 Who was Composer to the Chapel Royal and, from 1679, organist at Westminster Abbey?

Answers to QUIZ 475 – Pot Luck

1 Utilitarianism
2 Rascal
3 1970
4 Forget-me-not
5 Vistula
6 Will Young
7 Japan
8 *Candy Crush Saga*
9 Robert Pattinson
10 Opus Dei
11 *Frida*
12 Sweet Sensation
13 Fay Ripley
14 Pierre
15 Apple
16 Sir Walter Scott
17 Leo Sayer
18 Dakar
19 *Eldorado*
20 Ring

QUIZ 478 – Television

1 What was the name of the cat in the TV series *Rising Damp*?

2 In the US TV series *Numb3rs*, who played maths genius Charlie Eppes?

3 In which fictional village was the series *Hamish Macbeth* set?

4 Who won the first series of *The Voice UK*?

5 What was the title of the 2000-02 drama series about an internet start-up company?

6 Christopher Trace and Leila Williams were the first presenters of which long-running series?

7 What was the name of Aiden Gillen's character in the series *The Wire*?

8 In which year was *Casualty* first broadcast?

9 Who presented the UK version of the TV adventure show *The Mole*?

10 Which *EastEnders* character was originally played by Jo Warne for ten episodes in 1991 before returning with a new actress in 1994?

11 For what was the TV character of Kristin Shepard famous?

12 Who played Chloe O'Brian in the series 24?

13 Carbide and Eruption were amongst the winners of which TV competition?

14 Chris Lintott has presented on which programme since 2000?

15 Who hosted *Crackerjack* in its 1980s format?

16 The character of Helen Flynn, played by Lisa Faulkner, was controversially killed off in the second ever episode of which series?

17 Who is best known for playing Sandor "The Hound" in *Game of Thrones*?

18 The fictional research project The Dharma Initiative featured on which TV series?

19 Who played Pierre Bezukhof in the 2016 TV adaptation of *War and Peace*?

20 In which series did Amy Acker play Samantha Groves, nicknamed "Root"?

Easy

Medium

Hard

Answers to QUIZ 476 – Football

1 It was the first floodlit match
2 Denmark
3 Ada Hegerberg
4 Bert Trautmann
5 Gianpiero Combi (1934)
6 Hartlepool United
7 Danny Blanchflower
8 1967
9 Plymouth Argyle
10 Cyprus
11 Tom Finney
12 Arsenal FC
13 The Netherlands
14 1890s (1892)
15 Didier Drogba
16 McDiarmid Park
17 17
18 Switzerland
19 54
20 Internazionale

1 Who wrote "Hope springs eternal in the human breast"?

2 Which French general became Supreme Commander of all Allied Forces on the Western Front in the First World War in 1918?

3 "The woods decay, the woods decay and fall" is the first line of which Tennyson poem?

4 What was the title of the first record to be released on the Virgin record label?

5 Which American singer/songwriter's real name is Robert James Ritchie?

6 In which year was the speaking clock introduced in the UK?

7 Which environmentalist published *The End of Nature* in 1989?

8 Wat Chaiwatthanaram is a tourist attraction in which country?

9 In which year was Canada founded?

10 *What A Girl Wants* was a hit for Christina Aguilera in which year?

11 Lentigines is the medical term applied to what?

12 What is a sea lemon?

13 Who wrote *Sylvie and Bruno* (1889), a work which evolved from a short story entitled *Bruno's Revenge*?

14 Which play by Sheridan features Lydia Languish?

15 What kind of creature would be described as lumbricoid?

16 *A Moon Shaped Pool* is a 2016 album by which band?

17 In which country is Arlanda International Airport?

18 What is the capital city of Burkina Faso?

19 Which former Prime Minister once played cricket for Middlesex?

20 What is the name of the flying island in *Gulliver's Travels* (1726)?

Easy

Medium

Hard

Answers to QUIZ 477 – Pot Luck

1 Jamie Foxx
2 Simone de Beauvoir
3 New Zealand
4 *Hi Ho Silver*
5 Fungus
6 The Honeycombs
7 John Skelton
8 South Wales
9 Doha
10 Thomas Paine
11 Manuel de Falla
12 Signalling
13 Erato
14 Bahrain
15 Staying single
16 Tent maker
17 Caen
18 Alec Leamas
19 Barnsley FC
20 Henry Purcell

QUIZ 480 – Planet Earth

ANSWERS ON PAGE 482

Easy

1 Who founded the American environmental organisation The Sierra Club?
2 On Heard Island in the southern Indian Ocean, what is Big Ben?
3 What type of creature is a gelada?
4 Which is Scotland's deepest loch?
5 In which archipelago are Terceira, Pico, Faial, São Jorge and Flores?
6 Martha, who died in Cincinnati Zoo in 1914, was the last living example of which bird?
7 The Itatinga waterfall is in which country?
8 What is Spain's highest mountain, on the island of Tenerife?
9 Which is the main island of the Seychelles?
10 What is the "Alpide Belt" noted for?

Medium

11 A Pacific sea wasp is what type of creature?
12 What acid gives nettles their sting?
13 In which decade was the Great Barrier Reef listed as a World Heritage Site?
14 Which geological period immediately followed the Cambrian period?
15 The type of abalone known as a "paua" is found in which country?
16 Of which mountain range is Narodnaya the highest peak?
17 In which US state is the Mammoth Cave National Park?
18 The "Gaia hypothesis" is associated with which environmentalist?
19 Which is the longest river in Canada?
20 Which feathery-leaved plant is also known as milfoil?

Hard

Answers to QUIZ 478 –Television

1 Vienna
2 David Krumholtz
3 Lochdubh
4 Leanne Mitchell
5 *Attachments*
6 *Blue Peter*
7 Tommy Carcetti
8 1986
9 Glenn Hugill
10 Peggy Mitchell
11 She shot JR in *Dallas*
12 Mary Lynn Rajskub
13 *Robot Wars*
14 *The Sky at Night*
15 Stu Francis
16 *Spooks*
17 Rory McCann
18 *Lost*
19 Paul Dano
20 *Person of Interest*

QUIZ 481 – Pot Luck

ANSWERS ON PAGE 483

1 In which year did Frank Bruno win the WBC heavyweight title?

2 Who won four successive Olympic gold medals in the discus from 1956 to 1968?

3 Which Australian folk group had a hit in 1965 with *The Carnival is Over*?

4 Which geological period immediately followed the Carboniferous period?

5 Who wrote the play *Who's Afraid of Virginia Woolf* (1962)?

6 Which British composer wrote the 1968 opera *Punch and Judy*?

7 The Preakness Stakes, Belmont Stakes plus which other race make up the American Triple Crown?

8 *Who You Are* is a 2011 album by which singer?

9 What term was given to the 16th-century belief that herbs resembling specific body parts could be used to treat ailments in those body parts?

10 What is the flat rock on which tools are sharpened called?

11 Which 1957 Patrick White novel describes a journey into the Australian interior?

12 If you have coryza, from what are you suffering?

13 Who wrote the 1921 play *Six Characters in Search of an Author*?

14 What is a calpac?

15 What was the title of Britney Spears' fourth album?

16 The National Trust property of Erddig is on the outskirts of which town?

17 The sacred Hindu text *Bhagavad Gita* was incorporated into which epic poem?

18 Who topped the singles charts in 1970 with *Woodstock*?

19 Which French author wrote the 1949 novel *The Thief's Journal*?

20 What is the primary collection of sacred texts in Zoroastrianism?

Answers to QUIZ 479 – Pot Luck

1 Alexander Pope
2 Ferdinand Foch
3 *Tithonus*
4 *Tubular Bells* (Mike Oldfield)
5 Kid Rock
6 1936
7 Bill McKibben
8 Thailand (Buddhist temple)
9 1867
10 2000
11 Freckles
12 A sea slug
13 Lewis Carroll
14 *The Rivals*
15 Worm
16 Radiohead
17 Sweden (Stockholm)
18 Ouagadougou
19 Sir Alec Douglas-Home
20 Laputa

ANSWERS ON PAGE 484

1 Who wrote the 1794 poem *The Clod and the Pebble*?

2 *Tall, Dark and Gruesome* is the 1977 autobiography by which actor?

3 Which James Hilton novel is set in the fictional location of Shangri-La?

4 What is the name of Heidi's invalid companion in the classic 1881 children's novel?

5 In 1938, who was awarded the Nobel Prize in Literature?

6 *The Rachel Papers* (1973) was the first novel by which author?

7 What was author Ian Fleming's middle name?

8 The 2005 novel *The Book Thief* was written by which Australian author?

9 In 1935, which British publisher launched the first range of Penguin titles?

10 Although not made an official position until 1668, who became the first Poet Laureate in 1616?

11 Who created the Chinese detective Charlie Chan?

12 What are the forenames of Scottish author JM Barrie?

13 In 1697, who published *Mother Goose's Fairy Tales*?

14 Which literary figure was born in 1809 at Somersby Rectory in Lincolnshire?

15 What was the first name of writer F Scott Fitzgerald's wife?

16 The 2017 Man Booker Prize was won by which author for *Lincoln in the Bardo*?

17 Which hat is named after an 1894 novel by George du Maurier?

18 In Rider Haggard's 1887 novel *She*, who is the immortal queen?

19 Who wrote the 1961 sci-fi novel *Solaris*?

20 Which 1938 Evelyn Waugh novel features Lord Copper?

Easy

Medium

Hard

Answers to QUIZ 480 – Planet Earth

1 John Muir
2 A volcano
3 Monkey (baboon)
4 Morar
5 Azores
6 Passenger pigeon
7 Brazil
8 Teide
9 Mahé
10 Earthquakes
11 Jellyfish
12 Formic acid
13 1980s (1981)
14 Ordovician
15 New Zealand
16 Urals
17 Kentucky
18 James Lovelock
19 The Mackenzie
20 Yarrow

QUIZ 483 – Pot Luck

ANSWERS ON PAGE 485

1 In which country did the Morito and Chupaderos meteorites both land?
2 Who wrote *The Adventures of Peregrine Pickle* (1751)?
3 Which actor won Best Supporting Actor Oscars for *Spartacus* and *Topkapi*?
4 What is Peru's currency unit?
5 During the two World Wars of the last century, at which course was the Derby held?
6 Which singer topped the UK singles charts in 2015 with *Don't Be So Hard on Yourself*?
7 What is a cariole?
8 In July 2011, which space shuttle made its final flight?
9 Which football team plays at Kenilworth Road?
10 For what is oakum used on a ship?
11 What is the King of Naples' name in Shakespeare's *The Tempest*?
12 By what name is Bechuanaland now known?
13 What type of creature is a true lover's knot?
14 If someone is pandiculating, what are they doing?
15 What is a tava?
16 Which South Pacific island state was once called the New Hebrides?
17 In which city are football team PFC CSKA based?
18 Who won the Booker Prize in 1971 with *In a Free State*?
19 Which actress took the leading role in DW Griffiths 1915 film *The Birth of a Nation*?
20 In which city is the Mariinsky Ballet based?

Easy

Medium

Hard

Answers to QUIZ 481 – Pot Luck

1 1995
2 Al Oerter
3 The Seekers
4 Permian
5 Edward Albee
6 Harrison Birtwistle
7 Kentucky Derby
8 Jessie J
9 Doctrine of Signatures
10 Oilstone
11 *Voss*
12 Nasal inflammation caused by a cold
13 Luigi Pirandello
14 A hat (high-crowned cap)
15 *In the Zone*
16 Wrexham
17 *Mahabharata*
18 Matthews' Southern Comfort
19 Jean Genet
20 Avesta

QUIZ 484 – Inventors and Inventions

ANSWERS ON PAGE 486

Easy

1 Who invented the carpet sweeper?
2 Anthony Trollope is famous as a novelist, but which item of "street furniture" did he invent?
3 What is the name of the French inventor of the parachute?
4 Which Italian is said to have invented the modern pianoforte?
5 In which decade was Coca-Cola® invented?
6 What is Swiss engineer George de Mestral best known for inventing after cleaning his dog in 1941?
7 In which country was snooker invented?
8 Which household item was invented by James Spangler in 1908?
9 Douglas Engelbart invented which item of computer hardware in 1963?

Medium

10 What did Evangelista Torricelli invent in 1643?
11 What is the name of the English inventor who is often known as "the father of aviation"?
12 Who invented the digital camera?
13 For what purpose was Alka-Seltzer® first marketed?
14 What invention first appeared around 3500 BC and was originally used to shape clay?
15 What did the US company Diablo Data Systems invent for use on typewriters?
16 Louis Moinet invented which time measurement device in 1816?
17 Who invented the bifocal lens?
18 Clergyman William Oughtred invented which aid to calculation in 1622?
19 What was invented by Walter Morrison in 1946?

Hard

20 Who is often known as "the Father of English Clockmaking"?

Answers to QUIZ 482 – Literature

1 William Blake
2 Sir Christopher Lee
3 *Lost Horizon*
4 Clara
5 Pearl Buck
6 Martin Amis
7 Lancaster
8 Markus Zusak
9 Allen Lane
10 Ben Jonson
11 Earl D Biggers
12 James Matthew
13 Charles Perrault
14 Alfred, Lord Tennyson
15 Zelda
16 George Saunders
17 Trilby
18 Ayesha
19 Stanislaw Lem
20 *Scoop*

QUIZ 485 – Pot Luck

ANSWERS ON PAGE 487

1 Which German state has Wiesbaden as its capital?

2 Which British historian (b.1800) wrote *The Lays of Ancient Rome*?

3 Which country lies between Benin and Ghana?

4 What name is given to the small vestigial tube in the human intestine?

5 In which Scottish region is John o' Groats located?

6 Which Australian sportsman was nicknamed "The Rockhampton Rocket" in his playing days?

7 In 2001, the Gorillaz had a hit song about which actor?

8 Which rugby team played their home games at Knowsley Road until 2010?

9 What name is given to a clay tobacco pipe with a long, curved stem?

10 What type of creature is a great ramshorn?

11 In which year were the Dead Sea Scrolls found?

12 For which team did motor racing's John Surtees win his first Grand Prix?

13 Tristan Tzara is associated with which early 20th-century anarchist art movement?

14 Who was leader of the former state of Czechoslovakia from 1968 to 1969?

15 Which major river flows through France, Belgium and the Netherlands?

16 Which philosopher, author of *Also Sprach Zarathustra*, is known for his theories of the "superman"?

17 Andrássy Avenue is a World Heritage site in which European city?

18 On which Croatian peninsula are Pula and Rovinj located?

19 In which 1946 Hitchcock thriller did Cary Grant play a government agent called TR Devlin?

20 Which geological era saw the appearance of flowering plants and giant dinosaurs?

Answers to QUIZ 483 – Pot Luck

1 Mexico
2 Tobias Smollett
3 Peter Ustinov
4 Sol
5 Newmarket
6 Jess Glynne
7 A horse-drawn vehicle
8 *Atlantis*
9 Luton Town FC
10 Waterproofing (also called caulking)
11 Alonso
12 Botswana
13 Moth
14 Stretching while yawning
15 Frying pan (in Asia)
16 Vanuatu
17 Moscow
18 VS Naipaul
19 Lillian Gish
20 St Petersburg

Easy

1 Matthew McConaughey starred in which 1999 comedy film?

2 What was Walt Disney's middle name?

3 Which 1936 Hitchcock thriller is based on Joseph Conrad's *The Secret Agent*?

4 In the 2006 film *Factory Girl*, who played Andy Warhol?

5 What was the first name of Charlie Sheen's character in *Wall Street*?

6 Who directed the 1948 film *State of the Union*?

7 In the 1997 film *Anaconda*, which actress and singer played the lead role of Terri Flores?

8 What was the surname of silent-film star Theda?

9 Which 1973 film was Clint Eastwood's first western as a director?

10 In the film *Ghost*, what was Sam Wheat's profession?

Medium

11 Who played Rosalie Hale in the *Twilight* films?

12 Which film director was shot by an air rifle during a 2005 interview in Los Angeles with Mark Kermode?

13 Which actor won an Oscar for the 1952 film *Viva Zapata!*?

14 In the 2018 Marvel film *Black Panther*, who played the title role?

15 Who played Sarah Connor in the 2015 film *Terminator Genisys*?

16 Which Canadian actor played Evan in the 2007 film *Superbad*?

17 Which 2007 film featuring Emily Blunt was based on a novel by Karen Joy Fowler?

18 How was the actor Michel Shalhoub better known?

19 Who played Ted Striker in *Airplane!* (1980)?

20 For which film did Meryl Streep receive her first Oscar nomination?

Hard

Answers to QUIZ 484 – Inventors and Inventions

1 Melville Bissell
2 Pillar box
3 André-Jacques Garnerin
4 Bartolomeo Cristofori
5 1880s (1886)
6 Velcro®
7 India
8 Vacuum cleaner
9 The mouse
10 Barometer
11 Sir George Cayley
12 Steven Sasson
13 Cold cure
14 Wheel
15 Daisy wheel printer
16 Chronograph
17 Benjamin Franklin
18 The slide rule
19 Frisbee
20 Thomas Tompion

QUIZ 487 – Pot Luck

ANSWERS ON PAGE 489

1 Lake Tanganyika is bordered by the Democratic Republic of the Congo, Tanzania, Zambia and which other country?

2 Who wrote the children's book *The Very Hungry Caterpillar*?

3 Loch Ness and Oregon thornless are varieties of which fruit?

4 Who wrote the 1916 play *Hobson's Choice*?

5 What is the surname of *A Good Man in Africa* author William?

6 Who wrote the play *Chips with Everything* (1962)?

7 The battery was invented by which physicist?

8 What is the name of Jean de Brunhoff's cartoon elephant?

9 Which English king was known as "Beauclerc"?

10 Ricoh Arena is the home ground of which football team?

11 What was the name of the world's first electronic computer?

12 The travel memoir *Au Maroc* was written by which French author (b.1850)?

13 Which tree is the main food of the brimstone butterfly in caterpillar form?

14 The character of Professor Challenger was created by which author (b.1859)?

15 What is the longitude of the International Date Line?

16 In which country is the River Jumna?

17 To which family of mammals do civets belong?

18 What is South Korea's chief port and second-largest city?

19 Who wrote the 1989 novel *The Cloning of Joanna May*?

20 Who played Bernie in the 1999 film *Notting Hill*?

Easy

Medium

Hard

Answers to QUIZ 485 – Pot Luck

1 Hesse (Hessen)
2 Thomas Macaulay
3 Togo
4 Appendix
5 Highland
6 Rod Laver
7 Clint Eastwood
8 St Helens
9 A churchwarden
10 Water snail
11 1947
12 Lotus
13 Dadaism
14 Alexander Dubĉek
15 Meuse
16 Friedrich Nietzsche
17 Budapest
18 Istria
19 *Notorious*
20 Mesozoic

QUIZ 488 – Rock Music

ANSWERS ON PAGE 490

Easy

1 What was the title of Evanescence's second studio album, released in 2006?
2 Which band's cover of *The Sound of Silence* reached no.29 in the UK charts in 2016?
3 The 1992 album *America's Least Wanted* was by which band?
4 In the band name Kings of Leon, who is "Leon"?
5 Singer Myles Kennedy teamed up with which famous guitarist to form the Conspirators?
6 Which band featured Tony Iommi and Geezer Butler in its line-up?
7 Who released a 2016 album entitled *Braver Than We Are*?
8 Who was the original lead singer of AC/DC?
9 St Jimmy and Whatsername are characters in a concept album by which band?
10 Which hard-rock band released the 2003 album *St Anger*?

Medium

11 *Badge* and *White Room* were singles by which late 1960s rock band?
12 Which original band member joined Jeff Lynne in 2014 when he re-formed ELO?
13 Which singer collaborated with Robert Plant on the 2007 album *Raising Sand*?
14 Nickelback's 2001 single *How You Remind Me* was taken from which album?
15 2007's *Favourite Worst Nightmare* was the second album by which band?
16 Whose first solo album was entitled *Vigil in a Wilderness of Mirrors*?
17 The 2009 Westlife hit *What About Now* was originally recorded by which US rock band?
18 What was the title of the 2006 only UK no.1 single for My Chemical Romance?
19 M Shadows and Synyster Gates are members of which US hard rock band?
20 Which band released the 1980s albums *British Steel* and *Screaming for Vengeance*?

Hard

Answers to QUIZ 486 – Film

1 *EDtv*
2 Elias
3 *Sabotage*
4 Guy Pearce
5 Bud
6 Frank Capra
7 Jennifer Lopez
8 Bara
9 *High Plains Drifter*
10 Stockbroker
11 Nikki Reed
12 Werner Herzog
13 Anthony Quinn
14 Chadwick Boseman
15 Emilia Clarke
16 Michael Cera
17 *The Jane Austen Book Club*
18 Omar Sharif
19 Robert Hays
20 *The Deer Hunter*

QUIZ 489 – Pot Luck

ANSWERS ON PAGE **491**

1 The poisonous fungus *Amanita phalloides* is known by what common name?
2 Which London Tube station lies between Caledonian Road and Arsenal?
3 What is a jota?
4 Which branch of medicine is concerned with deformities of the bones caused by disease or injury?
5 Madeleine Wickham also writes "chick lit" under what pen name?
6 Between 1900 and 1908, which Olympic competitor won all the Olympic standing high-jump and standing long-jump events?
7 Which composer (b.1835) wrote the opera *Mademoiselle Fifi*?
8 In which country is the River Glåma?
9 What name is given to the principle that the simplest explanation is the most likely one?
10 Who scored two penalties in the 1994 FA Cup final?
11 Jimi Hendrix's former Mayfair house has two blue plaques honouring both him and which composer?
12 What was the first name of the sewing-machine inventor Singer?
13 "That is no country for old men" was written by which poet?
14 Which musician was backed by his Paramount Jazz Band?
15 Who wrote the 1911 novel *The Lair of the White Worm*?
16 In *Murders In The Rue Morgue*, who or what was the murderer?
17 Which UK group's first Top 5 hit was *Sha-La-La-La-Lee* in 1966?
18 Which French poet wrote the 1873 work *A Season in Hell*?
19 What is the largest freshwater lake in New Zealand?
20 In which East African country is the Ngorongoro Crater?

Easy Medium Hard

Answers to QUIZ 487 – Pot Luck

1 Burundi
2 Eric Carle
3 Blackberry
4 Harold Brighouse
5 Boyd
6 Arnold Wesker
7 Alessandro Volta
8 Babar
9 Henry I
10 Coventry City
11 Colossus
12 Pierre Loti
13 Buckthorn
14 Sir Arthur Conan Doyle
15 180 degrees (with several deviations)
16 India
17 Viverridae
18 Busan
19 Fay Weldon
20 Hugh Bonneville

QUIZ 490 – Mythology

ANSWERS ON PAGE 492

Easy

1 In Greek mythology, what was Tiresias' profession?
2 The Egyptian god Sobek took the form of which creature?
3 Which Cypriot city is the mythical birthplace of Aphrodite?
4 The tale of Culhwch and Olwen was originally written in which language?
5 How many worlds are there in Norse mythology?
6 In Greek mythology, which nymph of Artemis was changed into a bear?
7 Ops was the wife of which Roman god?
8 Who or what is Yggdrasil in Norse mythology?
9 Which word can refer both to all the gods of a religion, or the place in which they were worshipped?
10 In which country's mythology does the Moon deity Thoth appear?

Medium

11 What name was given to the Roman rite where images of the gods were set out as if at a banquet?
12 What is the name of Thor's hammer?
13 Who was the queen of the winter in Scottish folklore?
14 In Greek mythology, what was used to suspend the Sword of Damocles?
15 Who was the goddess of the hearth and its fire in Ancient Rome?
16 In Egyptian mythology, what role did Anubis have?
17 The Edda is a collection of poems from which mythology?
18 Which Roman god of war later came to be identified with Romulus?
19 The Dagda appears in the mythology of which country?

Hard

20 In Greek mythology, who were the parents of Rhea?

Answers to QUIZ 488 – Rock Music

1 *The Open Door*
2 Disturbed
3 Ugly Kid Joe
4 Their grandfather
5 Slash
6 Black Sabbath
7 Meat Loaf
8 Bon Scott
9 Green Day
10 Metallica
11 Cream
12 Richard Tandy
13 Alison Krauss
14 *Silver Side Up*
15 Arctic Monkeys
16 Fish
17 Daughtry
18 *Welcome to the Black Parade*
19 Avenged Sevenfold
20 Judas Priest

QUIZ 491 – Pot Luck

ANSWERS ON PAGE 493

1 What lived in the boiler of *Ivor the Engine*?

2 In the 1936 novel *Jamaica Inn*, what is the name of the vicar?

3 What is the alternative name for the earth-boring dung beetle?

4 Who was the French composer of *The Sorcerer's Apprentice* (1897)?

5 In which novel by Charles Dickens does the character Kit Nubbles appear?

6 Minestrone soup derives its name from the Italian "minestrare", which translates to what in English?

7 Who was the mythical wife of Odysseus?

8 Rarotonga is part of which island group?

9 In which US state is the Black Canyon?

10 Which ancient region and Roman province corresponds largely to modern Portugal?

11 What type of creature is a nyala?

12 The 1996 film *Up Close and Personal* featured which Celine Dion song?

13 Which group's first song was a no.1 hit entitled *Baby, Now That I've Found You* in 1967?

14 In which city is the Eden Park sports stadium?

15 Who wrote the 1739 work *A Treatise of Human Nature*?

16 In 1849, who invented the safety pin?

17 How was singer Dino Crocetti better known?

18 How many stomachs does a giraffe have?

19 *Blue Lines, Mezzanine* and *Heligoland* are albums by which group?

20 By what name has British Honduras been known since 1973?

Answers to QUIZ 489 – Pot Luck

1 Death cap
2 Holloway Road
3 A dance (from Spain)
4 Orthopaedics
5 Sophie Kinsella
6 Ray Ewry
7 César Cui
8 Norway
9 Occam's razor
10 Eric Cantona
11 George Frederick Handel
12 Isaac
13 WB Yeats (*Sailing to Byzantium*)
14 Acker Bilk
15 Bram Stoker
16 An orang-utan
17 The Small Faces
18 Arthur Rimbaud
19 Taupo
20 Tanzania

Easy

1 What was singer Perry Como's full first name?
2 Which baseball player was nicknamed "The Georgia Peach"?
3 How was singer and actor Terence Nelhams-Wright better known?
4 Which American state is nicknamed "the Garden State"?
5 What was the real name of Italian artist Botticelli?
6 Singer Frankie Vaughan had which original surname?
7 How was the consumer electronics company LG known before it shortened its name?
8 To what did Hollywood star Issur Danielovitch change his name?
9 What name did French playwright Jean-Baptiste Poquelin adopt as a pseudonym?
10 "The Land of the Long White Cloud" is the nickname of which country?

Medium

11 Betty Perske was the birth name of which American actress?
12 Which politician was born William Jefferson Blythe III?
13 By what name is Caryn Johnson (b.1955) better known?
14 Which UK city is also known as "the City of Discovery"?
15 What was the nickname of Edmund II, who was King of England for several months in 1016?
16 What were the first names of the author Baroness James of Holland Park?
17 Which creature is also known as the needlefish?
18 Whose Symphony No 4 is known as the "Italian" Symphony?
19 Which singer's birth name was Stevland Judkins?
20 The international CITES treaty is also known by what name, after the city in which it was created?

Hard

Answers to QUIZ 490 – Mythology

1 Soothsayer
2 Crocodile
3 Paphos
4 Welsh
5 Nine
6 Callisto
7 Saturn
8 A giant tree
9 Pantheon
10 Egypt
11 Lectisternium
12 Mjölnir
13 Beira
14 A single horse hair
15 Vesta
16 Leading the dead to judgement
17 Norse (Icelandic literature)
18 Quirinus
19 Ireland
20 Uranus and Gaia

QUIZ 493 – Pot Luck

ANSWERS ON PAGE 495

1 Lake Volta lies wholly within which African country?
2 What nationality was philosopher Arne Naess (b.1912)?
3 Which branch of theology is concerned with the end of the world?
4 In the 1999 sci-fi film *The Matrix*, what was the name of Neo's girlfriend?
5 What is the capital of the Isles of Scilly?
6 Victor Barna (b.1911) was five times world champion in which sport?
7 In which country did the game of chess originate?
8 What is the English translation of the title of the ballet *La Fille mal gardée?*
9 Grantley Adams Airport serves which island?
10 Which is the word for eleven bets, made up of six doubles, four trebles and an accumulator?
11 What is fear of rain called?
12 Colchester had what name in Roman times?
13 In sailing, what name is given to a lightweight, three-cornered headsail used to improve performance when sailing downwind?
14 The 1995 film *Sudden Death* featured which sport?
15 Which Czech city was the historical capital of Moravia?
16 Which freshwater mammal has the Latin name *Lutra lutra*?
17 In canoe polo, how many members of each team are in play at a time?
18 Who was the daughter of Oedipus and Jocasta in Greek mythology?
19 Menachem Begin founded which Israeli political party?
20 The Vagabonds are the backing band for which singer (b.1940)

Answers to QUIZ 491 – Pot Luck

1 Idris the Dragon
2 Francis Davey
3 Dor
4 Paul Dukas
5 *The Old Curiosity Shop*
6 Serve at table
7 Penelope
8 The Cook Islands
9 Colorado
10 Lusitania
11 Antelope
12 *Because You Loved Me*
13 The Foundations
14 Auckland
15 David Hume
16 Walter Hunt
17 Dean Martin
18 Four
19 Massive Attack
20 Belize

Easy

1 What is the capital city of Nicaragua?
2 In which country is the archaeological site of Chan Chan?
3 Sápmi is a region of Europe better known by what name in the UK?
4 What is the name of Melbourne's international airport?
5 Which Turkic language would be spoken by a native of Tashkent?
6 On the African mainland, which is the westernmost city?
7 The Devil's Beef Tub is one of the two sources of which Scottish river?
8 Which island off north-west France marks the southern entrance to the English Channel?
9 What is the name of the highest point in Yellowstone National Park?
10 What is the capital of Andorra?

Medium

11 Garuda is the national airline of which country?
12 The sand dunes of Maspalomas are on which holiday isle?
13 Which small Swiss canton lies between Zurich and Schwyz?
14 In Belgium, what is the capital of the region of Wallonia?
15 What is the highest mountain in Hokkaido, Japan?
16 Which South Pacific country was formerly called the Ellice Islands?
17 The kwacha is the currency unit of which country?
18 In which US city is the Gateway Arch?
19 On which island in the Tierra del Feugo archipelago is Cape Horn?

Hard

20 Which lough forms the boundary between the Irish counties of Longford and Roscommon?

Answers to QUIZ 492 – Also Known As

1 Pierino
2 Ty Cobb
3 Adam Faith
4 New Jersey
5 Alessandro Filipepi
6 Abelson
7 Lucky Goldstar
8 Kirk Douglas
9 Molière
10 New Zealand
11 Lauren Bacall
12 Bill Clinton
13 Whoopi Goldberg
14 Dundee
15 Ironside
16 Phyllis Dorothy
17 Gar (or garfish)
18 Mendelssohn
19 Stevie Wonder
20 The Washington Convention

QUIZ 495 – Pot Luck

ANSWERS ON PAGE 497

1 Who wrote the two collections of poems entitled *A Boy's Will* and *North of Boston*?

2 On which British island is Sumburgh Head?

3 The Bosnia-Herzegovina flag has what main colour?

4 What is another name for the Spider Bridge in Sheffield?

5 Which is the highest mountain peak in Russia?

6 Johnson Beharry won which military award in 2005?

7 Who composed the 1821 opera Der *Freischütz*?

8 In which year was the Lonsdale Belt introduced as a boxing prize?

9 Which country has the internet country code .is?

10 What was the name of the family living at 1313 Mockingbird Lane, Mockingbird Heights?

11 *Christmas in the Heart* was a 2009 album by which singer?

12 What dinosaur's name means "deceptive lizard"?

13 Which Nottinghamshire abbey was the home of Lord Byron?

14 Sergei Diaghilev founded which ballet company?

15 What is the surname of Amyas, hero of Kingsley's *Westward Ho!*?

16 What are sufferers of Sjogren's syndrome unable to do?

17 Under what name did Alexei Maximovich Peshkov write?

18 Who wrote *Prayer Before Birth*, that begins: "I am not yet born; O hear me"?

19 Which singer's real name was Eleanora Fagan?

20 Which mythological daughter of Tantalus was turned into stone by Apollo and Artemis?

Answers to QUIZ 493 – Pot Luck

1 Ghana
2 Norwegian
3 Eschatology
4 Trinity
5 Hugh Town
6 Table tennis
7 India
8 *The Wayward Daughter*
9 Barbados
10 Yankee
11 Ombrophobia
12 Camulodunum
13 Spinnaker
14 Ice hockey
15 Brno
16 Otter
17 Five
18 Antigone
19 Likud
20 Jimmy James

QUIZ 496 – Communications

ANSWERS ON PAGE 498

Easy

1 In which year was the first trans-Atlantic radio communication sent and received?
2 Which comedian made the first "public" mobile phone call in Britain at St Katherine's Docks in 1985?
3 What does the "AM" stand for in the term AM radio?
4 Which English king established the first "Master of the Posts"...?
5 ...and which king opened up the postal service to the general public?
6 In which year did Royal Mail complete the national roll-out of postcodes?
7 What name was given to the first US space satellite launched in 1958?
8 Which London church is known as "the journalists' church"?
9 In digital communication terms what does MIME stand for?
10 Cuneiform script was invented by which civilisation?

Medium

11 "What hath God wrought" was an 1844 message sent by Samuel Morse by which form of communication?
12 The Token Ring method of communication was used in which form of technology?
13 What does DLP stand for in relation to projectors?
14 Claude Chappe (b.1763) invented which method of communication?
15 Who published the 1837 pamphlet *Post Office Reform: Its Importance and Practicability*?
16 By what title is *The Daily Universal Register* now known?
17 Which was the first legal commercial radio station on mainland Britain?
18 The world's first scheduled airmail service flew between which two towns?
19 In which year was the Office of Communications (OFCOM) launched?

Hard

20 With whom did Marconi share the 1909 Nobel Prize in Physics for work in wireless telegraphy?

Answers to QUIZ 494 – Geography

1 Managua
2 Peru
3 Lapland
4 Tullamarine
5 Uzbek
6 Dakar
7 Annan
8 Ushant
9 Eagle Peak
10 Andorra la Vella
11 Indonesia
12 Gran Canaria
13 Zug
14 Namur
15 Asahi
16 Tuvalu
17 Zambia
18 St Louis
19 Hornos Island
20 Ree

QUIZ 497 – Pot Luck

ANSWERS ON PAGE 499

1 Who was the first player to win 20 titles at Wimbledon?

2 What technological item was invented in 1981 and named Osborne 1 by its creator Adam Osborne?

3 What is Bulgaria's currency unit?

4 What is the name of the desert region of southern Israel?

5 In *Under Milk Wood* (1954), what is the first name of the character Mr Bread?

6 What is the nineteenth book of the Old Testament?

7 A "muster" describes a group of which birds?

8 Which game was invented by unemployed Charles Darrow, that enabled him to retire a multi-millionaire?

9 What does the K stand for in the name of the author Jerome K Jerome?

10 On Glasgow's Subway, which station lies between St George's Cross and Buchanan Street?

11 Who was the human partner of Lenny the Lion?

12 What is the name of the U-shaped bone at the base of the tongue that supports the tongue muscles?

13 Which light cavalry regiment gives its name to a dance for eight or sixteen pairs?

14 Arrecife is a city on which island?

15 The choanoid muscles are found in which part of the body?

16 Who was the first female jockey to ride in the Grand National?

17 In the 1985 film *St Elmo's Fire*, who played Jules?

18 Who was the father of legendary Greek hero Ajax?

19 The Moluccas are part of which country?

20 St Anne is the administrative centre of which UK island?

Answers to QUIZ 495 – Pot Luck

1 Robert Frost
2 Mainland (Shetland)
3 Blue
4 Cobweb Bridge
5 Mount Elbrus
6 Victoria Cross
7 Carl Maria von Weber
8 1909
9 Iceland
10 The Munsters
11 Bob Dylan
12 Apatosaurus
13 Newstead Abbey
14 Ballet Russes
15 Leigh
16 Cry
17 Maxim Gorky
18 Louis Macneice
19 Billie Holiday
20 Niobe

Easy

1 The Volkswagen Golf was first introduced in which year?

2 Which make and model of car was named *Top Gear* Car of the Decade from 2000 to 2009?

3 Built in 1885, which vehicle is considered to be the world's first production automobile?

4 What make and model of car is Ecto-1 in the 1984 film *Ghostbusters*?

5 What is the full name of the company known as BMW?

6 The Lamborghini logo features which animal?

7 Which company is based in the town of Maranello?

8 Which manufacturer renamed its "Zhiguli" brand when exporting to other countries?

9 In which year was General Motors founded?

10 Which iconic British sports car was manufactured between 1961 and 1975?

Medium

11 The first model by which company was nicknamed "the Coal Scuttle"?

12 The company Nihon Sangyo, founded in 1928, used what name from the 1930s onwards?

13 What is the French name for the Citroën 2CV?

14 For what do the initials "Fiat" stand in the name of the car manufacturing company?

15 In the 2000 film *Gone in 60 Seconds*, what make and model is the car known as "Eleanor"?

16 Which car was awarded World Car of the Year and World Car Design of the Year in the 2016 World Car Awards?

17 In the 1974 film *The Blues Brothers*, what make and model of car is driven by Jake and Elwood Blues?

Hard

18 What model of car, made by Lotus Cars from 1996, was named after the granddaughter of the chairman of the company at that time?

19 The Vauxhall Astra was first introduced in which year?

20 What make and model of car, codenamed "BlueStar", was listed in *Time* Magazine's "Best 25 Inventions of 2017"?

Answers to QUIZ 496 – Communications

1 1901
2 Ernie Wise
3 Amplitude modulation
4 Henry VIII (in 1516)
5 Charles I
6 1972
7 *Explorer*
8 St Brides Church (Fleet Street)
9 Multipurpose Internet Mail Extensions
10 The Sumerians
11 Telegram
12 Local area networks (LANS)
13 Digital Light Processing
14 Semaphore visual telegraph
15 Sir Rowland Hill
16 *The Times*
17 LBC
18 Hendon and Windsor
19 2003
20 Karl Ferdinand Braun

QUIZ 499 – Pot Luck

ANSWERS ON PAGE 251

1 Which TV couple lived at 1164 Morning Glory Circle, West Port, Connecticut?

2 Eating cheese late at night can cause nightmares as it contains large amounts of what substance which affects the nervous system?

3 The 1838 work *Kinderszenen* by Robert Schumann has what English name?

4 *Seven Tears* was a 1982 hit for which group?

5 In which country is the Belmont Stakes horse race run?

6 What subatomic particles take their name from a passage in James Joyce's *Finnegans Wake*?

7 Whose hit 5-4-3-2-1 was used as the introductory music to the TV pop programme *Ready Steady Go*?

8 Which stately home is the seat of the Marquess of Exeter?

9 Grévy's and Burchell's are species of which animal?

10 "Q" was the pseudonym of which writer?

11 Which Hollywood film company produced *Citizen Kane* and *King Kong*?

12 Who created the detective Albert Campion?

13 Judith Durham was the lead singer with which Australian group?

14 Which constellation contains the star Thuban?

15 The mineral cobalt is what colour?

16 Which Irish rider (b.1952) won the Prix de L'Arc de Triomphe four times?

17 Who played Sue Storm in the 2015 version of *Fantastic Four*?

18 The Mindbenders were the backing group for which singer in the 1960s?

19 At which public school was squash first played?

20 Who wrote the 1965 novel *The Magus*?

Easy

Medium

Hard

Answers to QUIZ 497 – Pot Luck

1 Billie Jean King
2 Laptop
3 Lev
4 Negev
5 Dai
6 Psalms
7 Peacocks
8 Monopoly™
9 Klapka
10 Cowcaddens
11 Terry Hall
12 The hyoid bone
13 Lancers
14 Lanzarote
15 The eyes
16 Charlotte Brew (in 1977)
17 Demi Moore
18 Telamon
19 Indonesia
20 Alderney

QUIZ 500 – Science

ANSWERS ON PAGE 252

Easy

1 The Cretaceous period occurred during which geological era?

2 What does scotopic vision allow one to do?

3 In the 6th century BC, who realised the"Morning Star" and the "Evening Star" were one and the same?

4 What was astronaut Buzz Aldrin's original first name?

5 In a CAT scan, for what do the letters CAT stand?

6 What is the most abundant protein in the body?

7 What prefix indicates 10^{15}?

8 Sir Christopher Wren was a professor in which scientific field?

9 The lack of which vitamin causes the disease beriberi?

10 What is the name of the network of nerves and blood vessels behind the stomach?

Medium

11 In Einstein's formula $E = mc^2$, what does C stand for?

12 Which naturalist lived at Down House in Kent?

13 In 1938, which Italian-born physicist was awarded a Nobel Prize?

14 What is the SI unit of pressure?

15 In which year is Halley's comet next predicted to be visible from Earth?

16 What name is given to the minimum speed required to break free from gravity?

17 John Enders, Frederick Robbins and Thomas Weller jointly shared the Nobel Prize for Physiology and Medicine in 1954 for research into which disease?

18 Admiralty, cartridge and red are variations of which alloy?

19 Which is the largest object in the asteroid belt?

20 Which branch of medical science is concerned with muscles?

Hard

Answers to QUIZ 498 – Car Makes and Models

1 1974
2 Bugatti Veyron EB 16.4
3 Benz Patent-Motorwagen
4 Cadillac Miller-Meteor
5 Bayerische Motoren Werke
6 Bull
7 Ferrari
8 Lada
9 1908
10 Jaguar E-Type
11 Aston Martin
12 Nissan
13 Deux Chevaux (two horses)
14 Fabbrica Italiana Automobili Torino
15 Ford Shelby Mustang GT500
16 Mazda MX-5
17 Dodge Monaco
18 Lotus Elise (after Elisa)
19 1979
20 Tesla Model 3